Caligari's Heirs

The German Cinema of Fear
after 1945

Edited by

Steffen Hantke

The Scarecrow Press, Inc.
Lanham, Maryland • Toronto • Plymouth, UK
2007

SCARECROW PRESS, INC.

Published in the United States of America
by Scarecrow Press, Inc.
A wholly owned subsidiary of
The Rowman & Littlefield Publishing Group, Inc.
4501 Forbes Boulevard, Suite 200, Lanham, Maryland 20706
www.scarecrowpress.com

Estover Road
Plymouth PL6 7PY
United Kingdom

British Library Cataloguing in Publication Information Available

Library of Congress Cataloging-in-Publication Data

Caligari's heirs : the German cinema of fear after 1945 / edited by Steffen
Hantke.
       p. cm.
  Includes bibliographical references and index.
  ISBN-13: 978-0-8108-5878-7 (pbk. : alk. paper)
  ISBN-10: 0-8108-5878-9 (pbk. : alk. paper)
  1. Horror films—Germany—History and criticism. I. Hantke, Steffen, 1962–

PN1995.9.H6C37 2007
791.43'6164094309045—dc22   2006023867

Contents

**Part 5. Interviews: Three German Horror
Film Directors**

Postwar German Cinema and the Horror Film: Thoughts on Historical Continuity and Genre Consolidation

Steffen Hantke

The collection of critical essays you are holding in your hands tries to offer a corrective to the prevailing critical opinion that there is no such thing as German horror cinema after 1945. This claim may come as a surprise to readers who happen to be fans of horror film. As the lively and well-informed discussion on the internet and in the pages of fanzines illustrates, fans know very well that some great horror films have been coming out of Germany for the last fifty odd years.[1] Particularly in recent years, horror film fans have been developing a taste for—and, consequently, an expertise in—foreign productions, largely because they are left to their own devices by an American horror cinema that seems increasingly stuck in a rut of rehashing its own cinematic heritage as well as remaking horror films from around the world. From Italian *giallo* in the '60s and '70s, to the recent spate of outstanding Spanish horror films and the snappily nicknamed "J-Horror" out of Japan starting in the 1990s, fans of the genre have gone on to discover that virtually every country around the world with its own film industry has made horror films, and good ones, too. Germany is no exception. For years, fans have been doing heavy insider trading in names like Jörg Buttgereit or Christoph Schlingensief. More mainstream productions like Stefan Ruzowitzky's *Anatomie* (2000) and Robert Schwentke's *Tattoo* (2002) have brought larger audiences into the fold. Academics, however, have remained, by and large, focused on the type of German director who is a contender for Best Foreign Film at the Academy Awards, like Tom Tykwer and Marc Rothemund. If these critics do pay attention to popular film at all, it is to the type of film that draws large audiences, like Wolfgang Petersen's *Das Boot* (1981) and Oliver Hirschbiegel's *Der Untergang* (2004). Horror film, much like other cinematic genres with a dubious reputation, falls by the wayside; so much so, in fact, so that Randall Halle, in an essay on German splatter films, can state that there is "a certain urgency to have another look at horror film in Germany, given that contemporary studies of German film have largely disregarded the horror genre" ("Unification Horror" 281).[2]

Critical consensus among historians of German film concedes that there may be postwar German horror *films*, but insists that there is no postwar German horror *film*. In other words, critics are to acknowledge the existence of individual horror films, even of horror film cycles, but they refuse to acknowledge that these films add up to what can be called a genre. Their refusal to take the argumentative leap from the specific to the general, and the arguments delivered in support of this hesitation, makes for a story so compelling that it is well worth recounting.

There used to be German horror film before the advent of the Third Reich, or so the story goes. These were the golden days of German expressionist filmmaking. But this flourishing of the genre came to an end with the Nazis, who, like other totalitarian regimes of the 20th century that exercised absolute control over their respective national film industries, had no interest in the horror genre or were actively opposed to it. Joseph Goebbels' *Reichspropagandaministerium* (Ministry of Propaganda) was opposed to the "degenerate" excesses of German expressionism, its brooding introspection, its conflicted view of the human condition. At the movies, the Nazis preferred the light entertainment of costume and period drama, which would distract the population from politics and the increasingly terrifying realities of the war. Streamlining popular culture, the Nazis put an end to horror film during the twelve years of the Third Reich. Their efforts to root out the genre were so successful that, once the Zero Hour had passed and the film industries began to reconstitute themselves in East and West Germany, historical continuity had been severed. For a variety of reasons, both economic and ideological, there was no going back to prewar German cinema, no recovery of cinematic traditions. As the German film industry started to pick itself up from the rubble, the desire for distraction from the harsh realities of the historical moment, which used to be officially prescribed during the Third Reich, found itself confirmed and justified yet again. "The 'rubble films' of 1947–49 fit in with that down-to-earth positivistic model for 'coping with the past' that the Allies offered to the Germans; they relieved them of the task of radical self-analysis and thoroughgoing revisionism" (Kreimeier 377). Horror films, which appear to be relatively useless for such conciliatory politics, were no part of the production schedules. As it turned out, this condition was to be permanent. In effect, up to the present day, the horror film genre in Germany never recovered from having been so rudely interrupted at the height of its achievements. Every now and then, someone will make a film that qualifies as a horror film; occasionally, a horror film will hit upon a formula successful enough to initiate a cinematic cycle. But neither the quantity nor quality of these films justifies regarding them as elements functioning within the conceptual framework of genre. They remain statistical anomalies. They don't add up. Or so the story goes.

My goal in this introduction is not to steer head on against the flow of this historical narrative, trying to disprove or dismiss it altogether. For that, the narrative is too convincing, just as its authors have invested far more time and scholarly attention in its construction than I can possibly muster for the purpose of my own argument. As much as anyone can make sense of the historical data—the films, their contents, and the circumstances of their production, distribution, and consumption—the official historical narrative is, simply put, a pretty good account of what happened. But this narrative is also the product of an act of interpretation, or rather, a complex chain of deductions. And to the degree that the story is an interpretation of events, it is open to challenge. Recognizing the mechanisms of its construction, we might not only understand why the story goes as it does but might think of alternative ways of telling it. This is the goal of my argument: to take a look at how this argument is constructed; to find a foothold in its interstices for proposing a slightly divergent reading, and, ultimately, to propose a way of looking at postwar German film that allows for the existence of German horror cinema.

In a manner of speaking, I would like to open up the discourse on postwar German horror film to a more postmodern concept of genre, a more flexible and self-conscious understanding of how a cinematic tradition positions itself toward a concept that both facilitates and enables creative expression. Within this framework, genre would allow for more internal heterogeneity and external exchange than is commonly attributed to it. Genre would no longer mean an authoritative gesture of classificatory closure but rather a process of engaging with internal and external heterogeneity that helps to negotiate individual and collective identities. This reframing of the concept of genre strikes me as particularly relevant for the case of postwar Germany, a culture haunted by the historical trauma of the Third Reich, by unsuccessful attempts at suppressing this traumatic past rather than confronting it. Postwar Germany's search for a viable national identity is, in many ways, fertile soil for the horror film. With its multiple investments in the concept of trauma, and its interest in articulating the return of the repressed, horror film might be particularly useful in helping audiences, in Eric Santner's words, to "inhabit the heterogeneous language games that constitute the modest forms of community which mark the postmodern landscape" (7). In this broader sense, the anthology invites readers to contemplate "the shattered fantasy of the (always already) lost organic society that has haunted the Western imagination and to learn to tolerate the complexities and instabilities of new social arrangements as well as more hybrid, more "creole," forms of personal, sexual, cultural, and political identity" (Santner 7–8).

To open a way into this discussion, let me examine the validity of the official historical narrative by taking a closer look at its constitutive elements. The story revolves around three elements: the presence of horror films in the German film industry before the Third Reich, a period most closely associated with expressionist style and a small number of films that serve as its prime representatives; the rupture in historical continuity constituted by the Third Reich and the war years; and, finally, the absence of horror films from German film production after World War II. Let me address these elements one at a time.

First, critics assert that German filmmaking during the Weimar years played a crucial role in the development of horror film. Histories of the horror film often pinpoint the cinema of this period as an inventory of tropes and styles from which horror films have been drawing in all their national and thematic variations. This is the heritage of German cinema from the silent film era—films associated with the glory days of the Ufa and the Decla, with the stylistic influence of Expressionism, and with a thematic preoccupation with the darker aspects of the human psyche, best captured by Lotte Eisner's almost programmatic title *The Haunted Screen*. Equally programmatic is the title of S. S. Prawer's study of horror cinema, from which this book borrows its own title: *Caligari's Children: The Film as Tale of Terror*.[3] Horror film, Prawer suggests, emerged and consolidated itself as a genre in the wake of a single film, Robert Wiene's *The Cabinet of Dr. Caligari*, with the stylistic and thematic agenda it established. Prawer's analysis is too sophisticated to allow such radical reductionism, and so the title of his book, I believe, must be taken metonymically, referring to the seminal importance of the type of film *Caligari* represents—German filmmaking between the two World Wars. Looking back over the genealogy of horror film, we might recognize *Caligari* as the visual and thematic blueprint for every claustrophobic nightmare of dehumanization, just as Murnau's *Nosferatu* appears as one, if not *the*, seminal vampire film, *The Student of Prague* as the cinematic key-text about the Doppelgänger motif, Lang's *M* as the first serial killer film, and Lang's first two *Dr. Mabuse* films as foundational texts in the cinema of individual and collective paranoia.

Other critics, concurring with the basic conceit in Prawer's study, confirm the idea that German cinema during the Weimar years was, in fact, fertile grounds for the horror film. Summarizing the state of current research on the topic, Peter Hutchings makes the connection between horror film and the German films of the period explicit: "most accounts of horror history published in the past thirty years refer to the German productions *The Cabinet of Dr. Caligari* (1919) and *Nosferatu* (1922) as horror films" (3). To these two seminal films Hutchings also adds *The Student of Prague* (1913) and *The Golem* (1913), asserting that, taken together, these films "might well anticipate and be an influence upon later horror production" (9). David Skal, in *The Monster Show: A Cultural History of Horror*, picks up this theme of influence in his own discussion of cinematic history. Discussing German films of the Weimar years in the context of such modernist movements as Surrealism and phenomena like the French Grand Guignol, Skal ends the chapter entitled "'You Will Become Caligari': Monsters, Mountebanks and Modernism" with this tongue-in-cheek evocation of the influence German expressionist films were to have, especially on the American horror film:

> Whether Americans liked it or not, an enormous westward expansion of horrors was taking shape, a manifest destiny of the macabre. The dark beings that had used the European avant-garde to find a modern expression would soon begin crossing the Atlantic, in film canisters instead of coffins, waiting to be animated in darkened rooms through the application of artificial light. [...] Shaken out of their ancient crypts and castles by the mod-

ern concussions of war, they began seeking a new resting place, slouching inexorably toward Hollywood to be born anew. (Skal 60–1)

Similarly, Mark Jancovich considers German expressionist filmmaking as a "key moment in the development of the horror film" (3). It occurred in the wake of a brief pre-history of the genre during the silent era, and, in turn, preceded "the Hollywood productions of the 1930s," among which the Universal horror films are the most notable examples (3).[4] Though the Universal horror films were, according to Jancovich, more indebted in their choice of material and tone to the literary Gothic, they nonetheless "drew on some of the techniques of German expressionism" (3), demonstrating how deeply German filmmakers had written themselves into the further development of the genre. Style figures prominently in Jancovich's argument; he considers the "list of classics associated with the movement [of German expressionism] [as] particularly impressive" because of their "anti-realist aesthetic" (3), which was to become a hallmark of horror films thereafter (one might think of such wildly divergent examples as Charles Laughton's *The Night of the Hunter* and Brian Yuzna's *Society*).

Lesser critics, even if they have little of substance to add to the discussion of early German horror films, operate squarely within the chronology outlined by Hutchings and Jancovich, a chronology deeply invested in the formation of a canon for the genre of horror film. Attempting to describe, as its subtitle announces, the "Evolution of the American Horror Film," Joseph Maddrey's *Nightmares in Red, White and Blue* (2004) pays unquestioning homage to the canonical films of Weimar cinema. In fact, the chapter entitled (yet again) "You Must Become Caligari: German Expressionism and the Origins of Film Gothic" (7–10) opens Maddrey's historical survey, suggesting that American horror film—or perhaps even all horror film—starts with German expressionist cinema. Though Maddrey does little more than provide brief plot summaries of Wegener's *The Student of Prague* and *The Golem*, Wiene's *Caligari*, and Murnau's *Nosferatu*, it is the inclusion of these films in the book and their placement at such a crucial historical juncture that demonstrate how compelling the official historical narrative is.

Taken together, these sources make a strong case for the critical consensus among historians of horror film that German cinema before the Third Reich helped to bring about horror as a cinematic genre; that German filmmakers contributed works that were to become central to the canon of the genre, establishing a look, a style, and a mood for the horror film, as much as an inventory of themes and tropes, that were to persist during the further development of the genre throughout the rest of the 20th century and beyond. What we are dealing with here is a well-documented and well-theorized aspect of cinematic history.

Less well-documented and far less thoroughly theorized is the second element in the historical narrative of German horror film—the rupture that occurred during the Third Reich and the war years. Critical discourse has hardly addressed this historical turning-point at all. The absence of horror films from

German production between 1933 and 1945 is undisputed; perhaps it suffices to
point out the aversion of the official cultural bureaucracy toward the types of
radical artistic modernism that manifested itself in the showcase productions of
Weimar cinema. But this is to insist that German horror film and expressionist
style were inseparable, and that, somehow, horror film turned out to be virtually
the only cinematic genre that could not be absorbed and co-opted by the Third
Reich—both problematic assumptions for a number of reasons.[5] In this sense,
the question why the German film industry during the Third Reich did not produce horror films has never been asked. This is all the more surprising since
ample scholarship exists on the film industry of the Third Reich, as well as on
the transitional period between Nazi Germany and postwar German film production. But then again, if the historical narrative is correct, why would it be surprising to find film historians silent on the issue of German horror film after
1933; after all, how do you discuss something that does not exist?[6]

This argumentative conundrum aside, the takeover of the German film industry—as part of the process of *Gleichschaltung* (forced coordination) of all
aspects of society with the dominant ideology under the Nazis—was accompanied by a massive exodus of talent from the German film industry.[7] Many who
had been the inventors, promoters, and practitioners of the style and the cinematic genre most readily associated with it were no longer active participants in
the making of German cinema. Instead, their names begin to appear in the U.S.
film industry, in the credits of American film noir, but also of the Universal horror films in the 1930s and the RKO horror films of the 1940s, which were to
become the next stage in the history of the horror film, according to official film
history.[8]

Just as critical opinions on the crucial importance of prewar German cinema for the development of the horror film appear to be unanimous, so critics,
by and large, concur when they state that postwar German cinema no longer
featured horror films.[9] The standard history of German film, the *Geschichte des
Deutschen Films*, published in 1993, which works its way chronologically
through German cinema from the silent film era to the present, does not give a
coherent account of German horror films, the way it does discuss other film genres (e.g. the rubble film or the *Heimatfilm*). German director Jörg Buttgereit, to
whom the book you are holding in your hands is devoting two essays and an
interview, does not appear in the index of the *Geschichte des deutschen Films* at
all. Neither does Uli Lommel's *Tenderness of Wolves*, a film about serial killer
Fritz Haarmann, make an appearance in its index of film titles. It does mention
Christoph Schlingensief, but only once, and in this single case it refers to his
film *Das Deutsche Kettensägenmassaker* as "grotesque Horror*show*" rather than
a horror *film* (321, emphases added). Werner Herzog's *Nosferatu* is referred to
in the context of silent film (263), while Roland Emmerich is mentioned in passing as one of the younger German filmmakers in the 1980s interested not specifically in the horror film but, more broadly, "in current genres" (294).

If this conspicuous silence on postwar German horror film may seem a matter of German film critics representing their own history, let me add one more example from Anglo-American scholarship. Sabine Hake, in her book *German National Cinema*, published in 2002, does not feature an entry for horror film in its index either. Again, this is a conspicuous absence because Hake acknowledges the importance of genre cinema when she lists and discusses detective films, road movies, street films, science fiction, *Heimat-*, and mountain films. Confronted with individual films that could conceivably be categorized as horror films, Hake tends to distribute them across a variety of generic categories that operate adjacent to, or partially overlap with, the horror film (like the thriller). In reference to the filmmaking of the Weimar period, she traces postwar traditions in German cinema back to what she calls "fantastic films," which "incorporated visual and narrative motifs from romantic paintings and literature, as well as from the popular Gothic novels, to simulate the effects of what might be called the modern uncanny" (17–18). This term, "the modern uncanny," might be synonymous with horror film in the broadest sense. Nonetheless, it is significant that Hake, a meticulous and conscientious chronicler of cultural nuances, seems to shy away from the label of horror. As a ghostly presence, it lingers around the margins of her discussion whenever she discusses certain films, but it never rises above the threshold of visibility.[10]

This strategy also determines a conversation between Henrik Larsen and Harald Gruenberger, editor of www.metamovie.de, "a website dedicated to unusual movies," in which Gruenberger makes a number of observations that sound remarkably like Hake and the *Geschichte des Deutschen Films*. "There has always been a feeling of 'We can't do this in Germany,'" Gruenberger explains.

> We can't do Westerns, only Karl May. No horror movies, just Edgar Wallace. This self-diminishing way of thinking continues to this day [...] How many German horror movies have there been produced since the '50s? There are oddities like "Ein Toter hing im Netz/Horror of Spider Island" (more sexploitation than horror), the Wallace hybrids and occasional outcast flicks like "Schlangengrube und das Pendel" (yes, it IS a cute movie, but horrific?) or "The Head". Amongst the fans, the most popular German horror movies of today ("Anatomie" notwithstanding) are the amateur works of Buttgereit & Co. (Larsen n.p.)[11]

Ken Hanke, a critic who has written about what Gruenberger calls "the Wallace hybrids," comes to the conclusion that "the unfortunate thing" about them is that "they are insufficiently known and appreciated, even by fans of the stronger *gialli*, and, as a result, have never really gained and foothold in the history of the development of the horror film" (Hanke 123). Ironically enough, Gruenberger's argument does not hinge on a lack of popularity, which would constitute a matter available to empirical verification. In fact, Gruenberger is not lacking in examples to illustrate the non-existence of postwar German horror film, though every single example he mentions seems to be "almost," or "barely," or only "somewhat" appropriate. Gruenberger resolves this contradiction as a matter of irreconcilable categories: there are authentic horror films on the one hand and inauthentic imitations on the other (e.g. the series of films based on novels by Edgar Wallace, popular in the 1960s); there is the absence of a genre and the presence of individual films as "oddities" or categoric anomalies (e.g. sexploitation films like *Spider Island*); and there is the difference between what academic critics and what fans would consider a genuine horror film (e.g. the low- or no-budget films of Jörg Buttgereit and filmmakers like him). As in Hake's account, the disavowal of the existence of horror film is coupled with the assignment of individual films and filmmakers to other cinematic genres and categories. Again, horror film as a genre is written out of the historical record of postwar German film.

In order to suggest not empirical reliability but an interpretive mechanism, I have deliberately used the term "disavowal" in my discussion of these critical sources and their description of the conspicuous absence of the horror film from postwar German cinema. That is to say, an argument could be made that the non-existence of horror film in postwar Germany is the product of a rhetorical and argumentative strategy invested in ideological concerns about historical continuity, about the artistic and political integrity of postwar German cinema, and about the policing of the boundary between serious auteurist filmmaking on the one hand and light entertainment on the other. In order to create the space for an alternative reading, let me go back and point out the traces that interpretive choices have left on each of the constitutive elements of the larger argument.

In regard to the crucial importance of prewar German film to the development of the horror genre, almost all of the critics I have quoted earlier express concerns about the use of the term "genre." A sense of unease prevails in these discussions regarding the generic status of the canonical German horror films of the Weimar period. Mark Jancovich, one of the critics I cited earlier, registers this unease as a general concern with the "constructedness" of any history of the horror film, cautioning his readers that his own account "should not be seen as the history, but only as a history" (3). Instead of claiming that his own version of cinematic history is any more valid than any other historian's, he points to the difference between the "sense of how academics have understood that history" (2) and how fans might construe such a history.

Peter Hutchings extends the range of this argument by acknowledging that genre plays a role both not only in the consumption of films but also in their production and distribution. *The Cabinet of Dr. Caligari* and *Nosferatu* (1922) were not "produced [or] originally marketed as horror films but instead as 'art movies'" (3), and *The Student of Prague* and *The Golem* (1913), though they "might well anticipate and be an influence upon later horror production" were also not "deemed to be horror films when they first appeared" (9).[12] Given the fact that, "after WWII, unlike in the United States, German horror films never gained a mass audience," individual films failed to rally around themselves a strong sense of generic coherence (Halle, "Unification Horror" 281). Large audiences, secure in their expectations, would have helped to provide such a sense of coherence, as consumption patterns fed back into the production decisions of studios looking for predictable profits. A style and mood shared by a relatively small number of German horror films: apparently, this was not enough to generate the critical mass required for generic self-awareness to evolve.

> Comparing films like *Caligari* and *Nosferatu* (Murnau, 1922) to the Hollywood *Frankenstein* and *Dracula* films, it is clear that the German film industry produced films that in their generic qualities could be understood as related only in very broad terms of narrative development and horrific disruption, whereas Hollywood produced films that relied on a precise replication of the successful elements of a previous film. (Halle, "Unification Horror" 283)[13]

A conspicuous feature of these arguments about the lack of generic self-awareness of prewar German cinema is their reference to the Universal horror films of the 1930s. They all seem to agree that horror cinema "began in the early 1930s in the American film industry" (Hutchings 9). Randall Halle's phrase—the "precise replication of the successful elements of a previous film"—expresses the logic of this argument most poignantly: American film proceeded with filmmakers having a clear self-awareness that they were making horror films. German filmmakers, as well as the industry that supported them, did not. But is this a valid analogy, to measure the German film industry by the standards of the American film industry? To define the concept of genre by the shape it has been given in one specific set of economic, historical, and social circumstances, and then to apply it to other national traditions and industries?

Perhaps even more importantly, does it make sense to hold on to this narrow definition of the horror genre when even American horror film itself, especially since the 1970s wave of "neo-horror," has diversified to a degree that makes the old definition problematic, if not useless? When films without elements of the supernatural (like the serial killer films of the 1980s), films focusing more on the affect of disgust than horror, and highly idiosyncratic auteurist work like that of David Cronenberg and David Lynch are routinely considered examples of horror film, why then would we continue to measure postwar German horror cinema by the standards of the 1930s Universal horror films?

Still, diversity seems to pose a problem for those in search of genre. Klaus Kreimeier's history of the German Ufa, the production company most viewers would associate with prewar German horror film, puts the argument about missing stylistic coherence onto a more empirically sound foundation. Kreimeier suggests that the close association between "the 'gothicizing' films of the Weimar Republic" (109) and expressionist style has, in fact, been greatly exaggerated. Typical prewar productions, like those of the German Ufa, were more characterized by a work ethic, a set of interlacing production practices, which, in fact, led to what Kreimeier calls a distinct "lack of style" (152).[14] Ultimately, Kreimeier sounds a note that can also be heard in other works of cinematic historiography—that German expressionism, "this program against 'reality' and a dismissal of any form of realism" (125), only took shape "in, at the most, ten to fifteen works, which, as 'classic' German silent films, today are counted among the 'timeless heritage' of cinematography" (Kreimeier 126).[15] In other words, all arguments about the absence of a postwar horror film in Germany that start from the missing resurgence of expressionist filmmaking are flawed to the same degree as their initial premise.

The second aspect of cinematic historiography that is open to challenge is the trope of ruptures, which insists on German cultural history as a series of traumatic interruptions. This narrative has been challenged in regard to 1945, the so-called Zero Hour: for example, the "twenty-eight West German films of the years 1945–48 were almost without exception produced and directed by former employees of the National Socialist Ufa or of other Ufa companies" (Kreimeier 376).[16] But its application to the Third Reich as an exceptional period, a "time out" so to speak, is also problematic. Eric Rentschler's analysis of German cinema during the Third Reich concludes with a brief historical summary that emphasizes continuity rather than disruption, both in regard to the transition from the Weimar Republic to the Third Reich and from the Third Reich to the Bonn Republic. "Feature films in the Third Reich," Rentschler argues, "were principally the function of a genre cinema, which in turn was part of an elaborate mass culture. This cinema sported titles, figures, and materials well-known to Weimar film which would continue in the postwar era" (215).[17] Given the skewed equation of Weimar cinema and expressionist style Kreimeier and Elsaesser have noted, one might expect far more continuity from the cinema of the Weimar to the cinema of the Bonn Republic. That is to say, if there was a German horror film before 1933, there is little reason to assume that the twelve years of the Third Reich would have been able to kill it off once and for all.

In all these aspects of the official historical narrative, the horror film genre is present as a latent interpretive option, suppressed for a variety of reasons; in one case it may be an individual critic favorably predisposed toward "artistic" over popular cinema; in another case, a historiographic model predicated on the political exoneration of postwar German culture from complicities with that of the Third Reich. Pieces of the puzzle can be assembled one way or another, but in every construction, internal contradictions must be suppressed. Historians of postwar German cinema are not susceptible to the presence of horror films because they tend to devalue genre in favor of a more radically idiosyncratic and personal auteurist filmmaking. Historians of the horror film are not susceptible to its presence because, as scholars studying cinematic genres, their basic model of genericity is derived from the American film industry. Those who admit to the existence of a prewar German horror film will fail to recognize postwar German horror films because they assume that postwar horror cinema must be expressionistic; or they will fail to look for postwar horror films altogether because they assume that the prewar tradition has been interrupted once and for all.[18]

I am not suggesting a conspiratorial explanation of why no one has written a history of the postwar German horror film yet. In fact, the somewhat bewildering multiplicity of possible argumentative paths through the empirical landscape suggests that no single explanation exists, or that, if someone were to propose one, it would constitute a gross oversimplification. Also, a theory of single causes would probably require a single-author study of postwar German horror film; an anthology of critical essays by a number of different authors would be highly unsuitable to this purpose. The multiplicity of perspectives and voices in such an anthology is, however, very well suited to providing a tentative mapping out of alternative trails through this rough terrain. The essays in this anthology add up to something like an ongoing narrative, as much as their authors may disagree with one another on individual points of interpretation or weigh in differently on questions of aesthetic and political evaluation. Starting with three returning film exiles in the 1950s and wrapping up in the period following the momentous events of 1989, they cover the history of postwar Germany. They tell the story of films and their creators, the complex networks of influence that exist between them across time and generic boundaries, and the shared inventory of tropes and themes, styles and moods, affects and effects they deploy. Taken together, they map out what the title of this anthology refers to as the German cinema of fear—a phrase that acknowledges the contested nature of the genre label of "horror film" and makes room for lively exchanges in the margins of such an ill-defined term.

The first section of this anthology, entitled "The Long Shadow of Weimar: Expressionism and Postwar German Horror Film," weighs in on the theme of *Vergangenheitsbewältigung*, the coping or coming to terms with the traumatic past, that has haunted the immediate postwar years in Germany and persists as a trope in public discourse to the present day. The goal of this section is not, simplistically, to insist on thematic and stylistic continuities across the intervening years between 1933 and 1945, and thus on a German horror film tradition untouched by the rupture of the Third Reich; rather, it is to make such notions of continuity the subject of discussion. For this purpose, the section collects three essays that revolve around figures whose careers are strongly associated with the German film industry before World War II, with film exile in Hollywood, and with a problematic return to Germany after the end of the war—Fritz Lang, Peter Lorre, and Robert Siodmak. Two of them are often associated with horror film: Lang as the creator of paranoid nightmares revolving around the shadowy mastermind criminal Dr. Mabuse, and Lorre as the face of the psychotic child murderer in Lang's own *M* (1931), a role he would reprise numerous times in American films later on. Except for his contribution to *Menschen am Sonntag* (1930), Robert Siodmak did not, in the early stages of his career, figure prominently in German cinema. But this was to change when he emigrated to the U.S.

and began to make a name for himself, first with studio fare like *Son of Dracula* (1943), and then with noir masterpieces on the boundaries between horror, thriller, and mystery, like *Phantom Lady* (1944), *The Spiral Staircase* (1946), *The Killers* (1946), and *The Dark Mirror* (1946).[19] The trajectory of Siodmak's career—from prewar Germany to Hollywood, and back again to Germany after the war—is something he shares with Lang and Lorre. As returning exiles, all three provide case studies in historical discontinuity, raising questions about the transfer of expressionist style from one context to another. Each essay devotes itself to a film made after Lang, Lorre, and Siodmak had returned from the U.S. to postwar Germany. Blair Davis deals with Lang's film *Die Tausend Augen des Dr. Mabuse* (1960), in which Lang resurrected his prewar villain for the postwar audience, while Tony Williams takes on Lorre's sole directorial work in *Der Verlorene* (1951), in which Lorre created an opportunity for himself to insert his own American-made persona into a traumatic postwar Germany unwilling to confront its immediate past. My own piece, finally, focuses on Siodmak's film *Nachts, wenn der Teufel kam* (1957), in which Siodmak deploys a variety of styles he had continued to refine during his career as a versatile studio director in an attempt to outwit a recalcitrant postwar German audience.

The second section of the anthology, entitled "German *Autorenkino* and Horror Film: Influences, Dialogues, Exchanges," focuses on the fruitful, though conflicted relationship that exists between the German Autorenfilm, which frequently bears the burden of having to represent all of German cinema abroad, and the tropes and motifs of the horror film as a representative of genre cinema. As *Vergangenheitsbewältigung* serves as a leitmotif for the previous section, the boundary between auteurist filmmaking and horror film as a form of popular entertainment provides the theme that holds this section together. It is the purpose of this section to challenge the assumption that the two areas are mutually exclusive, and to suggest that a disdain toward the horror film on the part of influential German filmmakers would produce a critical misrepresentation of postwar German cinema. The section opens with Linda Badley's examination of the tumultuous relationship between one of the premiere filmmakers of the New German cinema, Werner Herzog, and his notorious star Klaus Kinski, entitled "The Shadow and the Auteur: Herzog's Kinski, Kinski's Nosferatu, and the Myths of Authorship." Badley's exclusive interest is not Herzog's remaking of Murnau's classic *Nosferatu*; this subject has been sufficiently discussed by other critics interested in horror film. Instead, Badley focuses on the trope of monstrosity that haunts notions of auteurist filmmaking and "inspired" acting, serving as an organizing metaphor for numerous recent meta-horror films. Richard Hand's essay "History, Homage and Horror: Fassbinder, Raab, Lommel and *The Tenderness of Wolves* (1973)" takes on, albeit obliquely, another figure central to the pantheon of German Autorenfilm, Rainer Werner Fassbinder, by way of Fassbinder's association with Uli Lommel and Kurt Raab, a director and an actor whose careers he helped to set in motion. Lommel's film about, and Raab's portrayal of, serial murderer Fritz Haarmann are, similar to Herzog taking recourse to Murnau, self-conscious attempts of new German cinema to define it-self in relation to canonical texts, tropes, and authors of German cinema—in this case, as Hand points out, through the intertextual play between *The Tenderness of Wolves* and Fritz Lang's *M*. Serial killer Fritz Haarmann, nicknamed the "werewolf of Hannover" by his contemporaries, appears yet again in the third essay in this section, Jay McRoy's "Joy-Boys and Docile Bodies: Surveillance and Resistance in Romuald Karmakar's *Der Totmacher*." As in the case of Herzog and Lommel, Karmakar comes to the inventory of the horror film as a highly idiosyncratic auteurist filmmaker. Through detailed analysis of cinematic technique, McRoy's essay positions Karmakar's auteurist filmmaking, with its indebtedness to the inventory of the horror film, in critical opposition to a mainstream cinema too eager to align itself with political consensus.

Following a rough chronology—from the theme of *Vergangenheits-bewältigung* in the first section (the 1950s to the 1960s), to the theme of auteurist versus popular film in the second section (the 1960s, starting roughly with the Oberhausener Manifest in 1962, to the 1970s)—the third section of the anthology, entitled "New German Horror Film: Between Global Cinema and the Hollywood Blockbuster," focuses on the boundary between national cinematic traditions and the larger context of global cinema. Phil Simpson's essay, entitled "Introducing 'The Little Spielberg': Roland Emmerich's *Joey* as Reverent Parody," frames this larger global context—in the figure of Roland Emmerich, Germany's gift to the American blockbuster—as 'Americanized' mainstream cinema. Ernest Mathijs' essay "To Die For: *Der Fan* and the Reception of Sexuality and Horror in Early 1980s German Cinema" discusses the rarely seen horror film *Der Fan*, which, in its peculiar amalgamation of graphic violence, celebrity casting, and 1980s pop aesthetics, captures a crucial moment in German cultural history. Meanwhile, Eugenie Brinkema's "Not to scream *before* or *about*, but to scream *at* death": Haneke's Horrible *Funny Games*" begins its investigation of the internationally successful filmmaker Michael Haneke with a theoretically sophisticated account of cinematic style. At first glance, Haneke does not seem to belong in this anthology—after all, he is Austrian, not German. But this is exactly Brinkema's point: her essay raises questions about national and cultural identity, the link between place and self, epitomized by the German terminology of "Heimat" and "Heimlichkeit" and its ideological implications.

The fourth section of the anthology does not offer so much an extension of the previous sections, though it lingers for a while in the 1970s and 80s, as it zeroes in on one specific aspect of postwar German horror film that, perhaps retrospectively, may appear to have been the representative manifestation of the genre. Entitled "Beyond Aesthetics, Against Aesthetics: German Splatter Films," this section collects three essays that each provide a unique take on the two most notable filmmakers of extreme, underground horror films—Christoph Schlingensief and Jörg Buttgereit. Chris Thomas-Vander Lugt's essay "Better Living Through Splatter: Christoph Schlingensief's Unsightly Bodies and the Politics of Gore" establishes an inventory of themes for the German splatter film.

More importantly perhaps, it also raises the question why, of all places, the splatter film should have flourished as much as it did in Germany from the 1980s on, linking it particularly to anxieties about German reunification and its aftermath. With these basic questions addressed, the second essay in this section, Mikel J. Koven's "Buttgereit's Poetics: *Schramm* as Cinema of Poetry" performs a reading of what one might call splatter aesthetics. Using Jörg Buttgereit's serial killer film *Schramm*, Koven demonstrates the basic visual and narrative mechanisms of splatter films and points out stylistic influences that link Buttgereit to more respected oppositional filmmakers, most notably Pier Paolo Pasolini. Focusing on the two films that established Buttgereit as the *enfant terrible* of postwar German cinema, Patricia MacCormack picks up the issue of cinematic style where Koven's analysis left off. Style, in MacCormack's analysis, is more a matter of collective than individual expression, an index of cultural obsessions and taboos. With the non-judgmental eye of the anthropologist, MacCormack's "Necrosexuality, Perversion and *Jouissance*: The Experimental Desires of Jörg Buttgereit's *NekRomantik* Films" provides a perspective on what, to many viewers and critics, is perhaps the most controversial aspect of Buttgereit's work—his preoccupation with the body after death.

The fifth and final section of the book, entitled "Interviews: Three German Horror Film Directors" gives three contemporary German filmmakers an opportunity to speak for themselves—Jörg Buttgereit, Robert Sigl, and Nico Hoffmann. While American readers may be somewhat familiar with Buttgereit, Sigl and Hoffmann are still relatively unknown outside of Germany, yet deserve wider recognition. It is their maneuvering between auteurist and commercial cinema, between directing and producing, as well as between film and television—more so perhaps than Buttgereit's more straightforward career path—that illustrates some of the problems for contemporary German filmmakers who operate in or around the boundaries of popular genres. In conversation with Marcus Stiglegger, all three, in discussing their careers and the social and economic circumstances under which their films were made, provide valuable insights into the current German film industry. All three interviews are made available in English for the first time.

For their hard work, patience, and perseverance, I would like to express my gratitude, first and foremost, to the contributors to this project. I am also greatly indebted to Jay McRoy and Donald Bellomy for editorial favors beyond the call of duty. My thanks also goes to all those friends and colleagues who have contributed ideas, criticism, and encouragement in casual and not so casual conversations over a long period of time, most notably among them David Willingham and Elisabeth Frazier, as well as Jack O'Connell. And, as always, I wish to thank my family, especially my mother, without whom nothing ever would have happened.

Notes

1. One example of such well-informed discourse, situated between journalistic or even fan discussion and scholarly analysis, is the web journal *Kinoeye: New Perspectives on European Film*, which has devoted considerable space to the discussion of new German horror films (see *Kinoeye*, at www.kinoeye.org/archive/country.germany.php).

2. Discussing the cycle of German horror films based on the Edgar Wallace adaptations in the 1950s and '60s, Ken Hanke echoes this sentiment when he states that his own topic, specifically, constitutes "one of the most under-explored areas of the horror genre, and quite possibly the ultimate in the realm of 'international horror cinema'" (Hanke 111).

3. Prawer admits that the "influence of Caligari on later film-makers has often been indirect rather than direct, mediated rather than unmediated" (Prawer 199).

4. One might want to add to these examples films produced by RKO, like Cooper's and Schoedsack's *King Kong*, as well as, a few years later, the films produced by Val Lewton at RKO. Tod Browning's *Freaks* also belongs in this list.

5. Thomas Elsaesser's magisterial *Weimar Cinema and After*, for example, opens with the statement: "The German cinema of the Weimar Republic is often, but wrongly identified with Expressionism" (3) Elsaesser's objection to this equation, which I myself have been embracing in my own discussion, is based on his rejection of its implied oversimplification. "No single stylistic label," he writes, "could hope to cover the many innovative ideas about film décor, the distinctive *mise-en-scène* of light and shadows or the technical advances in cinematography usually attributed to Weimar film makers" (3).

6. Individual critics have made attempts, in raising these questions, to demonstrate the relationship that exists between individual films made under the aegis of Goebbels' *Reichspropagandaminsterium* and the horror film (see, for example, Claire Sisco King's essay on the use of the dissolve in *The Eternal Jew* and *Jud Süss* and its relation to the same device in Weimar horror films, entitled "Imaging the Abject: The Ideological Use of the Dissolve," in *Horror Film: Creating and Marketing Fear*, Steffen Hantke, ed. (Jackson: University Press of Mississippi, 2004), 21–35. A systematic study of this phenomenon, however, has yet to be written.

7. For a detailed account of German film exile in the U.S., see Barbara Steinbauer-Groetsch, *Die Lange Nacht der Schatten: Film Noir und Filmexil* (Berlin: Bertz, 2000). It is important to note that the migration of German talent into the U.S. film industry did not exclusively affect film noir or the horror film, but that, cutting across a variety of popular cinematic genres tended to affect primarily mid-level and B-production—of which film noir, thrillers, and horror films were typical examples.

8. Let me raise one question in this context that strikes me as crucial for the assessment of horror film in general. While the question why German film production under the Nazis did not continue the tradition of horror film might have a concrete political and historical answer, the larger question why totalitarian regimes—from Nazi Germany to Stalinist Russia or Communist East Germany—have such an aversion toward horror films is more complicated. While none of these three film industries has a particular aversion to genre film per se, none of the three has contributed substantially to the legacy of horror film. The East German DEFA, for example, produced a fair number of Westerns—not exactly a genre that appears to be easily reconcilable with the pronounced anti-

Americanism of Cold War politics behind the Iron Curtain—but no horror films. Not a single one. Why not? Can horror film not be made to serve the interests of a totalitarian regime? Why do the monstrous abjections of horror cinema not lend themselves to the vilification of enemies of the ruling elite? Why does horror cinema appear to be useless to the requirements of political propaganda? These are questions for another time and place, yet questions that may be crucial for a critical assessment of the politics of horror film.

9. Exceptions to these accounts that place so much emphasis on German expressionist filmmaking tend to be thematic histories: Reynold Humphries' *The American Horror Film: An Introduction*, and Darryl Jones' *Horror: A Thematic History in Fiction and Film*. Both mention German expressionist films as examples of genre archetypes, themes, and stylistic idiosyncrasies, but are not interested in determining to what degree the style of prewar German filmmakers has had a lasting effect on the genre of horror film. See Darryl Jones, *Horror: A Thematic History in Fiction and Film* (London: Arnold, 2002) and Reynold Humphries, *The American Horror Film: An Introduction* (Edinburgh: Edinburgh University Press, 2002).

10. Klaus Kreimeier, in his history of the German Ufa, keeps using the expression "the 'gothicizing' films of the Weimar Republic" (109) instead of using genre terminology.

11. Gruenberger goes on to classify *Das deutsche Kettensägenmassaker* as political satire.

12. In *Dreadful Pleasures: An Anatomy of Modern Horror*, James Twitchell underwrites this notion of German horror classics as "art films" by contrasting directors like Murnau with those working in popular culture. An "important" film like Murnau's *Nosferatu* is not interested in "advancing the myth [of the vampire]" but instead "promulgate[s] one particularly self-conscious version" of this myth (Twitchell 141).

13. "...horror production by the German film industry [after the disruption of cinematic traditions during the Third Reich] did not return in any significant form until the late 1960s" (Halle, "Unification Horror" 284).

14. Kreimeier sees the Ufa style more as a set of production practices than a concrete and discernible set of visual conventions: "a strong capital base, squandered carelessly, a talent for large-scale organization and a tendency to go astray in microscopic detail; devotion to artistic excellence and to its perversion, which was empty perfectionism; a delight in the imaginative use of technology and in its reverse, which was mere technical slickness; a quest for philosophical power, but pursued in an intellectual vacuum; a 'will to form' that produced an amorphous ruin; craftsmanship, imagination, and diligence, and the waste of all those virtues through intellectual arrogance and the lack of a governing concept" (152). Kreimeier continues: "This interplay between perfectionism and inarticulateness, like that between mysticism and intellectual vapidity in the plot of *Metropolis*, was part of the 'Ufa aesthetic ...'" (155).

15. "... dies war ein Programm gegen die 'Wirklichkeit' und eine Absage an jeglichen Realismus. Seine Gestalt gewann dieses Konzept jedoch in höchstens zehn bis fünfzehn Werken, die als 'klassische' deutsche Stummfilme, heute zum 'unvergänglichen Erbe' der Kinematographie zu zählen sind" (Kreimeier 125–6).

16. For a more detailed discussion of film careers across the historical turning-point of the Zero Hour, see Sabine Hake, "The Legacies of the Past in the Cinema of Postwar Reconstruction," in *Popular Cinema of the Third Reich* (Austin: Texas University Press, 2001), 210–31.

17. If there was a rupture in continuity between Weimar and Bonn, it could perhaps be attributed to the films indebted to the fantastic, which constituted a significant part of prewar German cinema. "In contrast to its Weimar counterpart," Rentschler writes, "Nazi cinema denigrated the film of the fantastic as well as filmic realism. The former remained too open to irrational forces; the rightful place of the fantastic was to be an everyday of bright uniforms, hypnotic rituals, and dazzling spectacles" (216).

18. For this approach, I am strongly indebted to Thomas Elsaesser's discussion of the relationship between Weimar film and American film noir, which, as Elsaesser points out, "does not ultimately make sense as history if considered in terms of demonstrable cause and effect, agency and consequence" (420). Instead, Elsaesser suggests that historians read Weimar film through the lens of film noir, an ideological operation that serves "the function of simultaneously 'covering up' and 'preserving' the inconsistencies, multiple realities and incompatible entities named by German expressionist style, political exile and the Hollywood film industry, constructing an effect of self-evidence by giving them a single name and a cause-and-effect 'history'" (440, n6). To the degree that American film noir appears as a kind of "afterlife" of German expressionist film during the Weimar years, postwar German horror film could be considered a similar form of afterlife.

19. The haggling over the proper genre label makes Siodmak's case exemplary of the larger problem I have been discussing in the introduction. One critic, for example, refers to *The Spiral Staircase* as "a thriller-cum-horror set in 1906 New England and inside an effectively used Victorian-Gothic mansion" (Greco 74). Discussing the production history of *The Spiral Staircase*, Greco also points out that the film was considered a vehicle for Hitchcock and his idiosyncratic evocation of mood (74), and that producer David O' Selznick had considered Fritz Lang as his first choice of director (75). Another critic, Lutz Koepnick, cites Hollywood agent Paul Kohner calling Siodmak's style "vividly realistic" (169), but refers to *The Spiral Staircase* as meeting "the aesthetics of horror" (184) and being one of the "Hollywood gothics" (185). With reference to Lang and Hitchcock, Koepnick points out that *The Spiral Staircase* is essentially a whodunit (185), but that it also, very much like a neo-horror film, targets the sphere of the domestic, "contrary to [the] Victorian ideology" one might expect from its turn-of-the century New England setting, "as a space not of security and refuge but of terror and anxiety" (185). To qualify it further as a horror film, Koepnick also points out a scene in which a subjective shot literalizes the murderer's disgust at his victim's muteness by erasing the mouth from her face (he describes this as "surrealist iconography" 188), as well as the underlying process of forcing an audience to submit to, and perhaps ultimately enjoy, the killer's sadistic gaze (188). Sabine Hake has similar problems placing Siodmak's postwar film *Nachts Wenn der Teufel Kam* in a generic context. She classifies it as a "noirish thriller" (96), but suggests, albeit obliquely, a relationship to horror film by placing it next to Peter Lorre's *Der Verlorene* (by virtue of both directors being returned exiles) and then suggesting that both films use "the familiar Dr. Jeckyll/Mr. Hyde motif to evoke the disturbing image of a nation ravaged by guilt" (Hake 96).

Works Cited

Elsaesser, Thomas. Weimar *Cinema and After: Germany's Historical Imaginary*. London/New York: Routledge, 2000.

Geschichte des deutschen Films. Eds. Wolfgang Jacobsen, Anton Kaes, and Hans Helmut Prinzler. Stuttgart/Weimar: Metzler, 1993.

Greco, Joseph. *The File on Robert Siodmak in Hollywood, 1941–1951*. Dissertation.com, USA 1999.

Hake, Sabine. *Popular Cinema of the Third Reich*. Austin: Texas University Press, 2001.

———. *German National Cinema*. London/New York: Routledge, 2002.

Hanke, Ken. "The 'lost horror film' series: the Edgar Wallace *krimis*." *Fear Without Frontiers: Horror Cinema Across the Globe*. Ed. Steven J. Schneider. Godalming: FAB Press, 2003. 111–23.

Humphries, Reynold. *The American Horror Film: An Introduction*. Edinburgh: Edinburgh University Press, 2002.

Hutchings, Peter. *The Horror Film*. Harlow: Longman, 2004.

Jancovich, Mark. "General Introduction." *Horror, the Film Reader*. Ed. Mark Jancovich. Routledge Film Readers, Eds. Steven Cohan and Ina Rae Hark. London/New York: Routledge, 2002. 1–21.

Jones, Darryl. *Horror: A Thematic History in Fiction and Film*. London: Arnold, 2002.

King, Claire Sisco. "Imaging the Abject: The Ideological Use of the Dissolve." *Horror Film: Creating and Marketing Fear*. Ed. Steffen Hantke. Jackson: University Press of Mississippi, 2004.

Koepnick. Lutz. *The Dark Mirror: German Cinema between Hitler and Hollywood*. Berkeley: University of California Press, 2002.

Kreimeier, Klaus. *The Ufa Story: A History of Germany's Greatest Film Company, 1918–1945*. 1992. Transl. Robert and Rita Kimber. Berkeley: University of California Press, 1999.

Halle, Randall. "Unification Horror: Queer Desire and Uncanny Visions." *Light Motives: German Popular Film in Perspective*. Eds. Randall Halle and Margaret McCarthy. Detroit: Wayne State University Press, 2003. 281–304.

Larsen, Henrik. "'No Horror Films! We're German!': A Conversation Between Henrik Larsen and Harald Gruenberger." 2001. Accessed on August 15, 2005. www.cultmovies.dk /obskur/winnetou.htm.

Maddrey, Joseph. *Nightmares in Red, White and Blue: The Evolution of the American Horror Film*. Jefferson, NC, and London: McFarland, 2004.

Prawer, Siegbert Saloman. *Caligari's Children: The Film as Tale of Terror*. New York: DaCapo Press, 1989.

Rentschler, Eric. The *Ministry of Illusion: Nazi Cinema and Its Afterlife*. Cambridge: Harvard University Press, 1996.

Santner, Eric L. *Stranded Objects: Mourning, Memory, and Film in Postwar Germany*. Ithaca/London: Cornell University Press, 1990.

Skal, David. *The Monster Show: A Cultural History of Horror*. New York: Norton, 1993.

Twitchell, James B. *Dreadful Pleasures: An Anatomy of Modern Horror*. NewYork/Oxford: Oxford University Press, 1985.

Part 1:

The Long Shadow of Weimar: Expressionism and Postwar German Horror Film

Fritz Lang's *Dr. Mabuse* Trilogy and the Horror Genre, 1922–1960

Blair Davis

While Fritz Lang's Dr. Mabuse trilogy—1922's *Dr. Mabuse: The Gambler*, 1933's *The Testament of Dr. Mabuse*, and 1960's *The Thousand Eyes of Dr. Mabuse*—are not horror films in the traditional sense, they have enough elements of the horror to be considered entries to the genre at least in part. While the conventions of the horror genre used in each film are quite similar, the three films are distinctly different entities: the silent *Dr. Mabuse: The Gambler* resembles the crime-thriller serials of Louis Feuilliade such as *Fantomas* (1913) and *Les Vampires* (1915); *The Testament of Dr. Mabuse* has been declared the final film of the German expressionist cinematic movement; and *The Thousand Eyes of Dr. Mabuse* has more in common with the emerging spy film genre of the 1960s.

This essay will trace the evolution of the use of horror conventions in Lang's Dr. Mabuse films, with an emphasis on comparing the 1960 entry to the two previous films. Lang has long been celebrated as a director, perhaps even been counted among the true auteur filmmakers, and as such it is valuable to compare his treatment of the same narrative and visual elements across his career. Such a study is particularly useful in Lang's case, since the first Mabuse film comes relatively early in his career, while the final entry was the last film he ever made. The auteur theory promotes the study of directors according to recurring thematic and stylistic tendencies in their work, and so Lang's Mabuse trilogy makes a compelling case study in this regard: it is rare for an auteur director to make sequels to an original film, and rarer still to have a nearly thirty-year gap between such sequels.

The analysis will focus on the elements of the horror genre present in each of the three Mabuse films, as well as on how they are represented aesthetically on screen. Furthermore, the treatment of horror in each film will be examined in relation to what this speaks about the period in which it was made, with regard to how Lang's use of horror connects to larger trends in the genre in film history. In particular, the connection between the horror genre and expressionism will be examined in terms of how this relationship functions in both *Dr. Mabuse: The Gambler* and *The Testament of Dr. Mabuse*. This question will then be applied to *The Thousand Eyes of Dr. Mabuse*, as per how Lang's postwar filmmaking style differs from that used during the Weimar period, and as to how German prewar and postwar cinema differ in their validation of the horror genre and its

3

conventions. Lang is not traditionally associated with the horror genre, but he does utilize some conventions of the genre in regards to representing the supernatural in his Mabuse trilogy. Analyzing his utilization of these conventions will reveal how Lang approached the horror genre and its imagery, how the films were marketed, and what the implications of the Mabuse films are for the problematic of expressionism in Lang's career.

The Gambler, *The Testament*, and *The Thousand Eyes*

The question of genre is a complex one when it comes to studying Lang's Dr. Mabuse trilogy. The films defy easy categorization, as it is difficult to label them under one single genre that might wholly encompass their full range of thematic and stylistic elements. Together, the three films alternately resemble the detective or crime genre, the spy film genre, adventure serials, the suspense or thriller genre, and the horror genre, shifting back and forth between several or all of these various genres within each film. The latter genre, the horror film, is a significant presence in all three films, even though Lang uses its imagery and conventions sparingly. What I hope to show is that, while Lang's use of the horror genre may be relatively reduced in comparison to other genres represented in the Mabuse films overall, the cinematic techniques and supernatural images of the horror film that Lang utilizes are in fact quite crucial to the construction of the Dr. Mabuse character.

Though considered by modern critics to be one film, Lang's first Mabuse film, *Dr. Mabuse: The Gambler*, was originally produced as two films in 1922. Both bore the Dr. Mabuse name in their title, with the first subtitled *The Great Gambler: A Picture of the Times*, and the second subtitled *Inferno: A Play About People of Our Time*. Rather than being considered as one original film and its ensuing sequel, the two are now deemed to be one film separated into two volumes, much like Sergei Eisenstein's *Ivan the Terrible* or Quentin Tarantino's *Kill Bill*. Together, the two parts of *Dr. Mabuse: The Gambler* have a running time of nearly 4 hours, putting its length on par with any given chapter-serial film. Indeed, the film does feel quite similar to the serial films of director Louis Feulliade, such as *Fantomas* (1913) and *Les Vampires* (1915), in which sinister characters execute corrupt schemes, and drawn-out plots move from one cliffhanger to the next. It is a format Lang utilized when he made *The Spiders* in 1919, an adventure saga originally intended as a four-part serial. Lang only completed two chapters, but the film contains numerous cliffhanger perils and foreshadows the malevolent underworld of the later Mabuse films.

Another immediate parallel exists between the characters of Dr. Mabuse and Dr. Caligari from 1919's *The Cabinet of Dr. Caligari*, a film that had a distinct influence on the American horror films of the 1930s. Each character seemingly possesses supernatural abilities to control others, a trait that would later be utilized in the earliest films of the thirties horror cycle: *Dracula* (1931), *Svengali* (1931) and *The Mad Genius* (1931). Both Mabuse and Caligari even have a similar physical appearance at times; when Mabuse disguises himself as the old professor, he appears akin to Caligari's grotesque visage, sans glasses.

Just as the bug-eyed Caligari's intense staring creates an ominous feeling of menace, Lang uses shots of Mabuse's eyes for similar effect during several scenes in which characters are hypnotized by the evil doctor. Lang utilizes a close-up of Mabuse staring directly at the camera with intense eyes, his eyebrows arched forebodingly, and with dark make-up around his lower eyelids (similar to the expressionistic make-up used in *Caligari*) in order for the whites of his eyes stand out more starkly. The hypnotic result causes his victim to soon fall under Mabuse's control. The sinister quality of his eyes is described by several characters in the film with lines such as "He looked at me with his evil eyes, like a devil!" and "He had evil eyes, like a beast of prey!" During a later scene, Lang uses an extreme close-up of Mabuse staring directly into the camera, but blacks out the top and bottom thirds of the screen, so that all we can see are his hypnotic eyes. With the heavy make-up Mabuse uses in his old professor disguise, and the way the light catches his unkempt eyebrows that frame his eyes in this shot, Mabuse here appears feral, almost lycanthropic, as if ready to attack his victim. This kind of shot would be repeated in *The Testament of Dr. Mabuse*, with Lang placing shadows around Mabuse's eyes, while we hear someone describe how Mabuse "suddenly got an expression in his eyes, those eyes that leave you practically paralyzed!" This use of a close-up on the eyes for horrific effect would be repeated in several later Bela Lugosi films, most notably in *Dracula* (1931) and *White Zombie* (1932).

Other examples of horror iconography in *Dr. Mabuse: The Gambler* include the use of a séance, which would be repeated in *The Thousand Eyes of Dr. Mabuse*, making it one of the most distinctive images of the entire trilogy. Indeed, the cover of the video release of *Dr. Mabuse: The Gambler* (Image Entertainment, 2001) features an image from the séance, which establishes audience expectations before viewing that the film will contain supernatural elements, thereby connecting it to the horror genre in the viewers' mind. Séances would appear in numerous horror films, in particular the various 'old, dark house' films of the 1930s and 1940s, along with their parodies in the following decades. The séance as a generic convention of the horror film was popular with directors because it requires minimal set-up yet is both visually and dramatically compelling. That Lang decided to use a séance again decades later in his final Mabuse film, in which budgetary constraints are not so much an issue, is evidence of the continuing interest in the convention by filmmakers and audiences.

The séance in *Dr. Mabuse: The Gambler*, however, does not function according to its traditional usage in the horror genre. Lang downplays its supernatural quality by undercutting the scene's tension before the séance progresses very far. Prefaced with a title card reading "The other world," an establishing shot reveals eleven characters seated around a table as the scene opens, with their hands outstretched before them as they participate in the séance. A somber mood is quickly established, as the participants remain unmoving and contem-plative, mostly looking down at their hands upon the table. One character soon stands out amongst the group, however, as a young woman in the center-left of the screen starts to become restless, her upper body fidgeting slightly, with the slight trace of a smile on her face. The man to her immediate left soon turns and looks at her, seemingly distracted by her lack of attentiveness. Lang cuts to a medium shot of the participants, and pans left around the table to reveal each one. Each seems engaged in the event, alternately displaying anticipation, concentra-tion and concern. When the camera comes around the fidgeting young woman, her mood is revealed as being decidedly less serious than the rest of the group as she glances around, skeptically raises her eyebrows, laughs forcibly to herself and then struggles to regain her composure.

The leader of the séance, eyes cast upwards as she speaks, soon becomes distressed and clutches her face in horror. "An alien element is among us!" she declares. The séance becomes disrupted, as the members anxiously confer with one another and turn the room lights on. Yet Lang does not use this moment to create a sustained dramatic tension, as would typically be the case in the horror genre. Before the characters can determine what "alien element" might be among them, the young woman confesses her disbelief. "I'm afraid, ladies and gentle-men, the troublemaker is me!" she says. She excuses herself from the group as they consult busily amongst themselves, and Lang then moves to another scene.

As such, Lang does not utilize the séance for its potential as a trope of the horror genre; he is not interested in its possibilities in frightening the audience, rather he exposes the trope as perhaps being somewhat trite. By having the young woman snicker through the proceedings, Lang makes the other partici-pants seem rather gullible for taking the séance so seriously. Of particular note is how the leader of the séance has heavy dark makeup around her eyes—she is in fact the only member of the group to which Lang applies such expressionistic makeup. That she is exposed as gullible can be read as an attempt by Lang to undermine or perhaps mock the expressionist movement; this inclination will be seen more fully in *The Thousand Eyes of Dr. Mabuse*, in which Lang's position on expressionism is explored in more detail.

One of the most significant examples of horror iconography in *Dr. Mabuse: The Gambler* is also utilized in Lang's second Mabuse film, 1933's *The Testa-ment of Dr. Mabuse* (although not in *The Thousand Eyes of Dr. Mabuse*, for reasons that will be discussed later)—the use of supernatural apparitions. Several characters witness ghostly visions in the two films, and while it is open to inter-pretation whether these figures are literal or imagined, they nonetheless appear as ghosts to the audience. This is achieved through the use of superimposition, in which film is re-exposed either within the camera or with an optical printer, so that two or more images are placed over one another in the same frame. This allows each of the superimposed images to be sufficiently transparent to allow the other(s) to shine through, and can therefore be used to create the appearance of a ghost.

This cinematic technique had already been utilized to portray ghosts in hor-ror films for several years prior, such as in D.W. Griffith's film *The Avenging*

Conscience (1913), a loose adaptation of Edgar Allen Poe's story "The Tell-Tale Heart." In *Dr. Mabuse: The Gambler*, Mabuse is driving the character Count Told insane, who witnesses five ghostly doppelgangers come to life, sitting at a table while attempting to entice him with a game of cards. This scenario is repeated at the film's conclusion, when it is Mabuse himself who becomes insane, as his victims begin to appear to him one at a time in superimposed form, before finally becoming solid and drawing him into a similar game of cards at a table. They declare Mabuse to be a cheat, convicting him for his sins against them. As Mabuse stands up in a fit of rage, his victims simultaneously disappear in the blink of an eye.

One of Mabuse's victims in *The Testament of Dr. Mabuse*, Hofmeister, is also plagued by ghostly visions after being driven mad by the doctor. Yet after this occurrence the film's phantoms come only in the form of Mabuse himself, after he dies part way through the film. Mabuse returns after death to haunt Professor Baum, who had been treating Mabuse at his asylum and is now examining the dead man's notes. While Baum sits at his desk reading, Lang intercuts shots of various eerie artifacts that decorate Baum's office, such as rows of human skulls (including one which is smaller than the rest, yet with a disproportionately large cranium), and several tribal masks, figurines and what appear to be mummified or shrunken heads, replicas or otherwise. With voodoo hereby suggested, Lang then proceeds to bring Mabuse back from the dead as Baum reads Mabuse's writings out loud. As if reading a demonic incantation, when Mabuse's words are read out loud his power begins to take hold, and Baum's voice is soon replaced by Mabuse's. The sound of Mabuse's words takes on a frightful quality, as Michel Chion describes him as being "endowed with the eerie voice of an old witch" (31).

Lang then cuts to a medium point-of-view shot of a ghostly, superimposed Mabuse sitting in a chair across the table. He continues speaking the words that Baum had begun, yet we soon come to realize that Mabuse's face is altered from when last we saw it. The effect is reminiscent of a mask similar to those we have just seen on display. Lang cuts back to a close-up of Baum who appears half terrified and half possessed, with dark shadows around his eyes similar to those which Mabuse similarly had earlier in the film. This is followed by an extreme close-up of the spectral Mabuse's face, who looks much like a zombie; we can now clearly see how his eyes bulge extraordinarily, with his cranium resembling the human brain. This type of edit is known as a "shock cut," whereby something shockingly grotesque or violent is suddenly revealed to the audience. Shock cuts have long been a staple of horror films, having become standardized in the genre by 1925 with the Lon Chaney version of *The Phantom of the Opera* (Diffrient 52). By way of this device, Lang constructs Mabuse here as a hideous monster, assaulting the audience with the inescapable presence of his newfound deformity.

Lang follows this with a long shot of Baum and the spectral Mabuse sitting across the table from one another, but a second identical apparition soon rises from out of the first. The second Mabuse seems to teleport itself across the room—through the use of a quick fade out and fade in—and now stands immediately behind Baum, before moving forward to overlap with the professor. As Baum stares unflinchingly at the first Mabuse, the second begins to sit down in Baum's chair with the effect of entering his body, until finally both Mabuses disappear upon completion of the transfer. The specter returns at the film's conclusion, as Baum is being chased in his car by the police. Chaotic music begins to rise as a cue for the ghost's appearance, a standard convention of the horror genre. We first hear a whispered voice in the background before Mabuse slowly fades into view, seemingly hovering above Baum as he drives and commanding his actions by pointing forward towards their destination.

The frenzied music continues, with sharp strings repeatedly striking, similar to the effect that Bernard Hermann would use some years later in *Psycho* (1960). In his essay "Towards a Sign Typology of Music," Phillip Tagg describes this musical technique as an "anaphone that is at the same time sonic, kinetic and tactile." He goes on to show how the technique is particularly well-suited to the horror genre, analyzing the example of the shower scene in *Psycho*, whereby "the sonic anaphone is that of either a knife being sharpened or a repeated scream, the kinetic anaphone that of repeated, deliberate, regular movement (Norman Bates' multiple stabbing of Marion in the shower) while the tactile aspect is sharp, unpleasant and piercing…" (Tagg 372).

Once at the asylum, Mabuse leads Baum through several actions, and we hear the sharp, eerie note of an organ. The note is held for several beats as the scene progresses, once more following the conventions of horror film music as it creates an uncanny atmospheric effect. The use of a sharp musical note is present earlier in the film as well, prior to Mabuse's death. Michael Pinsonneault states in relation to film music that when the narrative presents elements that are "being challenged or destabilized … a range of more tense harmonic-melodic materials is generally used" in accompaniment (Pinsonneault 14–34). Hence, in foreshadow of the "destabilizing" events to come, as Baum stands over the still-living Mabuse in his cell a shadow quickly passes over the Professor and is followed by a single sharp musical note. The camera pans over to the corner of the room, where a ghostly image of Mabuse stands looking back at Baum, until the note and the image then begin to fade away. Baum rubs his eyes, glances back at the real Mabuse, and then looks again at the spot where the specter had just appeared. In both its dramatic pacing and use of cinematic convention, the scene creates the same feeling of tension and supernatural overtones as any of the contemporary American horror films of the period, particularly *Dracula* (1931) which is also set in an insane asylum.

These parallels with American monster movies seem even more significant considering the fact that Lang directly uses the word "monster" in describing his dramatic intent in creating Dr. Mabuse: "I had in mind a monster that controls people" says Lang, "a monster that hypnotizes people and forces them to do things that they don't want to do at all, to commit monstrous crimes" (McGilligan 87). Hollywood marketing departments took him at face value in 1952 when they released *Crimes of Dr. Mabuse*, an edited and dubbed version of *The Testament of Dr. Mabuse*. Their promotional material explicitly linked the film with the horror genre, thinking it the easiest way to sell the film: "Super-Man or Monster? You decide! More frightening than Frankenstein! Deadlier than Dracula! More hideous than Mr. Hyde! Madman? Monster? Murderer? Scientist?"(qtd. in Kalat 284)

The Horror of a Thousand Eyes

Nearly three decades would pass before Lang made *The Thousand Eyes of Dr. Mabuse* in 1960. It was a reluctant return for Lang, who famously declared, "I already killed that son of a bitch!" when asked to direct a new Mabuse film (Kalat 112). The film shares various elements with the two earlier films, yet there is a clear attempt to distinguish it from the prior entries, particularly regarding Lang's approach to representing the supernatural. With a plot centered around surveillance technology and nuclear theft, the film would seem to anticipate the emerging genre of spy films that would soon be popularized with the James Bond series. Indeed, the film's ultimate villain, Dr. Jordan, is reminiscent of a Bond villain with such lines as "I would have thrown the world into chaos with the rockets from your experimental plant. The famous push of a button ... I would have done it!" and describing Dr. Mabuse as "a genius, who wanted to throw this rotten world into a reign of chaos that could only be controlled by the one man who knows how to harness it for his own gain—me!"

In many ways, however, *The Thousand Eyes of Dr. Mabuse* can be read as horror film far more readily than its predecessors, despite Lang's intent otherwise. To begin with, the title is reminiscent of recent American b-movie horror films such as *The Beast with 1,000,000 Eyes!* (1955), *The Phantom from 10,000 Leagues* (1955), and *The Beast from 20,000 Fathoms* (1953). Lang's film is often referred to as *The 1,000 Eyes of Dr. Mabuse*, particularly in the film's advertising, as the use of a large number with ones and zeros was thought to give a film's title a distinct connection to the horror and/or science fiction genre, and also made for a visually compelling image on movie posters.

The American release of *The Thousand Eyes of Dr. Mabuse* allowed distributors to sell the film by its regular title or as *The Shadow vs. The Thousand Eyes of Dr. Mabuse*. Trade advertising for the film depicts the silhouette of a man, arms violently outstretched, and standing over a buxom woman. She appears to be dripping with blood, which pools beneath her. The ads tout the film as a "diabolical thriller," declaring, "Dr. Mabuse is on the loose! His evil and fiendish power unleashes a blood-bath of chemical and electronic terror!!" (qtd. in Kalat 128). Words such as "evil," "fiendish," "blood-soaked," and "terror" are traditionally part of the horror genre's promotional rhetoric, but are here used to sell a film that is only partially connected to the genre. In doing so, the American release can be seen as an attempt to retroactively rewrite the first two Mabuse entries as horror films, particularly given the way that the 1952 American release of *The Testament of Dr. Mabuse* was marketed in relation to such characters as Frankenstein and Dracula.

The opening credits confirm the expectation of "fiendish" imagery promised by advertisers, with the silhouetted image of a cityscape dominated by the kaleidoscopic presence of a dozen or more giant eyes swirling around the stratosphere. The effect is similar to the surrealist use of eyes in the unnerving Salvador Dali dream sequence of Alfred Hitchcock's *Spellbound* (1945), and establishes viewer expectation for the grotesque, the sinister and the supernatural. The audience is soon introduced to Cornelius, a self-declared clairvoyant who describes his abilities as "Magic powers [that] defy rational thought," whereby he has visions that appear to him "as if in horrible daydreams." Drawing a further parallel to "black magic," he soon removes his sunglasses to reveal his all-white eyes, giving him a decidedly inhuman appearance. Later in the film, Lang will frame Cornelius in a close-up shot as he gives a prophecy of death, staring directly into the camera. The shot is similar to that of the distorted and grotesque Mabuse in *The Testament of Dr. Mabuse*, and is utilized here for the same horrific effect, directly confronting the viewer.

The emphasis on the supernatural is further perpetuated early in the film with a police meeting, where it is said of Dr. Mabuse that, in 1932, "he died, insane. But if you talk to old-time criminals, they all say that Dr. Mabuse isn't dead! He can't die." As such, *The Thousand Eyes of Dr. Mabuse* sets the mood for the return of a villain thought dead at the end of the previous film—a convention utilized in most horror sequels. Besides the surrealist opening credits sequence, the opening of the film contains an attempted suicide, a dead body in a morgue, what the police describe as "a series of strange, unsolved crimes," a disfigured clairvoyant who apparently possesses magical powers, and the establishment of a possibly supernatural villain—all within the first fifteen minutes. Based on these combined elements, viewers are led to infer that the film belongs to the horror genre, adjusting their expectations from the opening to the film as whole.

The most significant difference, however, between *The Thousand Eyes of Dr. Mabuse* and the previous Mabuse films is Lang's utilization of cinematic techniques in his representation of the film's supposedly supernatural elements. The difference can be best analyzed in relation to the stylistic dichotomy between cinematic realism and formalism in the way that Lang portrays elements of the horror genre in the various films. *The Thousand Eyes of Dr. Mabuse* is relatively realistic in its use of cinematic style in representing the supernatural, as compared to the two other Mabuse films, which utilize the cinematic medium much more concretely in order to achieve the effect of the supernatural. In *Dr. Mabuse: The Gambler* and *The Testament of Dr. Mabuse*, Lang uses the stylistic device of the ghostly superimposition in order to suggest hypnotic influence and/or outright spiritual possession, as well as extreme close-up shots, cut-away editing to suggest hypnotic control, stylized makeup and the strategic use of shadows around his characters' eyes. In *The Thousand Eyes of Dr. Mabuse*, these types of formal techniques are not utilized in the same regard that they were in the previous films. Instead, there is more of a distinct attempt at realism in portraying the film's strange events more objectively. The diegetic world of the film is not broken by the use of formalist techniques to show supernatural events from an omniscient perspective, or one beyond the normal space and time that the characters in the film themselves inhabit. In the first two films, by contrast, the audience is able to see things that are not really there, or which could only truly be seen by the delusional characters themselves. In *The Thousand Eyes of Dr. Mabuse* this artifice is not utilized so as to preserve Lang's attempt at realism.

However, this dichotomy between realism and formalism reverses itself when considering the film's set design. In the first two films, the look of the film is relatively realistic, in that its settings are contemporary and reasonable for the period. Even during a scene with supernatural overtones, such as the séance sequence in *Dr. Mabuse: The Gambler*, Lang does not utilize the kind of heavily stylized art direction or cinematography that appeared in other contemporary expressionist German films dealing with similar subject matter. Instead, Lang stages the séance amongst the modern decor of a drawing room, with his actors' faces and outstretched hands shot with high-key lighting in order to eliminate any shadows. As such, the scene lacks the eerie atmospheric mood it would have had if it utilized a more heavily stylized expressionist visual technique.

In comparison, a séance also occurs in the major supernatural set piece of *The Thousand Eyes of Dr. Mabuse*, Cornelius's apartment. The decor of the room serves as a reflection of the character's mystical nature, in that the walls are covered with shiny stars, along with certain astrological figures arranged to match particular star patterns. When the lights are turned off for the séance, explicit attention is drawn to this design element through the cinematography, as there is a high degree of contrast between the luminous stars and the dark walls. As such, the design is almost expressionistic, in that it is an exterior projection of Cornelius's subjective reality—his professed nature as a supposedly supernatural figure is represented concretely in the room's decor. The design is much more similar to the expressionist set-pieces of *The Cabinet of Dr. Caligari*, which portrays the walls of an insane asylum with swirling spiral patterns on them to represent madness, than to anything in the previous two films. In fact, *The Testament of Dr. Mabuse* utilizes an asylum set but without this kind of expressionist design element.

Ultimately, in *The Thousand Eyes of Dr. Mabuse*, the supernatural is revealed to be fraudulent, as an undercover agent exposes Cornelius as a fake. By grounding the supposed supernatural events within the diegesis, Lang sets viewers up to fully accept the fact that these elements are indeed fake later in the film. Compared with the other films, we have not been shown anything that our eyes must accept as supernatural—i.e. the ghostly images that are unmistakably the iconography of the horror genre. Therefore, when the deceit is finally exposed, we have no reason to question the integrity of the narrative because of Lang's choice to ground the supernatural in the aesthetic mode of realism throughout the film. Indeed, we are told that we should have in fact been aware of the fraud the whole time, as the agent openly mocks Cornelius's affected mystical disguise and demeanor: "When you take off the sunglasses and stare into the distance—

very attractive! Really stylish. And the contact lenses—like in an American horror film!"

Thus, the conventions of the supernatural horror film are mocked, as if the film's mystical elements are to be viewed as absurd. This is in part a delicious moment of self-reflexive humor on Lang's part, but can also be seen as reflecting the director's desire to separate the film both from the horror genre as a whole, and more specifically from the supernatural overtones which have long been associated with the expressionist cinema of Weimar Germany, due to the enduring popularity of films such as *The Cabinet of Dr. Caligari* and *Nosferatu*. Although Lang's early films are often referred to as expressionist, several Lang scholars agree that this is a misnomer, and that only select instances within these films can truly be deemed expressionist. Lang himself resisted the label, even stating at one point that he and Bertolt Brecht "were the only people he knew who admitted that they did not know what Expressionism meant" (Gunning 147).

Furthermore, in *Dr. Mabuse: The Gambler* there is a telling exchange in which Countess Told asks Dr. Mabuse what he thinks of expressionism, to which he replies, "Expressionism is nothing but a game, but nowadays everything in life is a game" (qtd. in McGilligan 95). The line is alternately quoted by Thomas Elsaesser as reading "Expressionism!—it's a game of make believe! But why not? Everything today is make-believe" (Elsaesser 152)—an even more passionate critique. Lang's use of expressionism in the first two Mabuse films is mostly limited to the scenes depicting supernatural imagery. That he revised his method of representing the supernatural in *The Thousand Eyes of Dr. Mabuse,* opting for a more realistic approach in place of "make-believe," is therefore indicative of Lang's presumable desire to distance himself from the expressionist style associated with the trilogy's previous entries, a label that he never felt comfortable with having applied to his films throughout his career. By extension, it may be indicative of a further desire to distance himself from the horror genre, which much of German expressionist cinema has increasingly been associated with in film history.[1]

The State of Horror in Postwar Germany

The realism associated with the representation of supernatural imagery in *The Thousand Eyes of Dr. Mabuse* is also indicative of a significant trend in German cinema as a whole at the time of the film's release—the decreased viability of the horror genre. In the mid-to-late 1950s, the horror genre experienced a resurgence in many countries with the successes of director Roger Corman and American International Pictures in the U.S., and Britain's Hammer studios with new stars Christopher Lee and Peter Cushing. In Germany, however, the 1950s saw little to no production in the horror genre, symptomatic of an overall weakened film industry in the wake of the country's defeat in World War II. Unlike Japan, whose film industry soon thrived after losing the war, there were few film studios left in Germany by the 1950s, and those which remained were underfunded, mostly producing low-budget films. Instead of confronting the ghosts of the past within the discourse of horror film, Germany "fostered a genre of *Heimat* (homeland) films centering on sentimental domestic themes" (Sklar 455), which could be described as either attempting to pursue "a displaced dialogue with the past," or else simply producing films of "'limited and local character'" (Nowell-Smith 381–2).

With creative minds turned inwards to explore national identity, it is understandable that the horror genre was not prominent as Germany tried to come to terms with the real-life horrors that they had recently participated in. As evidenced from the lack of entries in such seminal horror film reference texts as *The Overlook Horror Encyclopedia* and *The Encyclopedia of Fantastic Film*, the 1950s saw no notable horror films produced in Germany, only a few thrillers and fantasy films with a faint resemblance to the genre.[2] Only by 1960 did the German film industry experience an upsurge in the number of thrillers produced in Germany, including such films that year as: *The Avenger*, which depicts the terrorizing of a movie studio; *The Hand of the Gallows*, in which a condemned criminal vows to return from the grave; the exploits of a sinister society in *The Fellowship of the Frog*; *The Red Circle*, in which Scotland Yard pursues a killer who leaves the title signature mark on his victims; the similarly premised *The Red Hand*; Scotland Yard versus the title killer in *The Strangler of Blackmoor Castle*; and *Dead Eyes of London* about a series of violent insurance murders. All of these films belong to a series of adaptations of stories by British author Edgar Wallace, and are set in London featuring British characters. As such, these films are even more symptomatic of an impoverishment in German cinema at the time, signifying a lack of versatility and diversity. Furthermore, by not presenting their audience with German characters or the imagery of Germany, these filmmakers made violent thrillers without necessarily providing any kind of cultural catharsis for German audiences in the wake of Nazism (or at the most producing such catharsis in the most oblique, roundabout way imaginable).

Lang's *The Thousand Eyes of Dr. Mabuse* came in the midst of this wave of thrillers, and in many ways can be considered to be the pinnacle of this new cycle of German filmmaking. It was a resounding success among German audiences, and led to the birth of a new series of Dr. Mabuse films under different directors in the years that followed. Producer Artur Brauner, who had recruited Lang to make a third Mabuse film, would deliver five more sequels between 1961 and 1964, and another in 1970: *The Return of Dr. Mabuse* (1961), *The Invisible Dr. Mabuse* (1962), *The Testament of Dr. Mabuse* (1962, a remake of Lang's original film), *Scotland Yard vs. Dr. Mabuse* (1963), *The Death Ray of Dr. Mabuse* (1964) and *The Vengeance of Dr. Mabuse* (1970). The films further combined the spy and horror genres, exploring the latter with far more interest—and more graphic violence—than Lang did in 1960. The alternate titles used to distribute these sequels readily evidence this fact, with such replacement monikers as *The Phantom Fiend*, *The Invisible Horror* and *The Terror of the Mad Doctor*. Not surprisingly, these films would return to the use of expressionistic visuals in their exploration of horrific imagery, drawing upon their nation's cinematic tradition in the hopes of recapturing some of its former glory.

As these sequels progressed, more new horror films began coming out of Germany as audiences once again found their taste for the macabre, in conjunction with a rising trend in horror production overall in European cinema. The year 1962 saw such German horror films as *The Door with Seven Locks* and the Mabuse imitation *Carpet of Horror. The Black Abbott, The Invisible Terror, The Phantom of Soho* and *The Strangler of London* followed in 1963. By 1964 the genre seemed to be in full resurgence, with more than ten horror films made that year, and dozens more by the end of the decade.

However unintentionally, Fritz Lang's *The Thousand Eyes of Dr. Mabuse* played a role in the rebirth of the horror genre in Germany in the 1960s. His Dr. Mabuse films were never horror films in the traditional sense, yet their imagery was often unmistakably linked to the genre. Lang may have resisted the genre, but he effectively utilizes its conventions in his representation of the supernatural in the Mabuse trilogy. The expressionist style, which is inherently based upon distortion, lends itself naturally to the presentation of horrifying characters and events; it is not surprising, therefore, that so many German films of the expressionist movement dealt in supernatural themes. In creating a new Mabuse film decades after the movement had ended, Lang sought to avoid the expressionist styles and techniques that had been overly read into his early films by many critics and viewers. As such, *The Thousand Eyes of Dr. Mabuse* is the story of a celebrated or auteur director taking back control over the meaning of his earlier films by making a sequel to them; in doing so, he is taking back control not from the studios but from those participating in the discourse on his films, from fans to film historians.

As such, Lang's final film serves to re-write the earlier films in the trilogy. *The Thousand Eyes of Dr. Mabuse* functions as a commentary on both the representation of supernatural imagery through expressionist means specifically, and on Lang's feelings on expressionism in general. Lang's use of horror in *The Thousand Eyes of Dr. Mabuse* is ultimately false; it is a shell game meant to deceive, but it is a rewarding deception nonetheless. In a way it is a fitting end to his Dr. Mabuse films, because this unveiling has been a long time coming for Lang. Raymond Bellour says of Lang that "there is no other filmmaker for whom vision is so nakedly and unequivocally the ultimate metaphor" (Crary 271), and Lang had in fact warned us from the outset of the trilogy that we are not to necessarily trust our eyes. "Expressionism is nothing but a game, but nowadays everything in life is a game," said Lang, via Dr. Mabuse. In his final film, Lang ultimately uses some sleight of hand to reveal the game to its players, and make his final statement about that magnificent "son of a bitch," Dr. Mabuse, who came to play a recurring role in the director's career.

Notes

1. Many film historians see expressionism as a distinct influence on the American horror films of the 1930s and 40s, and indeed many German emigrants such as Karl Freund and Robert Siodmak worked in the genre. Cinematheques and similar venues have also routinely chosen Halloween night to show such films as *Nosferatu* and *The Cabinet of Dr. Caligari.*

2. The most notable of these is the strongly anti-Nazi *Der Verlorene* (*The Lost One,* 1951), directed by and starring Peter Lorre.

Works Cited

Chion, Michel. *The Voice in Cinema.* New York: Columbia University Press, 1999.

Crary, Jonathan. "Dr. Mabuse and Mr. Edison." *Art and Film Since 1945: Hall of Mirrors.* Ed. Kerry Broughner. Los Angeles: Museum of Contemporary Art, 1996.

Diffrient, David Scott. "A Film Is Being Beaten: Notes on the Shock Cut and the Material Violence of Horror." *Horror Film: Creating and Marketing Fear.* Ed. Steffen Hantke. Jackson: University of Mississippi Press, 2004.

Elsaesser, Thomas. "Fritz Lang: The Illusion of Mastery." *Science Fiction/Horror: A Sight and Sound Reader.* Ed. Kim Newman. London: BFI Publishing, 2002.

Gunning, Tom. *The Films of Fritz Lang: Allegories of Vision and Modernity.* London BFI Publishing, 2000.

Hardy, Phil, et al., eds. *The Overlook Film Encyclopedia: Horror.* New York: Overlook Press, 1994.

Kalat, David. *The Strange Case of Dr. Mabuse.* Jefferson, N.C.: McFarland & Co., Inc., 2001.

McGilligan, Patrick. *Fritz Lang: The Nature of the Beast.* New York: St. Martin's Press, 1997.

Nowell-Smith, Geoffrey, ed. *The Oxford History of World Cinema.* New York: Oxford University Press, 1996.

Pinsonneault, Michael. "Social Dimensions of Hollywood Movie Music." Unpublished Ph.D. Dissertation. Simon Fraser University. 1999.

Sklar, Robert. *Film: An International History of the Medium.* Englewood Cliffs, N.J.: Prentice Hall, 1993.

Tagg, Philip. "Towards a Sign Typology of Music." *Secondo convegno europeo di anal si musicale,* ed. R. Dalmonte & M. Baroni. Trento: Università degli studi di Trento, 1992.

Young, R. G. *The Encyclopedia of Fantastic Film.* New York: Applause, 1997.

Peter Lorre's *Der Verlorene*: Trauma and Recent Historical Memory

Tony Williams

Returning to Germany after his period of exile in Hollywood, Peter Lorre encountered a cherished opportunity to direct for the first time in his career. He collaborated on a screenplay based on a real-life incident involving the murder committed by a doctor in the Elbe-Duwenstedt relocation camp and his eventual suicide. While Lorre underwent treatment for morphine addiction at an Alpine sanatorium, he met writer Benno Vigny, who suggested that they collaborate on a film based on Guy de Maupassant's short story "Le Horla" (Youngkin: 1998, 148–49; Kapcynski 157). Excited at the unexpected opportunity to direct a film, something he had attempted only on two occasions during his Hollywood exile, the distinguished actor also collaborated with journalist Egon Jameson on a screenplay which was rewritten at least six times and finally appeared in a serialized novel version in the *Münchener Illustrierte Zeitung* running for some twenty-two installments (Lorre: 1996; Kapcynski, 153, n.20).

According to contemporary reports, the production was riddled with problems. Lorre was inexperienced working behind the camera (Kapczynski 157). Lorre's co-star Karl John sustained an injury that resulted in a delay of eight weeks and heavy expenditure. Then there was the sudden death of producer Arnold Pressburger half way through filming, and the destruction of the edited film in a fire, which lead to Lorre's editor, C. O. Bartning, reconstructing the entire work from the surviving negative. The final product seems to lack narrative coherence. Lorre also appears to rely upon repeating his earlier performance of Hans Beckert in Fritz Lang's *M* (1931) to make a vague statement concerning past and present German history. Most journalistic accounts reproduced this perspective making the film's reception problematic. It did appear at the Venice Biennale Festival prior to its German release but then encountered mixed critical reception.[1] Subsequently, it only had a short run in German cinemas following its premiere at the Turm Palast in Frankfurt am Main on September 18, 1951. As several critics pointed out, German audiences were now seeking to escape both from the traumatic aftermath of the Nazi era as well as from those so-called rubble films, which revisited recent German history involving recognizable characters attempting to face the past in a devastated postwar landscape (Fehrenbach: 1995, 118–47, 149; Schandley; Kapcynski 160–61). Indebted to elements of German expressionist cinema and Italian neo-realist cinema, rubble films had already begun to lose popularity following the appearance of more escapist works, most noticeably *Heimat* films such as *The Black Forest Girl* (1950).[2] These films ignored the ugly lessons of the recent historical past to celebrate supposedly innocent and non-urban values existing within an unspoiled countryside. Unlike the products of the Nazi era, these films celebrated "Boden" without mentioning "Blut."

Following *Der Verlorene*'s mixed reception and the lack of further offers to work in Germany, Lorre returned to America, where he died in 1964. He had intended to work on further distribution of *Der Verlorene* to American audiences but the project fell through for unknown reasons. However, two years before his death, Lorre hinted that American desires to forget Germany's recent Nazi past in the Cold War era may have been responsible. "I have never and will not ever bring it over here. It would probably make money too. But there are times when an actor should know enough not to make money. I don't think the State Department would like me to indict any other country's politics." As well as quoting this statement by Lorre from a 1962 interview, Jerry Tallmer also mentions that Lorre was targeted by the House Committee of Un-American Activities between the years 1948–50. While visiting refugee camps and hospitals, the actor formerly known as Lazlo Lowenstein had tried to make sense of why the land of Goethe and Beethoven had become the slaughter house of Europe. This feeling undoubtedly occupied the minds of many in the Jewish artistic community who had fled Germany in the early Nazi period and later learned of the devastating fate visited on those who were not so fortunate to escape.

Lorre was not the only returning emigree to confront these issues. In 1948, the distinguished German-Jewish actor Fritz Kortner returned to his homeland to appear in the film *Der Ruf*, which he had also scripted. Directed by Josef von Baky, *Der Ruf* (*The Last Illusion*, 1949) featured Kortner in the role of Professor Mauthner. First seen living comfortably in his southern Californian exile, Mauthner decides to return to his old university in Germany wishing to re-establish his pre-Nazi sense of identity. As a German Jew he returns only to find that anti-Semitism and the forces which led him into exile are still rife. He dies totally disillusioned. As Schandley notes, *Der Ruf* "seeks to disclose the ugly German truths that even the terrible defeat of World War II did not change. It is not the mere existence of anti-Semitic tropes in the collective imagination that keeps the Nazi ghost from going away; but the fact that these old stereotypes and fantasies can, even after the defeat of Nazism, still serve as material for active Jew-baiting" (113). Like *Der Verlorene*, *Der Ruf* also operates in a different manner from the postwar rubble films. It avoids depicting the devastated urban landscapes of Germany in favor of more claustrophobic images emphasizing private, rather than public attitudes. The last sequence showing Mauthner's death from heartbreak moves away from techniques of classic cinematic realism used up to this point. "The cinematic style morphs from classical realism to a sort of psychological realism found most often in Weimar-era German film" (Schandley 114).

By contrast, *Der Verlorene* employs a complex series of flashbacks throughout a narrative which alternates between neo-realist images of the displaced person's camp where Lorre's Dr. Rothe now works under a new identity and past scenes of 1943 Nazi Germany. These past scenes often employ techniques of Weimar cinematic expressionism. Both Lorre and Kortner had worked in Weimar cinema and theater. While Kortner's Hollywood performances had not been affected by the demands of studios like those on Lorre to "[make] faces," his work in an American film noir style influenced by German expressionism was more limited than Lorre's (Tallmer). Kortner had played the nemesis of Conrad Veidt in *The Hands of Orlac* (1925), a role which Lorre would ironically repeat in the American version, *Mad Love* (1935), directed by Karl Freund. While Kortner's noir credits include only *Somewhere in the Night* (1946), *The Brasher Doubloon* (1947), and *Berlin Express* (1948), Lorre's Hollywood resume was far more extensive, including *Stranger on the Third Floor* (1940), *The Maltese Falcon* (1941), *The Mask of Dimitrios* (1944), *The Confidential Agent* (1945), *Black Angel, The Chase, The Verdict,* and *The Beast with Five Fingers* (all 1946). As Kapczynski notes, the

> despair and disillusionment typical of the noir vision (created by many of Loire's fellow exiles in Hollywood) must have seemed a good match for the barren world of postwar Germany. Lorre adopted key elements of noir aesthetics; he filmed in black and white, used high contrast lighting and canted camera angles, and established the film's overtly psychological tone on both the narrative and visual plane. (157)

Furthermore, Lorre was always to be identified with his title role in Fritz Lang's *M*, an identification that would lead to unfair comparisons with *Der Verlorene*. Such parallels do exist in certain scenes involving close-ups. But *Der Verlorene* operates on a darker and historically deeper level than Lang's earlier film. *Der Ruf* does refer to anti-Semitism in its narrative and thus, by implication, to the holocaust. Conversely, *Der Verlorene* does not. Yet, these historical facts do cast a dark shadow over the entire film, which, for example, the choice of lighting aptly symbolizes. By emphasizing visual techniques associated with German expressionism, which Hollywood adopted both for film noir and horror films (particularly, the 1940s Val Lewton RKO series), *Der Verlorene* is more symbolically powerful than *Der Ruf.* Kortner's Mauthner initially believes in the concept of German humanism. Lorre's Rothe never does. Although the film never explicitly refers to the Jewish Holocaust, it uses visual techniques to express postwar feelings concerning that event akin to later adaptations of *Macbeth*. Michael Anderegg sees Orson Welles's 1948 film version as "in many ways a post-Holocaust vision, a film fully conscious of the darkness at the center of the human soul, a darkness that Shakespeare, of course, had fully understood, but a darkness that awaited twentieth-century totalitarianism for its full realization" (85). Shakespearian scholar Jan Kott confirms this association, as did one of Welles's early critics, Maurice Bessy (Kott 85–97). Lorre even intended to follow up *Der Verlorene* with a contemporary film version of *Macbeth* set in postwar Germany emphasizing the character of a human being "with all his inner conflicts and suffering" (Lorre: 2004, 183).[3] However, the negative German response to *Der Verlorene* and Lorre's precarious financial position led him to return to America.

In *Der Verlorene*, Lorre engages in a counteroffensive against a culture in denial by creating, as director and lead actor, a traumatic text suggesting where the full responsibility actually lies. *Der Verlorene* engages in a social critique by means of a complex narrative structure that is not as confused as it may initially appear to be. Lorre's performance also evokes his earlier role in Fritz Lang's film *M*. During an interview conducted at the time of shooting, Lorre commented that the parallels between *Der Verlorene* and *M* were not accidental. His own murderer represented virtually the same character as that written by Fritz Lang and Thea von Harbou, but *Der Verlorene* emphasized the social implications of Lang's original character, giving Beckert a much more deadly relevance for the postwar era (Lorre: 2004, 182).

According to Christoph Fuchs, newspaper journalist Egon Jameson had not only inspired *M* but also the historical events behind *Der Verlorene* when he reported the mysterious suicide of forty-three-year-old Dr. Carl R., who may also have been responsible for the death of medical assistant Hannes R. from Kattowitz, a former chemical worker (167–8). This incident fascinated Lorre, who saw it as evidence of an unresolved national guilt originating from the Nazi era. Lorre also recognized the dramatic potential of the incident. Jameson worked on a serialized novel dealing with these events, which a Munich newspaper promoted on the basis of Lorre's name. This, he hoped, would lead to a film version he would also direct and appear in. Turning down an offer by Bertolt Brecht to play *Hamlet* in East Berlin, Lorre devoted his energies to his project, which disavowed traditional representations of good and evil as well as the familiar concept of the moral development of a character seen in postwar films such as John Brahm's *Die Goldene Pest* (1954) or *Der Ruf*.

However, Lorre never intended German audiences to indulge in the convenient forms of cinematic disavowal that later films offered when they projected guilt onto convenient scapegoats (such as a demonic SS officer in Robert Siodmak's *Nachts, wenn der Teufel kam* (1957)). Instead, he aimed at making his audiences confront those dark psychological collective mechanisms responsible for denial of the past. Returning to Germany, Lorre discovered that the spirit of fascism was still alive in a nation engaged in denial and self-pity. Like Orson Welles, he would never accept Germany's plea for forgiveness nor forget the crimes of the past (Youngkin: 1996; Leaming 280; Naremore 113).

Lorre's film does not offer stereotypical characters representing good and evil or depict a convenient moral awakening whereby characters would admit their guilt and thus serve as convenient scapegoats for audiences not wanting to admit their own. *Der Verlorene* attempted to challenge German audiences to make sense of a text that did not involve familiar narratives and identifiable characters and thus diverged dramatically from Hollywood films, German national cinema, and German rubble films such as Wolfgang Staudte's *Die Mörder Sind unter Uns* (1946). Although *Der Verlorene* can hardly be described as Brechtian, it is "alienating" in a particular manner, perhaps owing much to Lorre's association with both the playwright and his works.

Gerd Gemünden has noted an oblique Brechtian type of acting that Lorre brought to many of his Hollywood roles, which may also be relevant to understanding his performance in *Der Verlorene* (85–107). He also notices how Lorre's Hollywood performances often "provide a rupture in the complete immersion in the role on which Hollywood studio acting is premised. Employing the notion of gestus of his friend and mentor Bertolt Brecht, Lorre uses bodily posture, accent, and facial expression to exemplify social relationships" (99). Following Gemünden's insights one could also argue that the film's structure may even anticipate the more radical formalistic Brechtian experiments employed by Alexander Kluge in *Artists under the Big Top: Perplexed* (1968). According to Marc Silberman, this film "invites the spectator to initiate a dialogue by constructing a point of view from the parts offered, or more precisely, by filling in the spaces or gaps between the parts" (193). Kapczynski also recognizes Lorre's indebtedness to various influences, especially *M*. Lorre's "appearance on the postwar screen performs a doubled return of the repressed—reminding the audience not only of Jewish persecution under National Socialism but also the failure of German postwar society to address that legacy" (162). She also recognizes Lorre's use of generic motifs in concrete historical and political situations, as well as the actor's possible employment of those familiar double motifs from Karl Freud's *Mad Love* (1935), a Hollywood remake of that old German expressionist favorite *The Student of Prague*, itself indebted to Edgar Allan Poe's *William Wilson*. However, she never explains *why* the reference to Jewish persecution and the holocaust remains undefined in a film employing horror motifs in such a manner.

To contemporary audiences, *Der Verlorene* brings to mind Hou Hsiao Hsien's *A City of Sadness* (1989) in regard to both narrative structure and the concept of traumatic memory. Although set in the period leading to the historical events of February 28, 1947, when the Nationalist Government in Taiwan committed atrocities against the local population, *A City of Sadness* never explicitly depicts that incident. Instead, it engages in a sophisticated flashback technique juxtaposing images of past and present in an attempt to avoid a melodramatic recreation of these traumatic events in Taiwanese history. Robert Chi sees this ambiguity as a deliberate part of the film's strategy, making it a "historiographical rather than a historical film," which attempts to come to terms with the postwar Taiwanese White Terror that still remains a taboo subject (74). The term "historiographical" is not accidental in terms of its conflation of the autobiographical and the biographical elements involving an individual's attempt to confront historical memory, especially one involving individual and collective trauma. Chi sees such issues operating in *A City of Sadness*. The same may be true for *Der Verlorene*.

Differences certainly exist between *Der Verlorene* and *A City of Sadness* concerning national cinematic concerns, styles, and historical associations. But both employ a particular type of flashback device in connection with a traumatic memory in an attempt to awaken their respective audiences to personal and collective issues contained in recent history. The role of flashbacks is crucial. As

Chi notes, *City of Sadness* juxtaposes images of past and present to deny its viewers any escape into avoiding the traumatic implications of past national memory (74). Both films also avoid familiar cinematic images involving character representation and genre. During the American re-release of *Der Verlorene* in 1984 several critics such as Elliot Stein and John Morrone noted how Lorre appeared to depart deliberately from the usual cinematic conventions in order to make a film tapping his inner sadness.[4] Chi recognizes that Hou Hsiao-Hsien uses "flashbacks to suggest that the past in fact serves the present rather than vice versa" (59) in a historiographical film in "which the past as a memory flashes up in a moment of danger" (Benjamin 255, qtd. in Chi 63).

The moment of danger in *Der Verlorene* is Rothe's encounter with his former Gestapo assistant. After successfully concealing his real identity for some seven years, Rothe is forced to confront the past as well as his involvement in the Nazi era no matter how much he has attempted both consciously and unconsciously to deny it. This encounter leads to an intricate series of flashbacks which both structure the film and reveal past and present as indissoluble. Both *A City of Sadness* and *Der Verlorene* may be understood, despite their formal differences, as traumatic texts attempting imaginary resolutions of real contradictions by a particular use of flashback technique.

Commenting on the fact that the "fall of Hitler's regime forms the unspoken center of *The Lost Man*" and yet is "never made explicit onscreen," (147) Kapczynski further notes the film's use of a complex and fragmented narrative structure (149). Past and present are juxtaposed in twenty-one segments whereby ten memory flashbacks intrude into the film in a radical and disrupting manner. Citing Maureen Turim's reference to a flashback operating as an "ideological reframing of history" (105), Kapczynski remarks that *Der Verlorene*'s narrative structure is one where "the past cannot be neatly cordoned off, but repeatedly reasserts itself as it perforates the present moment. As Lorre's Rothe recognizes at the film's conclusion, "there can be no forgetting" (149). This is equally true for the understanding of trauma as it is for the narrative structure of *Der Verlorene*. Lorre departs from the traditional use of the screen flashback, which is most often used for personal confession or reframing historical memory through individual subjective experience. He instead uses it as a forum to debate social transgressions. Instead of having Rothe exclusively narrate the past, the film employs two narrative voices, as Hoesch (Karl John) often contributes to Rothe's past memory. As Kapcynski notes on several occasions, Rothe interrupts the flashbacks and although his voiceover continues,

> the film returns briefly to the frame narrative to show Hoesch alternately listening and sleeping through Rothe's account. These intrusions subject the past, like the present, to regular reevaluation and emphasize the framing intrinsic to the work of historical narration (while also indicating Lorre's scepticism about the willingness of some audiences to hear such stories). (150)

Furthermore, Lorre performs a unique, personal intervention into the narrative. He extends the boundaries of the traditional flashback by having his character entering into a debate with Hoesch during two shared voice-overs. They first discuss Rothe's wartime life before his murder of Inge and then debate Rothe's later accidental discovery of the attempted assassination of Hitler. Kapczynski sees this as the actor entering into "the ongoing debate about German guilt, and appears to incriminate even himself in his indictment of German society. In the role of the sociopathic doctor, the Jewish exile shoulders the burden of the German past" (150–1). Although Kapczynski's observations about the film's exilic perspective and Lorre's recreation of Hans Beckert, now firmly entrenched within the Germany of 1943, are both accurate and useful, the film's recreation of contemporary historical trauma and collective memory deserves further exploration. A closer analysis of *Der Verlorene* is necessary to reveal the particular manner in which Lorre interweaves past and present in his use of flashback.

The film's credits contain a caption emphasizing that the content is not fictional but "drawn from factual accounts of the recent past." It opens with a long shot of a train crossing a railway track. After the train passes, the barrier is raised and several people walk past, among them Dr. Neumeister (Lorre), who works at a refugee camp administering inoculations to displaced persons. As he walks through an area resembling a former concentration camp, another worker informs him that Novak (Karl John), a recent arrival, may be a possible assistant for his work. Neumeister comments about the need for more "serum and syringes" before he treats a refugee for an eye problem. These two references are by no means accidental. We later learn that under his former identity of Dr. Rothe, Neumeister was once a respected bacteriologist whose services were very much appreciated by the Nazi war machine. What these "services" were remains as deliberately vague in the film as many other historical references.

The 1943 sequences contain little reference to the Nazi era; no one, for example, ever presents the "Heil Hitler" salute. Instead, the flashback sequences depict a world of privation that is strikingly similar to postwar Germany. Frau Hermann (Joanna Hofer) is forced to embark upon outside shopping excursions for potatoes while the inhabitants of Hamburg mention the "ersatz" quality of many essential items such as handbags manufactured from dog skin and the enigmatic use of fish skins. These lines may contain ironic and oblique references to the "productive" ways in which war criminals such as Ilsa Koch (the "beast of Buchenwald") used skin from the dead bodies of concentration camp victims. After the death of Inge (Renate Mannhardt), Ursula Weber (Eva-Ingeborg Scholz) takes her place in the Herman residence due to being "billeted by the housing department," a detail that also suggests the lack of accommodation in the postwar era as seen in several rubble films such as *The Murderers Are Among Us* (1946). All characters in the film's past and present seem suspended in a limbo existence involving both denial and reluctance to change and face the implications of past and present history. In this uncanny present, Neumeister and Novak play the same professional roles of doctor and assistant as they did in 1943. The second encounter between Neumeister and the patient with the eye infection carries this metaphor of willing blindness even further. Neumeister comments that perfect vision will not be restored unless the patient really wishes this to be the case. There is no indication given that Neumeister's patient will follow these instructions. The same, Lorre seems to imply, also applies to *Der Verlorene*'s contemporary German audiences.

While administering an injection to a patient, Neumeister sees Novak for the first time. Both men recognize each other. Formerly Dr. Rothe's Gestapo assistant under the name of Hoesch, Novak tells Neumeister to control himself: "It couldn't be avoided." Rothe leaves, and the sequence ends with the camera tracking away from him as he walks on the railway tracks, his final destination at the end of the film. The next scene involves his encounter with Hoesch and the beginning of a complex series of flashbacks intertwining past and present not only by combining the voices of both men but also employing several visual gestures merging both time levels. For example, following Rothe's murder of Inge, the scene dissolves to revealing a cigarette on the floor which appears to belong to the past. However, the voice-overs of Rothe and Hoesch reveal that the narrative has returned to the present. Past and present blur in one scene with Rothe performing an identical gesture that initially makes it difficult to discern the correct time level. After informing Rothe about the death of Oberst Winkler (Helmut Rudolph), both men go to the canteen where the series of flashbacks begins.

Lorre uses German expressionist and Hollywood film noir techniques to depict Rothe's past world of December 8, 1943. German audiences would immediately recognize the period as anticipating the eventual fall of the Third Reich, with frequent bombing raids on Hamburg and the aftermath of the defeat of the German Army at Stalingrad. The first flashback begins with references to Rothe's affluent lifestyle at this time, and the first shot shows him on a crowded train. This is by no means redundant since the train has a particular metaphorical role to play in the film. When Rothe arrives at his laboratory, Winkler informs him that his fiancee Inge has been passing his research to London via her father now living in Stockholm. What Rothe's research involves remains perversely unclear in the film. However, enough indications exist to suggest that Gestapo interest in Rothe has nothing to do with disinterested scientific research and everything to do with the war effort. When Rothe draws blood from a rabbit, Winkler is squeamish. "No, no. I can't stand to see blood, especially when it's from little defenseless animals." His phrase evokes Himmler's reaction when witnessing the death by machine gun of Jewish civilians, an event which led to the search for a more "sanitized" method of extermination. Whether engaging in biological warfare experiments or attempting to find more efficient means than Zyklon-B for the "final solution," Rothe is definitely one of those Nazi doctors whose infamous experiments have been documented in key texts by Robert J. Lifton, Michael Kater, Arthur L. Caplan, and David A. Hackett. Rothe may even be working on perfecting Tablan, a lethal nerve gas used during World War II by German and Japanese doctors on prisoners (www.noic.com/biowatch). Although Rothe neither belongs to the Party nor directly engages in the type of experiments undertaken by

Mengele at Auschwitz, he is still responsible despite the fact that he chooses to deny any implications involving future use of his experiments. Rothe is a very important person in the Third Reich. Although a civilian, he is thought valuable enough to necessitate a Gestapo agent to keep him under surveillance both in the realms of his private and public life. Until he learns about Hoesch's seduction of Inge, he remains blissfully unaware—or chooses to do so—of his deadly contribution to the war effort. Despite lacking the notoriety of a Dr. Mengele, Rothe's disinterested scientist is still a dangerous person, as well as a figure of moral ambiguity. All sides in this war may have been interested in the fruits of his labor; Lorre may well have understood this as his later enigmatic remarks on the film's lack of American distribution suggest.

Once Rothe learns that Inge has sexually and politically deceived him, he creates his own epidemic of serial killings. His first murder is accompanied by a facial expression of tenderness and murder similar to the one he fashioned for his memorable role in Lang's *M*. These close-ups use techniques from German expressionism, the horror film, and film noir to express the nature of Rothe's "Lustmord," so much so that one early Frankfurt newspaper reviewed the film using the title, "Das Unheimliche Gesicht"—the uncanny face (Clipping service). The review also evokes those "bedside manner" expressions which often appeared on the faces of concentration camp doctors as many survivors have testified.

The film implicitly suggests that Rothe's murderous actions do not result from feelings of sexual betrayal but originate from his medical experiments in the service of the Third Reich. After learning about Hoesch's involvement in his betrayal, Rothe returns to his laboratory, puts his hand on a table he has earlier told an assistant to leave uncleaned, and moves to a mirror. Rothe sees his face in the mirror. Forehead and cheek are now smeared with the blood from the table. It is obviously contaminated blood from the "mutation" experiments he has been conducting. Rothe does not become a shambling monster or sleepwalking killer, produced by a criminal brain such as Victor Frankenstein's or Dr. Caligari's. He becomes his own scientific creation. On one level, he is affected by learning of Inge's political and sexual acts of betrayal. But the knowledge destroys his personal complacency and leads to his infection by the very virus he has developed for the Nazi war machine. His contamination results from forces he could have controlled. In Lang's *M*, Beckert emphasizes that he is motivated by irrational forces beyond his control. *Der Verlorene* supplies us with several reasons for Rothe's activities, the most important one being his "infection" by the very virus he has created for use by the German war machine. His murderous self becomes manifest in terms of a return of the repressed recognition overcoming the denial mechanisms he employs in his everyday life. Rothe denies the implications of his experiments in the same way that he will suppress the memory of his actual murders. These actions occur when Rothe's back blacks out the screen as he moves to kill Inge and later Helene (Lotte Rausch), the latter murder occurring, significantly enough, under cover of a *blackout* during an air raid.

This visual technique of blacking out the screen by using the back of the murderer is not just Lorre's formulaic or instinctive use of a cinematic cliché. It deprives the audience of viewing a murderous act and thus parallels the denial and convenient lack of memory affecting Rothe's character; after all, the murderous activities of the Third Reich supposedly occurred outside the perception of the German public. After Rothe recovers his senses following Inge's murder in the third flashback, he comments, "When I had finally come to, I could not remember anything." It is a comment ironically criticizing Germany's convenient collective postwar amnesia. While Rothe engages in irrational acts of murder, the State is pursuing the more deadly and equally irrational aspects of the Final Solution.

Like the very nature of the war never being explicitly referred to in both flashbacks and the present time of the film, Rothe's murderous activities are ignored by the State for its own reasons. After Winkler learns of the murder, he blithely remarks, "We'd have had to eliminate her anyway. This way, she'll still have a decent burial." He terms her death as "a clear case of suicide by strangulation with a black leather belt" effectively exonerating her murderer. The system needs Rothe. As Winkler remarks, "Do your work, Doctor." Eventually, Rothe refers to himself, Hoesch, and Winkler as "bacilli." All three are part of a deadly virus infecting Nazi Germany, a virus whose implications are denied by its host. Lorre's Rothe becomes the uncanny face—"das unheimliche Gesicht"—of Fascism, his actions motivated by an omnipresent system in which Hoesch often operates in a manner akin to Maupassant's "Horla." Kapczynski refers to this in regard to Inge's final moments when Rothe says in voice-over, "She wanted reconciliation. Would have worked, I think. But then something happened—the phone rang, you see. All of a sudden it was as if you were standing right there in that room" (164–65). However, the "Horla motif" is a convenient escapist device. Nobody can escape accountability for their actions, not even Rothe. He easily succumbs to Winkler's bland advice when he attempts to make himself accountable to justice for Inge's murder. Unlike the conclusion of *M*, Lorre's murderer will not be brought to justice. In the world of 1943, he is an important part of a war machine whose collective guilt leads it to deny the individual aberration of Dr. Rothe.

As noted, the film uses an interlocking series of flashbacks linking past and present. Rothe and Hoesch get increasingly drunk throughout the film, the latter falling asleep at one point only to be woken up by Rothe to continue the narration. After a bombing raid has destroyed Rothe's Hamburg apartment and everyone inside, he is able to declare his former self dead and go into hiding under the new identity of Dr. Neumeister to become, ironically, a "new master" of his former self. When the film finally returns to the present, Hoesch mentions that the Gestapo knew that he had survived but did not think him worthy of attention. Hoesch's statement echoes the manner in which, after the war, the American military authority turned a blind eye to the escape of figures such as Eichmann and Mengele. Rothe eventually kills his nemesis and commits suicide in front of a train concealing his face with his hand in a manner evoking that earlier mirror shot in the laboratory.

Lorre also criticizes the plot to kill Hitler as opportunistic. Winkler's involvement, as well as the plot's resemblance to a children's game, challenge its conventional historical interpretation. He regards the July 20, 1944 assassination attempt merely as any excuse to diminish German responsibility for the Hitler regime. *Der Verlorene* presents the incident as just another example of contemporary irrationality. As Hoesch states, "Everything was bizarre in those days." He also mentions Mussolini's rescue by German paratroopers, as well as Rudolf Hess's abortive 1941 secret mission to England. These were futile actions that never altered the course of history. Lorre also inserts himself as a fictional character in the narrative by sharing in his homeland's collective guilt. As Kapczynski notes, Lorre

> enters into the ongoing debate about Jewish guilt, and appears to incriminate even himself in his indictment of German society. In the role of the sociopathic doctor, the Jewish exile shoulders the burden of the German past. At the same time, this unusual multi-voiced narration can also be read as an attempt to stage a discussion with the nation he had left behind. The film initiates a fantastic conversation with the German past, and implies that historical narrative is subject to negotiation between victims and perpetrators. (150–51)

Lorre's oblique treatment of the Nazi era in *Der Verlorene* may be due to reticence over attracting more unwelcome attention by the American government. But another explanation is possible which may more appropriately explain *Der Verlorene*'s indirect mode of narration. Lotte Eisner had noted earlier that "this film's suggestive power is the fruit of devices which always have their origin in the situation. We have to read between the lines" (339). Like the previous rubble films, *Der Verlorene* also participates in postwar issues of collective memory whereby issues of what gets remembered and how it gets remembered represent issues of what Schandley defines as "intense contestation" (7–8). But it does so by employing a less familiar form of cinematic narration by leaving certain things unspoken and expecting audiences to fill in the gaps. Schandley refers to the work of sociologist Maurice Halbwachs (1877–1945), who was murdered at Buchenwald, in relation to his definition of rubble films. Although Schandley never refers to *Der Verlorene* in relation to these films, his application of Halbwachs's ideas concerning the role that present memory has in defining how the past becomes remembered is highly relevant here, particularly in the film's unique use of flashbacks where past and present merge and denial mechanisms operate during both eras.

Halbwachs was particularly interested in the social framework of memory through which individuals as group members engage in collectively remembering the past. He believed that such memories were often highly subjective rather than objective in preferring the comforting assurances of communal memory rather than their actual historical implications. *Der Verlorene* may also be compared with other postwar films that attempt to deny the implications of the recent past. Unlike Wolfgang Staudte's *Rotation* (1949), it does not regard the Nazi era as one of those inexplicable catastrophes which affect mankind, nor will it seek the timely anachronisms offered by Heimat films such as *The Black Forest Girl* (1950) to avoid unresolved contradictions involving the recent past. Unlike Pabst's *The Last Ten Days* (1955), *Der Verlorene* will not project any imaginary resolutions of the Nazi era resulting in the avoidance of any ugly recollections of the past that would undermine the ideological mechanisms governing popular memory of the recent past. Instead, the film employs its own special devices which often contradict particular trends in postwar German cinema noted by critics such as Fehrenbach and Silberman (97–142).

Furthermore, if we also see *Der Verlorene* as a text that provides the audience with a traumatic event in attempting to debate the issues of past and present German history, we can also understand it in terms of Maurice Halbwachs's arguments concerning how the present situation affects the selective perception of past history and how conceptions of the past are affected by the mental images we employ to solve present problems. Here Lorre's membership in both the German and the Jewish community plays a role in his attempt to deal with the trauma of recent historical memory that plays such a fundamental role in *Der Verlorene*.

Cathy Caruth notes that when Freud wrote *Beyond the Pleasure Principle,* following the aftermath of World War I, he observed the presence of what he termed "traumatic neurosis" involving the reenactment of an event which cannot be left behind. Applying Freud's ideas to literary and cinematic texts such as *Hiroshima Mon Amour* (1959), Caruth comments that

> each one of these texts engages, in its own specific way, a central problem of listening, of knowing, and of representing that emerges from the actual experience of the crisis. If traumatic experience, as Freud indicates suggestively, is an experience that is not fully assimilated as it occurs, then these texts, each in its turn, asks what it means to transmit and to theorize around a crisis that is marked, not by a simple knowledge, but by the ways it simultaneously defies and demands our witness. (Caruth 1996, 5)

She further remarks, in a sentence having several parallels to the cinematic structure of *Der Verlorene*, that questions concerning crisis and traumatic experience can never be asked in a straightforward manner but must "also be spoken in a language that is somehow literary: a language that defies, even as it claims, our understanding" (5). Unlike Staudte's *The Murderers Are Among Us* and Rossellini's *Germany, Year Zero* (1947), *Der Verlorene* is not an accessible film. Although employing postwar techniques of expressionism and neo-realism, it contains characters who are not as easily definable as those in most rubble films. *Der Verlorene* also employs a more sophisticated flashback structure than that used in Staudte's acclaimed film. Caruth (1995) also comments on the role of the flashback in relation to traumatic memory. She sees it as providing a particular form of recall surviving at the cost of willed memory or the continuity of conscious thought in a manner which may explain the oblique nature of historical memory in *Der Verlorene*.

> The ability to recover the past is thus closely and paradoxically tied up, in trauma, with the inability to have access to it. And this suggests that what

returns in the flashback is not simply an overwhelming experience that has been obstructed by a later repression or amnesia, but an event that is itself constituted by its lack of integration into consciousness. Indeed, the literal registration of an event—the capacity to continually, in the flashback, reproduce it in exact detail—appears to be connected, in traumatic experience, precisely with the way it escapes full consciousness as it occurs. (152–53)

This sheds much light upon *Der Verlorene*'s historical past, in which significant details appear mystified by recourse to techniques indebted to German expressionism, film noir, and horror cinema. It also provides another explanation for the suggestive nature of Lorre's film other than that supplied by certain critics. Eisner is correct in stating that we still "have to read between the lines" (339). By challenging its viewers in this manner, *Der Verlorene* manages to escape from those melodramatic devices, susceptible to indulging the audience's desire for denial, that were later used to demonize the Third Reich as an aberration in German history and conveniently to displace guilt onto individual scapegoats. In this way, it manages to avoid contemporary German cinematic tendencies resulting in a withdrawal from ideology achieved "through the insistence on individual rather than public morality and a preference for ethical rather than political categories of historical explanation" (Hake 96) by operating as a traumatic text of historical memory. As Hoesch says to Rothe during their first postwar encounter, in a line evoking the denial syndrome of the recent past operating both in German politics and cinema, "I only ask you to consider your silence as a reliable and permanent agreement … as a permanent and mutual pact between us." Rothe will keep his silence, but Lorre will not.

Caruth refers to Freud's example of the train accident in *Beyond the Pleasure Principle* in which the survivor walks away supposedly unharmed only to suffer symptoms of the shock several weeks later. She notes that "the recurring image of the accident in Freud . . . seems to be especially compelling, and indeed becomes the exemplary scene of trauma par excellence not only because it depicts what we can know about traumatizing events, but also, and more profoundly, because it tells us of what it is, in traumatic effects, that is not precisely grasped" (6). She further notes that trauma narratives do not just represent violence but also convey the impact of trauma's very incomprehensibility by those affected by it. The victims become haunted not by the reality of the violent event contained in these stories but by a particular form of narration in which the violence is not yet fully experienced. Thus the flashbacks in *Der Verlorene* do not give us all required information since they are as equally bound up in denial as the events of the present. However much Dr. Neumeister (Rothe) in his new identity wishes to escape from the past, his new occupation contains many ironic parallels to his former existence. As Kapcynski notices, the opening sequence of the film establishes its intrinsic connections to recent history. "The barbed wire fencing and watch tower that dominate our initial view of Rothe's postwar workplace suggest that the site once served as a concentration camp and recalls the Nazis' forcible deportation and murder of the nation's 'undesirable' population" (151). Furthermore, Rothe's new position sanitizing displaced persons ironically evokes images of those concentration camp doctors engaged in the darker realms of Third Reich medical practices. Also, the train used to convey displaced persons to Rothe's Camp evokes that ominous method of transporting undesirables to concentration camps during the Third Reich.

The train functions in several key scenes in the film. It occurs in the first scene passing the crossing before we see Rothe. Secondly, after Rothe recognizes Hoesch, the next sequence shows him walking towards the tracks. It ends with Rothe on the railroad tracks as the camera pulls away from him, anticipating the final scene in the film in which Rothe now stands immobile in the same spot, covering his face (as in the earlier mirror image scene in his laboratory) before the train hits him. Whether conscious or not, the role of the train strongly evokes parallels Freud makes between a railway accident and traumatic neuroses associated both with war and its aftermath. As Freud notes, no "complete explanation has yet been reached either of war neuroses or the *traumatic neuroses of peace*" (281, italics mine).

When Hoesch appears, Rothe is forced to confront the past. But the flashbacks do not explain everything as in the traditional manner. Instead, they avoid conventional methods of representation and instead convey veiled meanings utilizing non-realistic techniques associated with German expressionism, film noir, and horror. These flashbacks parallel Caruth's understanding of trauma as involving an indirect relation to references having a powerful impact upon the human personality. She sees "the return of the flashback as an interruption—as something with a disrupting force or impact [...] that cannot be thought simply as a representation" (115, n.6,7). *Der Verlorene*'s flashbacks have much in common with the remarks of critics such as Adorno, who stated that art was now impossible after Auschwitz, as well as with the feelings of directors such as Claude Lanzman, who reject typical representations of the Holocaust. As director and scenarist, Lorre thus avoids the normal and familiar aspects of cinematic narration. Furthermore, as a Jew traumatically affected by recent German history, Lorre could not be expected to remain objective and removed from the story he directed.

> No matter how much Lorre regarded himself as cosmopolitan and was generally a-political for most of his life, the actor's confrontation with the effects of a "Final Solution" from which he would not have been personally immune had he remained in Germany must have had some influence on the type of film he chose to make. (96)

Many American critics such as Judy Stone and Archer Winston commented on elements of the actor's sadness appearing in his performance, a factor which may have some associations with "survivor guilt."[5] Cathy Caruth again supplies some relevant comments.

> Not having truly known the threat of death in the past, the survivor is forced, continually, to confront it over and over again. For consciousness then, the act of survival, as the experience of trauma, is the repeated confrontation with the necessity and impossibility of grasping the threat to one's own life. (62)

She further states that individual trauma often contains within it the core of the trauma of a larger history also having collective associations (71, 136–37). By evoking his earlier role in *M* and placing it within a different narrative and historical context, Lorre may be engaged in a type of psychological "splitting" found not only in Freud's tale of the father and the burning child in a dream but also intuitively following disassociation techniques found in Lacan's reinterpretation of the dream as well as those found within Holocaust testimonies as documented by Caruth (101, 141–42). As she further notes, concerning Freud's reference to Tancredi's traumatic wounding of Clorinda in Tasso's story,

> we can also read the address of the voice here, not as the story of the individual in relation to the events of his own past, but as the story of the way in which one's own trauma is tied up with the trauma of another, the way in which trauma may lead, therefore, to the encounter with another, through the very possibility and surprise of listening to another's wound. (8)

The structure of *Der Verlorene* involves an impossible, but necessary, double narration constituting a particular form of historical witness. For a traumatic event to be historical "means that it is referential precisely to the extent that it is not fully perceived as it occurs; or to put it somewhat differently, that a history can be grasped only in the very inaccessibility of its occurrence." (Caruth, 1995: 19) This again explains the oblique nature of the flashbacks occurring in a film where, in Eisner's words, we have to "read between the lines." As Caruth further notes, "the painful repetition of the flashback can only be understood as the absolute inability of the mind to avoid an unpleasurable event that has not been given psychic meaning in any way" (1996, 59). Yet, at the same time, a memory of a traumatic experience may be paradoxical in the sense that

> the most direct seeing of a violent event may occur as an absolute inability to know it; that immediacy, paradoxically, may take the form of belatedness. The repetitions of the traumatic event . . . thus suggest a larger relation to the event that extends beyond what can be simply seen or what can be known, and is inextricably tied up with the belatedness and incomprehensibility that remain at the heart of this repetitive seeing. (Caruth 92)

Like the double imagery contained in Peter Lorre's one and only film as a director, *Der Verlorene* may be read in two ways. It can be admired for employing a quasi-Brechtian technique designed to alienate audiences, especially German audiences, separating them from their typical manner of reading a film in order to confront them with the grim realities of their recent historical past and a present, moving towards those denial mechanisms of the Adenauer era later criticized in the films of Fassbinder and others. Audiences can, or must, read between the lines of *Der Verlorene* in terms of its deliberately oblique references to a Nazi era whose dark nature cannot be revealed for one conscious reason or another. These may be ascribed to Lorre's own postwar sensibilities concerning both American and German political decisions to engage in denial of the past within the context of a new Cold War future and his intention to challenge audiences by eschewing typical modes of representation. But *Der Verlorene* also operates as a text of traumatic historical memory, combining both conscious and unconscious modes of narrative representation towards a particular goal. Like the many ironic references in the film, this goal evokes that old Nazi slogan, *Deutschland Erwache!* But this time, the aim is more ethical as the film attempts to confront audiences with past guilt in order to move towards a new direction where denial will no longer be necessary.

Notes

I wish to thank Stephen D. Youngkin, author of a forthcoming biography of Peter Lorre, for his generosity in supplying me with information and material from a clipping service concerning the reception of *Der Verlorene* cited in notes 1 and 3 as well as welcome critical comments on an earlier draft of this article. The clipping service has not always reproduced the relevant page number. But in view of the importance of this reference material, relevant citations will be accompanied by the definition "clipping service" below. The full references will appear in Youngkin's forthcoming biography of Peter Lorre to be published by The University of Kentucky Press.

1. For the problematic reception of *Der Verlorene* on its first release see Stephen D. Youngkin, James Bigwood, and Raymond G. Cabana, Jr. *The Films of Peter Lorre*, Secaucus, New Jersey: The Citadel Press, 1982, 204–5. Although the film's re-release in the 1980s was less problematic, it still encountered mixed reviews. Stanley Kaufman described it as a "disappointment, not nearly worth Lotte Eisner's praise in *The Haunted Screen*, but it's a poignant occasion in a poignant life" indebted too much to *M*. See "Stanley Kaufman on Films," *New Republic*, August 13, 1984. However, Elliot Stein regarded it as a "subtle and memorable film" recapitulating the realist and expressionistic styles of *M*. See "Lorre Lost and Found", *Village Voice*, August 7, 1984. During the film's re-release at the San Francisco Film festival, *San Francisco Chronicle* critic Judy Stone commented that there "is not one war movie cliché in the work which strengthens its symbolic import" and that Lorre "establishes a mood of genuine mourning, both in his restrained direction and in his eyes, filled with a terrible sorrow for a time when murder became the norm and there was no law to punish the guilty." See "Rare Lorre Film Highlights Festival," *San Francisco Chronicle*, February 16, 1985. Archer Winston also noticed Lorre's performance in conveying "an authentic note of internal suffering that cannot be questioned." See Winston, "Lorre's 'The Lost One' has been found again." *New York Post*, August 1, 1984. However, Vincent Canby found it a "curiosity" expressing "the frustration of Lorre's creative personality after his Hollywood dead end"; Rick Lyman regarded it as an erratic, self-conscious, but frequently thrilling attempt to bring the conventions of the German expressionist movement of the '20s into the world of postwar film noir thrillers"; while Sy Syna and Ernest Leogrande commented on its disappointing nature. See Canby, "Film: 1951 'Lost One,' directed by Peter Lorre," *The New York Times*, August 1, 1984; Lyman, "Film: 'The Lost One,' a long-lost Lorre work," *The Philadelphia Inquirer*, February 19, 1986; Syna, "Lorre's 'Lost One'

for fans only," *New York Tribune*, August 1, 1984; Leogrande, "Peter Lorre's 'Lost' Movie," *Daily News*, August 1, 1984. Finally, although William Wolf found the film faltering because "it is ultimately too melodramatic and because the musical scoring is heavy and clichéd in accordance with the habit of the time," he also regarded it as "an absorbing, evocative film that reminds us of a career and an epoch," especially in regard to the Nazi era. See Wolf, "The Lost One," *Gannett News Service*. August 1, 1984.

2. For the role of prewar German expressionism, melodrama, modernism, and literary influences as influences on East German cinema see Barton Byg, "DEFA and the Traditions of International Cinema," *DEFA: East German Cinema, 1946–1992*. Eds. Sean Allen and John Sandford, New York: Berghan Books, 1999, 26–35. *Der Verlorene* certainly combines all these elements, especially the melodramatic male crisis of Dr. Rothe, influenced more by history rather than the domestic environment of Hollywood melodrama, a sophisticated flashback technique and the attempted incorporation of the "Horla" motif. Sabine Hake also notes that German postwar cinema gradually moved towards "a depoliticized popular cinema whose visual and narrative strategies depended on the systematic suppression of politics in the discourse of humanism and the inevitable return of ideology in the form of a rabid anti-communism." She also recognizes how certain cinematic representations of the Holocaust such as *The Blum Affair* (1948), *Morituri* (1948), and *Der Ruf* (1949) were all affected by postwar politics. "The West subsumed the question of anti-Semitism under the category of crimes against humanity. The East incorporated the Jewish question into the grand narratives of anti-Fascism. In both cases, the creation of a postwar identity involved a complicated process of inclusion and exclusion, acceptance and denial." See Sabine Hake, *German National Cinema*. London: Routledge, 2002, 90–91, 96.

3. "mit seinen inneren Konflikten und seinen Leiden"

4. Stein notices a specific mode of unconventional "dedramatization" characterizing a "movie on the horrors of the Third Reich in which no one says 'Heil Hitler', in which the Gestapo is not seen as a troop of hammy villains or trimly uniformed heel-clicking hunks, but as a gaggle of baggy faceless wimps. Lorre's Gestapo is closer to Hannah Arendt than to Visconti...*All* of the scenes seem to be set in some sort of limbo—it is only halfway through the movie that the limbo is even geographically located as Hamburg." ("Lorre: Lost and Found," *Village Voice*, op. cit.) However, Lotte Eisner had earlier acclaimed *Der Verlorene* as a work of "very personal inspiration" whose quality "recalls that of the best films from the period 1930–32" acclaiming it for its tact and subtlety in representing the historical period of 1943. See Eisner, *The Haunted Screen*. London, Thames and Hudson, 1969, 339. John Morrone noted the film's hybrid style of "Expressionism by Hollywood by Expressionism" and commented further that no Lorre role since *M* and *Stranger on the Third Floor* (1940) ever "tapped his inner sadness quite so directly. He makes you wonder how much he absorbed of Nazi terror while living among Hollywood's expatriates far from the front and far from home." See John Morrone, "Unearthing a 'Lost One' by Peter Lorre," *Chelsea Clinton News*, August 2, 1984.

5. See note 1.

Works Cited

Anderegg, Michael. *Orson Welles, Shakespeare and Popular Culture*. New York: Columbia University Press, 1999.

Benjamin, Walter. "Thesis on the Philosophy of History." *Illuminations*. Trans. Harry Zohn.

New York: Schocken Books, 1968. 253–64.

Bessy, Maurice. *Orson Welles*. Trans. Ciba Vaughn. New York: Crown Publishers, 1971.

Byg, Barton. "DEFA and the Traditions of International Cinema." *DEFA: East German Cinema, 1946–1992*. Eds. Sean Allen and John Sandford. New York: Berghan Books, 1999. 22–41.

Canby, Vincent. "Lorre's 'The Lost One' has been found again." *New York Post*. August 1, 1984. (Clipping Service).

Caplan, Arthur. *When Medicine Went Mad: Bioethics and the Holocaust*. Totowa, New Jersey: Humana Press, 1992.

Caruth, Cathy. Ed. *Trauma: Explorations in Memory*. Baltimore: The Johns Hopkins University Press, 1995.

———. *Unclaimed Experience: Trauma, Narrative and History*. Baltimore: The Johns Hopkins University Press, 1996.

Chi, Robert. "Getting It on Film: Representing and Understanding History in *A City of Sadness*." *Tamkang Review* 29.4 (1999): 47–84.

Eisner, Lotte. *The Haunted Screen*. London: Thames and Hudson, 1969.

Fehrenbach, Heide. *Cinema in Democratizing Germany: Reconstructing National Identity After Hitler*. Chapel Hill: The University of North Carolina Press, 1995.

Freud, Sigmund. "Beyond the Pleasure Principle." *On Metapsychology. The Pelican Freud Library. Vol. 11*. Trans. James Strachey. Ed. Angela Richards. London: Pelican Books, 1984. 269–338.

Fuchs, Christoph. "Dr. Rothe trifft Dr. Holl: Entstehung und Rezeption der einzigen Regiearbeit Peter Lorres." *Peter Lorre: Ein Fremder im Paradies*. Eds. Michael Omasta, Brigitte Mayr, and Elizabeth Streit. Österreichisches Filmmuseum: Paul Zsolnay, 2004. 163–80.

Gemünden, Gerd. "From 'Mr. M' to 'Mr. Murder': Peter Lorre and the Actor in Exile." *Light Motives: German Popular Film in Perspective*. Eds. Randall Halle and Margaret McCarthy. Detroit, Michigan: Wayne State University Press, 2003. 85–107.

Hacket, Arthur, ed. *The Buchenwald Report*. Boulder, Colorado: The Westview Press, 1995.

Hake, Sabine. *German National Cinema*. London: Routledge, 2002.

Halbwachs, Maurice. *On Collective Memory*. Ed., Trans., and Introduction by Lewis A. Coser. Chicago: University of Chicago Press, 1992.

Kapczynski, Jennifer M. "Homeward Bound? Peter Lorre's *The Lost Man* and the End of Exile." *New German Critique*. 89 (2003): 145–71.

Kater, Michael. *Doctors Under Hitler*. Chapel Hill: University of North Carolina Press, 1990.

Kaufman, Stanley. "Stanley Kaufman on Films." *New Republic*. August 13, 1984. (Clipping Service).

Kott, Jan. *Shakespeare Our Contemporary*. Trans. Boleslaw Taborski. New York: Anchor Books, 1966.

Kracauer, Siegfried. *From Caligari to Hitler*. New Jersey: Princeton University Press, 1946.

———. *Theory of Film: The Redemption of Physical Reality*. New York: Oxford University Press, 1960.

Leaming, Barbara. *Orson Welles*. New York: Viking Press, 1985.

Leogrande, Ernest. "Peter Lorre's Lost Movie." *Daily News*. August 1, 1984. (Clipping Service).

Lifton, Robert Jay. *The Nazi Doctors: Medical Killing and the Psychology of Genocide*. New York: Basic Books, 1986.

Lorre, Peter. *Der Verlorene*. Ed. Michael Farin and Hans Schmid. Munich: Belleville, 1996.

———. "M kehrt zurück mit *Der Verlorene*: Peter Lorre im Interview mit Tom Granich (1951)." *Peter Lorre: Ein Fremder im Paradies*. Eds. Michael Omasta, Brigitte Mayr, Elizabeth Streit. Österreichisches Filmmuseum: Paul Zsolnay Verlag, 2004. 181–3.

Lyman, Rick. "Film: 'The Lost One,' a long-lost Lorre Work." *The Philadelphia Inquirer*. February 19, 1986. (Clipping Service).

Morrone, John. "Unearthing a 'Lost One.'" *Chelsea Clinton News*. August 2, 1984. (Clipping Service).

Naremore, James. *The Magic World of Orson Welles*. Dallas, Texas: Southern Methodist University Press, 1989.

Schandley, Robert. *Rubble Cinema: German Cinema in the Shadow of the Third Reich*. Philadelphia: Temple University Press, 2001.

Silberman, Marc. *German Cinema: Texts in Contexts*. Detroit, Michigan: Wayne State University Press, 1995.

Stein, Elliot. "Lorre Lost and Found." *Village Voice*. August 7, 1984 (Clipping Service).

Stone, Judy. "Rare Lorre Film Highlights Festival." *San Francisco Chronicle*. February 16, 1985. (Clipping Service).

Syna, Sid. "Lorre's 'Lost One' for fans only." *New York Tribune*. August 1, 1984. (Clipping Service).

Tallmer, Jerry. "Reel Finds: The Lost Film by Peter Lorre." *New York Post*. July 26, 1984. (Clipping Service).

Turim, Maureen. *Flashbacks in Film: Memory and History*. New York: Routledge, 1989.

Winston, Archer. "Lorre's 'The Lost One' has been found again." *New York Post*. August 1, 1984. (Clipping Service).

Wolf, William. "The Lost One." *Gannet News Service*. August 1, 1984.

Youngkin, Stephen D. "M like Morphine." Translated by Dita Taylor, in *peterlorre.com/files* from *Der Verlorene*. 1996. Eds. Michael Farin and Hans Schmid.

———. "Der Insider als Outsider: Die Emigration des Peter Lorre." *Peter Lorre: Portrait des Schauspielers auf der Flucht*. Eds. Felix Hoffman and Stephen D. Youngkin. Trans. Felix Hoffman and Ingrid Mylo. Munich: Belleville, 1998. 109–61.

———, James Bigwood, and Raymond G. Cabana, Jr., eds. *The Films of Peter Lorre*. Secaucus, New Jersey: The Citadel Press, 1982.

Hollywood Horror Comes to Berlin: A Critical Reassessment of Robert Siodmak's *Nachts, wenn der Teufel kam*

Steffen Hantke

Reception History

Based on the real-life case of serial murderer Bruno Lüdke, Robert Siodmak's film *Nachts, wenn der Teufel kam* fictionalizes the criminal investigation of Lüdke's murders and the brief aftermath of his apprehension in Berlin in the final year of WWII. The film opens with Lüdke (Mario Adorf) murdering the waitress Lucy Hansen (Monika John) during an air raid in Hamburg, and Willi Keun (Werner Peters), Hansen's lover and a lower-level party member, being arrested for the murder. Having returned from Hamburg to Berlin, Lüdke then makes the acquaintance of a Jewish woman who, hiding from the Nazis in a friend's apartment, looks like she will become Lüdke's next victim. Lüdke also meets a childhood friend, Anna Hohmann (Rose Schäfer), who is equally unaware of the danger she is in when she is in Lüdke's company. At the same time, Inspector Axel Kersten (Claus Holm) stumbles upon clues to what his superiors consider a string of unrelated murders but that he believes to be the work of a serial killer. Kersten is not a supporter of the regime, but when he is transferred, following an injury he incurred while serving on the Eastern front, from the civil authorities to the Gestapo and put under the command of SS-Gruppenführer Rossdorf (Hannes Messemer), he conscientiously fulfills his duties. Once on the trail of the killer, he quickly identifies Lüdke and has him arrested. Lüdke eventually confesses, but the official inquest never establishes a clear motive. Lüdke appears to feel safe from execution since he is officially labeled as mentally deficient under German law. How best to construct and exploit Lüdke's acts as ideologically significant becomes a point of contention for the Nazi propaganda machinery. This is all the more urgent because the war and the rapidly collapsing social order it precipitates are putting pressure on the authorities either to produce an ideologically coherent reading of the Lüdke case or expunge it from the public record altogether. Not only is the case unsuitable for raising public support for the government's eugenics program, but it also illustrates all too clearly the government's failure to protect the population from a danger emerging from the midst of the supposedly healthy German *Volksgemeinschaft*.[1]

Erroneously arrested as a suspect, Willi Keun, Lucy Hansen's lover, is framed for Hansen's murder and shot in a staged escape. Lüdke, after summary execution, is eliminated from official records and public memory. Since Kersten is privy to this cover-up, and even tries to stop it, he is ordered back to the Eastern front as a soldier—a transfer which, at this stage of the war, seems certain to cost him his life. As his troop transport pulls out of the station, Lüdke's childhood friend, Anna Hohmann, recognizes Kersten as the man who arrested Lüdke. When she asks about her friend, Kersten denies all knowledge that Lüdke ever existed. The film ends with a shot of the Bruno Lüdke file, labeled "top secret," being closed.

A detailed plot summary of *Nachts, wenn der Teufel kam* is necessary because, even though Siodmak's film was commercially and critically successful upon its initial release, it has been largely forgotten by today's audiences. This turnaround in public favor is surprising given not only the film's initial success, but also the multiple factors that speak in its favor. First, there is the work's sensational subject matter: a serial killer, the monster of numerous horror films and thrillers, using the chaos of the war's final years to cover his tracks. Additionally, the narrative device of the good cop working within Nazi Germany also has a certain appeal, as evidenced by the motif's successful adaptation in Len Deighton's *SS-GB* or Philip Kerr's *Berlin Noir Trilogy*. Furthermore, Bruno Lüdke's story had already proven commercially viable; Siodmak's film is an adaptation of a successful magazine expose written by journalist Will Berthold and published in the *Münchener Zeitung*. Important to the film's success is also its high-profile director. With a reputation reaching back to the Weimar years in Germany, and to a productive exile period in Hollywood, Robert Siodmak was certainly not an unknown in Germany. Then there is the German film industry's Film Award in Gold, which an impressive number of the contributors to *Nachts, wenn der Teufel kam* won in the category of Outstanding Individual Achievement.[2] Most notably among them is Mario Adorf, playing Bruno Lüdke, for whom the film stands as the beginning of a long and distinguished career as one of Germany's finest postwar actors. What's more, the crew that had signed on to Siodmak's project featured some of the most respected members of the film community in Germany at the time.[3] And, with a nomination for best foreign film at the Academy Awards in 1957, *Nachts, wenn der Teufel kam,* listed under the title *The Devil Came at Night,* looked ready to extend its success to the crucial American market.[4]

In hindsight, however, the context in which the film was made and released may have been more complicated, and some of its assets may not have been quite as dazzling as they appear at first glance. Siodmak himself, for example, was undoubtedly a director with name recognition. But unlike Fritz Lang, whose career often resembled his own—from the prewar career in Germany, to the Hollywood exile, to the problematic return to postwar Germany—Siodmak never succeeded in attaining the auteurist status that critics granted so readily to Lang.[5] There was also a sense that Siodmak had reached a career impasse within the Hollywood film industry and was returning to Germany not triumphantly, but out of expediency. "Siodmak has justified his farewell from Hollywood saying that he felt he American film industry was slowly but surely heading toward its demise," Hans Christoph Blumenberg explains, "but the farewell was most likely not voluntary" because Siodmak expressed "the desire to return to America and settle there once again" (9). Like other returning exiles—Peter Lorre's late directorial debut *Der Verlorene* comes to mind—Siodmak was confronted with an audience that may have harbored conflicting emotions toward those who had fled from the Nazis; to this extent, public opinion in Germany may have even been working against him. The glory days of Weimar had long passed, and those who had left Germany before the war could be suspected of having taken the easy way out. "Throughout the late 1940s and 1950s German reviewers spoke of Siodmak vaguely as a director who had once left his homeland to become a Hollywood star, as an uprooted wanderer between the worlds, as an artist German audiences might still recall from Weimar days" (Koepnick 194).[6]

The German reception of Siodmak's *The Spiral Staircase*, made in Hollywood in 1948, had already been somewhat less than cordial, not so much by larger audiences as by the film's reviewers. Some complained about the "absurd amalgamation of colportage and bogus psychotheraphy" (Koepnick 193), which they saw as a sign of mediocre American filmmaking. The rejection of the film included Siodmak as the director in either the critics' "moralizing anti-Americanism" (194) or their blanket rejection of the American domination of the postwar German film market.[7] Though this problem would not have arisen with *Nachts, wenn der Teufel kam*, which was a German project from beginning to end, "the ease with which Siodmak applied the techniques of film noir, which he had picked up during the '40s in Hollywood, to all kinds of subjects he was offered in Germany [constitutes in itself a] provocation through professionalism—this is where he makes the discrepancy obvious that exists between the film industry in America and the manufacturing of movies in Germany" (Goettler 184).[8] Not only did German audiences not want to be reminded of the political implications of returning film exiles, they also did not want to be made to feel inferior. "The Siodmak-touch of these dark postwar films has something almost professorial about it; they're not merely exercises, they're lectures about film noir" (Goettler 184).

In order to understand the current invisibility of *Nachts, wenn der Teufel kam*—that is, to understand not why the film *was* forgotten but why it has *remained* forgotten—it is best to look at the critical opinions expressed in contemporary reviews.[9] An American reviewer argues that the film's handling of politics and of narrative structure appears "reassuringly simple" to contemporary viewers (Hemingway); that is to say, it meets standards of political sensitivity that are germane to postwar Germany but no longer apply to contemporary Germany, and have never applied to an international audience. A German reviewer, Frank Ehrlacher, praises the performances of actors Mario Adorf and Claus Holm but notes that the film does not succeed in sustaining an intense gothic mood. The final result, Ehrlacher's review concludes, is "moving, but unfortunately not suspenseful." One anonymous critic also notes this lack of consistency, though this time the complaint is articulated not in regard to style or mood but to genre; looking at the film's shift from the police investigation to the political aftermath of the Lüdke murders, "one bewilderedly wonders how the movie got there [i.e. to "a clammy *1984* parallel"] from its horror movie beginning." Condescendingly, that same reviewer concludes: "That said, [the film is] not particularly thrilling, nor is it politically intriguing, so it never exactly succeeds with its contorted aims; it is, however, interesting enough, especially if you go in assuming it's just another *M* ripoff" (*Cinema Scale*).[10]

The recurring theme in these negative reviews, which plays itself out in a number of different registers, is inconsistency. Reviewers complain that the film does not fall into a recognizable genre. As a horror film, it loses sight of Bruno Lüdke too soon, so that the final reel, which deals with the political aftermath of the case, does not feature him at all. Siodmak also seems fairly disinterested in the staging of excessive violence, the depiction of abject imagery, displays of radical alterity, and other thematic hallmarks of horror cinema. Throughout the entire film, Siodmak only shows one single murder—that of Lucy Hansen. All other acts of violence are either psychological, social, or political in nature, presented in a morally ambiguous fashion, or take place off-screen. Though there is a pervasive sense of paranoia about the killer and the police operating within the setting of Nazi Germany, the film does not systematically sustain a gothic atmosphere. While the murder of Lucy Hansen is shot as a carefully staged expressionist set-piece, and Lüdke himself is occasionally represented within the visual and thematic conventions of the horror film, Siodmak often resorts to location shooting, using the actual ruins of postwar Germany as settings, a practice which gives the film a more sober, austere, and at times almost documentary feel.

For a political film—a satire about the postwar years (Goettler 184) which German audiences at the time would have recognized as a so-called *Problemfilm*—*Nachts, wenn der Teufel kam* seems to pursue an agenda that might have been comforting to German audiences in 1957, but that appears overly conciliatory to contemporary viewers.[11] Though the film places itself into the context of the collective cultural labor required from postwar Germany as it comes to terms with the historical burden of the Third Reich, it offers German viewers in 1957 a convenient exoneration from all complicity with the regime. It is important to remember that, at the time of the film's release, the vast majority of the German audience would have lived through the Third Reich. Axel Kersten, the film's tragic hero and the obvious figure of identification for the audience, can at best be blamed for being naïve. He represents the Good German, unwittingly drawn into a shabby political cabal by his sense of professionalism and his overly idealistic belief that the police in a fascist state can operate in the best interests of the people and independent from any overtly political agenda. His knee injury has him limp toward bitter self-realization, like the latter-day Oedipus that he is, accepting his own imminent death at the end of the film as a heroic penance, which, in turn, absolves both the film and its audience from the rather more complex question how one is to continue living with the guilt over one's complicity with the Nazis. Meanwhile, the film provides its audience with two easily recognizable villains—Kersten's superior, the SS officer Rossdorf, who represents the cruelty and elitism of fascist ideology, and the lower-echelon party member Keun, who stands for the laziness, cowardice and pompous self-importance of all those fellow travelers who were attracted to fascism by the opportunities it afforded them for social advancement. The ideological aristocrat and the petit bourgeois opportunist respectively, these two characters stand in stark contrast to virtually all minor characters that populate the film. Almost without exception, Siodmak shows these common people engaging in minor acts of political subversion—ridiculing the absurd claims of Nazi propaganda, trafficking in the black market, refusing cooperation with the intrusive regulations of the fascist state. In the final instance, the film appears to confirm the convenient fiction that the Third Reich consisted of a few perpetrators, exceptional in their violent pathology and ruthlessness; their victims, who would sacrifice themselves—not always effectively but always tragically or heroically—for the benefit of a democratic posterity; and a vast mass of ordinary citizens, none of whom was guilty of anything in the strict sense because they all opposed the Nazis on the sly. Critics who read the film in this manner, like Hemingway who calls the film "reassuringly simple," are correct in pointing out that Siodmak's strategies of narrativizing the experience of German fascism are, for better or worse, a product of their time. Since the process of German *Vergangenheitsbewältigung* is still stuck in its initial stages by the late 1950s, or so the argument goes, later generations will find its reflection in Siodmak's film overly simplistic.[12]

Critical Re-Evaluation: Inconsistency as Aesthetic Principle

To take a stand against this critical dismissal of the film and its director, and to initiate a process of critical re-evaluation in the context of the film's reception history, one would have to address this cluster of critical responses: the generic, the aesthetic, and the political. Because all three aspects are, in one way or another, related to each other, let me preface my re-reading of the film by looking more closely at the critical assumption that all three approaches have in common; namely, that inconsistency and impurity are at the root of the film's difficulty in securing for itself canonical status as either a horror film or a socially conscious political *Problemfilm*. Critical bias aside, inconsistency is in itself neither inherently problematic nor aesthetically displeasing. Taking it as the touchstone of Siodmak's failure as a director says less about the film and more about the gulf that separates mainstream cinema from high modernism—what constitutes failure for the former sets the high water mark of excellence for the latter. What appears as lack of consistency in Siodmak's film might very well fall within a self-conscious agenda that privileges fragmentation over integration, hybridity over purity, and local tactics over grand strategy.

As for the specific historical position that Siodmak's film occupies, internal inconsistencies could also be seen as a reflection of the film being determined by a framework of historical, social, and ideological forces all pulling in different directions. Understood in this manner, inconsistency may then register simply as a morphological feature of the film, beyond critical dismissal; or, it may even appear as a positive feature, showing the film's ability to carve out a textual space apart from the charted territory of established styles, clearly demarcated genres, and officially sanctioned political opinions—a space, in other words, from which this charted territory may be viewed and assessed with some degree of critical distance. Considered as a transitional work—in the career of Robert Siodmak, as well as in the history of postwar Germany—or as an interstitial work, suspended between different genres and narrative modes, *Nachts, wenn der Teufel kam* may, in fact, have a clearer view of German politics than some of the films which know exactly where they stand.

Generic Inconsistency

Fritz Goettler calls *Nachts, wenn der Teufel kam* "a bizarre shadow play of the 1950s" (184). Sabine Hake classifies *Nachts, wenn der Teufel kam* as a "noirish thriller" (96), but suggests, albeit obliquely, a relationship to horror film by placing it next to Peter Lorre's *Der Verlorene*—by virtue of both directors being returned exiles—which "uses the familiar Dr. Jeckyll/Mr. Hyde motif to evoke the disturbing image of a nation ravaged by guilt" (Hake 96). She traces such traditions in German cinema back to what she calls "fantastic films," which "incorporated visual and narrative motifs from romantic paintings and literature, as well as from the popular gothic novels, to simulate the effects of what might be called the modern uncanny" (17–18). The ambiguity within these critics' classificatory terminology reveals a corresponding ambiguity within Siodmak's handling of cinematic genres.

When critics like Frank Ehrlacher complain that *Nachts, wenn der Teufel kam* fails to sustain a gothic mood, one might point out that Siodmak's film is fairly open about its generic instability. Perhaps it is this frankness that cost it a clearly defined and committed genre audience. Even the film's title suggests an underlying nervousness or insecurity about genre. Though the use of the words "night" and "the devil" purports to announce a horror film, the signals turn out to be misleading. Bruno Lüdke is not much of a demonic figure; alternating between practical cleverness and infantile simplicity, he makes for a rather disappointing incarnation of absolute evil. His murders are committed as much during the day, as in the case of an earlier victim whose murder he re-enacts for the police during his interrogation, as they take place during the night, as in the case of Lucy Hansen. It follows that the title was chosen to promise the audience sensationalist pleasures that the makers and distributors of the text—both the articles in the *Münchener Zeitung* on which the film was based and the film itself—suspected they were not able to deliver.

From the privileged position of historical hindsight, the problem of generic inconsistency largely resolves itself if the film is placed in the context of a more contemporary genre. This involves counting *Nachts, wenn der Teufel kam* as a precursor—as a part of the generic prehistory, so to speak—of the American thrillers that have come to define critical and popular understanding of the figure of the serial killer. Concentrated in the period of the late 1980s and extending into the late 1990s, and finding its prototypical manifestation with Thomas Harris's novel *The Silence of the Lambs* and its cinematic adaptation by Jonathan Demme, the serial killer narrative evolved rapidly into a set of narrative, thematic, and ideological conventions—one of which is generic hybridity.

Critical assessment of the American serial killer during the latter days of the 20th century fits Siodmak's conception of Bruno Lüdke amazingly well. First, there is the problem of visualizing "an evil so abstract and essentialized as the serial killer," which requires "some form of reification" (Hantke 48). Lüdke appears to be an ordinary, harmless person moving unobserved through German society. Though his physical strength is at times unnerving, his apparent mental simplicity disarms those around him. This is a trait perhaps more crucial in a historical situation in which the need for concealing parts of one's self from public view is eminent, but the perception of duplicity can very well be fatal. Like the American serial killer films of the 1980s, *Nachts, wenn der Teufel kam* works hard at signaling Lüdke's monstrosity, showing him in the opening credit sequence as he is hiding from the police in a bog, his body rendered abject by being covered in slime and morass. *Mise-en- scène* also contributes to this classificatory labor. Lüdke is photographed in a vaguely expressionist style during a murder scene, and so are his makeshift quarters in a decrepit, partly bombed out stable in a Berlin courtyard. However, as in American serial killer films of the 1980s, this visual labor inevitably fails. Like Harris's and Demme's serial killers ("They don't have a name for it yet"), Lüdke remains an enigma. We never know with certainty what motivates him, and his death at the hands of the SS, though it erases him from public record, only serves to preclude genuine closure.

Hence, like his fictional heirs of 1980s and '90s popular fiction and film, Lüdke is, as Philip Simpson writes, one of the "revitalized and particularized mythic villains for an anomic world that is haunted by the macrocosmic specters of war, genocide, gynocide, terrorism, and random violent crime but ironically constructed from the institutionalized ideologies that make all of these possible" (2). According to Simpson, the serial killer is an amalgamation of archetypes and cultural stereotypes, some of which are derived from folklore, like the vampire (a label applied to Peter Kürten, the serial killer responsible for the death of numerous young women in Düsseldorf in the 1920s), and the werewolf (used to describe serial killer Fritz Haarmann in Hannover in the 1930s); other archetypes emerge from urban legend (the "Black Man" that the children in Fritz

Lang's *M* are singing about in the film's opening scene), and yet others from the inventory of popular culture (like the Jasons and Freddies of the 1970s slasher film). Adapting itself to this central character, the narrative about the construction of the serial killer is itself a hybrid entity:

> The "serial killer" as labeled by the FBI during the American 1980s and passed into the mass-media instruments of popular culture, ever quick to cater to the prevailing ideological winds, is a fantastic confabulation of Gothic/romantic villain, literary vampire and werewolf, detective and "pulp" fiction conceits, film noir, frontier outlaw, folkloric threatening figure, and nineteenth-century pseudo-sociological conceptions of criminal types given contemporary plausibility. (Simpson 15).

Other critics concur. Richard Tithecott, for example, sees "the serial killer [as] a continuation of the male heroes and antiheroes of, say, the Western, of the road movie, of the Gothic, of chivalry" (174).

If using Simpson's and Tithecott's definitions seems anachronistic in the context of German postwar film—after all, both are concerned with the 1980s and '90s as the heyday of the serial killer's "boom" in American culture—it is important to remember that the consolidation of this narrative into a hybrid genre not only rallies contemporary texts around a generic center and provides a prescriptive aesthetic for future productions. It also refocuses critical attention retroactively onto texts that previously were included in other genres or stood apart from genres altogether. Seen in the new context, these texts now appear as the predecessors in the lineage of the newly consolidated genre.

In their original context, such genealogical deliberations are still focused primarily on American culture of the Reagan years and its aftermath. Still, Simpson's description, especially in its discussion of the frontier and the millenarian aspect of American culture, fits the German context of Siodmak's film all too well: though there is no frontier mythology in German culture, the image of Nazi Germany in ruins, its social structure collapsing, and civilized behavior a hard choice rather than a socially enforced standard is highly reminiscent of a frontier situation. Simpson also points out the apocalyptic overtones of films like David Fincher's *Seven* and Dominic Sena's *Kalifornia*, which seem oddly prefigured in Siodmak's depiction of Germany on the verge of ideological, political, and military defeat in 1944. Apart from the historical fact of Germany's collapse, Nazi mythology itself even provides a millenarian reading of events, as Hitler steers the country toward an all-consuming *Götterdämmerung*. Similarly, Simpson's suggestion that the serial killer as outlaw is "ironically constructed from the institutionalized ideologies" at the root of all the world's evils rings true for Bruno Lüdke—a monster both better and worse than the judicial and ideological apparatus attempting to contain him.

The reviewer in *Cinema Scale*, who claims that *Nachts, wenn der Teufel kam* is "just another *M* ripoff" also engages in an act of retroactive genre historiography. However, by placing Siodmak's film specifically into the context of

German serial killer films, its position is defined by what it harks back to rather than to what it prefigures. If, indeed, the serial killer is constructed "with reference to various familiar genres of fiction and cultural paradigms" (Tithecott 174), the reviewer in *Cinema Scale* suggests that a German film from the late 1950s follows its own genealogy—a branch, perhaps, of the larger family tree. The reference to Lang's *M* links Siodmak's film to canonical German filmmaking, both by reference to a masterpiece of German cinema and to perhaps the outstanding auteurist filmmaker of the prewar period. Particularly fitting to Robert Siodmak's career, it circumnavigates the Third Reich and establishes a sense of continuity between German cinema of the Weimar years and postwar West German cinema.[13] Perhaps it is in part this uneasy suspension between genealogical reference points—back in time to a German film from which it is separated by the gulf of the Third Reich, and forward in time by a good thirty years to a cluster of films produced in another country and culture—that has made audiences uncertain what to do with *Nachts, wenn der Teufel kam.*

Aesthetic Inconsistency

If we listen to the complaints of the reviewers, it appears that this odd historical position of *Nachts, wenn der Teufel kam* has also left its mark on the film's aesthetic. Without an immediately available tradition to follow, Siodmak had to make aesthetic choices, none of which would have been obvious. His own career had supplied him with a variety of models: "the Grand Guignol of *The Spiral Staircase*," which, unfortunately, was "not typical of his work" (Greco 8); the "techniques of film noir he had appropriated for himself in Hollywood in the 1940s" (Goettler 184); "the heritage of Weimar film—chiaroscuro lighting, canted angles, narratives of male anxiety" (Koepnick 166); or, finally, a combination of two, or all three, of these traditions and styles he had at his disposal.

Given this wealth of possibilities, it is hardly surprising that Siodmak had, even earlier in his career, begun to be self-conscious about deploying generic tropes and stylistic devices. This stylistic self-awareness goes back, Koepnick points out, as far as Siodmak's American films during his years in exile. Confronted "with studio pressures, Siodmak may have recalled some aspects of German expressionist cinema—Weimar's film vocabulary of anxiety and paranoia, of visual stylization and theatrical excess" (Koepnick 167). Working on B-pictures (like the dreadful *Son of Dracula*), and operating with the diminished leverage of the recent arrival to the film industry, Siodmak would have had to improvise, think on his feet, and sacrifice authorial vision to studio demand if he wanted to survive in Hollywood. Consequently, "this reinscription [of one style within another] was discontinuous to say the least" (Koepnick 167).

Displaced yet again, this time from Hollywood to Germany, Siodmak had reason to continue thinking about style as a historically decontextualized element in his work.[14] Since "Siodmak had never been an expressionist in the canonical sense," Koepnick reminds us, "whatever was reminiscent of Weimar cinema in his Hollywood work"—and thus, conversely, of Hollywood and of Weimar in his postwar German work—"was highly performative; it recalled the past as pastiche and masquerade to challenge reified notions of continuity and historical determination" (199–200).

How far Siodmak's stylistic self-consciousness goes is visible in *Nachts, wenn der Teufel kam* during the scene in which Bruno Lüdke murders Lucy Hansen. Shot as a stylistic tour de force on a soundstage, the scene takes place on the bottom landing of a staircase in an apartment building. The staircase is constructed to be slightly off-kilter, an effect emphasized by dramatic low-angle lighting and camera angles which further add an element of visual distortion. An Allied bombing raid provides both Lüdke with the cover of darkness for the murder and Siodmak with a diegetic excuse to shoot in stark black and white chiaroscuro. The scene starts in the dark with Lucy Hansen entering the frame from the left and holding a candle. A spotlight effect is added as an overhead lamp casts oblique shadows through the slats of the overhead staircase banisters. Having tracked Lucy into the hallway, Siodmak has the camera dolly in on Lüdke as it enters the dark niche in the hallway where he is hiding. For a moment it holds on a dramatic medium close-up of his face, shot from a low angle, before Lüdke steps back into the shadows. A series of crosscuts—from interior to exterior, and from the staircase to the inside of Lucy Hansen's apartment—follows as the bombing raid begins. Then Lüdke steps out of the shadows; a panning shot shows him moving toward his victim before he grabs her.

Two details in this scene are remarkable. First, as Lüdke strangles Lucy, we see Lucy's lover Willi Keun getting dressed inside the apartment. He is similarly lit and lensed in the same ominous low-angle shot as Lüdke, which prefigures the very appearance of guilt that will lead to his arrest later when he comes under suspicion of having been Hansen's murderer. The first visual correspondence between the two men is confirmed when the air-raid warden shines his flashlight in Keun's face, trapping him in the spotlight just as Lorre's child murderer Beckert gets trapped in the beam of the flashlight in Lang's *M*. At that moment, Keun raises his hands up to his neck in the same manner as Lüdke readying himself for the assault on Hansen, a gesture that also obliquely prefigures Keun's fate as a victim of institutional judicial murder.

By way of the visual analogy between the two men—the psychotic serial killer Lüdke and the complacent, self-serving Nazi Keun—Siodmak raises the questions whether both men are equally guilty of murder, and how exactly the nature of the violence that both inflict differs from one case to the other. Once the moral correspondence between both men is established, Siodmak goes on to show both Keun and Lüdke being denied a fair trial. Regardless of their guilt, both men are killed in order to preserve the ideological agenda of the SS—Keun as a scapegoat to provide acceptable closure to the Lüdke case, and Lüdke to prevent public embarrassment for the authorities. If we are willing to grant Keun the status of a victim of political intrigue, wouldn't we then have to grant that status to Lüdke as well? Or do both men represent cases in which the status of perpetrator and victim are not, in fact, mutually exclusive? Is it perhaps the political rationale, as well as the system that enforces it, which is the true villain in this scenario? This diffusion or displacement of guilt—or at least the challenging of easy assumptions about guilt—returns the audience to the question that seems to arise from the film's title: who exactly is "the devil" who comes at night if Lüdke, initially the obvious choice, is revealed to be not such an obvious candidate for the epithet after all?

The second remarkable stylistic detail about the staircase murder scene is that Siodmak, in the middle of the murder itself, cuts to documentary footage of an Allied bombing raid over Germany. Within a matter of seconds, we go from the act of intimate one-on-one violence between Lüdke and Lucy to the massive industrial violence being unleashed by the war outside. We also alternate, at that moment, between a carefully controlled scene shot on a soundstage and lit in a non-mimetic, highly artificial style rich in historical associations for a film-literate audience, and pieces of film that come from an outside source, assembled with the presumption of artlessly documenting empirical reality. The montage stages a stylistic rupture so conspicuous and dramatic that, again, it raises questions about thematic continuity or the lack thereof. Diegetic necessity aside, does the montage of these two acts suggests that Lüdke's violence is a reflection of the war's violence, or vice versa? Does it suggest that Lüdke is actually not an aberration, but is acting in perfect synchronization with the world around him—that is, the world of the Third Reich, or the world of the war? And what does the difference in the ontological status between the two types of footage used in the montage tell us? What is the relation between the stylized, self-consciously gothicized violence of the murder, enacted by two actors on a set, and the mass slaughter that takes place outside as a matter of official historical record?

Siodmak sustains this selective and self-conscious deployment of style throughout the entire film, alternating between a highly artificial, gothicized style in some scenes, and a toned-down, bland, almost documentary style in others.[15] For example, the initial presentation of Lüdke as a gothic monster is maintained. In the scenes that show Lüdke in his quarters, his presence appears as vaguely threatening and ominous, first to Anna Hohmann and then to Axel Kersten. In both scenes, Siodmak frames Lüdke in oblique angles as a ladder diagonally cuts through the frame, and he has him step in and out of spotlit spaces in room. The association between the serial killer and his intimate space, a staple of American serial killer films of the 1980s, re-enforces the connection between the character of Lüdke and the expressionist style.[16]

At first glance, it might seem as if Siodmak reserves expressionist style for Bruno Lüdke, the film's monster. But we should not forget that Willi Keun, during the murder of Lucy Hansen, is also photographed in this manner. Keun is a morally dubious character, but he certainly is no monster on a par with Lüdke.

Still, Siodmak identifies him as afflicted with a form of violence as intimate and pervasive as that emanating from the serial killer. Another character who would make a suitable candidate for this kind of visual marking is SS-Gruppenführer Rossdorf, Axel Kersten's commanding officer and one of the masterminds behind the cover-up of the Lüdke case. Morally speaking, Rossdorf is a despicable character, more on a level with Lüdke than with Keun. Rossdorf's actions derive from the official ideology of the Third Reich, like Keun's. But unlike Keun, whose motivation seems mostly that of an opportunistic fellow traveler, Rossdorf is a cruel elitist and unfeeling, scheming careerist, one of the more frightening technocrats of fascism. He is the aloof, self-assured aristocrat to Keun's sweaty, pompous petit bourgeois.[17]

Surprisingly, however, Siodmak shoots Rossdorf in a more documentary style. Scenes in which he interacts with Kersten, and in which his presence announces the latent brutality of the regime, are almost always stylistically flat and unremarkable. This visual theme sets Rossdorf apart from the world of Lüdke, and from the violence he represents, and places him in closer proximity to the documentary footage of the Allied bombing raid. That is to say, Siodmak associates him with a less personal, politically motivated, and coldly rational form of violence—no less destructive than Lüdke's, but belonging to a less archaic, more radically modern universe. Rossdorf also may not be the "devil" in the film's title; but the historical association between the Gestapo practice of raiding and arresting in the middle of the night—the "Night and Fog" under cover of which undesirables were made to disappear—certainly places him among the list of suspects. There is an echo of "the banality of evil" in Siodmak's choice to photograph Rossdorf in a bland, self-effacing style, perhaps even an admission on the part of the director that no suitable style or tone exists within the vocabulary of popular film that would adequately represent Rossdorf as what he is.

In the context of reviewers like Frank Ehrlacher, who complain about the film's insufficiently sustained gothic mood, one might also notice that, during the film's final reel, Bruno Lüdke has virtually disappeared and Rossdorf appears more prominently. Viewers will be disappointed if they were expecting a narrative arc that, predicated on the suspense of the investigation, steered toward the climax of the killer's arrest or the detective's final showdown with the killer. These events occur, in a dramatically attenuated form, two-thirds through the film. At this point, Lüdke is given the opportunity to re-enact one of his earlier murders for the police. As he points to significant places and mimics his own actions in the absence of the actual victim, Siodmak's camera traces the invisible progress of the murder in empty space. This is not so much a lament about the death of the young woman, represented by the blank in the film's diegesis, as it is an eerie foreshadowing of Lüdke's erasure from both the official historical record and from the film itself—a transfer of properties between victim and murderer typical of the serial killer film. With this scene, Lüdke vanishes from the film. His execution, just like the frame-up that costs Keun his life, takes place off-screen. Similarly, as Kersten is sent to the Eastern front, his death on the battlefield is certain, yet it is deferred until after the film's closing scene.

Obviously, a new narrative aesthetic—this one based on ellipsis—has replaced the excessive visibility, the gothic spectacle of the Lucy Hansen murder in the opening sequences of the film. It is no less effective in its lethal consequences than the serial killer Bruno Lüdke, yet it operates on the principles of banality, invisibility, and bureaucratic legitimization. Despite the presence of specific representatives, like Rossdorf, it is essentially anonymous, impersonal, and procedural. Only in the film's final scene, which shows Kersten's departure for the front from the Berlin train station, does Siodmak resort to a more deeply textured, gothicized style. This time, it is reserved for the victims of this violence, because, after all, there are no clearly discernable perpetrators.

Politics: Conclusions

Ultimately, Siodmak's deployment of style returns us to the American serial killer films of the 1980s and the "representational crisis" that ensues with their tirelessly repeated, yet futile attempts at representing essentialized evil—not in regard to Bruno Lüdke but to SS Gruppenführer Rossdorf and the Third Reich (Hantke 50). American serial killer films, in dealing with a monster whose defining feature is his very normality, shift into a kind of semiotic overdrive, a "frenzy of the visible" to compensate for their inability to inscribe otherness on the monster's body. Whereas Lüdke can be contained within a style that makes a spectacle of evil, the Third Reich and its monsters cannot. Siodmak's self-conscious return to an expressionist style identifies Lüdke with a type of violence that shows a special affinity toward the cinema. Lüdke either represents an archaic form of violence that is pre-modern in nature though uncannily coexistent with modern society and activated by the collective descent into irrationality during the Third Reich, or he is a movie villain, a creature of deliberate artistic creation, whose evil pales in comparison with those committed under the aegis of rational modernity. Rossdorf's type of violence stands apart from these two options, and thus cannot be appropriately represented by a gothicized style. It either resists cinematic appropriation altogether, which would mean that Siodmak's choice of a less conspicuous style constitutes an admission of the failure of cinema altogether, or suggests that the only appropriate means of expression by which cinema can, in fact, represent German fascism is through what Siodmak sees as a "style of no style."

How one answers these questions in regard to Lüdke and Rossdorf also determines how one looks at Siodmak's film about the Third Reich within the political landscape of postwar West Germany in 1957. While it is true that the film superficially exonerates Germans from their complicity with the Third Reich, I hope I have made a convincing case that, upon closer inspection, it actually engages in a far less conciliatory, and far more radically questioning form of politics than many of the reviewers want to give it credit for. The film's engagement in the process of *Vergangenheitsbewältigung*, let alone its superficial moral and political simplicity, would have inspired a sense of dutiful observance or grudging respect on the part of the German audience in 1957. The oblique manner in which Siodmak undercuts the superficial reading he, admittedly, invites may have given this audience an excuse to stay on the surface. If it did recognize that the film also contained a more acerbic and ambiguous political stance, by way of visual style rather than character and narrative, Siodmak would have provided it with the possibility of disavowing this insight. Contemporary audiences, if they read the film carefully, will find it easier to embrace for just this complexity, or for its more radical challenging of easy moral distinctions. That the film's surface stance would not have aged well, and that the film's more radical politics would have eventually registered with the original audience might explain why the film faded from public favor after its enthusiastic opening.

German viewers in 1957 may have also started to suspect that *Nachts, wenn der Teufel kam*, together with Siodmak's other postwar German films, was, in fact, not so much about Nazi Germany but, uncannily, about the present. Though Siodmak himself has referred to the film in his memoirs as "a parable about the Third Reich" (233) and "a genuinely anti-Nazi film" (232), there is a sense that *Nachts, wenn der Teufel kam* is not entirely comfortable either with the newly democratic postwar Germany from which the film's audience emerged. "Normal people," Fritz Goettler has remarked—and I think he means all those major and minor characters in *Nachts, wenn der Teufel kam* who are likely to survive the Third Reich—, "appear more bizarre in this shadow play of the 1950s than the troupe of monsters" (184).

Who are, one might ask, the characters in the film that will survive the Third Reich and become the citizens of postwar Germany? Inspector Axel Kersten, the Good German who is about to become a casualty of the war's final phase, is a far less likely candidate for survival than SS Gruppenführer Rossdorf. Upon closer inspection, even Kersten's heroic parting speech to Rossdorf ("There will be a time when right will be right again. I don't know if we two will be around to see it") is ambiguous. At first glance, the future Kersten talks about looks like the postwar Germany that has dedicated itself to learning from the mistakes of the past. Similarly, the assertion that neither one of them will be around to see this future seems to suggest that Rossdorf himself will not survive the war either. As Kersten will pay with his own heroic death for the liberty of openly articulating this vision of a better future, Rossdorf and all those like him, in a turn of poetic justice, will become casualties of the war they themselves have started. But the poetic symmetry implied in Kersten's "we two" is hardly convincing. Kersten goes off to a war that is likely to cost him his life, but Rossdorf stays behind, in relative safety. And, in the light of the haphazard denazification campaign conducted by the Allied armies in their respective occupation zones after 1945, it is all the more likely that Rossdorf will survive unscathed. Hence, the ambiguity of the film's ending depends on the gap between the actual and the official historiographic representation of the end of the war—a gap that an audience in 1957 must have felt far more acutely and uncomfortably than audiences in subsequent years. The film's ambiguous ending thus leaves the audience with the unsettling possibility that postwar Germany is, in fact, *not* the brighter future (yet) that Kersten talks about because Rossdorf has, in fact, *not* become a casualty of the Third Reich but, rather, has gone on to transform himself—as many former party members, government officials, bureaucrats, Wehrmacht soldiers, and members of organizations like the SS, in fact, did—into the model citizen of the new West Germany. These ambiguities suffice if one were to argue that Siodmak's films "picture West German society as a dystopian space of repression and displacement haunted by a past that would not go away" (Koepnick 198).

It follows that the ending of the film, in which the Lüdke file is sealed, frames Siodmak himself as the muckraking journalist whose work reopens the case. It is this film that sheds light on the dark corners of the past, and thus forces his audience to confront a truth about themselves they would much rather forget. Siodmak himself has said, "I am not proud of the films I made after my return from America. With two exceptions: *The Rats* and *Nachts, wenn der Teufel kam*" (232). Granted, one might be bothered by the tone of self-congratulation in both the film's ending and Siodmak's statement. But it is difficult to dismiss the film, like some reviewers have, on aesthetic grounds. There are no stylistic inconsistencies here—Siodmak knows exactly what he is doing. Neither does the film flatter its German audience or indulge its smug complacency in coming to terms with a difficult past. Just as Siodmak's deployment of style is not a sign of lacking artistic control, it is not a self-indulgent display of technical mastery either. On the contrary, it demonstrates that Siodmak was acutely conscious of the sensitive nature of his material and his political stance. The film shows that he is looking for a way in which to address questions that his German audience in 1957 did not want to think about. The way he finds is sneaky and underhanded, which leaves an audience with the possibility of misreading the film, consciously or unconsciously, and ignoring its less obvious aspects, in case they are too unpleasant to consider, in favor of its more obvious ones, which happen to be more easily acceptable. The sugar-coating of the bitter pill worked. The accolades heaped upon the film by the German film industry upon its initial release in 1957 were perhaps less the product of enthusiastic endorsement, or the product of a guilty collective conscience, and more an expression of grudging admiration. They are earned by the film's subtlety as much as by its director's slyness. In either case, the fact that German critics and reviewers did find anything positive to say about the film *at all* is a sign that Siodmak prevailed where others—one might think of the critical and commercial disaster of Peter Lorre's *Der Verlorene*—failed. *Nachts, wenn der Teufel kam* stands as a remarkable piece of political filmmaking under difficult circumstances.

Notes

I would like to express my gratitude to the Sogang University Research Office, which supported the writing of this essay with a grant in 2005. I am also greatly indebted to Jay McRoy for his insightful comments on the rough draft of this essay.

1. This is the official Nazi terminology for the mythical concept of the "people's body," the coherent, unified racial and political entity of the German people.

2. Actors Hannes Messemer, Mario Adorf, Werner Peters, and Annemarie Dueringer, as well as cinematographer Georg Krause, production designers Rolf Zehetbauer and Gottfried Will received the award. So did screenwriter Werner Joerg Lueddecke, and, last but not least, director Robert Siodmak.

3. Georg Krause serves as director of photography. Having learned his craft in the last years of German silent film, Krause worked in the German film industry under the Nazis, shooting military action films and melodrama. While shooting *Nachts, wenn der Teufel kam* for Siodmak in 1957, Krause was also involved in Kubrick's *Paths of Glory* that same year. The same high caliber as Georg Krause is Rolf Zehetbauer, who served as Siodmak's set designer and received the Bundesfilmpreis for his work on *Nachts, wenn der Teufel kam*. Zehetbauer had started specializing in set designs of the Nazi period with his work on *Canaris* in 1945. He was to become chief set designer for the Bavaria Studios in Munich-Geiselgasteig in 1963 where he worked on the U.S. series *Inside the Third Reich* and on *Cabaret*, for which he received an Academy and a BAFTA Award in 1963. He also worked on Fassbinder's *Lilli Marleen*, *Veronika Voss*, and *Querelle*, as well as on Wolfgang Petersen's *Das Boot* and *Die Unendliche Geschichte*. Outstanding among the actors are Mario Adorf, who plays the serial murderer Bruno Lüdke, and Werner Peters, who plays Willi Keun, the man who was suspected of Lüdke's murders and unjustifiedly executed for them. Adorf, who was to go on to become one of the most respected actors in the postwar German film industry, working both in light entertainment and theater and Autorenkino, was not well known at the time Siodmak signed him on. He had made his first appearance in feature film in 1954/5 in Paul May's *08/15* films, based on Hans Hellmut Kirst's WWII military satire. Peters had made a number of films prior to 1957 for the East German DEFA, most notable among them in Wolfgang Staudte's *Der Untertan*, in which he played the epitome of the petit bourgeois "ugly German"—subservient to state authority and mean-spirited to those below him—so convincingly that he remained associated with this role for the rest of his career. Least remarkable, perhaps, among the cast is Claus Holm, who plays the detective in pursuit of Lüdke, the second lead role of the film. Though Holm was born in 1918, which places him, together with Werner Peters, closer to Siodmak's generation than Adorf's, his career had only begun to take off after 1945. Steadily employed, most of his films were unremarkable, however, ranging from sentimental "Heimatfilme" to light comedy. Even in the case of an unremarkable actor like Claus Holm, Siodmak's casting is inspired. Holm's good-natured blandness is beautifully contrasted with the intensity of performance by the dramatic leads Adorf and Hannes Messemer, as well as that of Werner Peters in a significant minor part.

4. Perhaps it was its losing out to Fellini's *Nights of Cabiria* that marked the turning-point in its reception history.

5. In his memoirs, Siodmak explicitly foregoes all claims to this status, presenting himself insistently, though perhaps not always honestly, as a director for hire within the studio system. See Siodmak, *Zwischen Berlin und Hollywood: Erinnerungen eines*

großen Filmregisseurs (101). Citing Siodmak's "versatility" and the fact that "he had worked practically in all genres" (14), Blumenbergh concludes, therefore, that "it is impossible to detect a definitive Siodmak touch—stylistic and thematic constants that tie together an entire oeuvre scattered over forty years and several countries" (13). Along the same lines, Lutz Koepnick states: "Nor had Siodmak ever been an auteur in the emphatic perspective of the postwar generation" (200).

6. Koepnick cites only Enno Patalas as an example to this dehistoricizing approach to Siodmak and his films during their postwar German reception (199–200).

7. That Siodmak himself would have been exempted from such criticism is surprising, considering that his years of exile in the U.S. would have made him, like Peter Lorre and Fritz Lang, problematic to German viewers. Yet Koepnick points out that such recognition of the directors' exile was slow in coming, granted reluctantly, or even altogether taboo (195).

8. All translations from sources originally in German are the author's own, unless otherwise identified.

9. Many of these reviews are written on the occasion of the film's release onto video and DVD. At the time of writing, the film has been available on DVD in Germany since May 2003, released by ARTHAUS, a distributor specializing in classics and German film. There is currently no English-language video or DVD release of the film.

10. The same sense of generic confusion, albeit without the judgemental pose of the reviewers, is also visible in Fritz Goettler's essay on postwar German film that makes reference to *Nachts, wenn der Teufel kam*. Goettler sees the film as being more closely related to "all the satires about the postwar years" than to any "moral drama" ("jedem moralischen Kammerspiel"), and finally settles on calling it "a unique form of cabaret" ("eine eigene Form von Kabarett") (184).

11. Though terminology tends to be somewhat vague in this case, the term "Problemfilm" loosely refers to a film with an overt social agenda, often commenting directly and didactically on pertinent issues of the day.

12. The term *Vergangenheitsbewältigung* is commonly used in postwar German political discourse to refer to the cultural labor of coming to terms with the Third Reich.

13. The title of Siodmak's memoirs is *Between Berlin and Hollywood*, tracing the cultural and professional arc of Siodmak's life as a filmmaker.

14. "Robert Siodmak's career is often told as a narrative of ruptures and fly-by-night departures" (Koepnick 168).

15. Joseph Greco, in one of the few book-length studies of Siodmak's work, characterizes the film this way:

> The subject was far more gruesome than anything Siodmak had handled before in his Hollywood *noirs*. Yet the visual style—high-contrast lighting, odd-angled shots, sinister close-ups, dangerous staircases—is powerfully reminiscent of those earlier films, most particularly in his disdain for documentary realism that has no appreciation of artistic composition and good taste. (173)

Clearly, Greco is a fan of Siodmak's, and this passage attempts to elevate *Nachts, wenn der Teufel kam* in a number of ways. It makes the film out to be expressionist in style, and it makes this style out to be consistent. Neither assertion is correct.

16. For a detailed discussion of this trope, see Steffen Hantke, "'The Kingdom of the Unimaginable': The Construction of Social Space and the Fantasy of Privacy in Serial Killer Narratives," *Literature/Film Quarterly* 26.3 (July 1998): 178–96.

17. If Siodmak is to be blamed for an overly conciliatory approach to the Third Reich for his postwar German audience it is in the presentation and casting of this character that I, for one, would find fault. By casting the slender, sleek, blond and blue-eyed Hannes Messemer, Siodmak does not so much fall back onto the stereotype of the Nazi, which I would find disappointing but forgivable, but he conceptualizes him within the visual framework of Nazi ideology. Messemer embodies an ideal of the SS officer as the Nazis themselves would have seen it. Himmler, Goebbels, and Hitler himself failed to meet these racial and aesthetic standards, yet popular iconography has rewritten German fascism as a coherent discourse, untroubled by its own inherent absurdities. How evasive this problem is can be seen in *Schindler's List*, in which Spielberg suggests, by recourse to stereotypical imagery, that German Jews really did look and dress, and thus *were*, different from the rest of the German population.

Works Cited

Blumenbergh, Hans C. "Der Schatten am Ende der Treppe: Die vier Karrieren des Robert Siodmak." *Zwischen Berlin und Hollywood: Erinnerungen eines großen Filmregisseurs.* Ed. Hans C. Blumenberg. Munich: Universitas/Herbig, 1980. 7–19.

Cinema Scale. "The Devil Strikes at Night." www.clcole.people.wm.edu/dsn.html. May 27, 2005.

Ehrlacher, Frank. "Nachts, wenn der Teufel kam." *Moviemaster.* February 27, 2004. www.moviemaster.de/index.htm?archiv/film/film.php?nr=3329.

Goettler, Fritz. "Westdeutscher Nachkriegsfilm." *Geschichte des Deutschen Films.* Eds. Wolfgang Jacobsen, Anton Kaes, and Hans Helmut Prinzler. Stuttgart: Metzlersche Verlagsbuchhandlung, 1993. 171–21.

Greco, Joseph. *The File on Robert Siodmak in Hollywood: 1941–1951.* Ph.D. Dissertation. 1999.

Hake, Sabine. *German National Cinema.* London/New York: Routledge, 2002.

Hantke, Steffen. "Monstrosity without a Body: Representational Strategies in the Popular Serial Killer Film." *PostScript: Essays in Film and the Humanities* 22.2 (Winter/Spring 2003): 34–55.

Hemingway, Bernard. "The Devil Strikes at Night." *Senses of Cinema.* November 2003. www.sensesofcinema.com/contents/cteq/03/29/devil_strikes_at_night.html. May 27, 2005.

Koepnick, Lutz. *The Dark Mirror: German Cinema between Hitler and Hollywood.* Berkeley: University of California Press, 2002.

Simpson, Philip L. *PsychoPaths: Tracking the Serial Killer through Contemporary American Film and Fiction.* Carbondale/Edwardsville: Southern Illinois University Press, 2000.

Siodmak, Robert. *Zwischen Berlin und Hollywood: Erinnerungen eines großen Filmregisseurs.* Ed. Hans C. Blumenberg. Munich: Universitas/Herbig, 1980.

Tithecott, Richard. *Of Men and Monsters: Jeffrey Dahmer and the Construction of the Serial Killer.* Madison: University of Wisconsin Press, 1997.

Part 2:

German *Autorenkino* and Horror Film: Influences, Dialogues, Exchanges

The Shadow and the Auteur: Herzog's Kinski, Kinski's Nosferatu, and the Myths of Authorship

Linda Badley

They were friends bound by fate and enemies driven by madness. Together, they changed movies forever. These six visionary collaborations between director Werner Herzog and actor Klaus Kinski are the legacy of the most fascinating and controversial relationship in modern cinema history. (DVD cover blurb, Werner Herzog and Klaus Kinski: A Film Legacy, *2002)*

Burdens, Dreams, Fiends

The recent (2004) re-release of Les Blank's *Burden of Dreams* (1982) as a feature-loaded Criterion Collection DVD was also a landmark, as film legacies go. As Paul Arthur and Scott Tobias have noted, this documentary about Werner Herzog's *Fitzcarraldo* (1982) was the first of a wave of feature-length films about directors and the making of their signature films, "crazed visionaries who, in creating art from chaos," venturing into the heart of darkness, "grew into uncanny reflections of their subjects" (Tobias). They included Fax Bahr, George Hickenlooper, and Eleanor Coppola's *Hearts of Darkness: A Filmmaker's Apocalypse* (1991, about Francis Ford Coppola's *Apocalypse Now!* originally released in 1979), Clint Eastwood's *White Hunter, Black Heart* (1991, about John Huston), Chris Smith's *American Movie* (1999, about sub-indie filmmaker Mark Borchardt's no-budget horror film *Coven* from 1998), and Keith Fulton and Louis Pepe's *Lost in La Mancha* (2002, about Terry Gilliam's abandoned *Don Quixote*). These documentaries were complemented by a pre-millennial wavelet of biopics on the uncannily similar subject of horror auteurs and their respective inspirations: *Ed Wood* (1993), *Gods and Monsters* (1999, about James Whale), and *Shadow of the Vampire* (2000, about F. W. Murnau and *Nosferatu*). As I have argued elsewhere, these films are about filmmaking portrayed according to a psychoanalytic, and very gothic popular understanding of the auteur theory.[1] This assumes filmmaking to be a "dark" business originating in obsession and personal and cultural trauma—the latter projected as the auteur's "vision" upon crew and cast, and featuring a monstrous auteur surrogate or double.

Burden of Dreams provided the model and the theme for many of the later films. A documentary about Werner Herzog's struggle on location to make *Fitzcarraldo* (1982), itself about the title character's struggle to build an opera house for Enrico Caruso in the Peruvian jungle, *Burden of Dreams* also established the legend that has hardened into stereotype with the passing years. Interrogating the director's psyche, the film featured Herzog's vision of reality or nature as a "harmony of overwhelming and collective murder," a horror greatly exceeded, however, by the filmmaker's hubristic act of chronicling "what we are." Herzog the auteur is found playing his favorite character: the mad dreamer—often a conquistador—who leads men to their doom. Beginning with *Aguirre, der Zorn Gottes* (1972, *Aguirre: The Wrath of God*), Herzog's films became known for being shot on location, where, confronting the dangers encountered by the characters, the shoot invariably became "the site of as much legendary pathos and drama as the films themselves" (Knipfel 4). This assertion is supported not only by *Aguirre,* about a demented sixteenth-century Spanish adventurer whose search for El Dorado deep within the Amazon ends on a sinking raft overrun by gibbering monkeys, but also by *Cobra Verde* (1987), about a nineteenth-century Brazilian bandit and Gold Coast slave trader who leads a war against a local king. It is also, most recently, supported by several of Herzog's documentaries including the acclaimed 2005 *Grizzly Man,* about grizzly bear environmentalist and filmmaker Timothy Treadwell, who was mauled to death by one of his subjects, as well as the mockumentary *Incident at Loch Ness* (2004), directed by Zak Penn, co-scripted and produced by Herzog, and starring Herzog as himself as the director of an ill-fated documentary about *The Enigma of Loch Ness.* In a hilariously deadpan performance of his legendary self, "Herzog" describes Nessie as the product of "our collective desires, our dreams": "We need our monsters," he says, concluding, however, that "Your film, John, the story of my life, ha[s] turned into some sort of a horror movie."

Thus Herzog admits to a compulsion to making feature films that are ultimately autobiographical and that are also "horrors." As documented by *Burden of Dreams* and confirmed by Herzog's commentary and interviews, *Fitzcarraldo* is a cross between metacinema and autobiography. It is a mad dream about a mad dreamer, the crazy document of a crazier performance project, as the Sisyphean task of making *Fitzcarraldo* perfectly embodied the protagonist's struggle to drag a three-decker riverboat over a mountain. Herzog's shoot, which involved hiring a second crew to make the documentary to immortalize the making of the film, resulted in armed conflicts between tribes, endangering the crew and cast and resulting in the deaths of several extras. In the end, the shoot cut a vast, muddy swath through the jungle and contaminated the indigenous cultures of the region, even as Blank's documentary showed Herzog mourning the loss. "I shouldn't make movies anymore," he admits in the final interview: "I should go to a lunatic asylum."

But the ultimate threat, both to the project and the people involved in it—or so argued Herzog's 1999 documentary *Mein liebster Feind*—was Klaus Kinski, Herzog's charismatic, volatile star in what have come to be recognized as the latter's greatest films. A cross between disclaimer and homage, this biography/autobiography focused on Herzog's collaboration, in that film and four others, with Kinski, who died in 1991. It portrayed working with Kinski as a primeval struggle during which Kinski would be raging for hours at a time, wounding extras in spear-and-sword-throwing tantrums, and threatening to leave the set. Herzog, in turn, would retaliate with death threats, leading to reports that he directed Kinski through the scope of a rifle. To Herzog's credit, Kinski made over 170 films but never worked more than once with any director except for Herzog, with whom he made a total of five films. The madder genius was Kinski, claimed Herzog, who added the "taming" of the "beast" to his achievements, while relinquishing some of his own mystique (and "inspired" authorship) to Kinski.

Informing the signature work of both men, this collaboration has become iconic, perhaps like no other. Additional testaments include Kinski's autobiography *Kinski: Ich Brauche Liebe (All I Need Is Love* (1991), translated and published in English as *Kinski Uncut* (1996), and Anchor Bay's *Werner Herzog and Klaus Kinski: A Film Legacy* (2002). Taking its keynote from *Mein liebster Feind*, which crowns the collection, *Legacy* includes five features— *Aguirre, Nosferatu, Woyzeck, Fitzcarraldo*, and *Cobra Verde*—with documentary featurettes and director's commentaries featuring Herzog with interviewer Norman Hill. Together these texts portray the relationship between the two men as a mutually self-reflexive Gothic psychodrama, with Kinski in the role of Herzog's demonic double or evil twin.

Nowhere is this line of reasoning more relevant than in Herzog's single horror film, *Nosferatu: Phantom der Nacht (Nosferatu: Phantom of the Night*, 1979), the noted remake of Friedrich Wilhelm Murnau's *Nosferatu, eine Symphonie des Grauens* (1922). On the surface, the choice of remaking Murnau's film might seem odd for a director of Herzog's originality and temperament. Remakes, like sequels, are undertaken by commercial directors interested in safe investments—a fact that adds to an impression that *Nosferatu* is a "minor" Herzog film. The same is true for Kinski. Compared to the more flamboyant roles of Aguirre, Fitzcarraldo, Woyzek, or Cobra Verde, Kinski's Nosferatu can seem a muted performance. Finally, Nosferatu paid homage not only to Murnau but to the Hollywood genre film, and a "low" and hackneyed genre at that, the vampire film. Although it had some crossover appeal, its recognition at the time reached nothing like that of Academy Award-winning

Volker Schlöndorff's *Die Blechtrommel* (1979, *The Tin Drum*) or Wim Wenders' *Paris, Texas* (1984). But it is precisely as a remake and a genre film, which aims at transcending its genre, and, most importantly, as a film authorized by Kinski, that this *Nosferatu* becomes Herzog's "testamental" film—a film that "speaks" to an unusual degree for the auteur.

A New Expressionism?

Herzog has spoken often and at length about Murnau and the expressionists as the lost and only legitimate patriarchs of a generation of New German filmmakers whose fathers (and mothers), working under the shadow of the Third Reich, had been disavowed. Of that generation of New German directors who collaborated in that disavowal, Herzog remains, more than most others, haunted by its shadow. This shadow, as it were, appears in the form of post-Kracauerian analysis which views the expressionists as facilitating, through their fascination with Faustian overreaches and archetypal tyrants, the fascist mythic mentality of the Nazi style. Herzog was fascinated with similar figures with which he populated quasi-historical epics like *Fitzcarraldo* and *Cobra Verde*. A longtime fan of German expressionist film critic Lotte Eisner, however, Herzog considered Murnau's *Nosferatu* the most important German film precisely for "prophesy[ing] the rise of Nazism by showing the invasion of Germany by Dracula and his plague-bearing rats" (Herzog, qtd. in Cronin 151). In *Nosferatu: Phantom der Nacht*, he attempted to produce a different kind of haunting with which he hoped to exorcise the Nazi ghosts by transposing the myth into a different key.

For Herzog, the film "was the final chapter of the vital process of 're-legitimization' of German culture that had been going on for some years" (Herzog, qtd. in Cronin 151) by building a bridge to the expressionist era. Returning to Stoker by way of Murnau, he was "not remaking *Nosferatu*," he emphasizes, "but bringing it to new life and new character for a new age" (Andrews 33). Eisner, for whom Murnau was the greatest of the expressionists, gave her blessing, announcing that the film is not being remade, it is being reborn" (Andrews 33). The image of rebirth, however, has an ominous ring, considering the film's central icon, the vampire, the rumoured insanity of the star actor, and the proclivities of a director who, in the words of Leonard Maltin, "shrouds himself in a cloak of self-fashioned mythology." As several critics have wondered, particularly in reference to this film, might Herzog's New German expressionism merely offer a new strain of Nazi-style mystification of the sort perfected by Leni Riefenstahl?

What is certain is that the occasion demanded Kinski, regardless of the trauma thus inflicted on cast, crew, set, and director, to impose Herzog's signature on Murnau's classic. Only what Herzog would end up calling his "best fiend" could evoke the sense of the primordial in the human, of "a pure creature out of the darkest layers" of the German and the collective psyche (*Mein liebster Feind*). An interrogation of the various texts, contexts, and myths surrounding the Herzog-Kinski saga and *Nosferatu,* this essay should also unearth some of the gothic, psychoanalytic, and Romantic ideologies underlying the popular concept of auteurist cinema.

Taming Nature, Framing Kinski

As vividly as any director now living, Herzog represents the problem at the heart of the auteur theory. Herzog has stated his official stance in an early autobiography, *Was Ich bin, sind meine Filme* (1979, *I Am My Films*), in which he advanced a version of the Foucaultian doctrine according to which the filmmaker's personality disappears into the work and is "ultimately dwarfed by the weights and energies it testifies to" (Corrigan, "Producing Herzog" 3). Herzog restates this position in *Mein liebster Feind,* concluding that neither the material struggle, nor the sacrifice (in human and animal lives), nor least of all "what happened between us [Herzog and Kinski]" mattered—and that "all that matters is what you see on the screen." This modernist platitude, however, is contradicted by the very personal nature of the film, whose title alone points out Kinski's role as Werner Herzog's friend, fiend, shadow, and mask.

The subject and theory implicit in *Mein liebster Feind* is more usefully explained by Linda Rugg's discussion of the auteur film, as defined by François Truffaut, in the context of autobiography. She quotes Truffaut's biographer Antoine de Baecque:

> What the critic sees in the film [...] is a (self-) portrait of the director, the auteur himself. An auteur, then, when all is said and done, is a director who allows his intimate self to be seen on the screen, either through a multiplicity of masks, like Hitchcock, or by revealing himself with complete frankness. (de Baecque 100)

In contrast to autobiography as traditionally understood, however, a film image takes on an uncanny, undead life of its own. As his "best fiend," a man he was fond of calling "a pestilence," Kinski provided an image which, according to Herzog, functioned as a mask and has become perhaps the central icon in the myth of his authorship. A rabid Kinski in Herzog's mad conquistador roles became the filmmaker's signature, turning *Aguirre* and *Fitzcarraldo* and especially Herzog's biography of Kinski, *Mein liebster Feind* (1999) into something approximating psychodrama, with Kinski as Herzog's id or shadow.

Rugg points out an obviously staged scene in the latter film in which, some eight years after Kinski's death, a cast member from *Aguirre* meets Herzog at the Lima airport with a sign reading "Herzog's Kinski," creating confusion between the actor and himself. This is a confusion, Rugg notes, that the documentary (and I would add, the *Legacy* collection as a whole) encourages throughout, and might be interpreted as an autobiographical assertion about his work as a whole (10).

The confusion extends to Herzog's account of his first uncanny meeting with Kinski when he was twelve, as Roger Ebert recounts it in 1999: "I was playing in the courtyard of the building where we lived in Munich, and I looked up and saw this man striding past, and I knew at that moment that my destiny was to direct films, and that he would be the actor." As Herzog restages the event, something in Kinski "called" him not only to make films but to capture his "innermost being"—to use a phrase Herzog often finds appropriate. Ergo Kinski: Ebert claims that when he asked the actor why he agreed to make *Aguirre* on location, under the most primitive and dangerous of conditions, he replied, "It was my fate." In turn, Herzog claims that he and Kinski "understood each other without words—almost like animals" and confesses that they "almost exchanged roles."

In fact, it was Kinski who at times was capable of creating "around him an attitude of complete professionalism"—and thus threw tantrums when his demands were not satisfied—while Herzog was equally notorious for his longwinded tirades. These exhausting monologues are recapitulated in the character of the demented German patriarch of a grotesquely dysfunctional family Herzog played in Korine's *julien donkey boy* (2002). Here the actor Herzog is also quite obviously "doing Kinski," his rages recalling the latter's legendary roles—perhaps most notably his "Jesus tour," a one-man show, staged in packed coliseums, in which Kinski claimed to be the embodiment of Christ, the "derided, misunderstood" iconoclast, and raged back at scoffers in the style of a 1950s poet.

Enhancing the myth of their composite nature, Herzog claims to have co-written parts of the latter's autobiography, using a dictionary to boost the most vituperative passages, all of which are rendered in an "eternal present" tense. Accordingly, "Herzog" is every species of "vermin" and "sticks [to Kinski] like a fly to a dungheap," dressing "in the same filthy clothes for weeks—even the camera lens is covered with slime. He bullies underlings and ties up a llama in a canoe and films it as it goes down the rapids to its death" (220). Kinski (or is it Herzog?) heaps curse after curse upon "Herzog," assuming the role of nature's revenge: "The huge red ants should piss into his lying eyes and gobble up his balls and his guts!" (220). In the course of one such diatribe, Kinski (and/or Herzog) ends up claiming that he is the real auteur of Herzog's films. Herzog's "so-called 'talent'" consists of nothing but tormenting helpless creatures and, if necessary, torturing them to death or simply murdering them. He doesn't care about anyone or anything except his wretched career as a so-called filmmaker. Driven by a pathological addition to sensationalism, he creates the most senseless difficulties and dangers, risking other people's safety and even their lives—just so he can eventually say that he, Herzog, has beaten seemingly unbeatable odds. For his movies he uses retards and amateurs whom he can push around (and allegedly hypnotize!) and he pays them starvation wages or zilch. He also uses freaks and cripples of every conceivable size and shape, merely to look interesting. He doesn't have the foggiest inkling of how to make movies. He doesn't even try to direct the actors anymore. [...] If he wasn't to shoot another take because he, like most directors, is insecure, I'd tell him to go fuck himself. [...] Every scene, every angle, every shot is determined by me, and I refuse to do anything unless I consider it right." (222–23)

Like Kinski's "autobiography," *Mein liebster Feind,* in spite of its various "voices," is essentially monologic, most of all when in "disagreement" with Kinski. It thus speaks for the two men's renowned "battle of wills" for control of the project, whatever that might be. To the extent that Herzog created Kinski and Kinski fabricated Herzog, the book, like the films they collaborated on, becomes a hall of mirrors.

Kinski's posturing here is an outward expression of the same egomania that Herzog associates with Kinski's uncanny ability to evoke the "primordial." Herzog's Kinski played human incarnations of extra-human nature, which Herzog "revealed" through a mystical perspective in which the landscapes in his films become characters and, more importantly, serve as authorizing presences. In its identification with the sublime, Herzog's camera mocks the human plight—think of the opening shot in *Aguirre* in which Pisarro's soldiers move in an antlike line down the vast side of a mountain, or the scene in *Nosferatu* in which Jonathan, having reached the Borgo Pass, contemplates the mountains and the sky, absorbed, alienated from the human and particularly the social world, transformed, as it turns out, into something alien himself. This state of alienated sublimity is not pretty when one looks at it closely; upon closer inspection, it often becomes abject and grotesque. Herzog pursues the same effect in *Burden of Dreams,* where he famously describes nature (or reality) as "vile and base, fornication, fighting for survival, rotting away. The birds are in misery. I think they scream in pain." Nature is "a harmony of overwhelming and collective murder." To the extent that nature is self aware, it is miserable in its compulsory vitality.

Herzog and Kinski competed to demonstrate their "instinctive" understanding of nature—Herzog in his landscapes and cinematic quests for the extra-human or "ecstatic" truth, which continue today in documentaries such as *Grizzly Man*; and Kinski in his nearly feral fits, or in his autobiography which, in its inherent violence and obsessive-compulsory sexuality, echoes Herzog's personality and agenda. In its inherent violence and obsessive-compulsive sexuality, Kinski's autobiography seems to reflect this vision. Described on back cover blurbs as "hyperbolically pornographic" and "totally fascinating" (*Newsweek*), the work of "an unregenerate id on two legs [. . .] a walking appetite" (*GQ*), it presents its subject, much as Herzog does in interviews, as a force of nature, incomprehensible even to himself. Kinski identifies himself with the "wilderness," which "isn't interested in arrogant bigmouth movie makers. It has no pity for those who flout its laws" (Kinski 223). Herzog, in turn, claims that in spite of Kinski's self-proclaimed "closeness" to "nature's children," the Indian extras in *Fitzcarraldo* found him intolerable and offered in all seriousness to kill him (*Mein liebster Feind*). Yet Herzog ends *Mein liebster Feind* with an extended take of Kinski courting a butterfly, a sequence that uncannily manages to suggest that the man (or is it the actor?) communes with the insect through some mystical sixth sense.

In the same way that he "communes" with nature, Kinski claims to be an instinctive, suffering actor who "becomes" the Other in Herzog's monstrous roles—most of all his role as the ultimate actor, partly provoked and duly documented by Herzog himself. Kinski, with characteristic modesty, concurs:

> I play parts involving what I have to experience myself but can barely endure. [...] Do I transfer other people's hells to my own life, or do I transfer my own life to the character I have to play? Does the event [...] occur in my own life through mystical force, so that I may suffer more deeply when I have to play the part? [...] In any case, it's part of the curse of being—as they put it—"The ultimate actor." (280)

Nosferatu appears as a cornerstone of such self-identification. Suffering from rejection (his wife divorced him during the shoot) and separation from his young son Nanhoi, Kinski identifies with Dracula as the monstrous outsider longing for love and unable to die. He sees people "uncamouflaged" and "grotesque," comparing them to the demons in Hieronymus Bosch's paintings. Kinski's attachment to Nanhoi, moreover, is vampiric: he lives only through Nanhoi, who is his perfected image reflected back to him. Separated from his son, he feels like a monster or the alienated figure in Edvard Munch's *The Scream*: "I have to see Nanhoi! I race along the quais, I keep turned away from the pedestrians and vehicles, I feel as if everyone were gaping at me. . . . A monster. An Elephant Man. Too disfigured not to be discovered. It is my *shriek* that dashes through the streets, not belonging anywhere" (279). As the bald, grotesque vampire, Kinski feels "exposed vulnerable, defenseless"—"not just physically (my bare head becomes as hypersensitive as an open wound) but chiefly in my emotions and my nerves. I feel as if I have no scalp, as if my protective envelope has been removed and my soul can't live without it. As if my soul had been flayed" (280). But the physical baldness is not the issue. "What I mean is the simultaneous metamorphosis into a vampire. That nonhuman, nonanimal being. That undead thing. That unspeakable creature, which suffers in full awareness of its existence" (280).

Speaking of Kinski's work on *Aguirre*, in spite of the struggle of the shoot that included the famous death threats, Herzog said that "somehow the beast had been domesticated after all, pressed into shape, so that his true madness and energy had been contained within the frame of a screen image" (*Mein liebster Feind*). It was *Nosferatu* in which the "madness and energy" of the two of them was most completely contained and reshaped. *Nosferatu* is an expressionistic and especially reflexive rendering of Herzog's semi-historical conquistadors such as Aguirre, Cobra Verde, and Fitzcarraldo. They are memorable through Kinski's ability to evoke what he internalizes most successfully in the role of Nosferatu: simultaneously their humanity and something irreclaimably alien.[2] As the challenge of remaking Murnau created a structure for Herzog, the character of the vampire itself, including the physical aspects of assuming it, which happened to include four hours a day of applying makeup, created a structure for Kinski. For Kinski, the role perfectly expressed the existential predicament of being trapped in the body of the beast. Paradoxically in the course of the discipline and suffering of "becoming" the vampire, Kinski embodied perhaps the most human role of his career.

"A Vampire Like No Other"

In *Nosferatu*, Herzog linked New German cinema with Murnau's great innovation, an expressionism that fused uncannily with a "documentary" naturalism through the symbolic use of natural settings and local non-actors. The result is a film that, like Murnau's *Nosferatu*, seems to subscribe to a belief in the vampire. As the embodiment of a vile but all-inclusive nature and of the existential human condition, Kinski's vampire epitomizes the pain that, as Herzog has explained, "all of my films come out from. [...] not from pleasure" ("The Making of Nosferatu"). However, this figure also stands in sharp contrast to Bram Stoker's Dracula, who is a conquistador indeed. Born of a Victorian fear of reverse colonization, Stoker's Dracula claims descent from Attila and, regretting the passing of Eastern Europe's bloodthirsty era, takes his campaign westward. He also departs from Murnau's Orlok, who, while ratlike and bestial, is "a cold and ruthless force," "arrogant and supremely self-confident," as William Luhr puts it (458). Herzog's vampire is as grotesque as Murnau's, but he is "at the end of his tether" and longs for death. He acts like "a lifelong hermit suddenly brought into social contract by desperate need, but lacking the social graces to conceal either his need or his desperation" (Luhr 458). With his grotesquely bald head, awkwardly held claws, and protruding fangs, he has the vulnerability of infancy, the pathos of extreme old age, and the bestiality of nature. Trapped by his instincts, he has eyes that radiate not only malice and madness, but also betray his fathomless sorrow and suffering.

An awkward, pathetically unsocialized beast-man, Kinski's Dracula is also a "nervous wreck," who, having lived too long, deriving no pleasure from his acts, is "as trapped by the evil he represents as his victims are" (Luhr 458). Ultimately Kinski's Nosferatu expresses the Cartesian split—the existential human condition of being an animal endowed with self-consciousness and tragically the worse for it.[3] In terms of Herzog's *oeuvre*, this figure combines both of Herzog's primary characters and themes: the madman or rebel, usually played by Kinski, and the manchild, idiot savant, or unsocialized outsider, most memorably embodied in *Jeder für sich und Gott gegen alle* (1974, *The Enigma of Kasper Hauser*) and *Stroszek* by non-actor Bruno S, a homeless street musician who had spent most of his early life in institutions (and whose "real" name, if he ever had one, Herzog refuses to reveal). Capable of embodying the "uncontainable" physical presence of inarticulate nature (Corrigan, "Producing Herzog" 10), Bruno S also evoked the deceptively simple young Bavarian mountain boy Herzog claims to have been.[4] But Bruno S lacked another facet of this character in which Herzog would project himself—a ferocity that suggested the predatory aspect of nature. Kinski could embody the furious torment of a wild animal in pain and desperation, especially in *Cobra Verde*, whose iconic image is the assaulting face of Kinski; only here, as Herzog admits in *Mein liebster Feind*, he was completely out of control. Together, Bruno S and Kinski came to represent different, passive and aggressive, aspects of the human predicament of existing within the ongoing futility of nature while being conscious of and alienated from it.[5]

Kinski's Dracula is in fact completely in tune with the sympathetic vampire heralded by Anne Rice's *Interview with the Vampire* (1976) and Barnabas Collins of the American soap opera *Dark Shadows* (1966–71)—a "pestilence" on the one hand, and, on the other, a creature cursed by his understanding the horror of his existence and his separation from fully socialized humanity. Commenting on an unrelated aspect of Herzog's work, Corrigan finds that, for Herzog, Christ is "an emblem of a human tragedy enmeshed in the forces of nature" (*New German Film* 132–33). In the same vein, Kinski's Dracula is Herzog's "ultimate iconoclast" (Corrigan, *New German Film* 131). A tortured soul trapped in his monstrous body, self-consciously encumbered by his claws and fangs, Kinski's Dracula, perhaps drawing on Kinski's "Jesus tour," is more suffering Christ than demon. Thus Herzog created a dialogue between the German expressionist avant-garde of the past, the contemporary art film, and the vampire genre film, whose increasingly sympathetic monsters begged for philosophically and aesthetically sophisticated and serious treatment.

The Hypnotic Gaze: The Politics of Vision

In spite of Herzog's many announcements that his version of Murnau's film was designed to "re-legitimize" German filmmaking, critics have been hard-pressed to find a German, much less a political subtext in *Nosferatu: Phantom der Nacht*.[6] In fact, filmed in Delft, Holland, which was chosen for its solid houses and tranquil canals, and in Czechoslovakia, with an international cast that included Isabel Adjani and Bruno Ganz in back-to-back productions in German and English, and distributed by Twentieth-Century Fox in an obvious bid for popularity in the West, *Nosferatu* has been considered one of Herzog's least "German" or political productions. Herzog seems to have been uninterested in the vampire as a political metaphor, argues Judith Mayne, any more than the titular character of *Cobra Verde* was a serious study of colonialism (120). Similarly, Brad Prager argues that Herzog's films distance themselves from the issue of German colonialism by projecting it onto conquistador figures, played by Kinski, from anywhere *other* than Germany (2–3). Kinski dominates Herzog's films, with issues of race and colonialism forming the backdrop for his posturing. Herzog is fascinated with the colonizer, who represents his own role as a pioneer/explorer who cuts a swath through "virgin" territory and domesticates the "natives" to make his monumental films.

In the same way, Herzog's fascination with the vampire played by Kinski dominates his *Nosferatu* and, as Mayne claims, furnishes a problematic metaphor for Herzog's myth of authorship. More troubling still is what Eric Rentschler calls Herzog's "reactionary modernism" which aligns itself with the Nazi style of Leni Riefenstahl: both "celebrate individual subjects in touch with the mysterious realm of the elemental" where they are "subservient to a larger destiny over which they have no control" (174). In interviews both Herzog and Riefenstahl have used the "jargon of authenticity" that Adorno depicted as "an irrationalism valorizing certain absolutes and at the same time embedded in a discourse denying the powers of reason and explanation" (Rentschler 174). In Herzog's films this realm is projected as an otherworldly no-man's-land through various disruptions of conventional narrative, including a roving, dislocated, extra-human perspective. Landscapes in particular take on what is often described as a dreamy, "hypnotic" effect, literalized in *Herz aus Glas* (1976, *Heart of Glass*), the film in which Herzog famously put the cast, except for the lead, under hypnosis throughout the entirety of the film.[7] In *Nosferatu*, this extra-human state is associated with the vampire's "land of phantoms" and his hypnotic power. This is all the more disturbing as the authorizing power of hypnotism recalls no expressionistic image other than Dr. Caligari, from whom Kracauer drew a direct line to Hitler.[8]

For Herzog, Mayne concludes, the vampire legend is appealing not for its role in German history so much as for providing a "myth of authorship," and "it is toward Nosferatu himself," already associated, from Murnau's film, with windows, mirrors, and shadows, "that Herzog is drawn as a fitting image" (128). The perspective of Murnau's vampire is opposed by the city scribe who opens the film and whose intertitles lend the film the authority of a historical record. Herzog's film creates a "single, all-encompassing" perspective which links disparate scenes: from the opening credit sequence, composed of shots of mummified corpses and accompanied by Popul Vuh's atonal choral chant that seems to emanate from their open mouths, to Lucy's scream, and shots of a bat swooping against a deep blue screen in slow motion (Mayne 128). This is reinforced as the characters one by one enter a hypnotic state that testifies to the vampire's—and, by implication, to Herzog's—power and is underlined by the coda, which comes full circle as Jonathan as Dracula's successor rides off into the shifting shadows of some fatally determined future.

Returning to the central problem represented by Herzog's authorial stance, Rentschler, Prager, and Mayne miss one point: they do not acknowledge the theatrical irony implicit in Herzog's style. Whether explicitly or implicitly, as Corrigan finds, a Herzog film "engages a viewer as a fellow producer of a staged world whose framework paradoxically only blocks that spectator's desire to see more" ("Producing Herzog" 9). The other side of the "mad visionary" auteur is Herzog as carnival barker, as attested by his inclusion of carnival scenes or motifs in the majority of his films and by such feats as *Even Dwarfs Started Small* (1970), Les Blank's *Werner Herzog Eats His Shoe* (1980), and *Incident at Loch Ness*. Moreover, in revising German expressionism, Herzog alluded to the filmic self-reflexiveness inherent in *its* realm of shadows and mirrors, as described in Eisner's *The Haunted Screen*. This, as J. P. Telotte argues, included theatrical or reflexive elements—carnivals, waxworks, replications, and, most of all, Dr. Caligari himself—designed to haunt or "trouble" viewers' perceptions and cause them to question their realities. For Herzog in 1979, tapping Kinski to play Dracula in his "re-legitimization" of Murnau's *Nosferatu* was a triply self-referential act. The 1999 release of the Kinski-Herzog *Legacy* collection including *Mein liebster Feind*, together with a separate DVD release in English in 2002, make it redundantly so. And certainly, as this essay's coda will venture to demonstrate, none of this was lost on Steven Katz and E. Elias Merhige when they made their metahorror film *Shadow of the Vampire*.

Like the original expressionists, Herzog attempts to create "an essential, inner reality [...] more accessible by deliberate distortion and *unreality*" (Furness 88). The estranged, defamiliarized landscapes are designed to invoke what he often calls "the inner landscape"—specifically the uncanny (alien and familiar) territory associated with the "poetic" or "ecstatic" "truth" of the shadow self. In *Nosferatu*, spectators enter this realm when Jonathan Harker (Bruno Ganz) passes from the greens and browns of the natural world through the sublime or "internal landscape" approaching the Borgo Pass as the palette deepens into shades of blue and blue-black, as epitomized in the long take of the phantom castle in silhouette. "You cross over into a different existence in which the shadows are more important than the figures," a "land of phantoms" and myth, Herzog explains in the DVD commentary.

Herzog also drew on elements from the genre film, which for him meant "an intensive, almost dreamlike, stylization on screen," which aligns it with the vampire genre and thus with "fantasy, hallucination, dreams and nightmares, visions, fear and, of course, mythology" (qtd. in Cronin 151). In particular, he raised Murnau's trademark, the expressionistic use of shadows, to an extreme level of stylization enhanced by the genre film, using bats as the vampire's authorizing signature. In Herzog's *Nosferatu*, shadows and bats merge expressively, indicating the hand of the auteur. From the beginning of the film, they alternate and then fuse insistently, as they might in a film with the subtitle "Phantom der Nacht."[9] The image of Lucy's hair spread out on the pillow like blue-black wings echoes the opening shot of the slowly swooping bat, which appears as an inky blue shadow against the sky. Yet Herzog conspicuously leaves out the most famous shadow scene of all, the one in which Murnau's Nosferatu, ascending the stairs to Ellen, casts the long shadow that, in effect, takes the place of the vampire itself. This imagery is altered and inserted into scenes that are not in Murnau's film in order to call attention to Herzog's authorial hand in the "remake." When a bemused Jonathan approaches the Borgo Pass, his own shadow looms ahead of him as he rounds the bend, foreshadowing the appearance of Dracula's shadow in Lucy's boudoir mirror before she turns to find him behind her. In reference to Murnau's equally signatorial low-angle shot in which Nosferatu traverses and is shown to dominate the horizon as limited by the ship, Herzog positions Kinski against a single sail upon which he casts a grotesque and gigantic shadow. As Prawer notes, in this scene Nosferatu emerges from the blue-black night, becoming in contrast to Murnau's vampire, the "Phantom der Nacht," the projection of an inner reality (32, 41). In such ways, Herzog pays homage to Murnau and trumps him at the same time. In fact, Herzog doubles Murnau's expressionistic use of the vampire's shadow by suggesting that Dracula is, in a Jungian sense, Jonathan's shadow, a projection of his real desire and a fulfillment of his destiny, to the extent that Jonathan becomes Dracula's double in the final scene.[10] This *Nosferatu* ends not with the defeat of the plague but comes full circle, with Jonathan fulfilling Dracula's quest: "Prepare my horse. I have much work to do." The irony is suggested in the fact that Herzog originally planned to include the grotesque images of the open-mouthed mummies in the closing credit sequence to underline the existential themes of the film. These equate the vampire with the plague and the curse of mortality.[11]

As Jonathan gradually discovers, the "ecstatic truth" to be discovered in the "land of phantoms" is far from sublime in the high Romantic sense. Nor is *Nosferatu*, as described by David Denby, a "conventional horror film (there are no shocks)"; instead, Denby calls it "an anguished poem of death" (89). It is

Herzog's vision of nature as "a harmony of overwhelming and collective murder" in which the birds "are in misery" and "scream in pain." Herzog's ontology approximates that of Jean-Paul Sartre's *Nausea* and is explained in Sartre's essay on "The Fantastic as a Language" for the human condition of existing as conscious subjects embodied within and alienated from the world of objects. The fantastic is "an entire world in which things manifest a captive, tormented thought that never manages to express itself" purely. That is to say,

> matter is never entirely matter, since it offers only a constantly frustrated attempt at determinism, and mind is never completely mind, because it has fallen into slavery and has been impregnated and dulled by matter. All is woe. Things suffer and tend toward inertia, without ever attaining it; the debased, enslaved mind unsuccessfully strives towards consciousness and freedom" (58).

Sartre insists that the fantastic is necessary for expressing states of being that cannot be articulated in "clear, distinct ideas." Although "wide awake and fully mature and in the midst of civilization," it resorts, like Herzog's films and Kinski's fitfully poetic monologues, to "half-formed metaphors" and "the magical 'mentality' of the dreamer, the primitive and the child" (58). In Herzog's existential humanist version of the vampire—one in which Kinski is the chief victim of the "evil" he himself represents—Kinski embodies the fantastic and conveys the "poetic" truth of the "inner landscape" of existence in nature. Kinski's performance brings the sublime that this film (as do Herzog's films in general) finds so fascinating down to earth, locating its "ecstatic truth" ultimately in the chthonic.

In Kinski's performance, as noted by Noël Carroll, "the familiar becomes arrestingly odd; ineffable mystery is presented as the basic condition of human life" (35). Rather than as a conqueror (as in Stoker, whose Dracula is propagating his race, or as in Kinski's other major roles), Kinski's Dracula comes merely as the bearer of the plague that is the human condition. To make this statement, Herzog turned Murnau's restrained and relatively linear treatment of the plague theme into an elaborately choreographed, pageant-like sequence in the town square, to which he introduced some 11,000 swarming rats.[12] Bringing the narrative to a standstill, this sequence calls attention to itself as a radical departure from Murnau or, for that matter, from any vampire film.[13] It begins with Lucy's encounter with the procession of coffins in three lines moving left to center, her tracking of the rats to the coffins in Dracula's house, and her return to the square where the processional has yielded to a dance of death and a funeral feast. As hooded monks in black robes kneel praying over coffins, people dance in the streets, reaching out to Lucy. Farm animals wander in the streets, and one man mounts a goat while attempting to dance with it. In the poignant final act of the sequence, expensively dressed men and women are feasting at a well-appointed banquet table as rats mass around their feet and over the next table, whose contents they have already devoured. This is their "Last Supper," the celebrants explain to Lucy, beseeching her to join them. As Herzog explains to Norman Hill on the DVD commentary track, the scene was inspired by the late medieval period where, during times of plague, "people would feast and dance as an homage to life and death itself and to the madness of the plague," which Herzog envisions as reality itself. In *Nosferatu*, it is these banqueters (as opposed to Herzog's usual conquerors) who have seen the "ecstatic truth."

Filmed in silence and accompanied by a choral dirge, this carnival sequence recalls Bakhtin's famous discussion of the medieval carnival, but more so the ritualized sequences of the existentialist films of Ingmar Bergman, most particularly *Det sejunde inseglet* (1957, *The Seventh Seal*). Murnau's vampire is "without a soul and looks like an insect," Herzog claims. "But from Kinski's vampire you get real existential anguish. I tried to 'humanize' him. I wanted to endow him with human suffering and solitude, with a true longing for love and, importantly, the one essential capacity of human beings: mortality" (qtd. in Cronin 155). And Kinski's vampire is the most physical of vampires, with a palpable presence often enhanced by the use of shadows, sound, and silence. Typical of this treatment is the scene in which we share his perspective of exclusion outside Jonathan's house, warmly lit from the inside, where a crowd of people are talking, and from which he is removed by his literal shadow (which precedes him), by the window, and by silence. Kinksi's Dracula does not shape-shift and must perform manual labor, serving Jonathan at table and efficiently moving his own rat-filled boxes. At the end of the film, blinded by the light, unable to breathe, writhing and wheezing in torment, he suffers a painfully naturalistic death. He is the only vampire that leaves a grotesque corpse, one whose almost fetal position recalls those of the mummies of the opening title sequence. The film does not terrorize; instead it evokes the plague that is mortality and the consciousness of death. Kinski's vampire embodies the subject's experience of the Cartesian division between consciousness and being-in-the-flesh.

Herzog used Kinski less to say something about German history than to reflect about his own characteristic themes and art. Able to internalize and subjectify the issue of alienation in nature that still is Herzog's main obsession, Kinski provides the film's chief contribution to the myth of the vampire and to the myth of the collaboration between Herzog and Kinski. At the same time, Kinski's presence put a strangely different spin on Herzog's sublimely "hypnotic" effect, producing a film that provokes tension and exceedingly "troubled perceptions."

Which *Nosferatu*? The Real Mythology behind *Shadow of the Vampire*

None of these elements in Herzog's *Nosferatu*, particularly Kinski's performance and the Herzog-Kinski myth, were lost on E. Elias Merhige when he made *Shadow of the Vampire*. On one level, the mythology "surrounding" the making of Murnau's film was ripe for deconstruction. The lives of Murnau and Schreck were relatively unknown even to the average film buff. *Nosferatu* (1998), Jim Shepard's fictional autobiography of Murnau, for example, takes its central idea from Murnau's signature film, confirming that in spite of his recognition as one of the great originals of filmmaking, Murnau himself is best recovered through his overdetermined signifier, *Nosferatu: Eine Symphonie des Grauens*. The lack of documentation about Schreck, complicated by Jamesonian historical amnesia, fostered the notion that the actor was a real vampire. Merhige has called his meta-film a "deconstruction of the mythology" surrounding the making of *Nosferatu* ("Interview with E. Elias Merhige"), but to the degree that elements of Herzog's film intrude upon the original, the question is: which *Nosferatu*?

The plot of *Shadow* concerns a megalomaniac director (John Malkovich as Wilhelm Friedrich Murnau) in league and at odds with his demonic star (Willem Dafoe as Max Schreck). Like the legendary Herzog (as opposed to Murnau), Malkovich's character is prepared to sacrifice anything, including the lives of cast and crew members, for the sake of authenticity and artistic effect. In the central conceit, cinema technology and authorship together constitute a kind of vampirism, a sacrificing of natural life to the image, which takes on an undead life of its own. This refers to Herzog, notorious both for his risk-taking and for his combination of dangerous Romanticism with high modernism to justify the sacrifices involved in making his films. *Shadow* also focuses on two other themes that echo Herzog's legacy: cinema as technological invasion/cultural contamination and the adaptation of "documentary" realism to an expressionistic aesthetic through destructive on-location shooting.

The opening title sequence evokes the theme of technological invasion: the camera penetrates the layers of an ornate frieze to reveal, in a survey of Modernist styles from Art Deco to Futurism, forward-marching armies, from the Greeks and Dracula's armies to the twentieth century. Recalling Walter Benjamin's "The Work of Art in the Age of Mechanical Reproduction" in the sequence's mechanistic stylization, the film equates the "march" of technology with war and imperialism. This motif is linked with the cinematic territorialism of the opening shot—an extreme close-up of a lens cuts to Murnau's eye, followed by contrasting low- and high-angle shots, one of "Murnau" on a platform and another from his point of view as he directs *Nosferatu*'s opening scene. While the sequence plainly uses the historical Murnau's camera to represent the "birth" of cinematic technology, it is enhanced by the memory of Herzog as a more recent and notorious symbol of cinematic territorialism.

In *Shadow*, as in Herzog's commentary, Murnau's expressionism is linked through Kracauerian hindsight with two world wars and German nationalism. However, Merhige renders Murnau's expressionism *itself* oppressive and downright gothic. Film technology is directly analogous to war machinery with the introduction of second cinematographer and pilot Fritz Wagner (Cary Elwes), who refers to the camera as his "weapon of choice" and shoots off guns to rouse the extras to authentic emotion. Thus the film refers cynically to Kracauer's thesis in which expressionist cinema provided prototypes and technology used by the Nazis. It may also draw on Shepard's fictional biography, which suggests that Murnau's experience as a World War I fighter pilot was the key to his filmmaking style.[14] But it cannot help but bring to mind the myth in which Herzog filmed Kinski through the scope of a rifle.

Shadow's "Murnau" regards himself as a pioneer, explorer, and scientist: "We are scientists in search of memory, memory that will neither blur nor fade," he intones as his train roars into Czechoslovakia; "our" art, he predicts, "will have a context as certain as the grave." Celebrated for "liberating" the camera and for "discovering" the use of on-location settings, Murnau here is portrayed as forging his way into territory as yet untouched by technology. But while this obsession with cinema technology and realism refers first to Murnau's pioneering, it recalls nothing so much as Herzog's monomaniacal quest for existential authenticity, familiar from *Burden of Dreams* and Herzog's more recent career as a documentary filmmaker. To facilitate this realism, and echoing both versions of *Nosferatu*, *Shadow*'s "Murnau" hires non-actors—servants and peasants—yet throws a fit when they inadvertently step into his frame. His usually quiet, detached demeanor—the cover for his monomaniacal and tyrannical disposition—becomes eerie when he proves capable of directing the out-of-control "Schreck." This of course mimics Herzog's direction of Kinski.

Like the real menace of Kinski, that of Dafoe's Schreck is necessary to the filmmaker's goals, especially when, in sudden feral bursts, he attacks and kills several crew members including the first cinematographer. Similarly an embodiment of the stereotype of the "difficult actor," he is both the method actor whose confusion between himself and his role gets dangerously out of control and the finicky perfectionist: he demands makeup, complains about the food (bottled blood), and refuses to sail.[15] And yet, like Kinski, Dafoe's actor-vampire can also demonstrate excessive professionalism, to the point of aspiring to control the shoot himself. This aspect of the figure becomes poignant in one scene in which he discovers the projector and, running through the dailies, becomes enraptured with the vision of the sunrise, which he is able to see for the first time in centuries.

Most tellingly, Dafoe's vampire is not so much noble and haughty, like Schreck's Orlok, but more grotesquely angst-ridden, lonely, on his last legs. He confesses that he is "too old" to remember when he became a vampire, much less to care. Impotent to "make more vampires," he feebly longs for love and for death (or the love that is death), quoting from Tennyson's "Tithonus" in a scene reminiscent of Kinski's uncharacteristically muted performance. Even so, he is neurotically consumed by his lust for the leading lady, demonstrated in protracted sucking scene. Asked how he became a vampire, he recalls that "It vas vooman. She came to me in the night, and then she went avay," which evokes the uncanny way both vampires, but more so Kinski's, resemble a grotesque child at its mother's breast.

Finally, at the end of the film, for the sake of cinematic authenticity, "Murnau" sacrifices not only the leading lady but also the vampire to his art and produces the ultimate "snuff" film. While *Shadow of the Vampire* thus alludes to a number of contemporary genre film sources, from *Psycho* and *Peeping Tom* (1960), to the slasher films of the 1970s, to *Snuff* (1976) and the *Guinea Pig* series (1985–1990), Merhige was likely influenced by Kinski's flamboyantly protracted and naturalistic death scene.

Ultimately Merhige refers to the aesthetic modernism to which Herzog famously ascribed and that took on sinister overtones after *Burden of Dreams*. In the scene's final moments, "Murnau" is hilariously restrained in his exasperation when Dafoe's frenetic "Schreck" won't stay in frame, controlling him instantly with the words, "If it's not in the frame, it doesn't exist." At last, after the vampire has killed or wounded all the crew members, consumed the leading lady, and has himself been absorbed by the technology of cinema ("burned to light"), immortalizing actor and filmmaker in the process, does "Murnau" stop cranking the camera. The final shot repeats the first, as he looks through the lens and lines up the camera with the end board: "There. I think we have it." With this flourish, Merhige inscribes his signature upon Herzog's incorporation of Murnau's incorporation of Stoker via Dafoe's virtuoso performance of Kinski, the "ultimate actor," who has claimed to have "become" not Schreck's Dracula but the vampire itself.

A web of intertextual exchanges, *Shadow of the Vampire* ultimately sends up itself as a vampiric text about the vampiric nature of cinema, and a late postmodern, high millennial gesture. In exploring the vampiric nature of cinema, Katz and Merhige also had the strange fate of the original *Nosferatu* in mind. The film had plagiarized Stoker's *Dracula* and was damned from the first to another kind of vampirism. Under the settlement with Stoker's widow, all prints and negatives of the film were destroyed; however the film surfaced outside of Germany and flourished underground and in the avant-garde of the 1960s, in a sort of undead or half-life until, through the miracle of video and DVD it was restored to a different kind of existence altogether by Renfield-like acolytes.

As an attempt to reconnect with their German grandfathers, Herzog's and Kinski's "remake" of Murnau's almost "lost" film proved yet another kind of unnatural rebirth. Viewed from *Shadow*'s cynical postmodern vantage point, Herzog's *Nosferatu* might seem vampiric in the petty sense because it incorporates Murnau's film to little specific political purpose other than to lend historical resonance and heft to Herzog's signature. But in adapting Murnau's expressionistic naturalism, Herzog brought his own cinema's fascination with the sublime down to earth, and in "taming" and internalizing Kinski, Herzog managed to express his generation's sense of its own loss, its own haunting, its sense of existential futility. By the same token, the role of Kinski in the horrific collaboration that produced *Nosferatu*, as *Shadow* suggests, may have ultimately been less vampiric than that of the director.

Finally, *Shadow of the Vampire* provides a useful measure of Herzog's and Kinski's mutual achievement. The scenes between Malkovich (as Herzog as Murnau) and Dafoe (as Kinski as Schreck) are among the most memorable in the film, and Dafoe is funniest and most poignant when he is more Kinski than Schreck. Playing intensely—whether as parody, comedy, or melodrama—these scenes remind us of how the cinema could provide a vampiric medium in what might be regarded as a positive sense. Oddly enough, *Nosferatu: Phantom der Nacht* created boundaries within which both Herzog and Kinski could find undiscovered territories within themselves. The medium and the legend surrounding it intensified that element in any relationship that allows two people to be different, momentarily, from their usual selves, yet ultimately most themselves. It is in this latter sense that, summing up the collaboration with his "best fiend," Herzog possibly meant: "All that matters is what you see on the screen."

Notes

1. See Linda Badley, "The Darker Side of Genius: The (Horror) Auteur Meets Freud's Theory." *Horror Film and Psychoanalysis: Freud's Worst Nightmare.* Ed. Steven Jay Schneider. Cambridge: Cambridge UP, 2004. 222–40.

2. Indeed, in Aguirre's final lines one can hear a hint of Stoker's Dracula, the ultimate gothic villain: "I, the Wrath of God, will marry my own daughter and with her found the purest dynasty known to man. Together we will rule the whole of the continent."

3. In contrast, Jonathan is a young man "like the villagers," who "cannot place [them]selves in the soul of the hunter," Dracula explains to Jonathan, predicting what the latter will become. He longs for death and for the love that Lucy and Jonathan share. "Will you come to me, become my ally? Bring salvation to your husband. And to me. The absence of love is the most abject pain." When Lucy refuses, he moans like a wounded animal and steals off into the night.

4. Born Werner Stipetić, seemingly of Balkan roots, Herzog grew up in a remote Bavarian mountain village and represents himself as largely self-taught and self-invented. The name Werner Herzog is itself a mask, one that asserts loyalty to a Germany whose traditions he admired but whose immediate past he deplored, as Prawer notes (13). Kinski, according to Herzog, invented himself in a different way, constructing a fictionalized impoverished childhood for his autobiography when in fact he was the son of middle-class parents (*Mein liebster Feind*).

5. Like Bruno S, says Herzog, "Kinski was not an actor—I wouldn't call him an artist either, nor am I. Of course, he mastered the techniques of being an actor, the technique of speech, of understanding the presence of light and of the camera, the choreography of camera and of bodily movements. Bruno S didn't have that and so had to be taught. But at the core of Klaus Kinski was not his existence as an actor—he was something beyond that and apart from it" (qtd. in Basoli).

6. Although the film is readable as being about the "continuous symptom of the unassimilated Nazi past, the always-already present capacity of evil" (Chaffin-Quiray), critics strain to find a political subtext, with Garrett Chaffin-Quiray and Prawer seeing in it a response to the socio-cultural and industrial-economic trends of the 1970s as opposed to the postwar era that produced Murnau's classic.

7. Herzog at first hired a hypnotist to work with the actors during rehearsals but dismissed the "New Age creep" after two sessions and took over the hypnosis in subsequent sessions (qtd. in Cronin 129). Herzog discusses his use of hypnosis in *Herz aus Glas* and elsewhere in Cronin 126–29.

8. "The capacity to act counts for very little" in Herzog's *Nosferatu*, Mayne stresses. Instead, narrative authority is "measured by the power to mesmerize—a power that is uniquely the vampire's. Put another way, the vampire is a kind of master narrator in Herzog's film" (126).

9. In contrast to Murnau's vaguely orchestral subtitle "Eine Symphonie des Grauens," "Phantom der Nacht" throws emphasis on the vampire, defining it specifically as a phantom or shadow self.

10. As noted by Mayne and detailed by Prawer, Herzog pays homage to and/or "tops" Murnau's film with a veritable catalog of his own signatures, employing them in scenes where they provide conspicuous variations from the original: the extensive use of non-actors, including peasants, gypsies, and dwarves, in scenes that recall Murnau's similar use of non-actors.

11. Murnau's vampire is strictly naturalistic, "like an insect." Drawing from Stoker and the vampire genre film, Herzog nods to the supernatural only to invert it into the absurd—he plants crosses that make Dracula cringe, if only momentarily, holy wafers that Lucy ineffectually disperses in the proper places—but as if only to indicate the death of God. As Lucy says to Van Helsing when advised to pray, she feels that God has deserted this plague-ridden world.

12. Murnau's *Nosferatu* had only a brief scene in which Ellen watches a line of coffins moving up the street from an upper window, followed by another in which the town crier marks crosses on the doors of houses with the plague.

13. In contrast, Luhr and others see this scene as representing the civil disorder the vampire brings (458, see also Prawer 73).

14. Shepard's Murnau discovers his calling as a virtuoso fighter pilot who supernaturally walks away from downed airplanes and conceives of the gun sight as a camera, a device for aiming with uncanny precision and simultaneously distancing

himself from carnage: "I am an icy scientist, and for me their war is a laboratory experiment" (65). See pages 63–65.

15. The latter point allows for an allusion to *Burden of Dreams* and *Fitzcarraldo* through the absurd image of a large ship stuck on the top of a hill. Crew members die unnoticed as Dafoe exsanguinates them and carelessly shoves them over the side.

Works Cited

Andrews, Nigel. "Dracula in Delft." *American Film* 4.1 (1978): 32–8.

Arthur, Paul. "In Dreams Begin Responsibilities." Program Notes. *Burden of Dreams.* Dir. Les Blank. With Maureen Gosling. DVD. The Criterion Collection, 2005.

Badley, Linda. "The Darker Side of Genius: The (Horror) Auteur Meets Freud's Theory." *Horror Film and Psychoanalysis: Freud's Worst Nightmare.* Ed. Steven Jay Schneider. Cambridge: Cambridge University Press, 2004. 222–40.

Basoli, A. G. "The Wrath of Klaus Kinski: An Interview with Werner Herzog." *Cineaste* September 22, 1999. Accessed January 5, 2006. www.cineaste.com/thewr.htm.

Carroll, Noël. "Creatures of the Night." *The Echo Weekly News.* October 11, 1979: 35.

Chaffin-Quiray, Garrett. "An Adaptation with Fangs." Werner Herzog's *Nosferatu: Phantom der Nacht (Nosferatu the Vampyre,* 1979). *Kinoeye: New Perspectives on European Film* 2.20. December 16, 2002. Accessed on January 12, 2005. www.kinoeye.org/02/20/chaffinquiray20.php.

Corrigan, Timothy. *Between Mirage and History: The Films of Werner Herzog.* Ed. Timothy Corrigan. London and New York: Methuen, 1986.

———. "Producing Herzog: From a Body of Images." Corrigan, *Between Mirage and History.* 3–19.

———. *New German Film: The Displaced Image.* Rev. ed. Bloomington: Indiana University Press, 1993.

Cronin, Paul. *Herzog on Herzog.* New York: Faber and Faber, 2002.

de Baecque, Antoine and Serge Toubiana. *Truffaut: A Biography.* Berkeley and Los Angeles: University of California Press, and New York: Alfred Knopf, 1999.

Denby, David. "Nosferatu." *New York.* October 22, 1979: 89.

Ebert, Roger. *"My Best Fiend." rogerebert.com Movie Reviews.* February 11, 2000. www.rogerebert.suntimes.com/apps/pbcs.dll/article?AID=/20000211/REVIEWS/2110305/1023.

Eisner, Lotte H. *The Haunted Screen: Expressionism in the German Cinema and the Influence of Max Reinhardt.* Trans. Robert Greaves. Berkeley and Los Angeles: University of California Press, 1969.

———. *Murnau.* 1964. Berkeley and Los Angeles: University of California Press, 1973.

Foucault, Michel. *Language, Counter-Memory, Practice: Selected Essays and Interviews.* Ithaca, NY: Cornell University Press, 1977.

Furness, Richard S. *Expressionism.* London: Methuen, 1973.

"Interview with E. Elias Merhige" (2000). *Shadow of the Vampire.* Dir. E. Elias Merhige. Saturn/Lion's Gate. 93 min. DVD. Universal.

Kinski, Klaus. *Kinski: Ich Brauche Liebe.* 1991. *Kinski Uncut: The Autobiography of Klaus Kinski.* Trans. Joachim Neugroschel. London: Bloomsbury, 1997.

Knipfel, Jim. *Aguirre, the Wrath of God. Werner Herzog and Kinski: A Film Legacy.*

DVD Program Notes. Anchor Bay Entertainment, Inc. 2002.

Kracauer, Siegfried. *From Caligari to Hitler: A Psychological History of the German
        Film.* Princeton, NJ: Princeton University Press, 1974.

Luhr, William."Nosferatu and the Postwar German Film." *Michigan Academician* 14.4
        (Spring 1982): 453–58.

Maltin, Leonard. "Biography for Werner Herzog." *Leonard Maltin's Movie
        Encyclopedia.* 1994. *Internet Movie Database.* January 9, 2006. www.
        imdb.com/name/nm0001348/bio.

Mayne, Judith. "Herzog, Murnau, and the Vampire." *Between Mirage & History: The
        Films of Werner Herzog.* Ed. Timothy Corrigan. New York and London:
        Methuen, 1986. 119–30.

Mein liebster Feind. Dir. Werner Herzog. 1999. DVD. Anchor Bay, 1999.

Prager, Brad. "The Face of the Bandit: Racism and the Salve Trade in Herzog's *Cobra
        Verde.*" *Film Criticism* 28.3 (Spring 2004): 2–20.

Prawer, S. S. *Nosferatu: Phantom der Nacht.* London: BFI, 2004.

Rentschler, Eric. "The Politics of Vision: Herzog's *Heart of Glass.*" Corrigan. 159–81.

Rugg, Linda Haverty. "Herzog's Kinski and Bergman's Liv: Cinematic Auteurism and
        the Shadow of the Vampire." *Communicación y sociedad* (2001).

Sarris, Andrew. *The American Cinema: Directors and Directions,* 1929–1968. New
        York, Da Capo, 1968.

Sartre, Jean-Paul. "'Aminadab': Or the Fantastic Considered as a Language." 1927. Rpt.
        in *Literary Essays.* By Jean-Paul Sartre. New York: Citadel, 1955. 56–72.

"*Shadow of the Vampire.*" *The Advocate.* January 30, 2001. Accessed on December 23,
        2000. www.advocate.com/html/video/849_vampire_830.asp.

Shepard, Jim. *Nosferatu.* New York: Knopf, 1998.

Stuart, Jan. "The Vampire Strikes Out." Review of *Shadow of the Vampire. The Advocate*
        January 30, 2001. Accessed on December 23, 2002. www.advocate.com/
        html/video/849_vampire_830.asp.

Telotte, J. P. "German Expressionism: A Cinematic Problem." *Traditions in World
        Cinema.* Ed. Linda Badley, R. Barton Palmer, and Steven Jay Schneider.
        Edinburgh: Edinburgh University Press, 2005. 15–28.

Tobias, Scott. "*Lost in La Mancha.*" *The Onion A.V. Club.* January 29, 2003. Accessed
        on January 12, 2005. avclub.com/content/node/6846.

Werner Herzog and Klaus Kinski: A Film Legacy. DVD. 5 discs. Anchor Bay, 2002.

History, Homage, and Horror: Fassbinder, Raab, Lommel and *The Tenderness of Wolves* (1973)

Richard J. Hand

"New German Cinema" (*das neue Kino*) is a term used to describe the films produced in West Germany from the 1960s to the early 1980s. As Julia Knight observes, New German Cinema as a whole "resisted clear generic delineation" (394). Moreover, from the prolific and eclectic body of work that is New German Cinema, the specific genre of horror is almost entirely absent. The two most notable exceptions are the remake of *Nosferatu* (Werner Herzog, 1979) and the factually based serial killer movie *The Tenderness of Wolves* (Ulli Lommel, 1973), the latter involving the close participation of Rainer Werner Fassbinder, one of the major *auteurs* of German cinema, as producer and actor. Fassbinder was one of the most extraordinarily prolific artists in the history of performance media. Fassbinder's films demonstrate that New German Cinema was not averse to genre cinema per se—one need only consider the thematic and structural influence of Hollywood melodrama, in particular the films of Douglas Sirk, in the Fassbinder oeuvre. However, the impetus behind New German Cinema generally reflected other preoccupations. The films of New German Cinema emerged out of a *divided* Germany and many filmmakers felt a responsibility to reflect the split identity—and geography—of the postwar "Germanies," and the bitter crises inculcated by the fiercely guarded border (in every sense of the word), whether in the form of military confrontation, the murder of East German escapees or the rise of West German terrorism. New German Cinema was radically different on a formal level but it also explored "contemporary concerns in a way that contrasted sharply and refreshingly with the 'escapist' nature of the German cinema of the 1950s" (Knight 400). However, a major part of this duty was also the need to investigate *how* Germany arrived at this situation: in other words, East/West Germany can only be understood by looking at German history. Therefore, films that explore the rise and fall of the Third Reich represent an important oeuvre which finds its supreme expression in the epic *Hitler, a Film from Germany* (Hans Jürgen Syberberg, 1977). In addition to direct studies of the Third Reich, a filmmaker such as Fassbinder would extend the implications of this to German national myth and identity, above all in his attack of the notion of "sentimental idealism," the late German Romantic quality he believed was responsible for the facilitation of fascism.

Even if New German Cinema avoids the obvious characteristics of generic horror, there is a case to be made that many of the films of New German Cinema are works of historical and social horror, works of "true horror." *The Lost Honour of Katharina Blum* (Volker Schlöndorff and Margarethe von Trotta, 1975) is a scathing portrayal of a West Germany diseased by the fear of terrorism which permits, between the state authorities and the media, the systematic attrition of the liberty of its citizens; as a study of paranoia it is not far from *Invasion of the Body Snatchers* (Don Siegel, 1955). In the Fassbinder oeuvre, *The Bitter Tears of Petra von Kant* (1972) is, on the surface, a satirical study of the bourgeois existence and worldview of its fashion designer protagonist. However, the relationship that forms the central narrative of the film—the romance between Petra and her protégée Karin—is increasingly stifling, sadistic and parasitical to the point of being vampiric. Indeed, the dreamlike mood and obscure time frame of the film, the languid and eroticized performances in the claustrophobic environment of Petra's garish and oppressive apartment lends the film a post-gothic quality. Similarly, despite having a glorious horror title, *Fear Eats the Soul* (Rainer Werner Fassbinder, 1973) is actually a love story about a multiracial and cross-generational couple; once again, the descent from *Gemütlichkeit* into a pitilessly cruel world of racism, disdain and alienation replicates a trajectory familiar in most horror narratives. Films such as these can be fruitfully analyzed as horror stories of the "real." These narratives are far from the realms of supernatural metaphor or "over the top" horror, and yet they employ a narrative structure, mood, and imagery that are akin to the horror genre. There may be, for example, scenes of explicit violence, an escalating mood of paranoia or an investigation into themes of mortality and "good and evil." It is in this spirit that we seek to define *The Tenderness of Wolves* as an unequivocal example of horror. Moreover, while *The Lost Honour of Katharina Blum*, *The Bitter Tears of Petra von Kant* and *Fear Eats the Soul* may share fictitious yet utterly believable stories, *The Tenderness of Wolves* is directly based on a grimly unlikely yet true story while making conscious allusion to precursors of the horror film genre and their formal features.

As a versatile and multitasking film creator of the "real" Germany, Fassbinder was, during his lifetime, variously described as either "The Messiah of New German Film" or "the thermometer up the arse of German culture" (qtd. in Rentschler 163). Fassbinder was always a provocative figure; he sustained, without compromise, a serious engagement with sensitive political, historical, social and gender issues in relation to contemporary Germany. The broad *political* dimension to his work could never be ignored. He was a political artist whose works consistently reveal a social dynamic, awareness and creativity. Assessing Fassbinder's success as a political artist, Leo A. Lensing argues that Fassbinder achieved this "more effectively than any German dramatist-director since Brecht" (Fassbinder, 1992, xiii). While Brecht may have believed that political art could change the world, Fassbinder knew that his plays and films would not.

would not. Nevertheless, he still felt that political provocation could yield results. "You can set up booby traps in such a way that the moviegoer, when he leaves the theatre, does not discard prejudices he brought in with him, but maybe is scared by his own prejudices" (Fassbinder, 1992, xvii).

What is interesting here is the sense of *scaring* the moviegoer: Fassbinder is expressing the belief that *fear* is an important device to trap the viewers and force them into self-reflection. Fassbinder's works are full of "booby traps": narrative episodes and even technical devices that problematize our aesthetic perceptions and ideological assumptions. For all his love of the conventions of Hollywood genres (such as the romance), Fassbinder rejected notions of escapism, always aiming to create works of performance in which the spectators "don't stop thinking, but rather actually begin to think" (Fassbinder, 1992, 150). *The Tenderness of Wolves* is not a film directed by Fassbinder but it does emerge from his "stable" and as such it has an unmistakable Fassbinderian quality. Not least, it is a work with its fair share of "booby traps" designed to scare us into challenging our perceptions and assumptions.

Before we embark on an analysis of the film, we need to establish two areas of historical context: the context of the making of the film, and the context of the historical event upon which the film is based. The film is directed by Ulli Lommel and is sometimes cited as his first feature although Lommel claims that it was his second film after *Haytabo* (Ulli Lommel, 1971). This is just one example of the numerous contradictions and conflicting accounts that will come to surround the film. Lommel, the son of the famous German comedian Ulli Manfred Lommel, had been a popular television, theatre and film actor since childhood. In his mid-twenties this already extensively experienced performer offered his acting services to Rainer Werner Fassbinder, which marked the beginning of an important professional relationship. Lommel appeared first in Fassbinder's first film *Love Is Colder than Death* (Fassbinder, 1969) and would appear in another twelve of Fassbinder's movies including the acclaimed *Effi Briest* (Fassbinder, 1974). Like Fassbinder's set designer and sometimes-actor Kurt Raab, he was part of the precocious and volatile *auteur*'s "remarkably stable infrastructure" (Elsaesser 264).

Thomas Elsaesser reveals that despite Fassbinder's spontaneity and idiosyncrasies (including his infamous psychological and physical violence towards his creative participants), Fassbinder benefited from a reliable and loyal production team and group of actors. This artistic entourage extended from individuals responsible for costume, editing, and sound all the way to financial accounting. With regards to performers, Fassbinder used a mixture of actors from his theater work, stars from commercial or international cinema, and non-professionals (usually friends and/or lovers). After *The Tenderness of Wolves*, Kurt Raab, an example of a non-professional actor, would return as an occasional but proficient actor starring in films like *Satan's Brew* (Rainer Werner Fassbinder, 1976)—yet another horror title this time for an absurd comedy—and the two-part television play *Bolwieser* (Fassbinder, 1976–77). It was Raab who was apparently obsessed with the case of Fritz Haarmann, a homosexual, pedophile, and cannibal serial killer. It was this case which was to form the basis of *The Tenderness of Wolves*. Hence, the fact that Raab would serve as production designer, script developer, and lead actor in the film was a *fait accompli*.

However, as Tony Rayns notes, when it comes to accounting for the development of *The Tenderness of Wolves*, "different people involved remember its genesis differently" (Rayns). Authorship of the film may always be contested between the creative triumvirate of Rainer Werner Fassbinder, Ulli Lommel and Kurt Raab. Likewise, the film continues to have a sometimes problematic reception. For some critics the film is "criminally underappreciated" (McRoy), while for others the film is flawed by "Lommel's generally rather inhibited direction of the camera" (Rayns). Similarly, the level of Fassbinder's involvement is always going to be disputed. For Christian Braad Thomsen, Fassbinder is critically absent. In his evaluation of the two films by Fassbinder's collaborators that the *auteur* facilitated—namely *The Tenderness of Wolves* and his production manager's effort *Game of Losers* (Christian Hohoff, 1978)—Thomsen contends:

> The results were disappointing. They were derivative works without the spark of distinctive artistic ideas. These clearly demonstrate that without Fassbinder's magical presence things fell apart, and his desire to delegate creative responsibility to others was ill-founded. (Thomsen 9–10)

In contrast, Tony Rayns argues:

> The film certainly sits more comfortably in Fassbinder's filmography than Lommel's, which fizzled out in American B-movies a few years later; the central view of Haarmann as a cypher for a society of "tender wolves" seems quite consistent with Fassbinder's attitude to German society at the time.

Lommel's "American B-movies" that Rayns dismisses comprise a number of cult and low-budget horror movies such as *The Boogeyman* (Lommel, 1980) and *Bloodsuckers* (Lommel, 1998). Given this later development of Lommel as a genre director, it is clear that *The Tenderness of Wolves* represents, if nothing else, Lommel's apprenticeship into the genre of horror.

What seems certain about the genesis of *The Tenderness of Wolves* is that it came into existence for economic reasons; Fassbinder was in a "use it or lose it" situation with a funding subsidy. Lommel explains, "When subsidies from the German government were about to run out ... Fassbinder was forced to make another movie" (Thrower). As Fassbinder was heavily involved in other projects, primarily *Effi Briest*, Lommel and Raab seized the opportunity and persuaded Fassbinder to let them develop and produce the Haarmann project. Perhaps astonishingly, it seems that Fassbinder was initially opposed to the project altogether because of the controversial subject matter. This does not prevent Thomsen from detecting a precursor to *The Tenderness of Wolves* in the Fassbinder oeuvre: in the second part of the five-part television series *Eight Hours Do Not Make a Day* (Fassbinder, 1972) a group of local housewives begins to worry about a local kindergarten having "heard about mysterious strangers, who lure children to kill them secretly and perhaps even sell them as meat" (Thomsen 128). Their fears prove to be unfounded but the film evokes a paranoia that reflects the social and historical anxiety triggered by having a genuine serial killer of Fritz Haarmann magnitude in not too distant history. Although the serial killer Jürgen Bartsch may have been more recent, having been arrested in 1966, the reference to cannibalism steers past Bartsch and reaches straight back to Haarmann. Despite his initial misgivings, Fassbinder finally acquiesced and participated as producer and actor. The film would include and feature the participation of most of the "Fassbinder family" in their habitual technical positions and, as performers, in principal roles and cameos. According to Lommel, "Fassbinder hated other directors" (Lommel Commentary) and so kept a low profile and often kept away from the production. He found it immensely difficult to work under somebody else's direction and, allegedly, resented witnessing Lommel's happy and successful work-in-progress. Consequently, he would often disappear from the set. However, we may prefer to give this a more generous interpretation in that Fassbinder may not have desired to interfere in Lommel and Raab's pet project. This was further compounded by the fact that Lommel claims he facilitated a very happy production and confesses that he even sacrificed the quality of the film to this end (Lommel Commentary), an issue we will return to later in this study.

Fritz Haarmann was known as the "Werewolf of Hannover," and his grisly crime spree occurred in the post–World War I period between 1919–24. One of the most prolific serial killers in history, Haarmann targeted adolescent boys and young men who, he would ultimately confess, he would kill by goring open their throats and drinking their blood before further cannibalizing their bodies, at one time allegedly selling the flesh in the market where he worked as a butcher. *The Tenderness of Wolves* includes a number of historical details that are based in fact. Haarmann was a known homosexual and worked as a police informer. The first human skulls to be discovered were dismissed by the police as thefts from the Göttingen anatomical institute, but the discovery of more body parts—including several hundred fragments of corpses in the river Leine—and the numerous reported disappearances of boys and men fueled a popular paranoia (which included the legend of a "Werewolf"). In 1924 the net finally closed around Haarmann.

Like other factual serial killers of the interwar period—Peter Kürten, the "Vampire of Düsseldorf" in the 1920s, or the "Torso" killer in 1930s Cleveland, Ohio—Fritz Haarmann was a murderer who exploited the "hard times" of social depravation and alienation to prey on the vulnerable. Obviously, this is a phenomenon that is not restricted to that particular epoch. From Jack the Ripper to Jeffrey Dahmer, these are killers who exploited the flaws in their social context. This accounts for Lommel's suggestion that there is a dereliction of duty by modern society which creates murderers to which it feeds victims: the double punishment of killers who have been turned into monsters by society and are then punished by society (Lommel Commentary).

Certainly, the fact that *The Tenderness of Wolves* is updated to a post–Second World War context is not in the least detrimental to the plot of the film, even if this was an expedient decision compelled by budgetary constraints. Indeed, by updating the Haarmann case to the late 1940s or early 1950s, the film not only saved production costs but it also lends *The Tenderness of Wolves* some of its Fassbinderian quality. The film becomes extremely provocative in its use of a real historical figure and many precise details from the actual murder case as it places these details within a very different historical period. As a result, the post–World War I era is given an equivalent status to the post–World War II epoch, linking both periods by analogy. The film, therefore, functions as a nightmarish and iconoclastic depiction of the burgeoning "Economic Miracle" of postwar West Germany, the same era Fassbinder will so ruthlessly debunk in *The Marriage of Maria Braun* (Fassbinder, 1978). The updated historical setting also enables the manufacture of the key turning-point in the film's narrative. As in real life, the police are nonplussed by the first grisly remains and the numerous disappearances of young men and boys. But while, in reality, the police eventually were forced into action under growing public pressure and the rise of the "werewolf" myth, in the world of the film, the authorities are only stirred into action when rumors spread that "the German police are working hand in hand with shady elements from the Nazi period." The suspicion that such cynical motivation might exist within state institutions reveals the overriding instinct of self-preservation—as irrepressible as Haarmann's bloodlust—in the upper echelons of the new hierarchy of postwar Germany.

In the way that Lommel presents the story, society is complicit in Haarmann's crimes. Partly, Haarmann exploits his social circumstances as he preys on deracinated young men in a society that is failing to resolve the crises of alienation and poverty. The film opens with hunger: we see one of Haarmann's neighbors in her nightgown in her ascetic apartment with an empty glass beside her. She knocks on the wall, expressing her desire for "a little of your meat." This illicit request is an ambiguous statement at this point. There is an unmistakable sexual inference to the line, which will prove ironic since Haarmann is overtly homosexual. It later becomes evident that Haarmann is selling meat (and is invited to partake in the feast). In a later scene he describes the delicious sausages he will make, although the film does not present the viewer with any "butcher" scenes. Tellingly, the chosen performer for the opening scene is not in the least emaciated. Haarmann's refusal and the vague promise of "tomorrow" precedes the turning off of the light, which may signify a denial of the audible pounding of sexual butchery or, perhaps more troublingly, serves as a conduit into the listener's personal fantasy. After all, society is afflicted with "a collective form of willful misrecognition" (McRoy). We see the rumors of werewolves beginning to circulate, as preposterous as the gossip that Haarmann sells the boys to the "Foreign Legion in Africa." In actuality, "your meat" says it all: arguably, the neighbors know the truth. Certainly there is no depiction of widespread food poisoning in the local community of the type that occurred when the Ed Gein case came to light in 1950s Wisconsin. If we accept this theory of complicity, suddenly the *gemütlich* family feast (and all its decidedly weird dinner guests) early in the film becomes a precursor to the cannibal feast of *The Texas Chainsaw Massacre* (Tobe Hooper, 1974). It is a legion of cannibalistic neighbors and self-serving policemen that are behind the closing of the net around the serial murderer. Haarmann's society is no longer tender but a rapacious pack of wolves, a more forceful metaphor than the myth of the lone wolf.

The *Tenderness of Wolves* is a remarkable nexus of allusion and influence. As an account of the Fritz Haarmann case, the film functions as a complex example of a late twentieth-century film animating earlier history and mixing principles of factual accuracy with substantial artistic license. As already indicated, Haarmann's crimes occurred in the same period as another infamous murderer, Peter Kürten, the "Vampire of Düsseldorf." The case of Kürten—who targeted girls—forms the subject of one of the masterpieces of interwar world cinema and a supreme example of "real" horror, *M* (Fritz Lang, 1931). The influence and legacy of *M* is hard to avoid in any example of the serial killer genre. Of equal importance to Fritz Lang's direction of the film is Peter Lorre's performance as the fictionalized Kürten character, "Hans Beckert." Lorre's performance arguably established Peter Lorre as the international icon of horror that he would be for much of his subsequent career. Because *M* is unavoidable, *The Tenderness of Wolves* includes a number of allusions to Lang's great precursor. Most obviously, there is the long tracking shot of Raab's shadow against the brick wall behind the opening credits. More broadly, as Ronald Bergan and Robyn Karney note, in *M* "fear permeates every brick of the dark alleys and crumbling buildings which form its background" (Bergan and Karney, 1988, 349). *The Tenderness of Wolves* finds a credible textural equivalent in its brickwork, train stations and encroaching shadows redolent with paranoia and melancholy. Although *The Tenderness of Wolves* is a color film, the qualities of what Jay McRoy describes as the "sickly hues of yellow, orange, brown and blue" render a social realm which is "economically and spiritually impoverished" (McRoy, 2004). This seems a surprising but effective equivalent to the grim black and white of *M* and its social register.

The most potent link between *M* and *The Tenderness of Wolves*, however, lies in the central performances of Peter Lorre and Kurt Raab. Although Bergan and Karney contend that Lommel's film allows Raab to demonstrate that he can muster up "quite a good imitation of Peter Lorre" (553), Raab's performance is emphatically not an imitation and certainly not in any way a pastiche of Lorre's. More accurately, Raab's performance is an intriguing homage to, and interplay with, Lorre's legendary performance.[1] In *The Tenderness of Wolves*, as McRoy writes, "Haarmann's ubiquitous trench coat and fedora clearly reference Lang's child-murderer in *M*." As well as "borrowing" Lorre's attire in an explicit allusion to *M* and its lead actor's iconic performance, Raab also bears a distinct physical resemblance to Lorre. However, Raab's characterization of Haarmann is in stark contrast to Lorre's Kürten/Beckert. Lorre plays the role predominantly as a social misfit, his eyes bulging, his gestures nervous, and his demeanor anxious (doubtlessly aided by his real life morphine addiction). Only when we see him securing his intended victims does he become charming and relaxed, overtly playing the kind, generous, and tenderly smiling "uncle." In contrast, for most of *The Tenderness of Wolves*, Raab is demure and urbane: he appears gentle and likeable and is, as McRoy observes, "the narrative's most sympathetic character." The non-diegetic music that surrounds Haarmann is J. S. Bach. Its meditative, pious, and melancholic airs are a far cry from the supernatural horror of Beckert's diegetic signature tune whistle, "The Hall of the Mountain King" from Grieg's *Peer Gynt*, which unambiguously refers to rampaging trolls and their man-eating appetite.

Our sympathy for Haarmann comes into play, even quite provocatively (and this must be a Fassbinder-style "booby trap"), when we see him alone with his intended victims. Some of the glimpses we catch of Haarmann's rituals and fetishism before the denouement of the film are not "horrific" but seem like a searching for meaning in an endlessly hungry and materialistic neighborhood. When Haarmann dresses as a woman in a dress and blond wig prior to committing murder, he is not Norman Bates in a schizophrenic frenzy. We know Haarmann is the killer, but he is a "tender wolf"—even his rapid strangulation of the victim before chewing its neck makes the murder become, albeit highly problematic and contentious, an act of "humane slaughter." He is also a figure of great power. During a police raid on his apartment at the beginning of the film, Haarmann's lover seems to be dead, only springing to life with an almost resurrectional ability when Haarmann tells him to leave. The violence of the character emerges only on rare occasions. It is revealed most startlingly in the climax to the film in which we see Haarmann in all his lethal ferocity, disconcertingly juxtaposed soon afterwards with his own final, pious words in a placid, measured voiceover. In that scene of brutality—Haarmann tearing out his victim's neck and then responding in fury as he is apprehended by the police—we see the transformation into werewolf taking place, complete with a trickle of blood oozing from the corner of his mouth. This obliteration of "tenderness" launches the character into the inhuman(e) and/or supernatural. It is at this moment that the other intertextual reference McRoy identifies comes most potently to life: "his shaved head, pale countenance and insatiable desire to rip open the throats of his victims with his teeth call to mind Murnau's vampire."

Lommel's film also abounds not only with intertextual reference to iconic figures of interwar German cinema, namely Peter Lorre and Max Schreck, but also with the immediacy of "living" or future icons. The man who performs "The Crocodile Bar" song, for example, is one of Marlene Dietrich's former pianists (Lommel Commentary). Fassbinder himself, who appears in a cameo role, is used as an increasingly iconic figure as New German Cinema disappears into history, as do the numerous Fassbinder "stars" who appear in the film, like Margit Carstensen, Brigitte Mira, and El Hedi Ben Salem. In fact, the degree of self-consciousness is so high that Hanna Schygulla being *not* in the film makes her conspicuous in her absence. The film also features Jürgen Prochnow, an international film star after *Das Boot* (Wolfgang Petersen, 1981), in his first film;

Lommel confesses that he would have made more use of Prochnow had he known that the actor would become such a celebrity (Lommel Commentary).

While *M* and *Nosferatu* may be common currency in cinematic allusion, the other examples of the film's mechanism of intertextuality rely on more "privileged" knowledge (and even sharp observation when it comes to the fleeting, sideways glance of Prochnow). Looked at in these terms, *The Tenderness of Wolves* can be seen as a film about film and the self-referential: just as it deliberately alludes to earlier German cinema, it cannot escape being a fascinating document of New German Cinema and the Fassbinder "family" in particular. The film is also distinguished by an interesting quality of established cinematic skill (Raab as designer and the input of other Fassbinderian figures in familiar roles) and new directions (Raab as actor, Lommel as director).

However, despite its filmic pedigree and resonance, *The Tenderness of Wolves* is a significantly extemporary work with an almost theatrical propinquity. Frequently in Fassbinder's films, movies and theatre tend to assimilate. Fassbinder explains: "In the theatre I always directed as if it were a film, and then shot the films as if it were theatre, I did that fairly determinedly" (qtd. in Thomsen 48). The same theatrical principle and aesthetic is similarly important in Ulli Lommel's direction and Kurt Raab's performance in *The Tenderness of Wolves*. Lommel admits that he utilized improvisation, often guiding the actors and the camera there and then without the benefit of a storyboard, a method that even led to the creation of the supreme shot of Haarmann framed by a split tree. Lommel also made use of people present in suitable locations as unpaid extras. Children we see playing amidst ruins in one scene were real children who happened to be playing in real ruins when the film crew arrived; the drunk at the train station was a real drunk who happened to be at a real train station and whom the crew dressed in an appropriate coat (Lommel Commentary). But although such moments are examples of verisimilitude, they ironically exacerbate the unreality of the film when they clash with moments of high stylization and artifice.

On an online film chat page a participant derided *The Tenderness of Wolves* as "worthless" and added, "Someone mind telling me what time period this movie is supposed to be set in? Anyone with half a clue, please e-mail me" (IMDb). Budgetary limitations were the primary reason the film was shifted from its original historical context to the era of West Germany's Economic Miracle. Although Lommel went so far as to borrow 1950s costumes from the dressing room of the local theatre, the film lacks historical specificity. Some clothes are 1950s and yet other images—for example, the children playing on the railway wagon—look distinctly 1970s with their flared trousers and long hair. McRoy cites the "white 1970s polyester jacket" of Haarmann's lover as another example of a "temporal displacement" that implicates Lommel's contemporary audience:

> [This] temporal displacement frustrates audience attempts at fixing the film's events within a stable historical moment, a maneuver made even

> more disconcerting by the text's schizophrenic visual style, which con-
> flates motifs from German expressionist masterpieces like Fritz Lang's *M*
> (1931) and F.W. Murnau's *Nosferatu: eine Symphonie des Grauens*
> (1922) with the intentionally melodramatic tone of Rainer Werner Fass-
> binder's darkest portraits of urban despair and spiritual isolation. (McRoy)

The "gaps" in the film's historical reconstruction and its visual schizophrenia may in part expose the movie's low budget and theatrical ethos and expediency. But they also help to create an eclectic timelessness. *The Tenderness of
Wolves* does not attempt an approximation of *Schindler's List* (Stephen Spielberg, 1993) with its "time tunnel" of black and white film and authentic period
reconstruction in costume and design. Ostensibly set in the 1950s, Lommel's
film embraces disturbing and disruptive fragmentation: the 1970s creep through
the gaps in the film in such a way that the theme of pedophile murder is not
safely compartmentalized into a historical era and specific case but undergoes a
troubling, unsolved extrapolation.

The "low budget" aesthetic can also offer other ramifications. One may
consider *Night of the Living Dead* (George A. Romero, 1968) and how its
"cheapness" may actually enhance its impact. In particular, one may consider
location filming, the use of black and white film stock, the inexperienced camera
work interspersed with occasional sequences of superb virtuosity, the unfamiliar
and (with Duane Jones as a notable exception) inexperienced actors: all these
factors contribute to make a film that combines, unsettlingly, the authentic with
the amateur, creating a work that is raw, unpolished and profound. Even the
paradigm of the "bad," Ed Wood, Jr., can be seen in a similar light. *Plan 9 from
Outer Space* (Ed Wood, Jr., 1958) is, for some viewers, the most terrifying film
ever made, among them the American visionary artist Joe Coleman, who saw
the film in his childhood. Habitually lambasted as one of the worst and most
risible films ever made, *Plan 9* struck the young Coleman as the ultimate in horror.

> Joe lived across the street from a cemetery, and in the film Ed Wood's
> limited budget (not to mention Bela Lugosi's untimely death) didn't per-
> mit Wood to match the night shots in the cemetery scenes. The shots with
> Lugosi are filmed in very brightly-lit conditions (bad day-for-night) in an
> actual cemetery, while the other shots for the scene are extremely dark and
> filmed in a very obviously fake cemetery (cardboard tombstones, etc.).
> Joe's childhood interpretation reasoned . . . that the more peripheral areas
> of the cemetery (where the cloaked Lugosi lurks) were flooded with day-
> light, while the deepest, creepiest interior of the cemetery somehow al-
> lowed no light to reach it! Joe says that this particular accidental element
> of the film is what terrified him as a child . . . (Jarmusch 8)

Arguably, the rough edges and contradictions of *The Tenderness of Wolves*
have a similar effect. Iconic actors mingle with real drunks; carefully composed
mise-en-scène (such as Haarmann's apartment) contrasts with the derelict ruins

and graffiti of the exteriors; the directness of full frontal male nudity and blood pulsing from a torn artery clash with the obvious unreality of the large but lightweight packages that are supposed to contain body parts yet nonetheless function as emblematic, even epic, devices.[2]

Features of *The Tenderness of Wolves* have acquired legendary status as the film drifts further into history. Kurt Raab and a number of the supporting players were to die in the first waves of AIDS. Other figures such as the young Moroccan boy Haarmann questions at the train station have an additional significance, as the child is one of Raab's adopted children. Similarly, the appearance of El Hedi Ben Salem, Fassbinder's lover and star of *Fear Eats the Soul* who would later commit suicide, is a cameo with legendary resonance within New German Cinema and the Fassbinder oeuvre in particular. However, the most potent legend fuelled by *The Tenderness of Wolves* is to be found in the presence of Fassbinder himself.

We have already suggested that Fassbinder's pervading presence has iconic status. Fassbinder is surrounded by a somewhat diabolical mythology. He was notorious for his prolific and voracious creativity; his unorthodox working practices and legendary aggression, often physical, throughout his professional career, and his sadomasochistic appetites in his personal life. Many of his personal relationships were destructive: two of his actor-lovers, El Hedi Ben Salem and Armin Meier, committed suicide. Fassbinder himself died of an alcohol and drug overdose at the age of thirty-seven—a tragically anticipated death for a man who was "expending his energies with life-threatening intensity" (Rheuban 23). In retrospect, Fassbinder looms over *The Tenderness of Wolves* like a "monster"; the historical figure of Rainer Werner Fassbinder is animated on the screen like the historical figure of Fritz Haarmann is reinvented for the screen. Indeed, Thomas Elsaesser describes the "fat body" of Fassbinder on celluloid as the image of an "unshaven, disheveled, beer-bellied monster" (Elsaesser 258). If Fassbinder is a monster he is as doomed as King Kong—a unique entity who is finite, terminal, and tragic, yet rises from the grave whenever the films of New German Cinema are repeated or appraised. Looked at like this, Lommel and Raab's Haarmann becomes an emblem for Rainer Werner Fassbinder himself. This reading has interesting implications regarding the role of the artist in postwar Germany. Fassbinder may be a major creative force but he is also a monster with an agenda of horror inasmuch as he forces the audience to confront not just the bleak recent history of their society but its living legacy in an unsatisfactory Germany. Like Haarmann, the postwar German artist can be seen as making the audience sup on horrors: they sit down to a feast and it is German flesh on a cannibal's table.

In *The Tenderness of Wolves* Lommel strove to investigate the "nature of evil and the complexity of it" (Lommel Commentary). The film is prefaced by, and concludes with, Fritz Haarmann's self-righteous words: his belief that his willing execution is a form of sacrifice that will serve as suitable reparation for his misdemeanors. In contrast to Peter Kürten's shocking desire to hear his own blood gush from his body after decapitation—the final act of sadomasochistic sex/death fetishism—Haarmann finds a Christian register, fashioning himself as a scapegoat for society. The fact that Lommel ends and begins his film with these words is the ultimate disruption: the story is endless, like the inadequacy and injustice of a rotten, duplicitous Western society which, in Lommel's view, will continue to create monsters of the type of Fritz Haarmann.

Notes

1. A similar mode of performative allusion can be found elsewhere in the Fassbinder/Lommel oeuvre: in *Love Is Colder than Death* (Rainer Werner Fassbinder, 1969) Lommel plays the lead role in direct homage to the image and style of Alain Delon in *Le Samourai* (Jean-Pierre Melville, 1967), a deliberate decision openly acknowledged by Fassbinder (Fassbinder, 1992, 5).

2. "Epic" is used here in a Brechtian sense: a form of theatre that appeals less to the spectators' feelings than their reason. In *The Tenderness of Wolves*, this would mean that we do not think that Haarmann's packages are literally filled with human flesh—or any meat at all—but function as props that serve a narrative and symbolic function. Haarmann's packages are body-shaped and might as well be labeled (a device frequently used in Brechtian theatre) "human flesh." The parcel sequence seems unsubtle and unrealistic but the purpose is not, at this point in the film, to be surprising or suspenseful but to develop the narrative trajectory in such a way that a rational rather than emotional response is elicited from the audience.

Works Cited

Bergan, Ronald and Robyn Karney. *Bloomsbury Foreign Film Guide*. London: Bloomsbury, 1988.

Elsaesser, Thomas. *Fassbinder's Germany*. Amsterdam: Amsterdam University Press, 1996.

Fassbinder, R. W. *Plays*. Ed. and Trans. Denis Calandra. New York: Performing Arts Journal, 1985.

———. *The Anarchy of the Imagination*. Eds. Michael Töteberg and Leo A. Lensing. Baltimore: Johns Hopkins University Press, 1992.

———. *The Marriage of Maria Braun*. Ed. Joyce Rheuban. New Brunswick: Rutgers University Press, 1986.

IMDb. February 3, 2001. "IMDb user comments for *Zärtlichkeit der Wölfe*." February 10, 2005. www.imdb.com/title/tt0070957/usercomments.

Jarmusch, Jim. "Why I Like Joe Coleman" in *Original Sin: The Visionary Art of Joe Coleman*. New York: Heck, 1997. 6–11.

Knight, Julia. "New German Cinema" in *An Introduction to Film Studies*. Ed. Jill Nelmes. London: Routledge, 1996. 393–428.

Lommel, Ulli. "Commentary" to *The Tenderness of Wolves* (DVD). Troy, MI: Anchor Bay, 1999.

McRoy, Jay. "Conspicuous Consumption: Ulli Lommel's *Zärtlichkeit der Wölfe (Tenderness of the Wolves*, 1973)." *Kinoeye: A Fortnightly Journal of Film in the New Europe*, 2.14 (2004). www.kinoeye.org/02/14/mcroy14.php.

Rayns, Tony. "Sleeve Notes" to *The Tenderness of Wolves* (VHS). London: British Film Institute, 1998.

Rentschler, Eric. *West German Filmmakers on Film: Visions and Voices*. New York: Holmes and Meier, 1988.

Thomsen, Christian Braad. *Fassbinder*. London: Faber, 1997.

Thrower, Stephen. "Insert Notes: Interview with Ulli Lommel" in *The Tenderness of Wolves* (DVD). Troy, MI: Anchor Bay, 1999.

Joy-Boys and Docile Bodies: Surveillance and Resistance in Romuald Karmakar's *Der Totmacher*

Jay McRoy

In the Realm of the "Consensus"

Critical discourse surrounding *Der Totmacher* (1995), Romuald Karmakar's commercially and critically successful cinematic recreation of the notorious serial killer Fritz Haarmann's interrogation at the Göttingen Mental Asylum in 1924, largely revolves around the film's quasi-documentary aesthetic.[1] In praising Karmakar for his "faithful" approach to exploring Haarmann's crimes, Gregory S. Burkart asserts that the director's camera is "completely—and wisely—objective," thus "leaving [audiences] to draw [their] own conclusions" (para 5). Similarly, many critics were quick to label Karmakar a "born documentarist" (Horwath para 13), and in his extensive survey of serial killer films, *Bad Blood: An Illustrated Guide to Psycho Cinema*, Christian Fuchs likewise recognizes a strain of *vérité* filmmaking in *Der Totmacher*. While acknowledging that Karmakar's film feels overtly theatrical at times, occasionally coming "very close" to blurring the "borderline between film and drama," Fuchs is quick to note that the director "rigorously" eschews the "cops vs. killer" motif so prevalent in contemporary horror cinema, representing the case's gruesome details "soberly and impartially" (88–89).

Such observations regarding the film's documentary authenticity, especially in popular reviews, are as typical as they are instructive. As I illustrate in the following pages, *Der Totmacher*'s formal elements, including its intersections with conventional documentary practices, are vital to understanding the film as a work of German cinema that, emerging amidst a neo-conservative "Cinema of Consensus" that privileges "[q]uestions of *Wirtschaftlichkeit* (commercial potential)" over virtually "all other [aesthetically and politically progressive] concerns" (Rentschler 267), nonetheless advances an important cultural critique. Drawing upon considerations of how filmic appeals to documentary authenticity influence spectator presuppositions, my essay explores how Karmakar's film not only locates the character of Fritz Haarmann as a construction of disciplinary power in its most conspicuous guises (the psychiatrist, the physician, the jailor),

but also posits Haarmann as a potential (albeit variably successful) model for
social resistance. In the process, this examination of *Der Totmacher* interrogates
Karmakar's positioning of the cinematic apparatus, including both the camera
and the screen upon which the film's images flicker, as valuable tools for
the construction of what Michel Foucault calls "docile bodies" (*Discipline*
135)—subject positions created, objectified, and policed in part through the very
compulsion to tell/"reveal" all—*and* as crucial weapons for challenging commercial cinema's predominantly recuperative inertia.

Romuald Karmakar, Punk Cinema, and the Shadow of Fassbinder

In the wake of Rainer Werner Fassbinder's untimely death at the age of
thirty-eight, the famed German critic Wolfram Schütte claimed that the New
German Cinema had suffered, metaphorically speaking, a case of cardiac arrest
that ceased, all-too-soon and all-too-immediately, the beating of the movement's
"pulsating, vibrating core" (qtd. in Rentschler 265). What followed, according to
scholars and filmmakers from Eric Rentschler and Alexander Horwath to Klaus
Kreimeier and Wim Wenders, was a dramatic restructuring of German national
cinema during the 1980s that parallels the neo-conservative agendas of politi-
cians like Friedrich Zimmermann and Helmut Kohl. As is the case with any
transformation in a nation's cinematic production, the contributing factors were
multiple and complex. The defining characteristics of many works of the German New Cinema, including the rendering of directors' personal artistic visions,
serious filmic engagements with Germany's *unbewältige Vergangenheit* (its
unassimilated Nazi past), and a recognition of the nation's increasingly heterogeneous social body, lost out to the allure of Hollywood- and Ufa-style glitz and
the appeal of copious box office receipts. Additionally, when one factors in the
impact of television capital upon decisions to subsidize even the least expensive
cinematic ventures, it is not difficult to fathom how "the possibility for political
interventions and the presence of alternative perspectives and formal experiments" steadily "diminished" (Rentschler 267). The result was a continued re-
duction of New German Cinema's already humble audience base nationally and
internationally, coupled with the emergence of a new generation of filmmakers
hungry to be anointed the next "Wolfgang Peterson or...Roland Emmerich"
(275).

By the early 1990s, a "Cinema of Consensus" (274) emerged that privileged
international funding and global marketability, presenting audiences, in the
process, with a plethora of upbeat, conventional narratives. Consequently, the
interventionist visions and critical politics that infused many productions by

prominent directors of the New German Cinema yielded to a mode of filmmaking increasingly informed by the aesthetic and cultural hegemony of major studio systems, most particularly that of Hollywood and its monotonous parade of flashy if formulaic offerings. Of course, this shift was by no means a phenomenon exclusive to German cinema. In her essay, "From a 'Prenational' to a 'Postnational' French Cinema," Martine Denan describes a similar phenomenon within the French film industry. In recent decades, she argues, "the desire to court an international audience" has corrupted the notion of a politically self-reflexive national cinema (240). Films, in other words, are meticulously crafted to "ensure that reference to national history does not detract from the international potential" of "French superproductions" (240). As with Rentschler's "Cinema of Consensus," such modes of production imperil the role of cinema as an art form concerned with specifically national, or national-historical, matters. As a consequence of late capitalism's global imperative, such alterations can not be underestimated; in Denan's words, "[w]ith the emergence of a film culture meant to succeed in a global economic system, the overall nature of national culture may be in the process of being altered" (243). Olaf Möller, in a recent *Film Comment* article, shares Rentschler's assessment of German cinema at the turn of the millennium. Film schools, he claims, "now guide their students toward ... straight commercial filmmaking," a practice that sublimates the importance of "talent and *vision*" to an understanding of cinema as motivated by an economic logic in which "'successful' has been substituted for 'good': big time, upscale, and international" (12).

This commercialist boom in contemporary German cinema, however, has not gone unchallenged by visual artists committed both to formal experimentation within the medium of cinema, and also to the proliferation of alternative cultural and political agendas. Created on often microscopic budgets and adopting a financially restricted and visually stark post-punk aesthetic reminiscent of Rainer Werner Fassbinder and Werner Herzog's edgiest films, the works of visionary filmmakers from Christoph Schlingensief to Connie Walther to Vanessa Jopp contest the cinematic status quo, albeit in productions too often limited to sporadic art house and film festival screenings. Among this new generation of "maverick" directors dedicated to revitalizing German cinema's socially progressive potential, Romuald Karmakar occupies a central and, given *Der Totmacher*'s commercial success, ultimately vital position. In fact, Alexander Horwath, one of the few scholars to engage extensively with Karmakar's emerging oeuvre, locates the German director as taking up "the threads of a bond broken by Fassbinder's death" (para 10) and as belonging to a "world of legionnaires and exile[d]" filmmakers existing "right in the middle of Germany" (para 32). From *avant-garde* short films like the brief but brilliantly subversive *Coup de boule (Headbutt*, 1987), in which a group of French and German soldiers assume a series of ridiculous (and seemingly unrehearsed) macho postures before charging headlong into the doors of metal storage lockers, to *Demontage IX*

(1991), in which a trussed, upside-down figure swings pendulously in an intentionally alienating extreme long shot, Karmakar exhibits a willingness to tackle extreme, exigent, and unconventional subject matter in an equally arresting, if not outright experimental fashion.

In *Demontage IX*, for instance, the shoeless and shirtless bound man is at once a captive and captivating entity as he swings between darkened walls that resonate with a distinctly industrial clamor when struck by his helpless form. Observed constantly by both an anonymous man who sporadically tugs upon the ropes that induce the trussed figure's swaying, as well as motion picture cameras (one of which is revealed to us in a reverse dolly shot seemingly intended to highlight even further the performance's outright artifice), the metronome-like body goes virtually unnoticed by a waltzing couple. Accompanied by a plethora of conspicuous sartorial and cultural signifiers—i.e. a tuxedo, an extravagant gown, flashy jewelry, and a classical score that renders the industrial clamor mute—the dancing couple occupies a bourgeois space against which the swinging man, at once always-already visible and invisible, silently clashes. A somewhat ham-fisted commentary upon the dynamics of class difference, especially disinterested stances towards labor exploitation, *Demontage IX* is perhaps most compelling in that the filmed performance itself transforms the human body into a variable commodity, an object of art for the consumption of others. Indeed, a similar intention informs the earlier *Coup de boule*. With its documentary aesthetic, a look informed by Karmakar's use of hand-held camera, his loosely composed close-ups and medium shots, and the narrative's overtly spontaneous and frenetically episodic structure, *Coup de boule* seemingly functions in a very different way than *Demontage IX*, especially given the latter's more conventionally formalized and largely static long shots and extended takes. Nevertheless, *Coup de boule* anticipates *Demontage IX*'s critical agenda not only in the configuration of the laughing, self-abusing soldiers' physiognomies as spectacles, but also in its revelation of the spectacles themselves as deliberate cinematic constructions designed to expose, through exaggerated displays of masochism, the operant logics of disciplinary power.

A self-proclaimed child of "[p]unk, football, and the *Werkstattkino*" (Horwath para 27), Karmakar is, as Horwath notes, an explorer "of defeat" and an analyst "of slippage" (para 17).[2] Certainly images like *Coup de boule*'s inwardly-directed violence and *Demontage IX*'s bound proletarian figure swaying above the waltzing bourgeois couple support such a description. Karmakar, however, is more than just a punk with a camera or an "explorer"/"analyst" of "defeat." He is also a visual seismologist dedicated to scrutinizing the all-too-conveniently ignored fissures beneath the polished sheen of a collective and politically sanctioned national re-imagining. As such, he exposes the cultural logics that, like quiescent fault-lines, pose a continual threat to those who, in the tradition of cultural anthropology, launch excavations designed to reveal the carefully constructed artifice that shields the public eye from the disciplinary matrix that simultaneously requires, and polices against, its own revelation. Hence, Karmakar's commercial and critical success, *Der Totmacher*, further develops the social critique advanced in these short films, exploring the ideological framework that requires—and thus "creates"—the very "deviant bodies" its "carceral archipelago" designates as "disruptive" to the functioning of a healthy social body.

"There's Not Much to a Human Being": Surveilling the Spectacle in *Der Totmacher*

As mentioned earlier, critical discourse surrounding *Der Totmacher* often foregrounds the film's quasi-documentary aesthetic, an approach informed by Karmakar's strategy of, in the words of Alexander Horwath, "dust[ing] off" the "records of the pretrial psychiatric examination of Fritz Haarmann" (para 21). Of course, collapsing/consolidating the content of such documents into a filmable screenplay requires strategic textual re-arrangements and compulsory erasures. Such manipulations for the sake of artistic vision at once violate the potential for an accurate representation of the source material and, as realist theorists from Bertolt Brecht and André Bazin to Mark LeFanu and Colin MacCabe have illustrated, contribute to the creation of cinematic texts, including those explicitly labeled as "documentaries," that purport to depict something "real." In other words, the combination of the knowledge, artistry, and technology at a director's disposal enables her/him to capture performances that render characters, whether historical or overtly fictional, as "convincingly human." Likewise, these devices allow directors to negotiate the treacherous, if not outright paradoxical terrain of so-called non-fiction filmmaking. In *Der Totmacher*, Romuald Karmakar has deliberately crafted a film that purports to represent "real events," causing spectators, through their recognition of a "kind" of authenticity, to suspend their disbelief. Such a practice locates both filmmakers and their audiences as active agents in the creation of artifice as "actuality," ultimately validating Karmakar's contention that, in cinema, "[e]verything documented is true and everything fictitious is not necessarily false'" (qtd. in Möller 13).

Thus, although many viewers understand *Der Totmacher* as "a fact-based portrait of a serial killer, with [Götz] George re-creating the 'authentic' Haarmann and Karmakar 'documenting' his 'shamanistic' performance," such a perspective overlooks Karmakar's directorial acumen, not to mention his "reputation for highly experimental documentaries on controversial subjects" (13). Like *Coup de boule* and *Demontage IX*, *Der Totmacher* allows for a reconsideration of the source documents' "political and cultural contexts" (Horwath para 21), while also shedding crucial light upon the circulation of disciplinary power in

many Western cultures. Karmakar's film, in other words, reveals the mechanisms of power that resulted in the creation of Fritz Haarmann as an infamous
historical figure, and that continue to enact the very "instrument-effect" Michel
Foucault situates as constituent of an "isolation, intensification, and consolidation" (*Discipline* 42) of marginalized subject positions against and through·
which normalizing social forces define themselves, perpetuating, in the process,
complex relationships of power and knowledge. In this light, Professor
Schultze's continued questioning of Haarmann's sexuality, a process during
which the professor requires his subject to provide ever more detailed explanations of his numerous homosexual (and eventually murderous) encounters,
seems to substantiate Foucault's assertion that "in order for a certain relation of
forces not only to maintain itself, but to accentuate, stabilize, and broaden itself,
a certain kind of maneuver is necessary" (206). Namely, psychiatrists had to
function as active agents in the "implantation of perversions...through the isolation, intensification, and consolidation of peripheral sexualities" (42). Indeed, it
was through such actions, Foucault argues, that the "relations of power to sex
and pleasure branched out and multiplied, measured the body, and penetrated
modes of conduct" (42).

   Der Totmacher's scope provides an excellent arena for Karmakar's investigation of the circulation of disciplinary power within Western culture. In other
words, *Der Totmacher*'s tiny cast and intimate setting contributes substantially
to the heightening of the film's dramatic, almost stage-like elements, as well as
to its intellectual impact. Set almost exclusively within a sparsely furnished interrogation room, with its dingy institutional-gray walls and barred windows, the
majority of the dialogue-heavy film's action transpires between three central
characters: the eponymous Fritz Haarmann, whose initial denial of the murder
and dismemberment of twenty-four young men yields to a delighted narration of
his violent acts and an awareness of himself as a media event; Professor Ernst
Schultze, the psychiatrist assigned to determine Haarmann's capacity to stand
trial; and Professor Schultze's stenographer, who records the sessions and with
whom Haarmann openly flirts. Romuald Karmakar's immersive camera work
and careful editing further contributes to the film's oppressive, claustrophobic
tone. Although the occasional long shot provides viewers with the opportunity to
orient themselves in relation to the interrogation room's layout, medium shots
and close-ups dominate the film's *mise-en-scène*. Furthermore, during several of
the lengthier interrogation sequences, especially those that transpire early in the
film, elliptical tracking shots slowly orbit Haarmann in an almost predatory
fashion. The extensive application of this cinematic technique visually reinforces the infamous killer's position as the subject of Schultze's clinical gaze,
while also providing a consistent visual tropology that, as the film progresses
and Karmakar's exploration of the complexities of disciplinary power and narrative cinema becomes more intricate, eventually turns at once less conspicuous
and more encompassing. This visual strategy allows, as will soon become clear,

for important two- and three-shots that question the dominance of certain authority figures, as well as the role of surveillance in the construction and maintenance of human identity.

Karmakar's predilection for long takes likewise contributes to the film's aesthetic and thematic structure. In a narrative like *Der Totmacher*'s, in which Professor Schultze's "incitement to discourse" (Foucault, *The History of Sexuality*, 34) dominates much of the film's dialogic content, long takes contribute to the film's deployment of the spectator's gaze. A staple of realist cinema, including films to which viewers readily attribute the label "documentary," long takes hearken back to the earliest motion pictures, some of which were composed primarily—and sometimes exclusively—of single shots. Long takes "are geared," as Mark LeFanu notes in "Metaphysics of the Long Take," towards creating a tone of "contemplative engagement" (para 18). This latter point is particularly noteworthy, especially if, as Patricia MacCormack posits, "[t]o gaze is to control" (para 10). From the film's opening line, in which Haarmann responds to Professor Schultze, who bears more than a passing resemblance to the iconographic psychoanalyst Sigmund Freud, by declaring that the professor "already know[s]" about him, Karmakar commences an analysis of the power of surveillance and the political function of telling (and re-telling) certain narratives. In this sense, *Der Totmacher* links the socio-political mechanics of power with the creation of deviant and, by extension, normalized and normalizing subjectivities. Curiously, with each successive battery of questions formulated specifically to elicit ever more graphic details of Haarmann's criminal deeds, the film's audience is propelled, like the professor and his stenographer, deeper into Haarmann's "deviant" mind until, as the film advances towards its climax, the alignment—and implication—of the audience's gaze (and perhaps their sympathies as well) grows increasingly problematic.

Additionally, the "contemplative engagement" evoked by Karmakar's adherence to the long take as one of *Der Totmacher*'s primary visual strategies contributes to the film's intrinsic theatricality. The result is a work that, in part, approaches realism through a distinctly Brechtian, counter-cinematic aesthetic that opens up the possibility of comprehending *Der Totmacher* as far more than merely a re-creation of a historical encounter.[3] Consider, for example, two brief moments from *Der Totmacher* in which Karmakar deliberately ruptures the film's established visual syntax of elliptical tracking shots, lengthy takes, and carefully composed crosscuts between Haarmann and, most frequently, Professor Schultze, who provides telling reactions to Haarmann's confessions by either posing further questions or passing moral judgments. These narrative disturbances consist of two almost identical shots that seemingly capture the stenographer's and the professor's considerably more intricately furnished offices. Importantly, although these interiors seem removed, at least geographically, from the main interrogation room, their drab color schemes and numbing institutional décor purposefully echo that of the main interrogation room. Filmed through the doorways that lead into their respective offices, these sequences, lensed as long shots, capture first the stenographer, and then Professor Schultze, at their respective desks. Alarmed, as if suddenly aware of being watched, each character turns to face the camera, with the professor going so far as to inquire: "Did somebody just knock?" Conspicuous in their radical break from the film's dominant visual rhetoric and apparent narrative trajectory, these shots dislocate the spectator by aligning the audience's perspective with the representation of suddenly intrusive gazes that, given their voyeuristic immediacy and intentional anonymity, at once foreground the cinematic apparatus and suggest that Fritz Haarmann is by no means the only character in the film whose actions are being policed.

As Foucault notes, Western societies are not defined, as Guy Dubord would have it, by the "spectacle"; rather, Western cultures are often cultures of *surveillance*:

> [...] under the surface of images, one invests bodies in depth; behind the great abstraction of exchange, there continues the meticulous, concrete training of useful forces; the circuits of communication are the supports of an accumulation and a centralization of knowledge; the play of signs defines the anchorages of power; it is not that the beautiful totality of the individual is amputated, repressed, altered by our social order, it is rather that the individual is carefully fabricated within it, according to a whole technique of forces and bodies. (*Discipline* 217)

In this sense, Karmakar equates Haarmann with his inquisitors in that both are revealed, if only fleetingly, as complicit in, and—importantly—subjects of, a disciplinary apparatus/gaze. Schultze's and, by extension, the stenographer's interrogation may construct Haarmann as a deep subject against which a matrix of normalizing forces are aligned and defined, but this function by no means removes them from similarly objectified positions within an endogamous web of surveillance. Far from canceling each other out, "pleasure"—as depicted by Haarmann—and "power"—as revealed through Professor Schultze and his stenographer—"seek out, overlap, and reinforce one another...linked together by complex mechanisms and devices of excitation and incitement" (Foucault, *History*, 49). Thus, this counter-cinematic rupturing of the film's visual rhetoric breaches conventional expectations on the part of the viewer. It is a gesture that purposely violates the film's quasi-documentary style, illustrating, in the process, Karmakar's allegiance to the experimental and socially critical agenda evidenced in his earlier short films, like the previously discussed *Coup de boule* and *Demontage IX*.

The sequence that stands out as perhaps Karmakar's most compelling and experimental disruption of the film's prevailing diegesis occurs approximately one-third of the way into *Der Totmacher*, when a session of questions from Professor Schultze is followed by a series of crosscuts that, like the intrusions upon the psychiatrist and his stenographer, gesture towards "making the mechanics of the film/text visible and explicit" (Wollen 122). Directed by off-screen voices to walk, turn, and then stand against one of the interrogation room's institutional green walls, Haarmann complies while dressed in a nondescript blue suit and peering occasionally into the glare of a bright spotlight. Karmakar then cuts to a tight two-shot of a police inspector and an unnamed photographer standing behind a motion picture camera, its lens aimed at Haarmann. Over the next minute and a half of dialogue with the aptly-titled "inspector," Haarmann is queried regarding the contents of meals ingested during his incarceration. In a particularly unsettling exchange, the inspector cunningly inquires whether a recently devoured roast could have been made with meat other than that originating from an animal. He winks conspiratorially at Haarmann, who refuses to "bite," suggesting that the practice of cannibalism is a fabrication.

This sequence, like the mysterious intrusions upon the stenographer and Professor Schultze discussed above, is crucial to an understanding of the larger social and political critique informing Karmakar's film. By positioning the inspector and photographer behind the camera directed at Haarmann, Karmakar identifies the most basic elements of the cinematic apparatus, namely the camera and the filmmaker, as components of disciplinary power. Like the guards in the watchtower at the center of Jeremy Bentham's Panopticon, the camera's lens directly affects the behavior of those upon which it focuses. As the sequence begins, for instance, Haarmann's awkward movements and postures signify his discomfort, an attitude elicited by an acute awareness of his objectification.[4] This depiction of the filmmaking process foregrounds the artifice behind any cinematic representation, including such filmic documents as "live" broadcasts or, as in the case of *Der Totmacher*, a dramatic re-creation largely based upon existing source materials. Furthermore, although the inspector's sly, strangely sinister insinuations regarding cannibalism and the potential content of the asylum's cuisine can be understood as playful baiting, his role as a law enforcer and director of a filmed document situates him as part of a larger matrix of legal, medical, and cultural authorities acting in concert to "produce" and "consume" individual and collective identities.

It is here that Karmakar's strategic editing and use of dialogue reveal a nuanced understanding of the construction and perpetuation of social power. In his depiction of the verbal sparring between Haarmann and the inspector, Karmakar composes and edits the interchange through a series of crosscuts between the visibly uncomfortable prisoner (shot from the inspector's/camera's POV) reacting to the inspector's commands, and the inspector, photographer, and camera framed from a slightly oblique angle that is clearly not aligned with Haarmann's perspective. As the exchange reaches its crescendo, with Haarmann still verbally frustrating his winking inquisitor's desires, Karmakar flash-cuts from a close-up of Haarmann to a two-shot of Haarmann and the inspector. Consequently, this sequence, beginning with Haarmann's compliance with the inspector's whims and culminating in the two-shot that visually reduces the power discrepancy

between the two figures, posits Haarmann both as resistant (if only momentarily) to operant power relations, and as a necessary component of a cultural dynamic in which disciplinary mechanisms define the parameters of, and the necessity for, their very existence through the creation of "aberrant," disorderly
identities.

    This sequence is by no means the only moment in which Karmakar deploys
carefully arranged compositions designed to challenge conventional power relations; as in the brief yet crucial exchange with the interrogator and photographer,
Karmakar's placement of characters within the frame alters throughout the
course of *Der Totmacher*'s multiple interrogation sequences. As the narrative
unfolds, Karmakar abandons the use of elliptical, almost predatory tracking
shots that, much like the interrogator and the photographer's camera and spotlight, variably position Haarmann as an object of critical inquiry and the target
of multiple disciplinary mechanisms. In their place, Karmakar substitutes an
increasing number of medium shots in which Professor Schultze and Haarmann
share space within the frame, their bodies frequently arranged so that the implied power relations increasingly vacillate or, to both borrow and modify Horwath's term for Karmakar's aesthetic and political agenda, "slip" (para 17).
Haarmann mimics Professor Schultze's professional demeanor by taking his
own notes and, in a vital scene towards the end of the film, both critically gloss-
ing the various judgments that punctuate the mail he receives from the general
public and aggressively challenging the professor's findings. Furthermore, Professor Schultze's numerous examinations and cross-examinations compel
Haarmann to place his thoughts and actions into a realm of discourse that inevitably results in reactions of conspicuous disgust followed almost immediately by
moral condemnation, the demand for further elaboration, or both. In one such
dialogue, Karmakar (assisted by Götz George's masterful performance) presents
Haarmann as a disturbed figure who seems both to enjoy the apparent power his
words have over the professor and stenographer—as evidenced by their dis-
gusted reactions—and to have internalized the logic of the culture of surveillance against which he struggles:

> Professor Schultze: Did you cut the eyes out?
> Haarmann: No, I covered them with a hanky. I didn't want them to look at
>   me.
> Professor Schultze: But they were dead.
> Haarmann: Yes, but they say the spirit lives on.
> Professor Schultze: You believe they could still see?
> Haarmann: Not if the eyes were covered.
> Professor Schultze: Could they see when they were dead?
> Haarmann: You're supposed to see everything.
> Professor Schultze: Nonsense. You're a fool.
> Haarmann: My mother used to say a dead person hears and sees every
>   thing! My sister, too. Go and ask my sister!

Beneath the professor's clinical gaze, Haarmann verbally acknowledges the expansive power inherent within a culture of surveillance—if only through the grotesque image of a corpse's lifeless stare—as well as the extent to which notions of an omnipresent panoptic vision permeates the larger cultural imaginary ("My mother used to say a dead person hears and sees everything! My sister, too. Go and ask my sister!").

Later, after Haarmann's gleeful recounting of the dismantling of his victims' bodies, accompanied by a manic bout of simulated chopping, has succeeded in causing the stenographer to become physically ill and the professor to voice his indignation, Karmakar shifts the focus and tenor of Haarmann's dialogues with Professor Schultze. In place of recursive explorations of Haarmann's "unnatural" predilection for "buggery" with "joy-boys" and the intricate details of his murderous acts, Haarmann deftly redirects the professor's questions until they give rise to discussions of Haarmann's status as a cultural icon, the validity and socio-political implications of judgments regarding his sanity, and the economic and cultural wealth the professor stands to gain from his patient's discourse. Through considerations of these issues, accompanied by a *mise-en-scène* that frequently invests Haarmann, Professor Schultze, and, at times, even the stenographer with an increasingly balanced dramatic weight within the frame, Karmakar ultimately accomplishes two goals. First, he effectively foregrounds "all those systems of micropower" that aim to "guarantee the submission of forces and bodies" ("Panopticism" 211), emphasizing the importance of and, ultimately, the necessity for, individual and collective identities that resist containment and, thus, require the intercession and perpetuation of multiple repressive apparatuses intended to create "docile bodies" (Foucault, *Discipline*, 135). In this sense, Karmakar's film reveals the very technology of power, including the ideological and political force of cinema itself, that too often go unexamined in contemporary film.

Second, by stressing Haarmann and Professor Schultze's interconnectedness—a relationship ultimately cemented by an exchange of anxious glances that, delivered in a pair of matching close-ups, precede the film's final fade to black—Karmakar provides viewers with an ambiguous finale that frustrates traditional conceptions of narrative closure and disallows easy alignments of audience sympathies. Long considered "invalid" by society, Haarmann wants only to be validated, to be found sane and fully responsible for not only his multiple murders, but also his acts of cannibalism—the latter being a practice that, as Anne Marie Olsen notes, obliterates "subject/object distinctions" by abolishing the "boundary between the One and the Other...between the subject eating and the object being eaten" (para 28). In the end, Haarmann elects to perform the function of the pre-Enlightenment "spectacle of the scaffold" (Foucault, *Discipline*, 32) rather than vanish from the public eye by being committed to an asylum and living out the remainder of his life as the submissive locus of countless modalities of coercive power.

Towards a Cinema of Ideas

As a complex consideration of film, genre, and the cultural logic of disciplinary power informing much of Western culture, *Der Totmacher* extends and
refines the aesthetic and political critiques informing much of Romuald Karmakar's work, including the short films *Coup de boule* and *Demontage IX*. Importantly, Karmakar accomplishes this through a narrative that elides both horror movie cliché and the didactic reductionism that regularly accompanies such
texts. In other words, *Der Totmacher* confronts audiences with a challenge that,
in Karmakar's own words, evokes "the motto of Immanuel Kant's enlightenment" (Fuchs 89). Namely, it compels viewers to "[h]ave the courage to make
use of [their] own mind[s]" and think for themselves (89). Of course, whether
the commercial success of Karmakar's film will engender an atmosphere in
which "[q]uestions of *Wirtschaftlichkeit* (commercial potential)" no longer in-
hibit explorations of "the darker side of German reality" (Rentschler 267) remains to be seen. However, if the creation and international distribution of
thought-provoking and visually arresting horror films like Robert Schwentke's
Tattoo (2002) and the Nuckleduster.com collective's *Splatbox* (2005) is any
indication, a return of a repressed cinema of ideas may some day challenge, or
even occupy a significant space within, the current "cinema of consensus" (267).

Notes

1. Christian Fuchs estimates that as of the publication of his book, *Bad Blood: An Illustrated Guide to Psycho Cinema* (Creation Books, 1996), Karmakar's film "has already
lured more than 500,000 people into the cinemas of Germany" (89). Additionally, Fuchs
ascribes much of the film's success to the presence of the German film star Götz George.
Such an assertion, though too dismissive of Karmakar's direction, is not without some
merit, as George won multiple awards for his performance of the infamous "Werewolf of
Hannover," including the Bavarian Film Award for Best Actor, the German Film
Awards' Film Award in Gold for Best Individual Achievement: Actor, and the Volpi Cup
for Best Actor at the 1995 Venice Film Festival.

2. Located in Munich, the *Werkstattkino*, or Workshop Cinema, provides a space for
cinephiles and filmmakers to view "underground" or "experimental" films (often several
in a row) that would rarely, if ever, play in larger, more mainstream venues.

3. See Peter Wollen's seminal essay: "Godard and Counter-Cinema: *Vent d'est*,"
Narrative, Apparatus, Ideology: A Film Theory Reader (New York: Columbia University
Press, 1986, pp. 120–29). Counter-cinema practices, for Wollen, include the privileging
of narrative intransitivity and multiply diegetic narratives, the foregrounding of the cinematic apparatus in an attempt to highlight film as constructed, and the use of aesthetic

techniques intentionally designed to increase the viewers' estrangement from the cinematic text(s) they encounter.

4. In one of *Der Totmacher*'s final moments—an intimate verbal exchange between Haarmann and Professor Schultze—Haarmann, anticipating the extent to which his murders and eventual execution will survive within the popular culture's imagination/memory, notes that "here [the Göttingen Mental Asylum] especially" he has had his words meticulously chronicled and his "photograph taken" repeatedly.

Works Cited

Burkart, Gregory S. "The Deathmaker (1996)." *Monsters at Play*, 2001–2004. www.monstersatplay.com/review/dvd/d/deathmaker.php.

Denan, Martine. "From a 'Prenational' to a 'Postnational' French Cinema." In *The European Cinema Reader*. Ed. Catherine Fowler. London and New York: Routledge, 2002. 232–45.

Foucault, Michel. *Discipline & Punish: The Birth of the Prison*. New York: Vintage, 1979.

———. *The History of Sexuality: An Introduction*. New York: Vintage, 1978.

———. "Panopticism." In *The Foucault Reader*. Ed. Paul Rabinow, New York: Pantheon Books, 1984. 206–13.

Fuchs, Christian. *Bad Blood: An Illustrated Guide to Psycho Cinema*. London: Creation Books, 2002.

Horwath, Alexander. "Bang Bang: Encounters with Romuald Karmakar and His Films." *Senses of Cinema*. June 2002. www.sensesofcinema.com/contents/02/21/karmakar.html.

LeFanu, Mark. "Metaphysics of the Long 'Take': Some Post-Bazinian Reflections." *P.O.V.*, no. 4. December 1997. imv.au.dk/publikationer/pov/Issue_04/section_1/artc1A.html.

MacCormack, Patricia. "Looking Away to See: Frazer Lee's Duty of Care Films." *Senses of Cinema*. June 2004. www.sensesofcinema.com/contents/04/32/frazer_lee.html.

Möller, Olaf. "On the Current State of German Cinema in the Wake of *Run Lola Run*." *Film Comment*, May 2001.

Olsen, Anne Marie. "Film as Metaphor: Cannibalism and the Serial Killer as Metaphors of Transgression." *P.O.V.*, no. 4, December 1997. www.imv.au.dk/publikatio ner/pov/Issue_04/section_1/artc1A.html.

Rentschler, Eric. "From New German Cinema to the Post-Wall Cinema of Consensus." In *Cinema and Nation*. Eds. Mette Hjort and Scott Mackenzie. London and New York, Routledge, 2000. 260–77.

Wollen, Peter. "Godard and Counter-Cinema: *Vent d'est*." In *Narrative, Apparatus, Ideology: A Film Theory Reader*. Ed. Philip Rosen, New York: Columbia University Press, 1986. 120–9.

Part 3:

New German Horror Film: Between Global Cinema and the Hollywood Blockbuster

Introducing "The Little Spielberg": Roland Emmerich's *Joey* as Reverent Parody

Philip L. Simpson

German-born Roland Emmerich has directed a number of big-budget, high-profile Hollywood films, including *Stargate* (1994), *Independence Day* (1996), *Godzilla* (1998), and *The Day after Tomorrow* (2004). These genre films, incorporating diverse elements of science fiction and horror, were released to luke-warm critical response at best, but generally earned enough money (over 100 million dollars each) to qualify as box-office hits. Emmerich's financial success in Hollywood in combination with his fondness for larger-than-life genre subjects has earned him the nickname of the "Swabian Spielberg" (so named for the Schwaben region around his native Stuttgart) or other variations on this theme, such as "Das Spielbergle aus Sindelfingen" ("Little Spielberg from Sindelfingen"). This label is at once salutary and derogative in that it acknowledges Emmerich's commercial success as an immigrant filmmaker but belittles him for his thralldom to "Spielbergian" popular cinema. The same dichotomy often found in critical appraisals of Spielberg's earlier work is evident in critical response to Emmerich's films: grudging respect for the filmmaker's ability to engage an audience through dynamic visuals in tandem with thinly veiled contempt for a supposed imperial agenda, the narrative promiscuity through sampling a little from this genre and a little from that genre, and choice of cinematic subject matter perceived as "adolescent" by high-minded critics.

Emmerich, through a Levi-Straussian type of bricolage, has essentially adopted the cinematic grammar of Spielberg and his ilk (Joe Dante, George Lucas, Tobe Hooper in the Spielberg-produced *Poltergeist*, and so forth) to forge Hollywood hits consistently. This commercial success presents an intriguing case of a European filmmaker from outside the American film industry thoroughly embracing some of its most critically lambasted methodology to follow what Emmerich clearly considers to be guiding or paternal influence. In this sense, it could be argued that Emmerich's co-option or seduction by blockbuster cinema is testament to the power of American cultural imperialism.[1] However, given the tendency of American popular film to appeal to the gamut of political spectrum within the course of a single accessible narrative, it is perhaps more instructive to focus upon Emmerich's aesthetic of what Christine Haase calls "transcultural appropriation and hybridization" (397) rather than any deliberately conceived political agenda on Emmerich's part.

Emmerich's American films are rife with visual and thematic homage to some of the most spectacular of 1970s and 1980s Hollywood cinema, particularly those works that blend the horror of large-scale, apocalyptic destruction into other genres such as science fiction. Such films include not only the work of Spielberg and Lucas but also "disaster" movies such as *The Poseidon Adventure*, *Earthquake*, and *The Towering Inferno*.[2] Additionally, Emmerich shows a less commented upon but equally obvious fondness for the work of horror writer Stephen King and the films based upon his novels. Emmerich himself unabashedly (or shamelessly, depending on one's point of view) acknowledges his debt to precedents such as American blockbuster movies: "*Star Wars, Close Encounters of the Third Kind*, those movies pretty much changed my life. Those are the kind of movies that influenced me to make the kind of films I do . . . I'm trying to reach a certain audience that I was a part of when I first saw those movies" (qtd. in Aberly and Engel 10). On the basis of such blatant referencing, Emmerich's harshest critics accuse him of cinematic plagiarism at worst, made even more egregious by being lifted from filmmakers who themselves are often accused of the same thing, and unoriginality at best.[3]

Critics are fond of leveling another, and related, charge at Emmerich—that in his eagerness to replicate larger-than-life Hollywood movies and his own pseudo-Oedipal drive to surpass what his genre fathers have done, he inflates his own work to absurd proportions of visual and narrative excess to out-shout the cinema of spectacle that inspired him.[4] From this angle, Emmerich's work can be thought of as radical and innovative, even though conservatively based on tradition and precedent. Again, Emmerich's own words are illustrative in outlining what we might call the "car-crash" aesthetic of filmmaking:

> The simple fact is that we constantly want to tell each other fairy tales and when we're telling each other stories, we usually embellish them. Like, if you had a little car accident on the way to work, you make a bigger deal out of it by the time you get to the office. We try to make it a more exciting story. In films, we have to entertain in an even bigger way than that and science fiction provides scenarios for the biggest possible stories. But, it all comes from fairy tales, the stories we tell each other around the camp fire, trying to entertain each other. We just have to do it in a larger way in films, to justify people going out of the house, getting in the car and driving to a movie theatre. (qtd. in Aberly and Engel 11)

From Emmerich's perspective, then, his detractors are missing the point. For Emmerich, his hyper-energized films are the purest and latest expression of the agenda of exaggeration of cinema narrative.

Emmerich, whose style of filmmaking undeniably privileges accessibility over subtlety, does seem at times to tread perilously close to parody in his rampant and self-knowing intertextuality.[5] However, giving Emmerich his due as a filmmaker whose commercial success demands some degree of critical understanding if not endorsement, one might consider his mainstream films as "parody" in the sense Linda Hutcheon defines a certain type of "serious" parodic text: a text that is reliant upon the codes of another pre-existing text for its own operation but does so in a reverent fashion and actually demands a fair amount of viewer knowledge of those codes for the second text to function fully (57). By relying on very popular and accessible American science-fiction and horror films, which are themselves parodies of earlier work in the same sense, for his own cinematic texts, Emmerich can generally count on his mainstream audience's sense of film historicity and perhaps even more importantly, his intended audience's acceptance of his playful appropriation of American and German texts. Consequently, this historicity is a joyously patchwork affair, exuberantly assembled out of flotsam of idiosyncratic import to Emmerich and his target demographic. Emmerich's scattershot strategy of reverent parody, in that it complements an industry tendency to privilege proven formula over untried novelty, accounts in part for his Hollywood success.

But Emmerich's self-referential strategy also owes much to the director's roots in the New German Cinema of the 1970s.[6] As indicative of an awareness of history (in this case, film genre history), Emmerich's sampling of the highlights of other film narratives is a technique widespread enough in recent German cinema for Anton Kaes to write: "History [in German film] no longer unfolds as a neat, self-contained narrative . . . As a 'bricoleur,' the author picks up fragments, selecting and assembling them" (118). Emmerich's work, at face value, is so concerned with unoriginal replications of adrenalin-charged moments from Hollywood blockbusters that it constitutes a paleo-conservative return to the accessible narrative of the kind found in deliberately ahistorical 1950s American and German popular cinema alike. Yet his films do manifest a more contemporary German concern with fragmentation, multiple perspectives, and de-centering, all grounded in a longer national tradition of non-realistic, expressionistic film technique. Filmmakers of Emmerich's generation, according to Robert Phillip Kolker, "have had to confront a past more complicated than that of any of their European colleagues, and out of the confrontation has come a cinema more informed by its past than any other . . . and more able to speak to the present because of this" (228). According to Kolker, this complicated past includes fascism, occupation, and postwar capitalistic success that led to suppression of any cinema deemed too leftist. Kolker then identifies, among others, one New German Cinema approach that is directly relevant to the present study—an obsession with American cinema. Brad Prager claims that, following the mainstream success of Wolfgang Petersen's submarine warfare epic *Das Boot* (1981), "many of the filmmakers associated with the [New German Cin-

ema] movement felt . . . that it was finally all right to make it in Hollywood"
(241)—a cultural exodus that Emmerich certainly was inclined to follow. Nor
are Petersen and Emmerich the only New German Cinema directors enamored
of American settings and subjects. For example, Kolker writes of the German
director Wim Wenders: "Even more than the young Godard, [Wenders] is obsessed by American things, American rock music, the American landscape, both
physical and moral, and its interactions with the German" (228). Kolker notes
that Wenders seems to be trying to "make and remake" the American road film
Easy Rider (229); similarly, Emmerich seems to try to make and remake *Star
Wars* and *Close Encounters of the Third Kind.*

     This strategy of remake or reverent parody, based in German artistic sensi-
bility but gravitating toward the American "event" film, can be seen in its embryonic form in Emmerich's 1985 German film *Joey* (the first from his production company Centropolis).[7] The film, essentially a horror movie about the
deaths of a father and his son, is not only a love letter to American blockbuster
cinema but also very much a product of latter-day German Romanticism in its
thematic concern with the lure of fantastical realms and the impact of the dead
past upon the present moment.[8] *Joey* is the story of a troubled young boy (the
title character) with latent psychic powers who makes contact with his recently
deceased father through a toy telephone, is menaced by a literal army of school
bullies and a diabolical ventriloquist's dummy, becomes increasingly ostracized
from his living mother in preference for his dead father, and eventually triumphs
over death itself. Somewhat incongruously for a film that is more horror than
science fiction, the original German version of the film is obsessively, aggressively obvious in its referencing of Spielberg, Lucas, et al.[9] Joey is surrounded
by *Star Wars* toys (a miniature Millennium Falcon), posters, and paraphernalia
(a *Return of the Jedi* blanket, an R2-D2 derivative robot named Charlie). One of
Joey's tormentors dons a Darth Vader helmet, and Darth Vader himself will
make an appearance toward the end of the film. Joey's toys, activated by his
awakening psychic powers in combination with his spiritual connection with his
dead father, come alive in the same way that Barry's do in *Close Encounters of
the Third Kind.* Yet the horror elements are just as strong or stronger than the
science fiction ones. The jarringly suburban American setting (Virginia Beach)
in this German film is similar to that of *Poltergeist*, as are the malevolent per-
sonifications of inanimate objects (the ventriloquist's dummy, the ringing
phones outside the Krispy Kreme shops, and so forth) and the climactic dimensional cross-over. The film seems to be little more than a string of homages to
other, better-known movies, as well as more subtle allusions to the literary work
of Stephen King. Yet in that the film is a reverent parody combined with a larger
emphasis on multiple narrative threads that defy cohesion, one can see Emmerich moving toward the strategy by which he will thrive in Hollywood.[10]

     Framed by opening credits in red lettering on stark black background, *Joey*
opens with the burial ceremony of Joey Collins' father. The scene is crucial in

establishing the controlling theme of the son's fantastical quest for the absent father and eventual reunion. This archetypal theme is much evident in Emmerich's films, especially in the interplay between David and Julius Levinson in *Independence Day* and the quest of the absentee father Jack to rescue his son Sam from New York City, rendered a flooded and then flash-frozen wasteland in *The Day after Tomorrow*. The theme is also prominent in many of those crafted by his cinematic mentors, Lucas and Spielberg.[11] One need only think of man/child Indiana Jones (significantly and often referred to as "Junior") reuniting with his remotely intellectual father Henry Jones, Sr., in *Indiana Jones and the Last Crusade*, or Luke Skywalker's reconciliation with the ultimate estranged father, Darth Vader, as depicted in *Return of the Jedi*—a film later visually referenced in *Joey* by the quilt in Joey's bedroom. The theme of paternal loss/reunion is announced rather portentously by the graveside minister, a figure promoted to shamanistic status by Emmerich's exaggerated text and who sanctions Joey's imminent quest with the imprimatur of divine purpose. The minister begins by stating (in the film's English subtitles): "We cannot always understand the need to remove a faithful husband from the bosom of a loving wife. Or a devoted father from the side of his only son." The minister counsels the grieving son, visually standing out from the other mourners through the camera's repeated focus on the boy, to accept the inevitability of loss by honoring but not fixating on his father's memory. Of course, for the purpose of the narrative's continuation and in keeping with the death fetishism that often underlies German Romanticism, Joey will promptly disregard this moderate advice and become obsessed with resurrecting his father through his own will. While, in the context of the narrative itself, the minister's words are a legitimate rhetorical device to lead into his attempt at consolation of the grieving, savvy audience members of the film know why this paternal amputation needs to happen—the son's quest to reconcile with the distant father is the dynamo that drives this narrative. Emmerich will return to this patriarchal theme repeatedly in later films, most notably in the father/son pairings of *Independence Day*, *The Patriot*, and *The Day after Tomorrow*.

After the funeral, Joey retreats to his picket-fenced suburban house, emblem of his father's modest social success, to seek his father's guidance from beyond the grave. In the scene that follows, the suburban father announces his resurrection through the animation of the son's toys: a reaffirmation of suburban materialism that this very scene simultaneously subverts through a poignant depiction of the desolate son's isolation amidst plenty. Again, not unlike Spielberg and Lucas, Emmerich ultimately celebrates the most conservative values of his mainstream audience. The post-funeral scene that shows us Joey's lonely inner sanctum within his father's house begins with an exterior shot of the orderly house enshrouded in swirling, oppressive fog at night, not only a stock horror-movie topos given fullest expression in John Carpenter's film *The Fog* but a fairly blatant recapitulation of similar imagery in *Close Encounters of the Third*

Kind and *E.T.*—both films in which remote or absent fathers loom large, revealing the emotional void at the center of suburban tidiness. A slow zoom into the house and a dissolve into Joey's room depict Joey amidst an abundance of toys that signify his material privilege but highlight his isolation and loss. Uncomforted by possessions, he speaks to his dead father, who is nonetheless symbolically present in the room not only through the numerous toys which his livelihood had bestowed upon his son but within a framed photograph of father and son that Joey holds in his hands. Joey begs his father to come back and remembers a happier time when his father played basketball with him—a scene rendered in ethereally lit flashback from Joey's subjective point of view. This memory now compels Joey to cross to his second-story bedroom window and look down at the basketball hoop and backboard mounted on the garage. Joey's overhead perspective on the silently beckoning hoop is almost literally Godlike and foreshadows the miraculous nature of the events to come. Much like the priest looking down at the grave in the film's opening scene, Joey entreats his father "to please come back." As Joey utters these words of invocation, a toy TIE fighter is conspicuously visible on the shelf behind his head, once again referencing for the audience the *Star Wars* mythos and its father-son leitmotif.

In answer to Joey's summons, the basketball that had figured so prominently in his memory of his father rolls across his room toward him and stops only when Joey commands it to do so. The film thus begins to establish that Joey's words carry talismanic force to control the supernatural and indeed penetrate the threshold between life and death—that his words literally succeed in a way that the minister's metaphors do not. The ball is coded as the film's visual signifier of this triumph over death. At this early stage, Joey has no comprehension of what his words are capable of unleashing and no control over this power. He is a neophyte, much like Luke Skywalker in *Star Wars* has no idea of what the galaxy has in store for him. The toys in his room, all in some way associated with Joey's *pater familias* longing, come to chaotic life at his unconscious behest. The toys coming to life around the child upon whom cosmic forces are converging is, of course, Emmerich's homage to the scene with Barry Guiler, the child destined to travel to the stars in Spielberg's UFO epic *Close Encounters of the Third Kind*. Barry's significance to the aliens is announced by their activation of the toys (including cars and a child's record player) in his room; thus too is Joey's importance signaled in another journey of discovery, in this case an exploration of the boundary between life and death. Other visual references to Spielberg abound—a toy shark on the shelf behind the toy gorilla reminds the audience of *Jaws*; the rubber balls moved by an invisible force to form a microcosmic solar system is a reconstruction of the title character's manipulation of the toys in Eliott's room in Spielberg's *E.T.*

But in Emmerich's March of the Possessed Toys, perhaps the most overt homage to another filmmaker is the introduction of the toy robot Charlie, which the audience will shortly learn was given to Joey by his father the previous

Christmas. The robot, coming to life like many of the other toys in Joey's room, emits expressive electronic beeps, chirps, and whistles that sound very similar to those made by R2-D2, the endearing droid from George Lucas's *Star Wars* films. Charlie, with his stocky cylindrical body, even looks like Artoo, at least in the scenes in *Star Wars* films when Artoo is waddling on two legs instead of rolling on three. In a veritable blizzard of referentiality, Emmerich next has the rubber balls orbit around Charlie, again reinforcing the visual link to *E.T.* Joey next reaches his index finger to Charlie's extended robotic arm in homage to the El-liot-E.T. tactile link in Spielberg's film—an earlier scene that in itself seems like reverent parody of Michelangelo's Sistine painting of God and Adam reaching toward one another in an act of mutual self-creation. Joey's tentative gesture of trust and interconnectedness with this token of affection from the father provides the catalyst for the moment of revelation promised by the toys' sudden anima-tion—when the dead father calls on the red toy telephone hidden amongst Joey's numerous belongings.

Picking up the phone and hearing the voice he most longs to hear, Joey ini-tially disbelieves the evidence of his senses. "Daddy, that's not possible," Joey cries out, and throws the phone away into the closet. The stage is set for momen-tary suspense—out of fear of the unknown, will the son after all reject the father who returned to the son's desperate summons? Joey flees to hide beneath his *Return of the Jedi* blanket, an abruptly self-referential visual cue to the knowl-edgeable audience that, as Luke Skywalker reconciled with his lost father in that film, so too will this boy reunite with his. A red glare, intercut by blinding rays of stroboscopic white light, originates from the telephone to radiate between the slats in the closet door—a sublime light show reminiscent of those that mark the boundaries between the ordinary and the fantastic in *Close Encounters of the Third Kind* and *Poltergeist*. Joey crosses to the closet door wrapped in his Jedi blanket. So garbed, he resembles an acolyte approaching a sacred but searing revelation. He opens the closet door to accept finally his father's call. The closet is the gateway between Joey's world and his father's world; Emmerich will use the dimensional gateway convention again in *Stargate*.

The effects of the interdimensional rift are felt far beyond Joey's room—or so the audience knows, even if no one within the narrative other than Joey per-ceives the true nature of the miracle. A shot from a hilltop looking down at the light grid of the city echoes similar visuals in *Close Encounters*, *Poltergeist*, and *E.T.* and suggests the ancient connection between the divine and high places away from the community; the electromagnetic forces spilling from the other dimension set a bank of payphones to ringing outside of the Krispy Kreme donut shops in town. The next day, the local radio will broadcast news of the distur-bance, and we will later find out that a special team of paranormal investigators has also noticed. Meanwhile, in the venerable narrative tradition of loving moth-ers who nevertheless just don't get it, Laura is outside in the hallway, oblivious to the magic that turned Joey's room into a blinding wind tunnel and set phones to ringing half a city away. She hears her son speaking and surreptitiously peers into his room, seeing Joey hidden beneath his blanket on his bed, his legs kicking contentedly at the air as he talks to his father on the toy phone and exhorts him to promise never to leave again. Apparently not taking note of the red glare shining from beneath the blanket, Joey's mother assumes her son is mad with grief and prays for God's help—a justifiable enough sentiment from her limited point of view, but in the context of the narrative a woeful lack of perception of the miracle that is occurring in front of her. In this ignorance of the miraculous, she resembles the kind-hearted mother in *E.T.*, who unknowingly sends an extraterrestrial hidden under a sheet out trick-or-treating with her children, or the mother in *Close Encounters* who is loving enough to her son Barry but as a grown-up nevertheless cannot go with him on his trip with the elfin aliens.[12]

At this point, the film introduces another well-meaning but rather clueless adult: Joey's teacher Martin, destined to become a potential mate for Laura and surrogate father for an extremely resistant Joey. Martin is introduced into the narrative the next day as the teacher who attempts to minimize Joey's ostracism by his classmates. Martin attempts to engage the class in dialogue about Joey's bereavement, a kind but naïve gesture in light of the contempt in which Joey's male classmates in particular hold him. The other boys mock Joey's claim that he can talk to his dead father via a toy telephone. Callowly invoking reason in the face of irrational prejudice and the underlying textual presence of the supernatural, Martin explains that Joey loved his father very much and is trying to keep his memory alive in any way possible. While Martin sounds eminently reasonable, the narrative context makes it clear that his rationality is a type of blindness peculiar to adults who have suffered the death of the imagination, and his scientific and psychological explanations for the supernatural events unfolding around him ultimately configure him as condescending to Joey.

Oblivious to this adult attempt to protect him from scorn, Joey uses his burgeoning telekinetic powers to levitate an egg from across the room to his desk. Just as the egg reaches his desk, Martin, exasperated by the other boys' gleeful malice, slams his hand down on Joey's desk to emphasize a point and smashes the egg. In that the egg symbolizes birth and the continuation of life, Martin's smashing of it suggests that his effort to replace Joey's father in the cycle of life is doomed. Whatever inroads into the children's collective conscience Martin may have been making are lost in the hilarity that greets his sudden transition into slapstick buffoonery. The moment also foreshadows the degree of resistance that Joey will exert toward Martin's attempts to inject himself into Joey's home life.

Moving out into the hallway after class, Joey notices a female classmate named Sally staying behind in mute solidarity for his plight. He demonstrates just a touch of his telekinesis—lightly feathering her pigtails back from her head. She is delighted by this psychic demonstration, and the growing friendship is cemented. While not abused by the other children, Sally too is a sensitive outsider in a child's world of casual cruelty, and thus the only figure in the narrative who can truly relate to Joey, if not totally understand him. Martin and Laura, while relatively sympathetic figures in the narrative context, simply are too ossified in their thinking and imaginative powers to truly help Joey. Of course, the inability of adults to comprehend the magical world or special emotional needs of children is a signature motif in the cinematic juvenilia of Spielberg that so influences Emmerich.

Having illustrated the depth of Joey's alienation in his ordinary routine, the film next establishes the film's central supernatural villain as the malevolent ventriloquist's dummy that Joey discovers in a suitcase secreted in the gloomy basement of an abandoned house conveniently located on the hill behind his house. The film has already signified hilltops as places of special, even divine significance, but this particular hill and sanctuary is a focal point for what we might as well call "the dark side of the force," as the *Star Wars* allusions are so prevalent. The embodiment of the Dark Side is the ventriloquist's dummy. As a simulacrum of humanity, the dummy's appearance is disconcerting. Its slicked-back hair, high forehead, large eyes, broad cheekbones, and shrunken jaw are exaggerations typical of such dummies but that also code it as wizened, in the fashion of archetypal older guides into magical realms. Yet as a puppet dependent upon someone else's actions for animation, the dummy's presence as an evil appendage to Joey's life implies that the enemy is not so much outside Joey as within him—an objective correlative for his Dark Side, in Lucas-speak.

If Joey's father represents the benign mentor or guide to the other world, this subterranean dummy is the other side of that coin—a malignant figure activated into sentience by Joey's powers who will put Joey through the trials of the underworld.[13] While these trials are a necessary part of Joey's spiritual development before he can reunite with his father, the dummy does represent pure evil and will act accordingly as it becomes animate. The dummy's appearance, hearkening back to the world of vaudeville in the 1920s through the 1940s, also suggests a sociopolitical subtext that, in light of Emmerich's background, is at once American and subtly German. The vaudeville dummy is a relic from the economically depressed times just prior to World War II, in which masses of people forgot their daily woes in nightly rituals of entertainment. Furthermore, Anton Kaes notes that the use of puppets is a fixture in German dramatic tradition, and German filmmakers such as Hans Jürgen Syberberg in his film *Hitler: A Film from Germany* have transferred "obvious physical and emotional traits" of Nazi leaders onto puppets to make the leaders "look ridiculous" (53). The puppet's grotesque appearance in *Joey* does seem reminiscent of any number of caricatures of European evil in numerous sources in Europe and America, from anti-Semitic cartoons to Hollywood depictions of Nazis. From this perspective, then, the animated dummy as a demonic holdover from the past, evil but nevertheless crucial in Joey's quest to reunite with his father, textually represents an attempt to reconcile with an unpleasant historical legacy—that of European anti-Semitism and fascism resulting in the social apocalypse of World War II.[14]

The dummy is slyly animate at first, revealing his consciousness and evil nature only to another toy, the robot Charlie. Joey does not see that the dummy is animate, let alone that it is evil. Joey's lack of perception is a necessary plot device for him to bring the dummy from this interstitial zone into the sanctity of Joey's own house, but also suggests that Joey's nine-year-old consciousness is not developed enough yet to recognize a true physical and spiritual threat. Once carried to Joey's room and placed with the other toys, the dummy continues to menace Charlie. Like Joey, the dummy possesses telekinetic powers, which he uses to besiege the hapless Charlie beneath a wave of stuffed animals. Thus, if the animated Charlie as an extension of Joey represents all that is innocent about the boy, the evil dummy embodies Joey's potential for inflicting evil.

The grieving Joey is quite vulnerable to negative impulses, as the following dinner scene with his mother makes clear. His mood is morose, even sullen, as his mother lectures him about watching television during dinner. He responds by telekinetically turning on the television in defiance of Laura and then moving a glass of milk across the table, and explains to Laura that he does these things with his daddy's help. Laura's effort to maintain domestic protocol at a time when all rules and stability have been exploded and magic is literally in the air codes her, at least at this moment, as an obstacle to Joey, which explains something of his resentment toward her. Also in terms of narrative structure, the child's resentment toward the remaining mother in the absence of the father is a governing character dynamic in the early Spielberg films that influence Emmerich. Little warmth is apparent between the mother and son in this scene; both seem a little weary, even annoyed, with one another. Laura is easily dismissed from her son's single-minded quest to recover his lost father, a fairly routine fate for female characters in the kind of quasi-mythological Hollywood narratives that Emmerich is smitten by. Laura is left alone in the domestic sphere represented by her kitchen and dining room, while her son goes upstairs to the liminal zone to practice his magic beneath his Jedi cowl.

The dummy reveals the extent of his powers to Joey in the next scene, ripping the phone from Joey's hands and flashing blue electrical arcs that resemble those spewed forth by the Emperor in *Return of the Jedi*. Then, the dummy levitates a television toward Joey, paralleling Joey's spiteful act with the television in the dining area, and literally "channels" the dummy's history to Joey as a show dimly visible behind an obscuring screen of static. As the television show explains in the mock newsreel fashion of another era, the dummy was part of a 1930's vaudevillian ventriloquist's show, Fletcher and Fletcher. The next television image the dummy conjures up for Joey is of a knife moving through the air toward Laura's outstretched hand on the doorframe, a scene undoubtedly inspired by a similar moment in Brian DePalma's film adaptation of Stephen King's novel *Carrie* when Carrie telekinetically kills her tyrannical mother with lethal kitchen implements. While Laura is not the evil mother of the King/DePalma text, certainly her psychically gifted son does carry at least some unconscious resentment toward her. The dummy Fletcher, as evil doppelganger to Joey, acts on this resentment of matriarchy. The malicious double, or Jungian shadow self, is a staple character type in Spielbergian cinema, from the competing archeologists Belloq/Indiana Jones in the early film *Raiders of the Lost Ark* to the bifurcated character of Goeth/Schindler in *Schindler's List*, a film that cemented for most critics Spielberg's supposedly more mature phase. In Emmerich's text, Fletcher as Shadow self, the murderer of his own creator and father, acts to destroy the constraints of family in equal counter-reaction to Joey's effort, aided by his dead father's guiding spirit, to restore family boundaries.

Both forces seem evenly balanced, as Laura's imminent skewering is averted by the ringing of a downstairs phone that compels her to move from harm's way. Joey's father is most likely responsible for this salvation, as the same series of shots that previously heralded his return from death are repeated here—the sacred hilltop and the jangling phone bank outside the Krispy Kreme shop. This second dimensional rift saves Laura and momentarily stills Fletcher. Joey initially refuses to tell his mother what is happening, but when she discovers an array of knives plunged into her kitchen wall and turns her frightened eye upon Joey, he explains that the dummy he discovered won't let him talk to his father anymore. Completely overwhelmed by the magnitude of her son's apparent psychological problems, Laura has to leave the house and her son for awhile to go for a drive. This brief maternal abandonment is necessary to establish the degree to which Joey's isolation builds the resentment upon which Fletcher feeds. Therefore, the film's narrative impetus toward reunification is held in stasis as Joey must confront and resolve his unconscious urge to destroy his family, an urge symbolized by Fletcher.

The next scene shows Joey's classroom tormentors spying on him the next day and digging up Fletcher, whom Joey has buried in an attempt to rid himself of the dummy's evil. The boys' neophyte militarism, betokened by their spying mission, military garb and lingo, and radio-controlled tanks with which they later attack and shoot the surrendering Charlie, is thus linked to Fletcher. The linkage between the youthful bullies and Fletcher as a symbol of European decadence and proto-fascism suggests a generational transfer of brutality—that the past continues to exert a baleful influence on the present. Though overt references to Nazism do not appear in the film, the subtext is that the boys' persecution of Joey is not dissimilar to that inflicted upon the Jews during the time of Fletcher and Fletcher. Of course, as this is a genre film, Joey is armed with a weapon not available to the Jews of Europe a generation past. Like Carrie White, he turns the power of his mind upon his persecutors, though in a much less spectacular fashion than King's psychic demigoddess. Joey explodes their toy tanks, effectively disarming the boys at this early stage in their military campaign against Joey. Momentarily defeated, Joey's enemies gather at the abandoned house on the hilltop, where they too enter the subterranean realm of Fletcher and quickly claim it as their secret clubhouse. Of course, this action cements their allegiance to the dark powers that Fletcher represents. One of the group's members, a silent girl carrying a doll, discovers pictures of Fletcher and Fletcher in the cellar. The parallel between the girl and her doll and the dead man and his doll is clear enough; this bullying group of embryonic Nazis is the next generation of evil.

In the face of such irrational hatred as that exhibited by the gang of children which wants to harm Joey, of what effectiveness is the type of liberal humanist philosophy represented by Martin? Going above and beyond what most teachers would do in such a situation, Martin shows up at Joey's house to inquire as to his health. Of course, through his uninvited solicitude, he unwittingly endangers the boy's health by completing what the bullies could never have done for all their malice—carrying the discarded Fletcher back into the house. In a scene that follows the narrative logic of Oedipal myth, Laura invites Martin to stay for dinner, thus replacing the absent father at the kitchen table with this surrogate father. Joey, who has lost a father and fended off an attack by bullies, now faces a terrible new threat to his emotional health and reacts, predictably enough, with overt resentment toward Laura and Martin. Here is another dimension of the patriarchal epic coveted by Spielberg and Lucas and Emmerich—what to do with the pretender or usurper to the father's place? In spite of his strong physical build, Martin is too intellectual and too ineffectual to be a suitable patriarch. Frankly, in the sexist world of male melodrama, he is coded as too feminized or soft. Besides that, his rationalizations are based on erroneous assumptions. Explaining rather condescendingly to Laura that poltergeist or psychic phenomena are commonly manifested around children entering puberty, Laura rightly responds that Joey has just turned nine, and thus is by no definition an adolescent. Meanwhile, Joey has to retreat to the magic cave—his room—to shut out his traitorous mother and the unacceptable pretender, placing a "Keep Out" sign on the door. He must then don his cowl—the *Return of the Jedi* blanket—to re-establish contact with his true father and express his hatred of Laura and Martin.

At this moment of greatest distress for Joey, Fletcher re-enters the narrative to tempt Joey to the Dark Side. The scene's dependence on Spielberg and Lucas is one of the most blatant such moments in the film. Fletcher's malign force rips the *Jedi* blanket away from Joey and directs the boy to the closet, the apparent portal between Joey's room and the realm of the dead. Fletcher then prevents Joey from leaving the room to go to his mother and fills the room with crackling blue lightning bolts nearly identical to those discharged from the Emperor's fingertips in *Return of the Jedi*; a poster showing the Imperial probe droid from *The Empire Strikes Back* is briefly visible on the wall at this moment. Not to slight Spielberg in favor of Lucas, Emmerich manages to encode *E.T.* into the narrative at this point. Fletcher teleports Joey's E.T. doll, slightly altered to include a small horn on his face (perhaps to avoid legal problems with Spielberg), from the closet to an outside garbage can, where it comes to life like many of Joey's other toys. A *Star Wars* poster showing two Imperial stormtroopers is clearly visible on the wall behind Joey, reinforcing for the audience that this struggle between Joey and Fletcher is analogous to that between Luke and the evil Empire. In fact, audience knowledge of Lucas's films is demanded in order to make any kind of sense of this film.

The temptation at this moment is for Joey to pit his own ability against Fletcher's in a personal power struggle, which parallels Luke's temptation by the Emperor and his puppet Darth Vader in the climactic *Star Wars* film. Like Luke, Joey rejects the offer to "play," but Fletcher replies simply, "We'll see." Fletcher knows what the audience knows—that also like Luke, particularly in *The Empire Strikes Back*, Joey is not spiritually enough developed for the audience to feel any kind of confidence that he will be able to resist such temptation. Sensing the danger to his son, Joey's father chooses this moment to try to reach him through ringing the telephone. Enraged by this intrusion, Fletcher pins Joey to the wall with the blue lightning bolts, leading Joey to call to his father for help against this stronger enemy. Of course, the scene is a replication of the one in which a defeated Luke, burned by the same kind of blue lightning bolts, cries out to Darth Vader in *Return of the Jedi*. Joey's unseen father does indeed help in the only way he can in his incorporeal form—he rings the telephone downstairs (incidentally setting off the phones in front of Krispy Kreme again) to summon Laura up to the room. Joey finally frees himself from the wall to wrestle Fletcher into temporary stillness. Thus, father and son, while not reunited, have nevertheless allied to win a small victory against evil. The scene concludes with Martin, the would-be father significantly prevented from being inside the magic room with Joey, going off for help while an overwhelmed Laura characteristically abandons her child.

The help arrives in a scene that is lifted more or less intact from *E.T.* In Spielberg's film, a hi-tech governmental team garbed in space suits descends upon Elliot's suburban house and quarantines it, in front of the goggle-eyed neighbors, to study the alien and its symbiotic link to Elliot. In Emmerich's film, a similar hi-tech governmental team garbed in space suits descends upon Joey's suburban house and quarantines it, in front of the goggle-eyed neighbors, to study Joey and his ability to communicate with the dead. The team cocoons the house in plastic and fills it with scientific apparatus. Accompanying the paranormal research team is the telephone company, investigating whatever force has been ringing all the phones in the city. This team, apparently summoned into overt action by whatever Martin did to secure help, is the extreme manifestation of Martin's teacherly inclination to chart, graph, photograph, quantify, and otherwise try to contain and rationalize the unknown.

Meanwhile, another threat to Joey rematerializes, as the bullies who threatened him before watch the quarantining of Joey's house. They cannot believe that all this fuss is "for that little idiot." Their leader William, whose imperialis-

tic dominance over the other children is emphasized by his U.S.A. shirt, says
that Joey will "now have to pay his dues," presumably for the sin of becoming
such a center of attention when he was supposed to remain downtrodden and
insignificant. William sets up his army's headquarters in the basement of the
abandoned house to plan an invasion of Joey's house. The call to arms resembles the briefing given by General Dodonna to the rebel pilots in *Star Wars* prior
to the attack on the Death Star. The children don various masks in preparation
for battle, and *Star Wars* characters are well represented. One of the children
wears an Emperor mask. Others wear C-3PO and stormtrooper disguises. William as imperialistic leader dons a Darth Vader helmet and concludes his rally-
ing of the troops with a pop-cultural prayer: "May the Force be with us." Like
the Rebel X-wing fighters of *Star Wars*, the children's army ascends from the
underground and then descends upon the technocratic bubble enclosing Joey's
house. At this point in the film, Emmerich has clearly abandoned any pretense at
narrative plausibility and lets his fondness for *Star Wars* iconography completely dictate the form and direction of his text.

Warned by Sally, Joey has run with her ahead of the advancing army into
the inner sanctum of his room. Finally cornered, and urged by Sally to "play the
game" and use his powers in self-defense, Joey opens his closet door to tap into
the dimensional forces beyond. In a startling image reminiscent of the standard
punishment handed out to fascist and Nazi war criminals at the end of World
War II, Fletcher is bound and hanging from a noose in the closet, presumably
rendered powerless by Joey's father. At the same time, the rest of the toys,
which had mysteriously vanished when the scientific team arrived, spill out in a
torrent that symbolizes the unleashing of all the power at Joey's command. William in his Darth Vader mask enters Joey's room first. In a fitting moment of
poetic justice, a toy All-Terrain-Transport walker (one of the elephantine war
machines first introduced into the *Star Wars* cosmology in *The Empire Strikes
Back*) laser-blasts William, sending him running back out into the hallway and
screaming for "Mommy," all in full view of his astonished minions. He is pursued by a toy replica of Han Solo's ship, the *Millennium Falcon*, which in turn
is chased by two TIE fighters in another scene grafted from *The Empire Strikes
Back*—the scene in which the *Falcon* is chased through an asteroid field by Imperial fighters. The hallway fills with flying toys looking for escape, all wit-
nessed by mesmerized children and adults who record the magical event.

Within the room, Joey and Sally sit atop his levitating bed, with Joey aiming a toy rifle at any and all enemies who enter the room. The image is both Hollywood iconic and uncomfortably charged with latent sexual imagery—the nas-
cent couple, with the male defending his woman and his territory in patriarchal
Western hero fashion. Joey, allied with his invisible father and abandoned by his
earthly mother, has finally unveiled his powers to an extent that not even the
most skeptical child or adult can deny. Literally, he is "coming out of the closet"
and into his own as an adept practitioner of the wild talent with which he is

gifted. His manipulation of the *Star Wars* toys to defeat an attack by "Darth Vader"—the manifestation of the Dark Father or Shadow self in *Star Wars* mythology—marks the moment at which he becomes for all narrative intents a Jedi, fully accepted as such by friends and former foes alike. Joey's newfound status as "Jedi knight" is underscored by an image of Yoda on a wall poster behind his head.[15]

The scene that follows shows the little girl with the doll, under the malign influence of Fletcher, freeing the dummy and initiating a series of events that will place her and four of Joey's former tormentors at the mercy of Fletcher in a vast underground labyrinth. The final phase of the narrative presents Joey with his first mature test of his newly acquired power against the Shadow. Like Theseus descending into the Minotaur's maze, Aeneas into the underworld, or Luke Skywalker into the cave "heavy with the dark side of the force" in *The Empire Strikes Back*, Joey and his consort Sally must enter this maze to prove Joey's moral integrity and newfound maturity by rescuing his former enemies.

The children that are lost in the labyrinth encounter a variety of threats, in much the same way that the youths in *The Goonies* do. In this instance, the threats are conjured up by Fletcher and individually tailored to each child's idiosyncratic fears. This portion of the film strongly resembles Stephen King's novel *It*. An elemental monster made of rock menaces the little girl; a movie-monster mummy emerges from the shadows; a giant cheeseburger with teeth threatens the overweight boy of the group; and Darth Vader himself, light-saber in gloved hand, appears to William. By the time Joey and Sally find the children, William and company are completely terrified and all too relieved to accept Joey as their leader through the maze. They have not yet entered their home dimension; however, one doorway remains between them and their world. It is conspicuously marked by an "EXIT" sign, but between it and them is a chair, with Fletcher sitting on the arm of the chair with his back to the children.

It is up to Joey, once again, to win the children's safe passage from Fletcher. This last obstacle will prove to be the defining one of Joey's role as former exile turned culture hero (at least in the sense that he is the champion of his classroom peers). The human Fletcher, summoned from the afterlife by Joey's increasing power and looking quite disoriented in the transition, appears in a nimbus of white light beside the dummy Fletcher. Momentarily, it appears as if this return, the reassertion of history into the narrative, will miraculously correct the imbalance that the unrestrained puppet Fletcher has created. However, any hope that the former master could contain the puppet's power is lost, as the dead Fletcher's will seems quite disorganized in death and is powerless to stop the crumbling of the house around them. But the dead Fletcher as an emissary from the other dimension does provide Joey with one climactic bit of information he needs to defeat the puppet's evil, reunite with his father, and save his friends. He directs Joey toward the exit door and says, "I don't have to help you. You have a friend who will." Sally understands immediately the implication of Joey crossing that threshold between the dimensions and begs him not to go, but for Joey the attraction to find his lost father again is too strong and for director Emmerich too crucial to the thrust of the patriarchal fantasy narrative to be denied at this late point. Joey enters the dimensional gateway, an action that unleashes enough power to burn the evil puppet to ashes and reinsert Joey's friends back into their world. A subjective point-of-view shot shows the audience what Joey sees, as his astral self is propelled away from his body through an ethereally lighted tunnel toward another open door. Entering fully into the other dimension through the door, Joey sees his father (though the audience does not) again and greets him: "Daddy." Father and son, like Luke and Vader, have been brought together again in the spirit realm, and the narrative is quickly brought to denouement.

A search party finds Joey unconscious in the ruins of the house on the sacred hill and brings him down to his own house, where Sally, the other children, and Laura and Martin watch the scientific team attempt to revive the dying boy. Again, the visual allusions to the scenes in *E.T.* where the doctors work to save the mortally ill extraterrestrial and Elliot are deliberate. The resuscitation efforts (CPR and electro-shock), shockingly visceral in their impact upon Joey's small body, are similarly jarring in E.T.'s death scene. Yet for all the sorrow of the death scene that Emmerich creates from a template provided by Spielberg, the overall tone is somehow reassuring, even redemptive of the formerly intimidating, overly mechanical members of the scientific team. The doctors and technicians become humanized individuals in their earnest but futile efforts to save Joey. The team's female leader, Hayden, formerly icy and formidable, is reconfigured as a much more sympathetic character in her consolation of Sally.

As does E.T.'s death, Joey's death provides an occasion for the filmmakers to revel in a great deal of maudlin sentimentality gilded by religiosity. Joey's lifeless body is portrayed with his arms outstretched in standard crucifixion iconography. When Hayden announces Joey's death to the assembled crowd outside the house, the lamentation and group self-excoriation begins. All is emptiness and desolation as the mourners leave Joey's room and Hayden softly orders her team to pack up and leave for good. Yet just as Spielberg miraculously resurrected E.T. back from the dead, so too does Emmerich completely reverse the melancholia of the past few minutes of screen time and return Joey, at least in spirit, to the world of the living. The narrative returns full circle to the images that signaled the father's return. Toy balls on the floor of Joey's room begin to move and form orbits around each other on their own. Clouds form rapidly in the sky over the house—a visual effect rather pitifully aspiring to the roiling clouds of *Close Encounters of the Third Kind*. As some of the team members begin to exhibit fear at this latest manifestation, Sally happily proclaims, "I'm not afraid. It's only Joey." Charlie, recognizing the presence of Joey, rolls toward Joey's room with mechanical arms waving wildly in greeting. The toy *Millennium Falcon* returns to the house, the children cheer, and Laura's tightly clutched toy telephone glows cherry red. As Sally moves toward the light radiating from Joey's room, her figure is outlined in halo like Barry Guiler standing innocent and unafraid before Spielberg's *Close Encounters* aliens. "He's back," Sally cries out in a more positive reworking of the signature statement, "They're here" from *Poltergeist*, and Emmerich's narrative thus concludes what has to be one of the cheeriest child's-death scenes ever filmed. Any of the film's earlier unsettling questions about patriarchal tyranny, fascism, family tensions, etc., are erased by the triumphant ending—a narrative closure often manifest in popular film and a sure indicator of Emmerich's Hollywood aspirations.[16]

So too ends the film, undoubtedly the strangest of all tributes to the Hollywood work of Spielberg and Lucas. In one sense, Emmerich's film is refreshing in that it makes no effort to disguise its conservative agenda to replicate iconic moments, storylines, and images from earlier foundational texts. The ubiquitous referencing of *Star Wars* and *E.T.*, as well as other films, is so over-the-top in the film that it would be parodic in most texts. But Emmerich is playing it straight here, with obvious love for the source material and a sincere desire to recreate those films' attractions on his own terms, as any "loving son" might do in homage to a father's example. There is none of that sense of ironic detachment so crucial for the hip postmodern tone. This seriousness of homage, combined with an almost childlike delight in being able to retell a beloved story in a different context, is what makes Emmerich's film *Joey*, along with his later blockbuster Hollywood epics, a work of reverent parody.

Notes

1. In all of Emmerich's cinema, perhaps the most blatant moments of American triumphalism occur in *Independence Day*, in which the threatened nations of the world defer to the American president's military strategy and the President himself (seemingly an amalgamation of Bill Clinton's youth and his predecessor George H.W. Bush's aviation combat experience) in a superficially unifying but aggressively nationalistic exhortation to the troops deeming the American Fourth of July a "world" holiday.

2. Emmerich's love for disaster movies finds fullest expression in his 1996 film *Independence Day* and his 2004 film *The Day after Tomorrow*.

3. For example, Richard Schickel says rather contemptuously of *Stargate*: "One thing [the film] definitely proves . . . is the old adage, if you're going to steal, steal big. If you're caught, you can always claim you were doing an homage" (par. 2). Of the film *Independence Day*, Michael D. Friedman more genteelly writes, "One of the most prominent features of director Roland Emmerich's blockbuster . . . is the movie's highly allusive quality" (par. 1).

4. Gary Westfahl diagnoses what he considers to be a major aesthetic malady of Emmerich's films: "Emmerich wishes to emotionally connect with every single person in his audience and he will, in the course of a single film, briefly try almost everything he can think of in order to do so. . . . The problem with this approach is that all these disparate motifs are given too little time, and are so visibly contrivances unsupported by conviction, that they cannot possibly have any emotional impact" (par. 1). David Hudson

complains that "[Emmerich's] movies wear the absurdity of their premises and spectacles on their sleeves. They swagger and shout: This is escapist entertainment at its best because its [sic] just too plain crazy to ever actually happen" (par. 2). In the same breath, however, Hudson notes that the post-9/11 world jibes in a disturbing fashion to the landscapes of destruction that Emmerich visualizes. The real-life terrorist destruction of American architectural icons and the melting of polar ice caps related to global warming is coming uncomfortably close to intersecting with Emmerich's apocalyptic fantasy vision.

5. One need only think of the characters of the bumbling mayor and his aide from Emmerich's version of *Godzilla*. The characters are obviously modeled on film critics Roger Ebert and Gene Siskel, who had disliked *Independence Day*.

6. Some critics have taken note of the German influence in Emmerich's American films, such as Christian Caryl, who writes that the plot of *Independence Day* comes straight from the Brothers Grimm and that ". . . there's nothing intrinsically American about . . . *Independence Day*. O.K., fine, so the movie was shot in Hollywood with Hollywood actors. But the idea, the script, the direction, the camerawork, and many of the special effects came from Germans" (par. 2). Similarly, Sabine Thuerwaechter tracks through Emmerich's films many features of the "Storm and Stress" movement in German literature of the 18th century.

7. There are two extant versions of Joey—one the American 79-minute theatrical cut (dubbed in English) and the 98-minute German original. This discussion focuses on the German original, in which the various allusions to American filmmakers are more numerous and developed at greater length.

8. Though writing of another film, Linnie Blake's words apply to *Joey*: ". . . at the heart of German subjectivity there lies a tragic will to self-destruction that manifests itself in failed relationships with the living, and a mordant, though necessary, festishization of the dead" (par. 17). As for the film's unlikely juxtaposition of necromancy and *Star Wars*, Anton Kaes argues that this too is a symptom of "the never-ending longing for other worlds that links German Romanticism to modern fantasies of space travel" (61).

9. Gregory Burkart states, rather strongly, that he sees in *Joey* "the first inkling of the talent which would become Emmerich's trademark: stealing the hell out of other people's movies. . . . Emmerich's lucky his movie premiered in Germany, or Spielberg would have eaten his ass alive for stealing entire chunks of plot, character, and cinematography from 'Close Encounters,' 'E.T.' and 'Poltergeist'" (pars. 1, 2). Unverifiable speculation about Spielberg's intentions aside, Burkart's commentary sums up about as well as any the degree of antipathy that Emmerich arouses in some of his audience.

10. Kage Alan, for one, notes Joey's de-centeredness but attributes this quality to artistic lack of control: "[*Joey* is] a confusing story that seems to cross a number of genres in search of its own message and way of delivering it" (par. 6). But certainly it is arguable that the film's diffuseness is very much under Emmerich's control.

11. If one accepts Peter Biskind's contention in *Easy Riders, Raging Bulls* that the New Hollywood represented by Lucas and Spielberg overthrew the hoary traditions of the Old Hollywood to ironically create a new established order or film empire, then Emmerich is the next generation of filmmaker who will both honor and displace the likes of Spielberg. The Oedipal drama continues.

12. Of course, some critics see a darker, misogynistic streak in Emmerich's work that is part-and-parcel of an over-arching fascistic agenda. Teresa Santerre Hobby, for example, argues that "Independence Day reveals the resurgence of the right-wing attitude

toward women: Stand by your man and shut up" (53). From this perspective, then, Laura is rightly punished by her son's disapproval for the cardinal sin of allowing the father to be dead in her thoughts. Or put another way, the narrative rewards the death fetishism of the son.

13. Such an occurrence is common in Stephen King's earlier work, but the most obvious connection here is between Joey and Danny Torrance, the psychic little boy trapped in a haunted hotel in *The Shining*.

14. This aspect of Joey corresponds to what Linnie Blake identifies as "one of the core subjects of recent German film—*Die Unbewältigte Vergangenheit*—the past that has not been adequately dealt with" (par. 3).

15. The image is yet another in a series of eternally mutable *Star Wars* pictures on the wall that signify key moments in Joey's development. The pictures change from scene to scene without any apparent regard for continuity, but Emmerich's aesthetic does not require such literalism as unchanging wall posters.

16. Christine Haase, in her comparison of German cinema to American popular cinema, elaborates: ". . . in Hollywood action films [family] conflicts usually appear for dramatic arching and ultimately are resolved happily, without leaving loose ends or really questioning social institutions like marriage or parenthood" (415). In *Joey*, for example, the potential "loose end" of a son's grief for a dead father, or a mother's devastating loss of a husband and son, is rendered moot by the fairy tale return of the subject of mourning from the fantastical realm of the dead.

Works Cited

Aberly, Richard, and Volker Engel. *The Making of Independence Day*. New York: Harper Paperbacks, 1996.

Alan, Kage. "DVD Review: *Making Contact (Joey)*." *Modamag*. July 15, 2004. www.modamag.com/makingcontact_dvd.htm.

Biskind, Peter. *Easy Riders, Raging Bulls: How the Sex, Drugs, and Rock 'n' Roll Generation Saved Hollywood*. Simon & Schuster, 1999.

Blake, Linnie. "Sex, Selfhood, and the Corpse of the German Past: Jorg Buttgereit's *Nekromantik* (1987) and *Nekromantik 2* (1991)." *Kinoeye* 3.6 (May 26, 2003). June 4, 2004. www.kinoeye.org/03/06/blake06.php.

Burkart, Gregory S. "*Making Contact* (review)." *Monsters at Play*. July 15, 2004. www.monstersatplay.com/review/dvd/m/makingcontact.php.

Caryl, Christian. "German Farewells." *The New Criterion* 15 (March 1997): 40–45. *First Search*. WilsonSelectPlus. Brevard Community College Libraries, Palm Bay, FL. July 15, 2004.

Friedman, Michael D. "*Independence Day*: The American Henry V and the Myth of David." *Literature Film Quarterly* 28.2 (April 1, 2000): 140–9. EBSCO Host. Brevard Community College Libraries, Palm Bay, FL. July 15, 2004.

Haase, Christine. "You Can Run, but You Can't Hide: Transcultural Filmmaking in Run Lola Run (1998)." *Light Motives: German Popular Film in Perspective*. Eds. Randall Halle and Margaret McCarthy. Detroit: Wayne State University Press, 2003. 395–415.

Halle, Randall, and Margaret McCarthy. *Light Motives: German Popular Film in Per-spective.* Detroit: Wayne State University Press, 2003.

Hobby, Teresa Santerre. *"Independence Day:* Reinforcing Patriarchal Myths about Gen-der and Power." *Journal of Popular Culture* 34.2 (September 2000): 39–55.

Hudson, David. "The Treatment." *Greencine* (2004). July 15, 2004. www.greencine. com/article?action=view&articleID=19.

Hutcheon, Linda. *A Theory of Parody: The Teachings of Twentieth-Century Art Forms.* London: Metheun, 1985.

Kaes, Anton. *From Hitler to Heimat: The Return of History as Film.* Cambridge, MA: Harvard University Press, 1992.

Kolker, Robert Philip. *The Altering Eye: Contemporary International Cinema.* Oxford: Oxford University Press, 1983.

Prager, Brad. "Beleaguered under the Sea: Wolfgang Petersen's *Das Boot* (1981) as a German Hollywood Film." *Light Motives: German Popular Film in Perspec-tive.* Eds. Randall Halle and Margaret McCarthy. Detroit: Wayne State Univer-sity Press, 2003. 237–58.

Schickel, Richard. "Indiana Jones, Space Linguist." *Time* (November 21, 1994): 116. EBSCO Host. Brevard Community College Libraries, Palm Bay, FL. July 15, 2004.

Thuerwaechter, Sabine. "A Tale of Two Nations: Friedrich Schiller's *The Robbers* and Its Retelling in Roland Emmerich's *The Patriot.*" 2005 Annual Conference on Literature and Film. Florida State University. Turnbull Student Center, Talla-hassee. January 29, 2005.

Westfahl, Gary. "Roland Emmerich." *Gary Westfahl's Biographical Encyclopedia of Science Fiction Film.* July15, 2004. www.sfsite.com/gary/emme01.htm.

To Die For: *Der Fan* and the Reception of Sexuality and Horror in Early 1980s German Cinema

Ernest Mathijs

"Was sich liebt, das neckt sich"
Old German folk saying

"I know where you are": New Wave, German Style

Imagine a film that ends like this: a teenage girl kills her pop star idol, then elaborately carves up and freezes his body, then eats parts of him, shaves off her hair, and, to an eerie *Eraserhead*-ish soundtrack, confides to her journal, "I know where you are. Don't fear," before a final fade to a bright red screen. When this film also happens to be made in West Germany in the early 1980s, and when it is full of references to Nazi-style imagery, electro pop, and when the girl and pop star remain completely nude throughout the slashing scene, one thing is clear: the filmmaker is courting scandal. The film, directed by Eckhart Schmidt, is *Der Fan,* a notoriously explicit and curiously unknown horror film from 1982. It has only recently received DVD-releases, and its video versions have been reported as out of print for more than a decade. Yet everyone old—or unlucky—enough to have been a teenager in or around Germany in the early 1980s seems to remember the film and the controversy surrounding it.[1]

The public status of *Der Fan* is at the centre of this essay. In what follows, I will first sketch the place of *Der Fan* in studies of German cinema culture (or rather its lack of a place), with special consideration for approaches towards popular and exploitation culture. Next, I will discuss its reception, particularly the controversy it caused and the place it occupied within contemporary pop culture at the time, especially as part of the so-called *Neue Deutsche Welle* (literally: the New German Wave). I will single out the most characteristic features of this trend: its cultural politics of anti-Americanism, its aesthetic affiliation with expressionism, its feminist sensitivity, and its representations of misfits and misogyny. I will also describe the platforms through which the trend became publicly visible, focusing on the attempts to integrate cultural commodities beyond medium-specific boundaries. Finally, I will discuss the film's most essential property, its portrayal of sex and violence through the salient motives of nudity and orality, and ask why this property is of pressing importance for understanding German popular culture of the early 1980s.

Der Fan and German Horror Cinema

Horror cinema is an integral part of popular culture, and as such it needs to be discussed as incorporated with other forms of popular culture, such as music, television, cartoons, writing, and performances. Much the same way *Nosferatu, eine Symphonie des Grauens* (Murnau, 1922) is mostly seen to acquire a certain significance in relation to other cultural products of its era, postwar German horror needs to be treated similarly: through its connection with contemporary popular culture, both in its local and global perspectives.[2]

No one can doubt *Der Fan* is a horror film. It tells the story of a seventeen-year-old girl, Simone (Désirée Nosbusch), who is madly in love with R., a teenage heartthrob and successful pop singer (Bodo Staiger). She writes to him fervently, but never manages to get a reply. Desperate to get him to notice her, she sets herself a deadline of seven days. If R. does not reply by then, she will go find him. In the meantime she ignores attentions from potential boyfriends, resists advice from her parents, and neglects her schoolwork. After seven days, Simone sets out to Munich, to meet R. at a television recording session. She almost gets raped on the way, but finally makes it to the city. Outside the television studio, amidst a crowd of fans, she meets R., and faints (one assumes from sheer excitement). He takes her into the studio, and during rehearsals they begin to flirt. After the performance R. takes Simone to a friend's house. They have sex, after which he tells her that he needs to leave. Simone hits R., kills him, cuts his body to pieces, and eats some of them. She stays in the house for an indefinite amount of time, grinds some of the bones to powder, then returns home. When she arrives home the television news broadcasts a story about the missing pop star R. "I know where you are," she says to herself, "Don't fear. I won't betray you. For no money in the world. I have not yet had my period. It is four weeks overdue. I will bring you to the world. We will be happy. I know you love me. And I love you too." She repeats the last two sentences in writing in her diary. The doorbell rings . . . fade to red.

A film with these obvious properties should not be difficult to frame. The slow start of the film is a typical technique in horror film, especially in realist horror. It takes a while before there is any sign of disturbance. The trained viewer knows that, sooner or later, this disturbance is bound to arrive, and thence details, especially those of the characters, become crucial. It is a feature *Der Fan* has in common with many American horror films, most notably *Psycho* (Hitchcock, 1960), *Last House on the Left* (Craven, 1972), and *The Texas*

Chainsaw Massacre (Hooper, 1974). Yet in a peculiar way, it also shares this characteristic with Joseph Conrad's *Heart of Darkness*. Early on in *Der Fan* the character of Simone almost seems to be a synthesis of Hitchcock's Marion Crane, of Mari and Phyllis in *Last House on the Left,* and of Conrad's Kurtz. With Marion Crane, Simone shares a stubborn desperation and a neurotic anxiety, which manifests itself as near autistic behaviour. This is a characteristic not uncommon for active female characters in films, and one well criticized as ultimately resisting, and containing, on-screen female liberty.[3] Whereas Marion gets slaughtered, though, Simone gets revenge, and the methodical way in which she executes her designs aligns her with Estelle, Mari's mother in *Last House on the Left.* But in the first forty-five minutes of the film Simone is more like the two girls getting brutally murdered in that film: she seems slow minded, numbed, confused, unable to grasp what is happening; one wonders whether perhaps she is simply naive, like Mari and Phyllis. Mari and Phyllis do not understand why they are tortured, while Simone does not understand why R. fails to answer her letters and why, once they have met, he rejects her after using her. Mari and Phyllis do not survive this abuse, and, in a way, neither does Simone. While her body remains active, her personality has clearly been destroyed. With Kurtz she shares not just the bald head and the descent into madness, but also the fact that her revenge on the world is disproportionate. Immoral beyond boundaries, their behavior is also consistent with an obsessive ideology, a worldview admittedly more explicit in Kurtz's semi-public monologues than in Simone's private ones. From innocent teenager to psychopath, in their victimization—or the evil they represent—Simone and Kurtz are never admired or understood, always finding themselves at a distance from the audience's perspective.

Der Fan mimics plenty of other classical horror narratives and repertoires: the inability of the protagonist to relate to friends and relatives, the disconnection from moral values, the travel/descent into hell, murder as a form of catharsis, the representation of sexuality as abject, and the inner monologue—they are all core features of the horror genre.[4] But, as pointed out above, an aesthetic understanding of *Der Fan* as horror is not enough to explain the particular place it occupies in early 1980s Germany. To understand this position, a larger cultural framework is required. This is where a problem occurs. As Jennifer Fay and Steffen Hantke have observed, the study of German film seems to have an ambiguous attitude towards taking a popular culture perspective.[5] At best, it seems that many critics regard particularly the period of the 1970s and the early 1980s primarily, or even exclusively, in the context of art cinema. At first glance, this period is best known for its "new wave" of auteurist, modernist cinema, culminating in Volker Schlöndorff's Academy win with *The Tin Drum* (1981), and Margarete von Trotta's *Die bleierne Zeit* (1982) as the high points of a cinema characterized by overt politics and left-wing ideologies, seriousness and a critical attitude towards German culture and history. Much of the rest of German cinema is often seen as the antipode to this aesthetic and political program: farcical, trashy, exploitative, and/or reactionary. This shows itself in different ways, from pure neglect of anything outside the New Wave canon (e.g. in Sabine

Hake's 2002 history of German cinema), to unfounded and dismissive remarks on other forms of German cinema. Thomas Elsaesser's comment that the sex film—one of Germany's main film industries, at least quantitatively—eradicated family audiences and turned educated audiences away from films outside the New Wave, is one example of this attitude (69).

But not all German cinema outside the New Wave is aesthetically inferior, politically reactionary, and culturally and historically irrelevant. Many films of the period deserve the same kind of critical attention usually reserved for the New Wave, and indeed represent similar anxieties and concerns as its finest examples. As Jennifer Fay has shown, the semi-pornographic and immensely successful *Schoolgirl Report* films of the 1970s carry the same, if not more pressing, issues of guilt, repression, and reconstruction of personal history that many of the New Wave films are said to be foregrounding.[6] The neglect is remarkable when it concerns postwar horror cinema. With the exception of Werner Herzog's *Nosferatu, Phantom der Nacht* (1978), a homage to the original more than a horror film, German horror movies hardly ever receive critical attention, neither by academics nor by writers.[7] For instance, in essays about German and Austrian horror respectively, Hantke and Jürgen Felix & Marcus Stieglegger regret the lack of systematic attention that critics pay to the relation between horror movies and local cultures.[8] They observe how this lack forces them to address an "American" point of view when discussing horror. This is most poignantly exemplified by their assertions, made independently from each other, that discussions of serial killer movies do not really need the elaborate affiliation with an American legacy and heritage (Ed Gein, Jeffrey Dahmer, etc.), because they can just as well be directly linked to local culture and history. There are exceptions, of course, and journals like *Kinoeye*, *Splatting Image* and *Testcard* testify to a very recent increase in attempts to take a cultural studies approach to German horror—a hopeful development this essay hopes to join and strengthen.[9]

The Reception of *Der Fan*

Let us pick up the gauntlet then. How does *Der Fan* associate with the local culture of its time? In the case of *Der Fan*, the cultural link contains two main components: the controversy it generated, and the connection with the Neue Deutsche Welle. Both components are, of course, tied to each other. Let us have a look at the controversy first.

Der Fan premiered on the 4th of June 1982, amidst wide controversy.[10] Nude publicity pictures of Nosbusch preceded the general release, and she and her manager took legal action, trying to prevent the film from being shown. When interviewed she claimed that this was not because nude pictures of her were available; after all, she had already done a nude scene in *Nach Mitternacht* (Gremm, 1981). She insisted that she liked the story because it was so close to her personal experiences as a presenter of a pop music television show. Rather, they sued because the producers had not kept their promise to refrain from over-publicizing the shock-effects of the films. They took particular offence to Schmidt going on record about the sex/killing scenes, detailing them, and suggesting that they were shot "as in a furious dream" so that they acquired "almost antique dimensions" as in Greek tragedy (240).[11] Unsurprisingly, when Nosbusch and her manager sued the distributors and producers, the subsequent press attention fuelled the controversy even more.

Beyond the court case, however, the overall impression of the reception of *Der Fan* is characterized by absences. There was a general disdain for the film, and, as could be expected, the film's explicit imagery features prominently as reason for this disdain. The mutilations, the cannibalism, and especially the explicit ways in which it was being shown led reviewers to condemn the film; out of thirty-five reviews, only five gave it some credit. And yet, the scenes which were meant to be so controversial invoked nowhere near the moral outrage one would expect. At its most moderate, they led to a bland aesthetic dislike: in *Die Zeit*, Hans-Christoph Blumenberg called the slow start of the film "fürchterlich" (dreadful) and the slasher scenes "hardly convincing"; and in the *Fischer Film Almanak 83* the film was seen as being "without psychological depth, but with screenwriting shortcomings and bizarre details."[12] This was the position taken by most film-specific magazines. At its fiercest, it involved the so-called Regenbogenpresse, the German equivalent of tabloids, calling the film straightforward rubbish, exhibitionistic, and unacceptable. In the teen magazine *Bravo*, one of the publications that had pictured Nosbusch topless, and one which usually took a fairly liberal stand towards nudity (they had a weekly "confessions" section which carried a full page picture of a nude girl), the film was described simply as "stupid." In most cases, however, reviewers did not see themselves as creating controversy: by attacking the film by way of the "Nosbusch vs. the producers" scandal, they took a seemingly descriptive approach, as if they only observed a developing scandal. But, as the interview with Nosbusch in *Blitz-Journal* shows, much of the longer-term controversy was the result of a consistent appropriation of the initial dispute to either push through a conservative agenda, which was definitely the case for tabloids like the *Bildzeitung*, or, more likely, cunningly to cash in on it by publishing the risky photographs, and thus, indirectly, publicizing the film.[13] An efficient technique in this latter case was the use of irony; the fact that Schmidt himself was a former film critic who used to accost filmmakers about their craft is a dead giveaway in this context.

In itself this is nothing new; the German press is not much different from that of other countries in this respect. But it also meant that there was really no moral component to the outrage after all. Rather, there was some kind of bemusement about a cultural development in which front page scandals and cinematic nudity seemed to go hand in hand (as asserted by Felis Umbruch in *Film-faust*). This acknowledgement would have been well suited to considerations of *Der Fan* as horror, and it would have enabled an explanation of the film's politics, beyond the scandal. Interestingly enough, however, and contrary to the film's obvious alignment with characteristic features of horror cinema, many reviews (*Die Zeit, Filmfaust, Kino*) refuse to call *Der Fan* a horror film. If nothing else, this reluctance shows German reviewers' prudence towards the term. But it also means that they do not manage to fit the film into a genre framework. It demonstrates, once again, how low on the cultural radar horror was at the time. It also means that the equally obvious cultural connection a horror framing would have enabled—such as seeing how the film comments on pop-culture excesses, how it uses the post-sex (and post-rejection) violence to critique gender inequalities—was absent.

Der Fan and the Neue Deutsche Welle

But there is more that is absent than just a discussion of horror's cultural relevance. *Der Fan*'s equally obvious connection to the Neue Deutsche Welle and its attempts to portray and address contemporary youth culture also goes, to a large extent, unmentioned—a most surprising lack of recognition of the film's public status. *Der Fan* abounds with references to 1980s pop music, celebrity culture, and art styles. It consciously revisits earlier forms of popular culture to evoke a sense of rooting, of historical awareness, retrofitting it with a critical attitude. What makes *Der Fan* particularly interesting is its clever (some say cynical) affiliation with a distinctive trend in German popular culture, namely that of the Neue Deutsche Welle, a relatively close-knit and networked youth and pop culture development that put German pop music on an internationally acclaimed level. At least in Europe the Neue Deutsche Welle received much popularity, particularly for its success in altering the perception of German pop culture as outmoded (visible, e.g., in the legacy of the first generation of German rock music, affectionately nicknamed "Krautrock"). This affiliation makes *Der Fan* more than a symptomatic *cause célèbre* of horror: by connecting horror with popular culture, the film can lay claim to a more obvious cultural relevance. Yet no critic seems to pick up on this.

Partly this can be the result of the critics' refusal to deal with the horror genre. Much of the connection between horror and pop culture is established by the fact that the extensive scenes of sex, nudity, violence, and mutilation in the film are performed by two well-known youth pop culture icons, who are, after all, supposed to be role models for teenagers. Désirée Nosbusch, who plays the part of Simone, was a presenter of hugely popular television shows like *Music Box* and *Hits von der Schulbank*, and looked like the embodiment of the bourgeois ideal of teen culture: fresh, keen, smart, fashionable, cheerful, and unspoiled. Bodo Staiger, who plays the part of the pop singer R., was the lead singer of the highly successful electro-pop band Rheingold, a poster boy whose picture could be found on the walls of many teenage girls' bedrooms. Both were seen as exponents of a new confidence of German youth culture, and their recurrent appearances on the cover of youth magazines such as *Bravo* made them instantly recognizable. To place these two at the center of a sexually explicit horror narrative was to insist on a link between pop culture and horror themes. From a press seemingly bent on ignoring horror, a refusal of such an acknowledgement might be expected.[14]

Beyond the personalities of Nosbusch and Staiger, *Der Fan* also affiliates itself, almost by default, with the politics of the New Wave. By and large, these politics are derived from 1970s activism in the German left-wing movement, though much of their anarchistic radicalism had been replaced, by the time the film was made, with a turn towards trash aesthetics (an admiration for exploitation culture, including horror) and commercial pop culture (not just an admiration for shrewd business sense, but also a desire to carve out alternative economic patterns within the pop culture industry). An example of this is the insistence on being active in more than one expressive medium or the demand for artistic and commodity/exhibition control. In this latter sense the Neue Deutsche Welle often comes across like an electronics-obsessed branch of the punk movement.

The combination of politics and pop was not always comfortable, however. Symptomatically, Staiger's band Rheingold claimed to have no political viewpoints, yet explicitly used Third Reich references in much of its public performance. It serves to show how, for the Neue Deutsche Welle, the issue of activism is less a moral one, and more one of meaningful (maybe cynically postmodern) posture, which allows for creative combinations rather than politically meaningful exclusions. While perhaps not an aesthetic achievement of the highest order, *Der Fan* also manages to combine commercial elements with this contestation and activist culture. But this appropriation of countercultural interests does not mean that the film is any less useful as a cultural critique. As the reviews indicate, much of the film's notoriety is related exactly to its refusal to take a moral stand.

Der Fan embodies four major themes of the Neue Deutsche Welle: a critique of what is perceived as an American domination of popular culture; a homage to expressionism; an acute obsession with gender issues, combining, like so much horror cinema, feminist sensitivities and an exploitative take on portraying women and sex; and, finally, an interest in the representation of misfits and misogyny. Throughout these themes, one senses the ghostly presence of Nazi Germany, in image and/or sound.

Before showing how *Der Fan* uses these themes and offering an explanation of why the German press might have wanted to ignore its connection to popular culture, it is essential to elaborate on the themes of the Neue Deutsche Welle. A key ingredient was its desire to break away from a perceived Anglo-American domination of popular music, exemplified by bands like Boney M and Baccara, and American politics, in favour of a return to local roots. Since the U.S. was often seen as creating a cold-war rhetoric that prevented local culture to develop, bands and performers of the Neue Deutsche Welle were, confidently or even defiantly, writing and singing in German. Bands like Slime, who titled one of their albums *Yankees raus* (1982), or even Nena, with *99 Luftballons*, combine an anti-war stance with anti-U.S. politics. Bands like the Spider Murphy Gang and DAF (Deutsch-Amerikanische Freundschaft) are other examples of this concern. It is important to note that the return to local roots is not an uncritical one, nor is it always free of moralizing. A tone of self-criticism prevails, especially in looking at history. BAP, from Cologne, extended the language issue to singing in the local dialect. The fact that their greatest hit "Kristallnach" critiques Nazi Germany, is not unusual. The use of expressionist aesthetics, and its moral ambiguity, is essential in this tone. Both the purist expressionism of Herzog's films, and the modern one of Kraftwerk, Der Plan, Palais Schaumburg, Wirtschaftswunder (a reference again to the American domination), or Einstürzende Neubauten are among its exponents. Rheingold combines the two: its name evokes Wagnerian allures, yet its music brings Kraftwerk to mind. Film is always a close ally in these efforts: Herzog worked consistently with Popol Vuh, Rheingold provided the soundtrack for *Der Fan*, Nena contributed to the commercial *Gib Gas Ich Will Spass* (Büld, 1983), and so-called collectives like Unter Viele Andere, Notorische Reflexe and Der Kulturelle Einfluss tried to combine film and music. Another example is *Die Letzte Rache* (1983), a film by Rainer Kirberg, commissioned by state broadcaster ZDF, which features a pastiche of expressionist films from the 1920s. The feminist element of the Neue Deutsche Welle is a direct heritage from the 1970s, and is perhaps best exemplified in the person of Nina Hagen, Germany's most prominent female punk singer. As I will show below in relation to *Der Fan*, it permeates many of the narratives of the Neue Deutsche Welle. As these cultural critiques merge expressionist elements with feminist sensitivities, horror is never far away.

The theme of misfits and misogyny brings us even closer to contemporary horror. Much of the self-presentation of the Neue Deutsche Welle bands relies on anti-hero worship and immobile stage performances. In *Der Fan*, we witness R.'s performance during the television show, which, in its use of mannequins and models, clearly references both Holocaust imagery and Kraftwerk-inspired science fiction (even Lang's *Metropolis* is given a passing nod). *Der Fan* is not alone in this. We find a similar fascination in a contemporary horror film, *Angst* (Kargl, 1983).[15] Both films share an austere realism (admittedly in *Der Fan*, one that is much more injected with expressionist references), a cold and detached look at gruesome deeds, and one which Hantke, in an essay about the "German experience" of the serial killer, equates with a decidedly German approach to murder and horror (Hantke 56–57). Simone might not be serial killer, as she only kills one person, but the way she goes about the murder she commits, and her psychological profile, seem very close to that of the serial killer. Maybe too close?

All in all, *Der Fan* clearly positions itself at the center of the Neue Deutsche Welle. Consequently, the denial of this fact in the film's official reception, as if critics were trying to ignore the entire trend or distance themselves from it, is all the more significant.

Gendered Horror: Sex and Death—Nudity and Orality

As most of the reception tells us, *Der Fan*'s narrative and style seem to boil down, if one can use that word here, to those twenty-five minutes in which Simone and R. meet, have sex, and she then kills, mutilates, and eats him. Since there are only two people in these scenes, a male pop star and a teenage female fan, it is impossible not to address this section in terms of gender representation. This is, as I had pointed out above, an element very close to the heart of the Neue Deutsche Welle. It is this section that should have outraged critics. But it didn't. Although critics did single out these scenes in their comments, they did so by addressing the court case controversy, the row—genuine or staged—over the nude pictures, or the perceived aesthetical clumsiness. No one discussed the cultural significance of these scenes directly. Why? I would like to propose that they shied away from discussing it because doing so would have necessitated cultural framing. This is exactly what reviewers wanted to avoid because to allow such a framing would have turned their reports and reviews into comments on society.[16]

What then is there in that section of the film that might be culturally framed? First and foremost, the section is all about the gendered association between sex and violence, as well as the representation of Germany's cultural attitudes towards it. As Fay has pointed out, representations of the sexual perversion of casual innocence are a recurrent trope in postwar German cinema, especially in exploitation movies. They suggest a close connection between sex and horror, and thus point to possible dangers lurking behind the facade of society. In arguing how even a liberal view towards sex and nudity might get tangled up in this complex of themes, Fay quotes Dagmar Herzog: "the release of the libido might be, not just liberatory, but rather dangerous, and [...] the pursuit of pleasure might lead, not to social justice, but to evil" (398). This gradual move towards evil, away from normality into a world of outcasts and misfits, is paralleled by Simone's journey, both mentally and physically. This is apparent even before the section begins. On her way to Munich Simone almost gets raped, and once arrived she witnesses drug trafficking. She also watches, with what could be seen as more than just casual interest, two girls take a nude dip in the city park pond. This latter moment is a curious pre-empting of the emphasis on nudity later on; it happens at a key moment, exactly thirty minutes into the film, when Simone has more or less settled in Munich. There is a glimpse of hope to be seen in her posture; she seems less desperate, and the glorious sunlight that envelops the two bathing girls emphasizes that. By all standards, this is a weird scene: the girls take their clothes off and take a quick dip in the pond, after which they stare into the camera, as if acknowledging the viewer's/Simone's gaze. It is also a bit clumsy; the dip itself is shot using a telephoto lens, and the way we see one girl almost sneakily get into the water, quickly run a few meters, and then rapidly get out again gives the impression of candid footage—as if the shooting was semi-illegal, which would link the scene to the *Schoolgirl Report* films Fay discusses.

The move also indicates Simone's ambiguous relationship towards sexuality. Like the school girls and teenagers in the *Schoolgirl Report* films, Simone is not really innocent. Her entire presence is permeated with sensuality. Her brooding stares convey that she is not just a girl admiring her idol; her passion extends beyond boundaries of admiration into obsessive appropriation and attempts to dominate R.. She is not interested in R. as a subject, only as an object, as a toy of some kind. At the same time, she herself is a toy to R. When he picks her up after the show he treats her like a groupie, casually letting her into her dressing room, ignoring her while talking to managers and assistants, and swiftly ushering her into his fire-engine-red Rolls Royce. Their intentions are clear: they want to dominate each other, and their relationship will be the clash of two strong-willed people rather than a fusion of minds or personalities.

As said before, at the core of *Der Fan*'s notoriety is a twenty-minute section, spanning the first love scene between Simone and R. and her return home. These twenty minutes contain the major horrific acts most reviewers take as their main points of contention: the murder of R. by Simone, and her subsequent mutilation of his body. The section breaks down into two main acts. In the first, shorter act, Simone and R. have sex, after which he refuses any further dealings with her, clearly treating the sex as a one-off act and resisting her attempts to cuddle and embrace him. In the second act, Simone cuts up R.'s body, then freezes parts of it, eats it—or at least part of it, since it remains unclear just how much of his body she consumes—and leaves the house to go back home.

In a sense, both acts in this section are pre-signalled in the preceding scene. When left alone for a second in the bathroom Simone presses her face against her own reflection in the mirror and kisses and licks it with fierce intensity. This not only shows Simone's lust for R., emphasized by her state of excitement. It also reminds us of how her idolatry is not really about R. but about herself and her own search for identity. In a similar gesture, earlier on, Simone remains in the car when R. stops at a gas station. Again alone for a few moments, Simone stares blankly ahead, then opens her mouth, as if to check her lipstick. As she opens her mouth wider and wider, the camera suddenly moves in, and Simone's mouth swallows the camera. This may strike some viewers as a quasi-perfect simulation of James Williamson's *The Big Swallow* (1901), one of the first films to demonstrate how an exaggerated sense for reality (the close-up of the mouth) leads to distortion, not just graphically (the mouth becomes grotesquely big) but also in narrative impact (its engulfing of the frame is unsettling, introducing a first sense of the horror to come). We are warned: Simone's desire can get out of hand.

Two tropes stand out here: nudity and orality. During both of the final acts of the film the characters are prominently naked. Their bodies are on full display, with only the smallest possible shades covering the closest shots of the genital areas, and with numerous close-ups of torsos, heads, faces, shoulders, necks, and limbs. There are hardly any background props, and stark lighting prevails throughout the sequence. While there is some soft lighting in the sex scene, the mutilation of the body takes place in the kitchen under harsh pseudo-neon lights, leaving nothing to the imagination. It is here that the influence of modern expressionism on the Neue Deutsche Welle becomes most strikingly visible—the whole scene breathes harshness. As if to emphasize this, the few props we do get to see—the tools Simone uses to cut up R.'s body—are state-of-the-art modern consumer objects: a freezer, a modern saucepan, and an electric kitchen knife, which insinuate a witty equation of meat and flesh.

Nudity is not a new trope in German cinema; in fact it comes loaded with the particular weight of the Freikörperkultur and its appropriation by the Nazis. Back then, it represented the freedom of the body from social constraints, in direct touch with nature, most prominently celebrated in the opening of Leni Riefenstahl's *Olympia* (1938). Based on this historical association, nudity, and especially full-out nudity without direct sexual activity, as during the scene in which Simone cuts up R., might appear as a historically and ideologically suspicious trope. While this did not prevent Germany from running one of the most active erotic and porn film industries in Europe, it explains why Elsaesser found it easy to denounce the exploitation industry, and German reviewers are carefully avoiding the topic in their discussions of *Der Fan*.

Still, the nudity we find in *Der Fan* is of a somewhat different order. It does not show a "liberated, nude body, free of the trappings of capitalist consumer culture [which] could function as a signifier of [...] victimization and guilt" (Fay 40). Rather, we see nudity here when the characters are least free, first in the almost compulsory and compelling execution of desires that have regulated the exchanges between Simone and R., then as signs of the one character's death and the other's descent into madness. We can use two other instances of nudity in the film as contrasting examples to press this point: the concern with nudity in *Der Fan* is less about the liberated nudity of the two girls in the park and much more about the constrained nudity of the mannequins at the television show performance. This also happens to be the scene in which, as if to complicate matters even further, *Der Fan* literally celebrates its connection with the Neue Deutsche Welle, and the one in which R. wears a distinctly Gestapo-inspired uniform. After having first viewed the liberated two nude girls in the park, the television performance nudity, with its unnatural plastic eroticism, evokes references of the Holocaust. The few real live models among the mannequins emphasize that even more. Chillingly, the way the performance is shot (as a video clip, again a reference to the Neue Deutsche Welle), makes it, after a while, almost impossible to distinguish between the mannequins and the models, the fake and the real, the live and the dead. Given these loaded scenes earlier on, it should be no surprise that violence follows sex, and extreme cruelty follows nudity. No wonder reviewers steered clear of this affiliation. It silences them.

The trope of orality is firmly connected to that of nudity. Both form a schizophrenic double, feebly attempting to comment on each other, offering a legitimization that turns out to be pathological. The most obvious way in which orality is used occurs during the act of cannibalism. Simone eats part of R.'s body, tasting him (not for nutritional reasons, it's safe to assume) while disposing of him. By orally internalizing his body she copes with the hurt he caused. Beyond this specific metaphor, it is Simone's mouth which is at the center of all oral symbolism. She hardly speaks during the entire film. Even the voice-over is surprisingly downbeat, consisting more of short utterances (matter-of-fact statements like "if R. doesn't answer in seven days, I will act") instead of explanations. When she first meets R. outside the television studios, she is unable to speak, even when R. walks up to her and asks her name. She opens her mouth, and her lips move, but no sound comes out. It is interesting to observe, in this respect, how earlier in the scene, when R. is signing autographs for his fans, we see Simone watching, and suddenly a close-up of her lips and half-open mouth is inserted. Unwarranted by any narrative necessity, the insert shot only stresses how Simone stands in awe of her idol. At the same time it uncannily announces the focus on orality later in the film.

Instead of text or dialogue, it is the music that seems to be doing all the talking. Throughout the film Simone wears headphones. If she does not have them on to listen to music—R.'s music, we presume—then they serve as a prominent prop, the black earpieces outlined against her white shirt. In line with common concerns at the time about how the Walkman disables proper conversation and thus curtails proper meaning, Simone's earphones do indeed give her an excuse not to talk, and hence not to engage in the world. They suggest that there is no real explanation, only tunes floating in and out of consciousness, seemingly without ideological and moral weight. Again, this brings the Neue Welle into the picture, its music in Simone's ears but also to ours, offering the non-moralistic commentary of the time, perfectly in tune with its non-moralistic politics.

The ending of the film invites the same interpretation: when she arrives home, she only says one thing: "Tomorrow I am going back to school." It is the first line of dialogue she speaks in more than twenty-five minutes. When the television news announces that the famous pop star R. has gone missing, her voice-over adds: "I know where you are. Don't fear. I won't betray you. For no money in the world. I have not yet had my period. It is four weeks overdue. I will bring you to the world. We will be happy. I know you love me. And I love you too." She repeats the last two sentences in writing in her diary, while the electronic soundtrack rises in volume. Completed by the fade to a bright red screen upon which black letters appear, the scene serves as a final reminder of how Simone, while verbally docile in accepting her place in society as a school girl, carries on a deeper level a dark secret which makes her both victim and perpetrator, as if no one can really be innocent in this context. With no possibility to move away, she becomes a fitting demonstration of Michel Foucault's observation that the disciplining of sexuality is always linked to guilt.[17] In this case, the link is established not just through Simone's personal guilt, but through associations with and references to the legacy of guilt in a larger culture that endlessly regenerates itself within teen and popular culture.

Drawing Conclusions

It would be a stretch to say that this endless re-representation of a dark, secret past—explicitly and implicitly through horror and references to the Neue Deutsche Welle, and crystallized in the tropes of nudity and orality—is representative of all German cinema of the early 1980s, even within the horror genre. But I do think the sensitivities this imagery provokes are not limited to *Der Fan*. Its closeness to the Neue Deutsche Welle implies that the entire movement addresses that very secret; that, regardless of some of its optimism, the Neue Deutsche Welle is, in fact, permeated by this secret. Since the early 1980s were indeed an era in which music, film, television and other popular culture outlets—and even high-culture ones like the Nouveau Fauve trend in painting (Anselm Kiefer, Georg Baselitz, A.R. Penck)—seemed to be striving towards integration with each other, it makes perfect sense to insist that German horror films of the time should be seen in the context of the wider popular culture, even when they are clumsy in assembling cultural references into a larger pattern. In a time without explanations, at the beginning of the end of the cold war, *Der Fan* does not offer any explanations either. This is either what the press seems to miss altogether, or what reviewers understand all too well when they discuss *Der Fan* in contexts that are only tenuously related to the film itself. In claiming neutrality when it comes to controversy, reviewers open the door to accusations of complicity by refusing to offer explanations. They do not even offer an acknowledgement of uncertainty. Perhaps this is not a big deal to them, but, having experienced this uncertainty myself, I cannot help seeing them as partly responsible for the kind of ambiguity they like to rage against.

Notes

1. I owe a very big thank you to my dear friend and colleague Bert Mosselmans, of the Roosevelt Academy in Middelburg, The Netherlands. He grew up in Germany, I came from the east of Belgium, near the border. It was his insistence on reminiscing about German music from our teenage years that prompted this research. When he subsequently sent me the Swiss DVD version of the film, I could not resist writing about it. This research is based upon all available documents on *Der Fan* in the Royal Film Archive in Brussels, whose staff I thank once again for their kind assistance, and on searches in the British Film Institute, in the Margaret Herrick Library of the Academy of Motion Picture Arts and Sciences in Los Angeles, and through Imdb Pro. After the re-

lease of the Swiss DVD edition in 2004 by the German company Marketing Films, *Der Fan* has also become available through an English distributor, Oracle Home Entertainment. Many of the DVD reviews refer to the film's English-language release title, *Trance*.

2. See Elsaesser, 2000: 3–5.

3. See Williams, 1984/1994.

4. See Wood, 1979: 1–9; Kristeva, 1980.

5. See Fay, 2004: 39–52; Hantke, 2005: 56–79.

6. See Fay, 2004: 39–52.

7. See Chaffin-Quiray, 2002.

8. Hantke, 2005: 56–79; Felix & Stiglegger, 2003: 175–182.

9. See for instance Linnie Blake on Buttgereit, or David Del Vale on *Der Nackte und der Satan* (*The Head*, Trivas, 1959) ; Blake, 2003; Del Vale, 2002.

10. Ominously, this happens to be the month in which Romy Schneider, Curd Jürgens, and Rainer Werner Fassbinder, three icons of pre-1980s German cinema, died. It is also the month in which *Das Boot* (Petersen), *Fitzcarraldo* (Herzog), *Lola* (Fassbinder), *Die bleierne Zeit* (von Trotta) and *Der Zauberberg* (Geissendörfer) received the *Bundespreis* for film. In short, it was a time when German cinema seemed to be at the top of the cultural agenda.

11. See Schmidt, 1982: 240.

12. See Blumenberg, 1982; Schobert et al, 1983. No page numbers are available.

13. See Lehman, 1982. No page numbers are available.

14. The Neue Deutsche Welle is not to be confused with New German cinema of the 1970s. Granted, the films of Rainer Werner Fassbinder, Wim Wenders, Werner Herzog, Volker Schlöndorff, and Margarete von Trotta are of relevance to the movement. They share many of the same attitudes towards politics, both local and international, and they have thematic, stylistic and historical legacies in common. The New German Cinema even functioned as a noteworthy source of inspiration for the Neue Deutsche Welle, or at least as a touchstone. But neither movement is identical with the other. One of the main differences is that, at least in public perception and popularity, New German Cinema was more of a high culture phenomenon, whereas the Neue Deutsche Welle includes a greater variety of media and has a firm base in popular or even low culture. Often its intentions are clearly commercial, which occasionally make it downright exploitative. Its broadness has extended debates about high versus low culture to disagreements about taste and aesthetics *within* the larger trend, leading to a differentiation between more avant-garde and more commercial exponents. I will pass on those distinctions and treat the Neue Deutsche Welle much in the same vein as most overviews of German pop culture from the early 1980s tend to do.

15. For a discussion of this film, see Felix & Stiglegger, 2003: 175–182.

16. For a similar argument with regard to another horror film, see Mathijs, 2004.

17. See Foucault, 1990.

Works Cited

Anonymous. *Ich Will Spass. Die Neue Deutsche Welle.* November 25, 2005 www. ichwillspass.de/index2.htm.

Blake, Linnie. "Sex, Selfhood and the corpse of the German Past." *Kinoeye*, 3.6. May 26,

2003. Accessed on November 25, 2005. www.kinoeye.org/03/06/blake06.php.
Blumenberg, Hans-Christoph. "Im Kino: Annehmbar." *Die Zeit.* June 11, 1982. n.p.
Chaffin-Quiray, Garrett. "An adaptation with Fangs." *Kinoeye,* 2.20. December 16, 2002. Accessed on November 25, 2005. www.kinoeye.org/02/20/chaffinquira20.php.
Del Vale, David. "The Thousand Ties to Dr. Ood." *Kinoeye,* 2.6. March 18, 2002. www. kinoeye.org/02/06/delvalle06.php. 25 Nov. 2005.
Elsaesser, Thomas. *New German Cinema: A History.* NJ: Rutgers University Press, 1989.
———. *Weimar Cinema and After. Germany's Historical Imaginary.* London: Routledge, 2000.
Fay, Jennifer. "The Schoolgirl Reports and the Guilty Pleasure of History." In Ernest Mathijs & Xavier Mendik (eds). *Alternative Europe: Eurotrash and Exploitation Cinema since 1945.* London: Wallflower Press, 2004. 39–52.
Felix, Jürgen and Marcus Stiglegger. "Austrian Psycho Killers & Home Invaders: The Horror-Thrillers *Angst & Funny Games.*" Ed. Steven Jay Schneider. *Fear Without Frontiers: Horror Cinema Across the Globe.* Godalming: FAB Press, 2003. 175–82.
Foucault, Michel. *The History of Sexuality; Vol 1.* New York: Vintage Books, 1990.
Hake, Sabine. *German National Cinema.* London: Routledge, 2002.
Hantke, Steffen. "The Dialogue with American Popular Culture in Two German Films about the Serial Killer." Eds. Steven Jay Schneider and Tony Williams. *Horror International.* Detroit: Wayne State University Press, 2005. 56–79.
Herzog, Dagmar. "Pleasure, Sex, and Politics belong Together: Post Holocaust Memory and the Sexual Revolution in West-Germany." *Critical Inquiry,* 24 (1998): 398.
Kristeva, Julia. *The Powers of Horror.* New York: Columbia University Press, 1980.
Lehmann, Henry. "Interview with Desiree Nosbusch." *Blitz Journal.* May 1982. Reproduced as extra on DVD *Der Fan.*
Mathijs, Ernest. "Nobody Is Innocent: Cinema and Sexuality in Contemporary Belgian Culture." *Social Semiotics* 14.1 (2004): 85–101.
Pflaum, Hans-Günther. "Midlife Crisis 1981/82." Ed. Hans-Günther Pflaum. *Jahrbuch Film 82/83.* München: Carl Hanser Verlag, 1980. 39.
Schmidt, Eckhart. "Der Fan." Ed. Hans-Günther Pflaum. *Jahrbuch Film 82/83.* München: Carl Hanser Verlag, 1982. 240.
Schobert, Walter, Rüdiger Koschnitzki, Wilhelm Roth, Ronny Loewry and Jürgen Berger. *Fischer Film Almanak 1983.* Frankfurt/M: Fischer, 1982.
Silberman, M. *German Cinema: Texts in Context.* Detroit: Wayne State University Press, 1995.
Williams, Linda. "When the Woman Looks." *Re-vision: Essays in Feminist Film Criticism.* Eds. Mary-An Doane, Patricia Mellencamp, and Linda Williams. Los Angeles: American Film Institute, 1984. 83–99.
———. "Learning to Scream." *Sight and Sound* 4.12 (1994): 14–17.
Wood, Robin. "Return of the Repressed." Eds. Andrew Britton, Robin Wood, Richard Lippe & Tony Williams. *The American Nightmare; Essays on the Horror Film.* Toronto, Festival of Festivals, 1979.

"Not to scream *before* or *about*, but to scream *at* death": Haneke's Horrible *Funny Games*

Eugenie Brinkema

Michael Haneke ist nicht hier einheimisch. Twice over, actually. For the great Austrian film director would appear to be as ill-fitting, as *nicht hier zuhause*, in an anthology about German cinema since 1945 as in an anthology about horror films, a category under which none of his works would traditionally be classified. And yet, *hier ist er.* The not-quite-German, not-quite-horror director is both familiar and strange to this anthology, *unheimlich* to its very workings—a positional parallel to the concerns imbricated in his films from the past fifteen years. Less a matter of life imitating art, this is life unimitating, unmatching, unlinking art. This is precisely where we begin—outside the text; stranger to Germany, stranger to horror cinema, stranger to the anthology. Rest assured, the *heimlich*-strange always becomes the *heimlich*-familiar, but, of course, at a certain cost.

When Freud wrote of "the narcissism of minor differences" in *Das Unbehagen in der Kultur (Civilization and Its Discontents)*—"a convenient and relatively harmless satisfaction of the inclination to aggression, by means of which cohesion between the members of a community is made easier"—he was referring to the aggression levied by nations with adjoining territories against each other in the desperate attempt to locate difference where, precisely, there is little to begin with: North and South Germany he mentions, and, of course, we might now say Austria and Germany (Freud, *Discontent* 27). But genre in the field of film studies is no less national in structure than nations proper, bound together in shared difference from others. Genre: kind, in like kind; etymologically sutured to gender, that primary system of differences, that primary system of aggressivity. Horror films no less virulently bind their boundaries, defend their borders, than do nations, ever more threatened by the seemingly tiny differences, the ineluctable flow of citizens from elsewhere into the *Heimat*. Horror is not only about the home (that duel *heimlich*, which means both "familiar" and "threatening"), but as a genre, it also *is* a home, vulnerable to invasion, penetration and violation from without. Freud's prescient pronouncement about the violent lengths to which nations will go to distinguish themselves from their proximate and similar brethren is more relevant than ever in the era of globalization. Likewise, never has genre been under greater threats of dissolution than in the anarchic free-for-all of the postmodern. Difference for horror is now dependent on ironic distance, the parodic dimensions of the genre replacing fully invested performances of horror in the desperate attempt to hold on to nothing more than one's own final gasps at distinction. Thus, we find ourselves in the early twenty-first century at a moment when one can speak of the difference between Austria and Germany, but find great difficulty locating precisely what or where that difference is—it is no longer, for example, dependent on any materially real boundaries. One may speak now of horror as bounded, finite, different from, but locate oneself in the same epistemological dusk as above, desperate to distinguish, able to do little more than point mutely and stare with hollowed-out critical eyes. Into this void, I emplace Michael Haneke—not quite, a little off, close but not identical to the very categories bounded by this anthology, that the visitor might reveal a hidden truth about the very home into which he bursts, intentions unknown.

Perhaps it is not so surprising to begin to rethink horror from the site of the home, given not only the centrality of the home (its recesses and secrets; hidden terror and exposed perversion) to the genre as traditionally formulated, but also, of course, the truest horror implied by the uses of the term *Heimat* in the twentieth century. *Heimat* was itself a genre in 1930s Germany, designed principally to provoke patriotism and its obverse, virulent racism against *die heimatlose Juden*. But *Heimat*, also, in a way, underlies all generic attempts to find and defend a formal and historical homeland. Returning to Freud—it seems as if the insistent return of horror to psychoanalysis makes all horror, at heart, Austrian—in his 1919 essay "Das Unheimliche" ("The Uncanny"), we find that Freud begins his reading of E.T.A. Hoffmann's "The Sandman" by criticizing aesthetic studies "which in general prefer to concern themselves with what is beautiful, attractive, and sublime—that is, with feelings of a positive nature," and it is this turn to negative affect that has made this essay so potently useful for studies of horror in literature and cinema (Freud 194). Freud locates in the etymology of *heimlich* two entirely compatible meanings which nonetheless stand in opposition to each other. The term suggests home, hearth, family, the familiar, the pleasant and comforting; it also suggests that which is concealed, hidden, strange, malicious, gruesome. The word is not emptied of signification through this turn of self-negation. Rather, it becomes full, excessive, paradoxical—a locus of surplus precisely where one would expect a semantic canceling out. Freud spends much of this famous essay in a structure of return, repeating himself, creating nuances, insisting on difference where none appears to be (*minor* differences, no less), while still never fixing on one thing that we might point to and call "the uncanny." It is precisely the place of that nothing, that absence of knowledge and affect that comes to characterize, through the performance of the essay, the terms it un-describes.

Freud identifies key features of the uncanny, talking around rather than naming precisely this affect—the central trait of the term itself is a dimension of non-reciprocity, a relation "incapable of inversion" (Freud 195). During the etymological digression on the correspondence of *heimlich* (homelike) and *unheimlich* (unhomelike), Freud notes that "we are tempted to conclude that what is "uncanny" is frightening precisely because it is *not* known and familiar. Naturally, not everything that is new and unfamiliar is frightening however" (195). In other words, if the uncanny is frightening because it is not known, this does not imply that all unknown things are uncanny. Yet Freud ultimately sees a conversion of meaning—*heimlich* comes to mean *unheimlich*: "among its different shades of meaning the word 'heimlich' exhibits one which is identical with its opposite, 'unheimlich.' What is *heimlich* thus comes to be *unheimlich*" (199). The temporality of the uncanny, its historical gesture, is one of return, the non-reciprocity of the intrusive past into the present. The uncanny comes to name "nothing new or alien, but something which is familiar and long-established in the mind and which has become alienated from it only through the process of repression" (217). I begin here not, actually, to use this essay or its workings to talk about horror or even Haneke—indeed, much, perhaps too much, has already been written in horror studies on the uncanny "return of the repressed"—but for one reason, one reason in two letters.

When Freud makes his case for the *unheimlich* naming what was once familiar (the mother's body, in his analysis), he writes "the prefix '*un*' ['un-'] is the token of repression" (Freud 222). What Freud takes from his language, I take to mine. In proper uncanny form, Freud's familiar "un-" will become unfamiliar in this essay and yet insistently return to defend its boundariless boundaries. For what Michael Haneke's films do, I contend, is problematize the very language by which we describe horror films, German or otherwise, though certainly the question of description and definition is never far from the question of a national cinema. This problematization takes the form not of the prefix *un*- but otherwise, in its linguistic double, *Doppelgänger* twin and stranger to itself, in a displaced suffix. For Haneke makes, not horror films—as I have said, he is not *heimisch* in this collection—but *horrible* films, and it is the suffix *-ible* that marks the workings of his particular brand of cinema as much as Freud's token of repression characterizes Hoffmann's stories. That mark of repression indicates the temporality of return, repression always contracting for the future guarantee of its eruption. So too does Haneke's suffix indicate a temporality (though not of return, we will see) and a tension of presence/absence. Crucially, though, displaced into the afterthought of the word, it hides itself at the moment of its appearance, secreting away its pernicious workings—the making-strange of the very word it attaches to like a parasite, bloody and hungry for meaning.

This is not, I insist, I insist this is not a question about genre, but a problematization of that very taut family of films that must be read symptomatically as a primary working of the *horrible*. For if *un*- makes impossible an epistemic certainty about the term it precedes, *-ible* makes impossible a semantic certainty about the term it displaces, heralding its vampiric attachment at the very moment one safely thought the word had neared its articulated end. Writers on Haneke unanimously struggle against the bounded space of genre definition (see, for example, Christopher Sharrett's insistence, expressed in his interview with Haneke, that his films are works of "contemporary horror" because of their focus on the bourgeois family in dissolution), pointing to the absence of monsters (or the overpresence, thereof, in the threatening quotidian—rest assured, both observations retain a similar error at their core) or the relatively thwarted visibility of acts of violence in his works.[1] These defenses—and the more vocal they are, the more they do precisely this—effect little more than securing the entity "horror films" against intrusion by ways of imagining that very field otherwise. For in defining Haneke's films against, one simply secures the present opposite. The *horrible* is not the opposite of *horror*; their relation is not one of similarity, contiguity, opposition or even proximity. It is another relation altogether, and precisely in formulating it, one sees the dangerous workings of the terms' rubbing against each other, a frictional frisson that is, itself, *horrible*.

Haneke positions his films as enacting a troubled relationship to genre, characterizing, in separate interviews, but with identical language, his 1997 *Funny Games* as "a parody of the thriller genre" (Sharrett, Interview) and his 2001 *La Pianiste* (*The Piano Teacher*) as "a parody of a melodrama" (Foundas, Interview). He elaborated in the latter interview: "the genre film is, by definition, a lie. And a film is trying to be art, and therefore must try to deal with reality...If films are just business, then you can lie" (Foundas, Interview). The problem with genre, for him, resides in a problem with the cynical marketing of expectations as a palliative for an unthinking, uncritical audience. But the status of truth is at stake here as well, as his films are positioned as counterweights to the "lies" of genre. It is tempting to read in this doubled articulation of "parody" a carte blanche to the postmodern camp to locate in his films playful irony, the triumph of the simulacrum, and the dissolution of the category of the lie (correspondingly, of course, the breakdown of truth as well)—but this would be a great error. For his quibble seems not to be with the lie that genre sells (the lie of coherence) but the lie of genre as the locus of a privileged formal truth. We might lose control of this term very quickly—from genre to gender to like kind to race to species. But grasping it at the very moment it loosens its hold, we can insist that far from positioning his films within a genre (horror, melodrama, the thriller, the art film, new Austrian cinema, postwar German cinema, postmodern cinema), we would be wise to note how his films challenge the hegemony of the concept itself. This is not to propose an alternative schema—would that not identically lead us back to classification, to genre proper? Rather it is to insist that classification is itself suspect in relation to the field of truth that Haneke expounds. One final insistence: this is not to fall back yet again into the argument for Haneke as a postmodernist, as *parody* is as stable and fixed a term as any other, but rather as *something else*, something marked by the deferred temporality of the suffix that forever changes the word and world that came before.

Haneke, as a former student of philosophy, and native speaker of German, philologically privileged as it is with an overabundance of concepts, has named as one of the primary gestures of his films *Entwirklichung*, which might be translated as reality losing its realness.[2] Inextricably linked with this feature is what I term *Entgreuelung*—horror losing its horror-ness. That loss is what is re-found in the supplement *-ible*. Crucial to the movement of both terms, the *-ung*, is a process, a movement, a perpetual unbecoming and undoing. The suffix *-ible* is etymologically derived from the category of *-ble* suffixes, which form adjectives that bear the meaning "given to, tending to, likely to, fit to, able to" (OED 144). *Horrible* thus terms an ability, likeliness, or tendency of its root *horror*. The same text indicates that "adjs. in the *-bili, -ble*, were originally active (and neuter) as well as passive," and it is this twin identity as bringer about of horror and passive plane for the reception of the conditions for its existence that so troubles the agency of the horrible. The *horrible* implies a realization in a potential and future time and place, a condition for the possibility of horror. Its temporal logic is precisely the opposite of the retrograde repression/eruption of *heimlich*—the horrible is squarely placed in the temporality of what is likely, able, or fit to come; as opposed to the reemergence of what has formerly remained hidden (*unheimlich*), the horrible names the potential bringing into existence of what has formerly remained hypothetical and unrealized. The question of unstable epistemology on which the *unheimlich* so resolutely depends is rendered, here, a question of ontology, of the conditions for the very being (its *Dasein*) of horror.

Horror suspends, it delays its own abstract conditions as a noun—it holds its own meaning at bay. The *horrible*, saturated with the burdens of its suffix, its word-past and word-future, indicates not a repression but a realization; it brings into existence the very plenitude by which the horror genre insists on its own lack. But if horror delays and the horrible insists, what takes up the space of that temporal suspension? What structural gap in horror films is violently realized, closed and brought far too close, in horrible films? We will approach an answer obliquely, tracing the contours of the conditions for possibility so resolutely refused in the one case, so resolutely and cruelly rendered real in the other, through Haneke's cinema. In its overproximation to the horrible, we glimpse more correctly what must have gone missing from horror, so threatening in its newly formed realization. This thing that has gone missing is nothing less than the primacy of the cinematic image itself.

After many years directing numerous programs for television—not an uncommon beginning for Austrian film directors—Haneke staked his claim for an art-cinematic legacy with his 1989 *Der Siebente Kontinent* (*The Seventh Continent*), a ninety-minute exposition, rich in detail, that traces the gestures of an Austrian family as they destroy their possessions and prepare for a shared suicide. Properly modernist in its self-consciousness—from the shocking thickness of time as a formal category itself, to the use of Alban Berg's violin concerto, dedicated "To the Memory of an Angel"—it was the first film in his three-part trilogy devoted to the portrait of *"emotionale Vergletscherung"* ("emotional glaciation"), followed by *Benny's Video* in 1992 and *71 Fragmente einer Chronologie des Zufalls* (*71 Fragments of a Chronology of Chance*) in 1994. Like all of his works, these films are formally obsessed with close-ups of hands, quotidian gestures of domestic business (performing chores, daily tasks, etc.), Austrian music, the status of representation—in particular, television—and the ever-in-process dissolution of the bourgeois family (Austrian, at times, though not universally). These concerns are continued in 2001's *La Pianiste* (*The Piano Teacher*) and 2003's post-apocalyptic *Le Temps du Loup* (*The Time of the Wolf*), both of which mark his partnership with French screen diva Isabelle Huppert, and a more general production move to France. An extension of his aesthetic language of fragmentation to the increasingly fractured world of globalized Paris is found in *Code inconnu: Récit incomplet de divers voyages* (*Code Unknown*), released in 2000.

Between the *emotionale Vergletscherung* trilogy and his more recent work in France came a strange little film from 1997, *Funny Games*, which begins as many horror films do—though this is entirely irrelevant—as a family leaves the city for the country. In their house by the water, mother, father, son and their dog are terrorized by two well-dressed young men whose intrusion into the house is universally mischaracterized in Haneke criticism.[3] The point is that they are invited in by the family when they arrive to "borrow some eggs," as social rules dictate. The two men play a series of sadistic *Spiele* with the family, ranging from betting that the family will be dead in twelve hours (a wager shared, in a close-up aside and wink, with the audience), to dares involving the mother's undress, childlike "warm/cold" alternations in a hunt to find the murdered family dog, and a vicious game of hide and seek with the young son, who escapes only to be caught and then indifferently shot minutes later. The son is murdered off-screen as we watch one of the visitors make a sandwich. The father, wounded from the beginning, is casually dispensed with; and the mother, despite escaping, is returned and, without fanfare or triumph, drowned at the end of the film, as the two killers politely approach another family to begin their "funny games" anew. Logic and causality are not central to the narrative—and criticism that attempts to draw strict lines of plausibility inevitably turns sour with frustration. Nor is this a canonical horror film in any regard, as the victims levy little to no satisfactory power against their killers: they are reserved throughout—with one notable exception—desperately attempting to locate in liberal discourse the bargaining rights of contract (what do you want? what can we give you? we'll give you our word we won't tell, and so forth) that might make the violence end.[4] The failure of the contract is linked here to the failure of the visible, for these strategies of mutual cooperation are as shunted aside within the narrative as full visual knowledge is within the frame. Indeed, each attempt at contract leads to a concession, and each concession leads to yet another, in the infinite reflective logic of sadism.[5] The "final girl," theorist Carol Clover's term for the figure in horror who escapes the killer and with whom audiences identify strongly, is killed, unceremoniously. I mean that quite literally: horror films regularly surround their deaths with ritual, suspense, delay, anticipation, chase, flight, but here ceremony and ritual are dispensed with for the over-quick unremarkable annihilation. Death is important in and to traditional horror films—it is screechingly feared, tirelessly pursued, sneakily avoided—but in the move to the *horrible*, death becomes more than ordinary or banal, it becomes trite, mundane, boring.

Funny Games is one of Haneke's more violent films—situated in the horrific overexposed daylight of *I Spit on Your Grave* territory—though *Benny's Video* could certainly vie for that title as well. Like many thrillers, much of its violence is psychological and much of it is glimpsed only in its effects. None of this matters at all. For *Funny Games* leads us into this anthology by way of a deviation that eschews any consideration of violence, murder, blood splattered on the wall, or generic battles about the difference between horror and thrillers. *Funny Games* is—like many of Haneke's films with far less gore—properly *horrible* in the violence it effects nowhere on the screen, but somewhere else entirely. In the move from horror to the horrible, in our detour away from this collection to Haneke and back again, the image has lost something crucial. The severe privileging of the visual realm one can glimpse—in an example not indifferent to this collection—in Siegfried Kracauer's *From Caligari to Hitler: A Psychological History of the German Film* ("films are able, and therefore obliged, to scan the whole visible world ..." (6) speaking of the features that will come to prefigure fascism in Germany: "huge mass displays, casual configurations of human bodies and inanimate objects, and an endless succession of unobtrusive phenomena" (7) is no longer a valid basis for defining, delimiting, or differentiating horror. *Horrible* cinema locates itself elsewhere than in the image.

Much can be said about the opening of *Funny Games*, as the family car is seen driving through the forest.[6] In fact, much can be *said*, for saying, speaking, speech, sound is what is properly *shown* in this opening scene. Mascagni's *Cavalleria Rusticana* plays on the soundtrack, but this comes to constitute the entire visual field, as close-ups of hands stopping the CD player in the car to change discs effect a diegetic break in the music. We hear voices articulate the terms of their game (the husband and wife try to trick each other with difficult musical selections), but these are disembodied, bodies reduced to the hands changing discs. A few minutes into this opening sequence, the first murder occurs—Händel's "Cara Salva" is killed off by the ferocious avant-garde heavy metal of John Zorn, which rapes into the text as loudly, violently, vilely penetratingly as any object into any body. Haneke has said in interviews that the Zorn is not meant to be the "killer's music" and the refined Händel and (later) Mozart the family's aural sanctuary (Sharrett, interview). This strikes me as entirely correct, for to imply that sound here is a question of possession or a mere leitmotif is to entirely miss this significance—that the soundtrack in this film escapes and exceeds all attempts to marshal its representational pull. *Funny Games* is an aural horror film, but this does not mean that horror is produced in or through the soundtrack, but that the aural realm is itself the locus of the horror, the problematization of horror that realizes the horrible. The soundtrack in Haneke's films—the music, the voices, the speech, the screams—is that suffix that displaces the meaning that precedes it and problematizes all temporalities in a forever about-to-arrive affect.

Throughout *Funny Games*, voices are insistently severed from their loci of enunciation. Numerous scenes in the opening of the film allow us to hear voices of characters, but without seeing their mouths, lips, teeth—the messy materiality of articulation. At times, the voice sources are offscreen entirely and the camera lingers on an empty hallway or space anticipating visual plenitude. At other times, the hands of the speakers, busy with domestic duties, are shown in close-up while their presumed owner partakes of spoken language. This severely limited visual field effects a double parsing: of the body, newly fragmented into zones of labor, and of the voice from the face. Language comes to exist completely in the realm of epistemological doubt, for there is always a gap (temporal, spatial, epistemic, at the very least) in which the non-coincidence of voice and image is possible. Here a mistake may be made, and the visual image may play a primary *Spiel*: the body we take to be enunciating may turn out not to be the speaker's body after all. What we suppose to be a sutured whole—mind and body, voice and mouth—comes to be unmade, then, into a series of partial objects, available for re-description and re-appropriation. The image no longer guarantees a certainty about speech and language; it no longer can be found to offer a match between what is spoken and who speaks. In other words, Haneke's aural universe confesses a model of subjectivity in which there is an irreducible division between the language that is enunciated and the subject of any spoken statement. It implies an erasure that inevitably comes to privilege language as a representation for being, a subjectivity whose first move is to rend the subject in two, torturous, murderous, a violence in loss that necessarily makes impossible the return of the subject to the self. Is it not a torture on par with the wound to the flesh when one of the killers demands of the Father "What's this?" (answer: a golf ball), forcing him to produce speech—produce, that is, the loss that constitutes his status as a subject alien to itself.[7] We begin, then, with this loss. It will not always be a loss.

The son is murdered, having won a child's game of pointing—this "win" is misrecognized by the less viciously intelligent of the two killers, Peter (sometimes called Tom by his partner), as a loss, the most vicious loss of life reduced to a misrecognition of the rules. When it happens, we are in another room, with the other intruder, Paul, as he calmly fixes himself a sandwich. We hear the shot, the mother's scream, a struggle—all the time, seemingly held at bay from the scene of horror. When we return with Paul to the room in which the family is being held captive, blood covering the TV screen fills out the narrative for us in a sudden shock. The film seems to too quickly come to an end—"So: have a good evening ... bye ..." rush the killers and they leave the house. The son's body lies in a corner, unremarkable really, and unrelentingly distant, as the camera refuses a close-up, to the point that his form is nearly lost in the imagery, and must be hunted for, located, searched out. Time passes. The son, dead in the right corner, father limp, wounded, shocked, in the left, bookends to the horrors of the room. The long take is so very long, so very long, so very long—it is not the repetition you just read, it is undifferentiated, thick not with suspense but with the unbearable load of finitude's irreversible certainty. We wait. Time passes. Time expands, expansive, so very, very long. It has taken seconds—maybe thirty in all—since you read above of the boy's end. In the film, it takes endless minutes—a paradoxical phrase, no doubt, but you will have time to figure it out. The mother, still bound, makes her way to the television set to turn off the sounds of car racing. The room becomes a field for a different relation to visuality. Forms are made out where there were none. The enormous blood splatter on the wall takes on the fuzzy certainties of a Rorschach blot. Silence undoes itself, amplifying the tiniest rustle. The father's growing wails and moans fill the void of the time that passes, which remains otherwise vacant. Agony, awful, anguish—the truly horrible is being forced to coexist alongside other people's pain. And yet it goes on, it goes on—there is no producing here the experience of time listening to parents grieving. There is no formulation in language proper to the taut nausea of trauma. You cannot imagine it either; reading this essay, you will falter in the face of any description and cannot go in search of its meaning. You must experience it; the parent's pain must find you.

Of course, it is not a moment—there is no antonym for moment, for one has to excerpt oneself from whatever that unnamable thickness is to name it as such, returning to the moment proper—but this un-moment (unmomentous) experience of time appears often in Haneke's work. In *Le Temps du Loup*, various scenes that consist of little more than women screaming hysterically—screaming in and at time, unlike the silly punctuated shriek of traditional horror—produce aurally the claustrophobia that the gray *mise-en-scène* produces visually. *Le Temps du Loup*, as well, regularly refuses to show the subject enunciating—bodies are cloaked in prohibitive darkness, faces are turned away from the screen, hands take the place of the face in the close-up, etc.—instead producing speech that cannot be tied to any specific body. The visceral wailing of a mother at the death of her child in the post-apocalyptic chaos goes on, again far too long—as does, let us admit, all grief to those who endure its witnessing. The temporality of horror is the temporality of the moment (the shock, the surprise, the sudden); the temporality of the *horrible* is the temporality of grief—a temporality of already-too-long, a temporality that can never catch up to its origin, a temporality *unheimlich* to itself.

The centrality of time to Haneke, or sound to Haneke, cannot be stated, for it is the centrality of *time to sound* and *sound to time* that his work takes up, already partnered, already heavy with the burdens of the other's meanings. Throughout *Funny Games*, sound is connected to the unendurable sense of time itself as a formal principle. The heaviness of silence when the family first enters the house is punctuated by the mother's observation that the clock has stopped. Time has become impossible in its progressive dimension, but not in its affective one. Though the killers keep asking each other what time it is and though the film itself is structured by the twelve hours of the death wager, this concept of time as a marker of difference is a red herring for the more significant indifference of time—the mother is killed before her twelve hours are up, just because. And it is this question of the affect of time that binds it so insistently to sound.

Sound ought not to be reduced to language in either Haneke's corpus or the psychoanalytic one: the centrality of language to Lacan cannot be overstated—and indeed, the impotent *Che vuoi?* to the big Other is everywhere apparent in *Funny Games*: "Why?" insists the modernist family; "Why not?" reply the postmodern psychopaths. But it is not in language that we turn to Lacan, that we might return to Freud and the uncanny. Rather, we must look to his work on the invocatory drive, for adding to the legions of thinkers who have noted the peculiar status of the ear as that which cannot lid itself shut, defending against or ignoring external influence.[8] Lacan insists on one thing more—it is not simply that the ears have no lids, and thus that they cannot close shut against the world. But more so, being perpetually, constitutively open, the ears are the privileged organ in relation to the unconscious. In his 1964–65 *Seminar XI: Les Quatre Concepts Fondamentaux de la Psychanalyse (The Four Fundamental Concepts of Psychoanalysis)*, Lacan intones that "the invocatory drive, which has, as I told you in passing ... the privilege of not being able to close" (Lacan, *Fundamental* 200) is thus "the closest to the experience of the unconscious" (104). The total vulnerability of the ear, its inability to defend against penetration from without and the insistence of its message to effect affective causality, creates a phenomenally different (and I mean this very literally—it is phenomenologically different) mode of horror address, a mode that resides at the rotting heart of the horrible. Emptying out the realm of the visible, and thus refusing Kracauer's mandate to *show all*, Haneke relocates meaning in a barrage of aural puncta.

It would be disingenuous to say that what happens after the son's death, what occurs *next* in the narrative, is this: the mother tries in vain to get the phone to work, gets dressed, leaves the house to find help, escapes over the fence, hides from a passing car, tries to chase down help, and then is returned by the killers to the husband in order to determine the outcome of the bet. It would be disingenuous not because that is not what takes place, but because the narrative is but punctuated by—and not at all dependent on or even very interested in—this brief reprieve. The mother's return to the house is not a narrative progression but inevitable from the very beginning. The scenes of escape are mere distractions from the work of the film, which is a game—and games are centered, simple, and repetitive; they do not have narrative depth, but simply insist on the cruel binary of winners and losers. Insisting that "we want to offer the audience something," and asking the audience in direct address "Is that enough?", Paul determines that the audience would prefer a "real ending," locating this decision in the look to the camera, a complicity not unfamiliar to the horror genre, invested as it is with the ethics of watching violence. Paul establishes a final game, "The Loving Wife," in which the mother/wife is offered the chance to take the husband's place and/or determine the weapon used to finish him off. At a crucial moment—the Final Girl's first, and final, appearance—the mother grabs the gun and shoots Tom with what the narrative presents as the last bullet. Paul grabs the remote control for the family's television, rewinds the film, unvanquishing the "final girl"'s role in the narrative through repetition, grabs the gun this time and shoots the husband instead.

There are four moments when Paul address the camera directly: when playing the "warm/cold" game to find the family's dead dog he winks at the camera and the audience; after making the central wager of the film—that in twelve hours the family will be "*kaputt*"—he asks us: "Who will you bet on? Do they have a chance?" Before the rewinding scene, he asks us "Is that enough?" And finally, at the end of the film, when the mother is unceremoniously dropped into the lake behind the house, as the two men approach the next house to "borrow some eggs," again he smiles and looks out into our world. These asides are routinely identified in Haneke criticism as moments of Brechtian distanciation that produce a critique of our own investment in violent films such as Haneke's.[9] Such readings entirely miss the point and the conservative function of such eruptions in the totality of the film. For though seen as offering a moment of spectatorial anxiety (one has been "seen" by the film, and implicated in the otherwise protective darkness of the theater), in reality, these asides to the audience suture together the very thing rendered asunder in the course of the film: body and voice. The *méconnaissance* of these moments as eruptions of the real operates in ignorance of the more radical proposition that these moments are indeed *defenses* against the anxiety that constitutes the majority of the film.[10] In returning the voice to the seen material body, verified in the close-up on Paul's face during these asides, these four scenes return to the film—perhaps solely to make the remainder just bearable enough. They return language to the speaker. In doing so, as opposed to effecting a rending of representation, they bring about a return to a scenario of lack. This is the lack of the speaking subject in relation to his or her enunciation. The specific election of this film *not* to show us that lack means, in essence, to eliminate lack, produce the lack of lack in relation to a fullness of some affect, in some elsewhere. *Funny Games*, for most of its duration, is thus overproximate to some presence that has comfortably gone missing in normative voice/body dualisms and in normative horror. Properly traumatic, this overproximation matches precisely Lacan's formulation for anxiety. Opposed to Freud's assertion that it takes no object (unlike fear), Lacan reads anxiety as taking as its object nothingness. This nothingness—I will soon argue—is the material void of the scream.

The significance of anxiety—that affect which "does not deceive," and is the realization of a "complete response" (Lacan, *Anxiety* 10)—to Lacan's thinking cannot be overemphasized: he dubs it the nodal point, we might say the navel, of his psychoanalysis, and locates in this affect a significant revision of the subject's relation to the Other. In his *Seminar X: L'angoisse (Anxiety)*, he radically rejects Freud's notion that anxiety does not take an object, proposing rather that the object of anxiety is precisely the void, the *objet petit a*. This punctum, which touches on the real, erupts in the symbolic as frustrated representation. In his return to Freud, in the move from anxiety to the uncanny, Lacan finds in *das Heimliche* that moment in which "man finds his home in a point situated in the Other beyond the image of which we are made and this place represents the absence where we are" (Lacan, *Anxiety* 5) What the uncanny exposes is precisely the subject's current place as absence—for it is elsewhere he is found. At stake in anxiety is not what we normally think of as fear-provoking: it is not the integrity of the body or even the imaginary defenses of the ego, but rather the status of the subject itself.

Anxiety threatens from, and takes as its object, the place of nothingness. It is not a response to the lost object (the mother's lost/absent penis, the mother herself) but arises paradoxically *when lack fails to appear*. Anxiety occurs in relation to an overproximation to something from which a symbolic distance is normally maintained. Thus, the famous Lacanian explanation for anxiety's impetus—"when lack is lacking"—has to do with the disappearance of an otherwise normative gap: "if all of a sudden all norms are lacking, namely what constitutes the lack—because the norm is correlative to the idea of lack—if all of a sudden it is not lacking … it is at that moment that anxiety begins" (12). As an experiment, let us take Lacan literally:

> It is this emergence of the *heimlich* in the frame that constitutes the phenomenon of anxiety. And this is why it is wrong to say that anxiety is without an object. Anxiety has a completely different sort of object to any apprehension that has been prepared, structured, structured by what? By the grill of the cut, of the furrow, of the unary trait, of the "that's it" which always in operating as one might say closes the lips—I am saying the lip or the lips—of this cut which becomes the sealed letter on the subject in order…to send him off under a sealed cover to different traces. (6)

These words betray the true subject of the discourse—not in the frame, the cut, the language of cinema, but in the closing of the lips. Anxiety resides in the opening up of the cut, the opening that reveals some unexpected token of the real. The scream, sound in time, unlinked to a wailing, bloody body, is the locus of a properly Lacanian anxiety in Haneke's films. It is this mark that fully severs horror films from horrible films. The disembodied scream produces an overproximation to the plenitude of speech normatively absent in punctuated yells and discourse, no matter how fragmented or tortuous. The site of anxiety in *Funny Games* is specifically *not* in the scenes in which Paul talks to the camera (conducting a normative production of the lack of language in relation to its speaker), but where such lack disappears, where lack goes missing in the speech without a source, in the scream without a body. This is trauma: the scream with no origin, and hence, no end. And in our impossible relation to sound, our inability to shut it out, we receive not the affect proper of *horrere* (not bristling hairs) but the anticipatory arrival, the coming into being of the Real—that resistance to the symbolizing work of the film, that resistance to horror's suspension, that bringing into being of the truly *horrible*.

In his meditation on painter Francis Bacon, *The Logic of Sensation*, Gilles Deleuze writes that what "directly interests [Bacon] is a violence that is involved only with color and line: the violence of a sensation (and not of a representation), a static or potential violence, a violence of reaction and expression," and that "this is not the relationship of form and matter, but of materials and forces; to make these forces visible through their effects on flesh" (xxix). Deleuze argues that Bacon was drawn to the idea that "a man ordered to sit still for hours on a narrow stool is bound to assume contorted postures. The violence of a hiccup, of a need to vomit, but also of a hysterical, involuntary smile..." (xxix).[11] There is a material trace in Bacon's paintings of the "there is" of real pain. There is the sensation of the wound inscribed onto the paintings and then produced anew in the viewer. Deleuze identifies a violence of representation in Bacon's work ("spectacles of horror, Crucifixions, prostheses and mutilations, monsters" (xxix) as well as a violence of sensation. Both Bacon and Deleuze deride the violence of representation for being cheap and degraded and pandering, and celebrate the violence of sensation.

The body in Bacon, crucial to this project of a violence of sensation, undergoes a particular type of deformation: "Bacon thus pursues a very peculiar project as a portrait painter: *to dismantle the face*, to rediscover the head or make it emerge from beneath the face" (Deleuze 19, italics in original). This dismantling of the face—though Deleuze would not precisely characterize it as such—is also a dismantling of the face's relationship to speech production, to being a source for and yet unable to defend against sound. Deleuze writes,

> This is what Bacon means when he says he wanted "to paint the scream more than the horror." If we could express this as a dilemma, it would be: either, I paint the horror and I do not paint the scream, because I make a figuration of the horrible. Or else, if I paint the scream, and I do not paint the visible horror, I will paint the visible horror less and less, since the scream captures or detects an invisible force. (51)

Realism does not imply an opposition here to symbolism, simply an affinity with sensation. And indeed it is not in realism, but in the Real, that we locate Haneke's contribution to the cinema of sensation. Deleuze figures a rendering visible of the trauma in Bacon as this radical gesture: "not to scream *before* or *about*, but to scream *at* death" (52). This interest not in representing or approaching violence (the *raison d'être* of horror—the violence of representation), but in engaging with it on a sensorial level and encountering it directly is as close as Haneke gets us to true affect, the mark of the horrible, the conditions for possibility suspended in horror delayed no longer. Lacan's Real is that which resists (no reason not to bring him and Deleuze together on the plane of Haneke's films, as their twin contributions give us the scream and its affect), and as the horrible resists horror, so too does it insist on its own production of affect (the violence of sensation), of an experience in and of time that does not deceive, that does not suspend, but that arrives, all too soon, all too insistent in its fierce fullness. This arrival should remind us to look at our own departure more closely: for although Haneke *ist nicht hier einheimisch*, this in no way means that his intrusion is unwelcome. We have, after all, invited him in ourselves.

Notes

1. See, for example, Mattias Frey, *Michael Haneke*, www.sensesofcinema.com entry. Accessed October 20, 2005. Available at: www.sensesofcinema.com/contents/ directors/03/haneke.html.

2. See, for example, the following interview from 1997. Accessed October 20, 2005. Available at: www.berlinonline.de/berliner-zeitung/archiv/.bin/dump.fcgi/1997/0911/ber linberlin/0007/.

> Berliner Zeitung: Herr Haneke, ist "Funny Games" ein Kinofilm, der sich gegen das Fernsehen richtet?
> Michael Haneke: Ausgangspunkt des Films ist die Entwirklichung der Gewalt im Mainstreamkino, im normalen Actionfilm. Gewalt wird da zum Konsumgut gemacht. Aber der Film richtet sich gegen die Medien als Ganzes. Wir leben zu 90 Prozent über Abbilder der Wirklichkeit. Wir haben uns in ein mehr oder weniger synthetisches Abbildungsreich zurückgezogen.

3. Tarja Laine writes, for example: "well-educated young men...force their way into the holiday residence...", in "'What are you looking at and why?': Michael Haneke's *Funny Games* with his audience," *Kinoeye*, vol. 4, no. 1. Accessed October 20, 2005. Available at: www.kinoeye.org/04/01/laine01.php.

4. In *Le Temps du Loup*, the same breakdown of contractual language is seen: the father says to the intruder in his house, "What I propose is this..." promising a future cooperation, and is shot point blank—not in answer, but as a filling in of precisely what the father leaves unsaid.

5. One is tempted to read in this scene a political allegory about the twentieth-century failure of containment and conciliation.

6. This is a recurring trope in Haneke's work, a modern fairy tale corpus, no doubt.

7. Throughout, the killers insist—not unlike the analyst—that the family freely produce speech: "You really can speak to us openly," Paul implores. Producing speech in the other comes to signify the first, primary violence, replicated in later scenes on the flesh.

8. Jean-Jacques Rousseau writes, in *Essai sur l'origine des langues* (*Essay on the Origin of Languages*): "these [musical] accents, which cause us to shudder, these accents to which one cannot close one's ear and which by way of it penetrate to the very depths of the heart, in spite of ourselves convey to it the emotions that wring them, and cause us to feel what we hear" (Paris: Flammarion, 1993: 58).

9. See, for example, Laine.

10. Lacan's Real is not to be confused with the film-theoretical notion of realism. See, for a discussion of the latter concept, Brigitte Peucker, "Effects of the real: Michael Haneke's *Benny's Video*," *Kinoeye*, vol. 4, no. 1. Accessed October 20, 2005. Available at: www.kinoeye.org/04/01/peucker01.php.

11. I return to Haneke with this language—this need to vomit—as an alternative to disembodied speech is performed in nearly all of his films, most dramatically in *Funny Games* and *Le Temps du Loup*, with a scene where a woman vomits uncontrollably, surprisingly, as a reaction to the loss of speech—or, properly, vomit as another form of speech.

Works Cited

Deleuze, Gilles. *The Logic of Sensation*. Trans. and Intro. Daniel W. Smith. Minneapolis: University of Minnesota Press, 2002.

Foundas, Scott. "Interview with Michael Haneke." *Indiewire*, December 4, 2001. Accessed on October 20, 2005. www.indiewire.com/people/int_Haneke _Michael_ 011204. html.

Freud, Sigmund. *Civilization and Its Discontents*, Standard Edition, Vol. 21. Trans. James Strachey. London: 1930, New York: 1962.

———. *Writings on Art and Literature*. Eds. Werner Hamacher and David E. Wellbery. Stanford, CA: Stanford University Press, 1997.

Frey, Mattias. *Michael Haneke*, www.sensesofcinema.com.entry. Accessed on October 20, 2005. www.sensesofcinema.com/contents/directors/ 03/haneke.html.

Kracauer, Siegfried. *From Caligari to Hitler: A Psychological Study of the German Film*. Princeton, NJ: Princeton University Press, 1947.

Lacan, Jacques. *Anxiety, Book X*, 1962–65, unpublished translation by Cormac Gallagher from unedited French typescripts.

———. *The Four Fundamental Concepts of Psychoanalysis*. Ed. Jacques-Alain Miller. Trans. Alan Sheridan. London: Vintage, 1977.

Laine, Tarja. "'What are you looking at and why?': Michael Haneke's *Funny Games* with his audience," *Kinoeye* 4.1. Accessed on October 20, 2005. www.kinoeye.org/ 04/01/laine01.php.

Oxford English Dictionary, 2nd Edition, compact. Oxford, England: Oxford University Press, 1991.

Peucker, Brigitte. "Effects of the real: Michael Haneke's *Benny's Video*," *Kinoeye* 4.1. Accessed on October 20, 2005. www.kinoeye.org/04/01/peucker01.php.

Sharrett, Christopher. "The Horror of the Middle Class," *Kinoeye* 4.1. Accessed on October 20, 2005. www.kinoeye.org/04/01/sharrett01.php.

———. "Interview with Michael Haneke." *Kinoeye* 4.1. Accessed on October 20, 2005. www.kinoeye.org/04/01/interview01.php.

Rousseau, Jean-Jacques. *Essai sur l'origine des langues*. Ed. Catherine Kintzler. Paris: Flammarion, 1993.

Part 4:

Beyond Aesthetics Against Aesthetics: German Splatter Films

Better Living through Splatter: Christoph Schlingensief's Unsightly Bodies and the Politics of Gore

Kris Thomas-Vander Lugt

*"Tastelessness appears in this context to be
the only possible answer to Germany."*[1]

In the summer of 2004, to the great horror of devout Wagnerians worldwide, the enfant terrible of the German art scene Christoph Schlingensief came to Bayreuth to direct the epic masterpiece *Parsifal*. What ensued was a bizarre spectacle that included a menstruating Grail, Arthurian knights in blackface, and the putrefying flesh of dead rabbits, in short: a splatter opera. In an effort to revivify the fading spirit of the Bayreuther Festspiele, the organizer of the festival—and grandson of its namesake—Gottfried Wagner had engaged Schlingensief to mount the production of *Parsifal*, a choice which ultimately did have the effect of repopularizing the event, though perhaps not in the manner originally hoped. Reactions ranged from outrage and disgust to appreciation and admiration to simple confusion—reactions that are typical for Schlingensief's work in general. While the Bayreuth spectacle launched him into the eyes of the educated middle class to an extent unprecedented in his previous work, *Parsifal* is only the most recent installment in a long line of splatter fare that goes back to the very beginning of Schlingensief's cultural production. From his earliest endeavors in horror film to more recent theatrical and street-art projects, Schlingensief has populated his visual universe with bodies that bleed and bodies that bludgeon, oozing bodies, disabled bodies, bodies in ecstasy and bodies in decay—unsightly bodies that form a part of an overall oeuvre that revolves around splatter as an aesthetic, political, and even ethical element. His roots in horror film remain evident in his later work, which, in addition to *Parsifal*, has covered the gamut of "bad taste," ranging from a public call for the death of the German chancellor ("Kill Helmut Kohl!" 1997)[2] to a xenophobic reality show that lured foreigners with the promise of citizenship ("Foreigners Out! Please Love Austria," 2000).[3] For his exaggerated parodies of German fascism, right-wing radicalism, and the East-West divide (to name a few), Schlingensief has been criticized as merely "recycling stereotypes" instead of combating them. His works are characterized by an almost schizophrenic mixture of allusions, quotations, and intertexts.

From Big Brother to Shakespeare, Tobe Hooper to Pier Paolo Pasolini, Schlingensief's works mix "low" and "high," "art" and "trash," making it difficult to identify a consistent aesthetic or politics. Furthermore, these strategies of appropriation and citation often make it difficult to defend his art against accusations that it replicates the violence and spectacle it seems to want to critique. The extent to which his representations of right-wing violence—for example, in works such as *Hamlet* (2001), which used "real" neo-Nazis as actors—serve to destabilize representation through subversion is a question that cuts to the heart of Schlingensief's political project.[4] At the same time, the very indeterminacy that characterizes his work, coupled with the processual nature of his peculiar brand of *Aktionskunst* most especially, is for some critics a source of subversive potential. As Mark Rectanus notes, it is precisely the investment of passion, spontaneity, and radical unpredictability in Schlingensief's "action-art" that becomes a source for "collective transformation" into a "radical democratic project":

> Performative process defies the fixity of representation, which corporate media and cultural politics utilize to frame culture and politics and which postmodern culture attempts, but often fails, to destabilize. [...] Because performative process can be initiated at any time or place (websites, the street, rock concerts, demonstrations) and may have an indeterminate start and termination, it becomes an unknown and unforeseen variable that may alter commercial event culture by linking it to political passions—from the right or from the left. This fusion of performance, process, and politics may indeed infuse political passions back into cultural spaces but without a predictable outcome. (249)

While there has been a great deal of attention—from both the public and the critics—devoted to Schlingensief's more recent work in the realm of performance art and theater, his earliest endeavors in film, specifically horror film, are rarely discussed by critics and academics, but have flourished in an underworld of aficionados devoted to what Jeffrey Sconce has termed "paracinema" or trash aesthetics.[5] Focusing on his horror films, specifically a trilogy of films made between 1989 and 1992, this paper unravels Schlingensief's paracinematic strategies as part of an (anti-)aesthetic project aimed at confounding boundaries of taste that are simultaneously bound up with politically, culturally, and socio-economically inflected "proper" and "improper" ways of dealing with violence—past and present—in Germany. In this context, splatter is engaged as an intervention into a certain liberal construction of national identity in the wake of (re)unification, that is, (West) Germany's self-understanding as a post-fascist liberal democracy: a state constructed not only *after* fascism in a temporal sense, but also more significantly *out of the ruins of* fascism. To the extent that postwar German identity is *constituted* by the principle that "human dignity shall be inviolable," instated as the first and most fundamental article of the Basic Law

[*Grundgesetz*], liberal democracy in West Germany is underwritten from its outset by the shadow of inhumanity, that is, it defines itself very specifically against German fascism.[6] In this sense, German national identity is inherently spectral: it is haunted by the spectre of fascism. Indeed, as Steffen Hantke notes, "the Holocaust is always already in place for most Germans."[7] Against the backdrop of this spectrality, the excessive over-production value of camp-horror á la Schlingensief works, in the German context, toward a violent refusal of repression.

Splatter History

As an aesthetic that refuses to "hide" or sublimate violence, especially bodily violence, splatter is a critical part of Schlingensief's decidedly political approach to art. Using confrontation and provocation to stage both his art and his own personage as spectacle (where he himself has become a kind of artistic phenomenon, using himself as an artistic object, inserting himself as an actor into his plays and films, referencing his art as "self-provocation") he advances an ethical dilemma with works that are simultaneously progressive and reactionary.[8] Indeed, the ambivalent status of politics in his works—which finds expression in reception that either praises Schlingensief as an heir to Fassbinder and '68er revolutionary progressivism or maligns him as reactionary, pubescent, and hysterical—is par for the paracinematic course, in particular for horror films. Ambivalence, as it were, is what horror film is all about. Traditionally, it invites critiques that are both progressive and conservative, often within the same film.[9] It is in this mode that Schlingensief is at his finest.

Splatter is defined above all by its hypermedia(liza)tion of the body-in-pain and excessive depictions of violence—"mutilation is the message," as John McCarty famously described it.[10] The intended effect (and affect) is not fright or suspense, but mortification: "Splatter movies, offshoots of the horror film genre, aim not to scare their audience, necessarily, nor to drive them to the edges of their seats in suspense, but to *mortify* them with scenes of explicit gore. In splatter movies, mutilation is indeed the message—many times the only one" (McCarty 1, emphasis in original). Louis Kern identifies splatter as a "transitive element" that appears in various combinations and "lends [...] gerundive quality. It serves notice as to intent and technique—brutal sexual violation, the casual rending of human flesh, dismemberment, the dripping, spilling, and spewing of bodily fluids and internal organs, and coloring the whole, hogsheads of dark, hot blood—the 'wet work' of contemporary horror [...]" (48). As has been discussed in some depth with regard to horror film, Kern notes that this element of splatter—its "wet work"—can be regarded as a "direct lineal descendant (transmitted through films of extreme violence and explicit sexuality) of the French dramatic tradition of the Grand Guignol" (48). Founded in 1895 by Oscar Méténier, *Le Theatre de Grand Guignol* sought to "awaken the deadened soul of its audience" through nightly performances that focused on the macabre, enacted in grisly and graphically often very violent fashion (48). Both splatter and Guignol, then, have come to describe an aesthetic that is characterized by grisliness, explicitness, and shock, often including "the element of humor amidst incredible carnage [...], humor that seeks to invert socially conditioned expectations of behavior and to parody the logic and smugness of cozy bourgeois sensibilities. It is subversive and at times anarchic humor rooted in violent fantasies of status reversal and the un-masking of cultural hypocrisy" (Kern 49). It is this mixture of horror and black humor that give both Grand Guignol and splatter film an element of "schlockiness"—gore taken to such an extreme that it becomes a parody of itself.

Thus, the transgression of boundaries that is prototypical for horror films in general is ratcheted up in splatter until the boundaries virtually disappear, resulting in what Stefan Höltgen terms an "an aesthetic of loss-of-distance" (Höltgen, n.p.).[11] That is, splatter takes Brechtian distanciation and reverses it, bringing the viewer into direct—and violent—confrontation with trauma, loss, and the returned repressed.[12] Instead of making the line between actor and spectator, fiction and reality explicit, splatter not only blurs the line, it threatens to annihilate it. This blurring becomes more apparent in Schlingensief's theatrical projects, in which actors frequently pervade the "fourth wall" and mingle amidst the audience (or vice versa). Splatter's confrontational style is also characteristic of paracinema, which—like New German Cinema before it (though not as sublimated)—is "founded on the recognition and subsequent rejection of Hollywood style" (Sconce 373).

Keeping in mind, then, the double function of splatter as aesthetic and ethic or politic, I will examine Schlingensief's parodic *German Trilogy*, a collection of three films which trace German violence from post-fascism through post-communism in the mode of camp-splatter, detailing the horrors of the last hour of the suicidal Führer (in *100 Years of Adolf Hitler: The Last Hour in the Führer's Bunker*, 1989), the first hours of the East Germans' traumatic re-unification with the West (in *The German Chainsaw Massacre*, 1990) and the ongoing legacy of attacks on foreigners (in *Terror 2000*, 1992). By placing violent nationalism and racism in a framework that is at once comedic and horrific, the trilogy unmakes reunification's dream of a multiculturalist Western-styled liberal utopia as a farce, and launches a harsh critique of contemporary left-wing responses to (continually increasing) right-wing violence in Germany. Schlingensief departs from "politically correct" avenues of social critique, most especially from discourses of tolerance that arose in the postwar and post-reunification context. Instead, Schlingensief recognizes conflict and confrontation as being at the center of contemporary debates and works from within the logic of violence to explode it from the inside out. As *Terror 2000*'s corpulent detective explains, infiltration is the surest method toward extermination: in his search to destroy a band of neo-Nazi rabble-rousers, he must become one of them and implode their organization "from the inside out."[13]

Inserting the "unsightly"—the racial, ethic, sexual Other; the disabled; the deviant—into mediated versions of violent realities made hyper-visible by the graphic aesthetics of horror, he uses splatter to expose the grisly realities of contemporary Germany. As Kern explains, splatter's use of "grisly descriptions of torture and slaughter constitutes a stylistic focus that is intended to outflank the natural impulse to deny the dark, brutal underside of the human mind" (49). Thus, where DuPont once cited chemistry as the means to "better living," Schlingensief engages splatter as a means to clearer vision of the present as history: *Gegenwartsbewältigung* in living color.[14]

Horror as Cultural Memory

Schlingensief made his first movie at the age of eight—a mystery, tellingly. Since then he has directed a score of other films, the contents of which his own website sums up succinctly and fairly accurately as films "in which Hitler, rapists, and homicidal maniacs get into orgiastic mischief."[15] "Getting into mischief" is, of course, what Schlingensief does best. In this regard, he shares, along with other cinematic horror "bad boys" such as Jörg Buttgereit, Olaf Ittenbach, and Andreas Schnaas, the reputation of a post-Fassbinder "*enfant terrible* of German cinema."[16] Together, these directors' films fit within a larger body of underground films from the period directly before and after German Reunification, films which consciously flaunt the political correctness of other more popular films from this period and which re-present German history in the mode of horror.[17]

As noted on his "official" website, Schlingensief's aesthetics are partially rooted in the same anti-establishment impulse that characterized New German Cinema:

> Schlingensief's filmic methods reveal his aesthetic affinity to Fassbinder: the desire to bring the treatment of the subject matter back around to a flash of insight or to a contemporary situation, anarchy and abandon in the economy of the scenic depiction, the spontaneity of play as an inferior imitation of everyday reality[,] and also a frivolous, disturbing penchant for aggressivity. Imitation and confusion are key. It's about finding the shortest path toward the documentation of a unique, unrepeatable event that thereby carries with it theatrical qualities. His films are personal expressions, not just about the time in which they occur, but also and especially about the time of their making.[18]

Yet, whereas New German Cinema (NGC) tended to aestheticize violence and worked more often in the mode of melodrama than horror, Schlingensief's depictions of murder, suicide, and bodily harm are much cruder and his references to fascism tend to be much more obvious. With some exceptions—Werner

Schroeter, Hans Jürgen Syberberg, and the female directors most notably—NGC
tended toward a "high" cultural aesthetic, veering away from the trivial, the
kitschy, or the overtly gory. Furthermore, the body of nation for New German
Cinema was predominantly female: from Sanders-Brahms' *Germany Pale
Mother* to Fassbinder's *BRD Trilogy*—in which Germany is embodied, respectively, through the three central characters Maria, Lola, and Veronika—
Germany was a woman, wounded.[19] For New German Cinema, then, *Vergangenheitsbewältigung*—the mastering, conquering, (sur)mounting of the past—is
often articulated through the female body or female desire.[20] For many of Germany's postwar horror directors on the other hand (Schlingensief, Buttgereit,
Schnaas, Ittenbach, Karmakar), German history is located—and becomes stag-
nant—in the putrid entrails of the dead, dying, or pathologically perverse male
body. In this sense, Schlingensief's films bear less resemblance to the highbrow
artiness of New German Cinema and more to a subgenre of European horror
film from the sixties and seventies: sex-horror, or what Joan Hawkins terms
"horrotica" (96). Hawkins identifies tendencies within European (most notably
Italian, French, and Spanish) "low" horror that explicitly referenced Nazism in
the vein of erotic horror, noting that "[d]uring the sixties and seventies, Italian
horror directors made a string of low-budget SS sexploitation horror movies,
frequently set in concentration camps. And the Nazi doctor (just where exactly
had all those sadistic physicians gone?)—showed up with increasing frequency
in medico-horror tales" (87).[21] While "fascinating fascism" (Sontag) was re-
emerging on the big screen further to the west and south, young German filmmakers sought to get beyond the escapist, nationalistic fantasies of the 1950s
Heimatfilm, proclaiming the death of "dad's cinema" with the 1962 Oberhausen
Manifesto.[22] In New German Cinema, postwar anxiety bubbled at low to medium heat beneath a surface of sublimation, hygienic in comparison to the splatter aesthetic of directors like Franco, Franju, and others dabbling in the genre of
Nazi/SS sexploitation.[23]

In Germany, European sex-horror has always been subject to stringent legal measures intended, so the letter of the law, to protect the youth population.
Already in 1949, West Germany established the *Voluntary Self-Inspection*
(*Freiwillige Selbstkontrolle* or FSK), a system by which films were "kontrol-
liert" or tested, primarily for Nazi content, and subsequently assigned certain
age restrictions or even seized (films in Germany since this point are designated
as, for example, FSK16 or FSK18, according to these ratings). C. Weinrich explains that the intensification of violence in both European and American horror
films starting in the late '50s and early '60s moved legal authorities' attention
from pornography to horror, and many horror films were banned:

> If sexuality was still cause for censorship into the 50s and 60s, the picture
> changed with the rise of the "new" horror movies. The new quality of the
> representation of violence and sexuality occasioned a morality debate and
> highly controversial opinions of the spectator. In 1973, the "Rubber Para-
> graph" §131 Section 3 was passed in Germany, and a new instrument for

censorship was created. Representations of violence (glorification of violence) [...] is from now on criminalized. [...] A number of films were restricted or even forbidden due to the strict criminal code. On the side of youth protection, words like "disorienting to youths," "desensitizing," "endangering morality" or "glorifying violence" became buzz words, and, with the video-wave being hyped-up in the media, a virtual "violence-paranoia" erupted.[24]

Based on Paragraph 131, Germany's "Law for the Protection of Youth" [*Jugendschutzgesetz* or JuSchG] provides for a special division to oversee media production, the "Federal Inspection Agency for Youth-Endangering Media" [*Bundesprüfstelle für jugendgefährende Medien* or BPjM], which may restrict films, ban them from sale or distribution, or confiscate them. All films that are deemed "youth-endangering" are placed on the "List of Youth-Endgangering Media" (colloquially referred to as the "Index").

So far, Schlingensief's films have managed to elude censorship, due perhaps in part to a certain level of illegibility with respect to genre. Combining elements of the underground European sex-horror tradition with a sort of tongue-in-cheek nod to "high" culture (with respect to technique, intertextuality, casting, and so on)[25] Schlingensief's films straddle the often precarious line between trash and art, and so, fall under an exception to the *Jugendschutzgesetz* that protects representations of violence when it serves the interests of "art":

A medium may not be added to the list 1) solely because of its political, social, religious, or ideological content, 2) when it is in the service of art or science, research or teaching, 3) if it lies in the public interest, unless the mode of representation is objectionable.[26]

In terms of "art," Schlingensief's own brand of cinematic violence blurs the line between "high" and "low" quite literally. In *100 Years of Adolf Hitler: The Last Hour in the Führer's Bunker,* the underworld of Nazi sexploitation (located literally "underworld" in the dark recesses of Hitler's bunker) is melded with the "legitimate" surface culture through the conflation of present and past, high and low. Underground, we see Hitler and his cronies watching New German Cinema master Wim Wenders on the bunker TV set, a medium that bridges outside and inside. Wenders is speaking—on the outside, on the "high ground"—at Cannes, calling for cinematic revolution: "to make the world's pictures better, in order to make the world better."[27] The film suggests, in this scene and in others discussed below, that attempts by the liberal left to "better the world" occur within a context of image manipulation that mirrors liberalism's dark Other, fascism.

"Hitler bin ich"—*100 Jahre Adolf Hitler, Die letzte Stunde im Führerbunker* (1989)

As the "100 Years" in the title suggests, Schlingensief's bizarre retelling of the Führer's "last hour" is framed as a celebratory work, marking the passing of one century since the birth of the man who sought to purify the German race by means of mass murder. It references a timeframe that begins with Hitler's birth (1889) and ends with the reunification of the two German states (1989), a reconsolidation of power which Günter Grass famously anticipated with foreboding by remarking, "The monster wants to become a superpower."[28] Schlingensief's staging of Hitler's last hour at the very moment Germany stood ready to reclaim superpower status (inserting, for example, contemporary television clips into the film) suggests that Schlingensief feels a similar foreboding regarding reunification. At the same time, he confronts Germany with the image of its (horrific) past and links it with the present, suggesting that Hitler is not a monster that can be quickly, efficiently, and permanently killed, but rather, an element that lingers on in the living present. Dietrich Kuhlbrodt, in a review of the film, suggests that

> *100 Jahre Adolf Hitler* corresponds to an actual need to no longer treat Hitler as a phenomenon of evil (although it was comfortable indeed to segregate him temporally and locally, so that one could then explain complacently that one had nothing to do with it). Today it counts much more to say: "I am Hitler" (André Glucksmann). Taking courage for himself (and for us), Schlingensief willfully overcomes fears of contact, as disgusting as that is and as deviant as it may be considered today, and he conjures that which is uncomfortable. By activating myths of silent film, he binds the old expressivity, which he—like Werner Schroeter—had set free, to the generation of the fathers, grandfathers, and their predecessors. And that makes him unique in German cinema.[29]

Not only does Schlingensief suggest that Hitler lives on in every individual German, echoing in some ways Hannah Arendt's argument about the banality of evil, but also, by using techniques reminiscent of silent film, he links German cinematic history to the (hi)stories of the fathers and grandfathers, the generations of the Third Reich: *From Caligari to Hitler* set to film. Schlingensief considers himself a descendant of fascism, hardly confident of his own pacifistic nature. After telling a friend he believed he would make an "excellent guard in a concentration camp,"[30] Schlingensief relates his friend's reaction and explains his own anxiety regarding his personal inheritance:

> He was like "Now what's that supposed to mean?" but no, I'm telling you, […] I have this fear, I probably have those molecules, maybe at some time there was—I'm a few steps removed from Goebbels, my grandmother's maiden name is Goebbels, it was the cousin of a cousin or something like

that, maybe there are molecules in me, [...] hopefully, they won't come into effect, so I've got to use it up from the outset, before it maybe puffs itself up later on and says, "There it is now, I've returned" or something like that.[31]

Schlingensief's anxiety about some sort of latent hereditary fascism links up with the general historical anxiety that found expression in, for example, the historian's debate [*Historikerstreit*] in the mid-1980s.[32] Focusing on the representation of the Holocaust in the historical identity of contemporary Germany, the debate set up binaries of "continuity" and "singularity" as well as "imitation" and "original." As Ernst Nolte, one of the "Band of Four" of conservative historians prominent in the debate, asked, could it not be that "the so-called extermination of the Jews by the Third Reich" was "a reaction or distorted copy and not the first act or the original"?[33] Nolte considered the Gulag Archipelago the "blueprint" for Nazi crimes, and argued for a "continuum" of German history that situated the Holocaust within a larger geographical paradigm of twentieth-century mass murders. Jürgen Habermas, the most prominent liberal voice in the debate, countered that such a denial of the singularity—the monstrous original-ity—of the Holocaust was paramount to relativizing or "normalizing" it. Schlingensief's conflation of past and present enters directly into this debate. As *100 Years of Adolf Hitler* suggests, the repression that enables the current status of liberal democracy in Germany involves not only the suppression of Holocaust memory but also the casting away of shadows thrown by the spectral image of democracy: the irrationality, intolerance, and inequality that democracy seeks—through often violent means—to suppress. Having ignored (or sublimated) the fascination with Hitler, whose continued existence Schlingensief locates in low culture, the mainstream culture has essentially guaranteed that Hitler will return in another form. As he relates in an interview:

That's also the problem with the whole neo-Nazi scene and all those things, it's not worn out, Hitler hasn't been worn out since '45 unfortu-nately, we haven't used him up, we haven't said, leave that shit or any-thing like that, wear it out, use it, and then it'll spin out into nothingness and become tattered und no one will have any interest in putting on this ruined jacket. That doesn't happen, because of course the high-society-culture always comes in and says "No, for God's sake, cover it up, build a temple, madness, careful, beware, not one wrong word" and so on.[34]

By locating the problem in "high-society-culture," Schlingensief suggests that the process of *Vergangenheitsbewältigung* is not only psychologically based, but class-inflected as well. Moreover, it suggests that the disciplining of para-cinema and other "low" modes of representation—disciplining that is written into the legal codes that surveil trash and horror—is not only about "protecting youth" but also, perhaps more significantly, about protecting "proper" ways of channeling a traumatic past.

Das Deutsche Kettensägenmassaker (1990): Reunification as Mass Deception

Schlingensief's "nightmare of reunification,"[35] *The German Chainsaw Massacre* (1990), begins with a grainy, home-movie-style portrayal of a jubilant reunification celebration at the foot of the Brandenburg Gate.[36] Directly following comes a series of shots in which we see a car speed past a woman who has been cut in half, entrails dangling, singing incoherently while intertitles relate: "It happened on October 3rd,"[37] using the vocabulary and tone of a midnight monster flick or sensationalist news magazine to recall the official date of German reunification. The camera pans past the disemboweled woman toward a sign welcoming us to the GDR, which is promptly knocked down by the speeding car, and a second intertitle relates: "Since the borders opened on November 9, 1989, hundreds of thousands of GDR citizens left their old home. Many of them live to this day unacknowledged among us. Four percent never arrived."[38] The idea of "not arriving" in West Germany plays both literally and figuratively. As the narrative unfolds, we discover that these four percent were in all likelihood literally ground into wurst and devoured by a West German family of butchers. But the phrase also plays on another meaning of "never arrived"— there were some East Germans who did manage to make it to the West with their bodies in one piece, but never "arrived" in a metaphorical sense, that is, they failed to adapt to capitalism and fell through the cracks of the system.

The plot of *The German Chainsaw Massacre* is a bizarre twist on the basic formula for the so-called slasher film.[39] Schlingensief's German massacre begins, as does Tobe Hooper's *The Texas Chainsaw Massacre* (1974), with a journey from home (here, East Germany) to a place that is "not-home" or, what Carol Clover calls "The Terrible Place" (here, West Germany). After arriving at the Terrible Place (a West German slaughterhouse), the protagonist Klara encounters a family of psychotic killers who, like the Sawyers in *TCM* "have taken up killing and cannibalism as a way of life." Also in homage to *TCM*, the patriarch is "an aged and only marginally alive grandfather," the sons are "awkward symbols of arrested development," "permanently locked in childhood" by their "cathexis to the sick family," and a poorly preserved corpse is treated as a regular family member (Clover 27). As Clover reminds us, "the horror" that derives from the basic slasher formula "lies in the elaboration" (24) and so, in Schlingensief's Germanized version, the cannibalistic family is West German and East Germans form the victim pool, whose numbers are enriched by influx of "new meat" occasioned by the fall of the Wall. Further historicizing Schlingensief's German variation on the slasher theme, the family corpse is dressed in a Nazi uniform and the protagonist—Clover's plucky "final girl" who is typically transformed from innocent, prudish bookworm to weaponized avenger during the course of the narrative—is tainted from the outset by sexual depravity and violence. Furthermore, although Klara, like *TCM*'s Sally, "manages to escape to the highway, where she scrambles into a pickup and is saved" (Clover 24), her safety is only an illusion; in the second-to-last scene, we see the driver(s) of the pickup truck: son Alfred and the Nazi skeleton. The body of the film is framed by two images that, together, form an apocalyptic vision of the effects of reunification: the first image we see is the West German flag fluttering amidst a sea of jubilant citizens and smiling dignitaries; the last image is a Trabbi, the iconic automobile of the former East Germany, engulfed in flames, thus framing reunification as misguided idealism that ends in (or indeed leads to) the literal engulfing of East Germany.

Like *TCM* before it, *GCM* is rife with social commentary, in particular the critique of capitalism. As Jeffrey Niesel notes with respect to Hooper's sequel *The Texas Chainsaw Massacre 2*, the original Sawyer family represents the epitome of successful entrepreneurship; the homemade "chili" produced in their slaughterhouse hides the conditions of its productions and, notably, is a symbol of "good taste" in at least two senses: first, culinarily, and second, as an aesthetically appealing product marketed to mainstream consumers, who define themselves not least through the appeal to taste and the ability to practice discerning judgment:

> For Sawyer the ideal product doesn't reveal the exploitation and bloodshed of its production. The Sawyers' chili is a perfect example of the way consumer culture covers the violence of commodity production. The chili is made from human flesh, yet it wins awards because of its aesthetic appeal (72).

As Niesel also notes, in the mode of horror, capitalism is understood as being constantly under threat by (classically, feminine) sexuality. In *GCM,* when capitalism is contaminated by sexuality (notably, more often a perverse masculine desire in German horror), violence erupts. For example, the perverse capitalist desire inherent in the Western system is parodied near the beginning of the film in the scene that introduces "final girl" Klara, who later becomes the main target of the cannibalistic West German family. In this scene, we see her sexually ambiguous husband enter their modest East German apartment, describing to her with almost orgiastic fervor his excitement about the fall of the Wall and a possible trip to the West, which promises to bring new job prospects. Whether she wants to break out unencumbered by her spouse, or whether there is some other underlying motive for what happens next, remains unclear. Klara suddenly pulls out a butcher knife and stabs her husband—and their dog—to death. Klara travels into the West to meet up with her West German lover, who tries to have sex with her against a tree as soon as she steps out of her car, exclaiming, "You're in the West now, Klara!"[40] In addition to associating the West with sexual depravity or perversity (the husband's sexual arousal while dreaming of his prosperous life in the West, not to mention his gender confusion, the eagerness of Klara's West German lover, etc.), this scene displays a lack of underlying motives for murder—a lack that characterizes all the ensuing murders as well. In *GCM*, neither Klara's murder of her husband and their dog, nor the ensuing attacks on East Germans by the West German family are framed politically or as cause-and-effect; rather, they are depicted as outbursts fueled by psychosexual perversion and pure blood lust. And yet, the psychosexually perverted subject fueled by pure blood lust is also potentially politically situated. In this sense, Schlingensief's depictions of violence depart from New German Cinema representations not only by virtue of the sheer bloodiness of violence, but also in the sense that Schlingensief's framing of violent acts focuses less on the causes of violence—fascism or the dialectic of enlightenment—and more on the ineffectuality of explanatory apparatuses descendant from the Frankfurt School critiques popular with NGC, such as postmodernism or, in Jameson's terms "the cultural logic of late capitalism." While the film works from within a certain mode of Marxist critique in terms of its exposure of socio-economic inequalities between East and West, it also plays with, and to a certain extent, makes fun of, theory. Stylistically, through the use of montage, for example, thematically, through the valorization of fragmentation, and textually, through the use of parodic or satirical elements and through intertextuality, *GCM* both imitates postmodernist and avant-garde approaches to cinema and, at the same time, ridicules them.[41]

The film ends without the resolution and return to normative values typical of most horror films. Instead, we see Klara ostensibly escaping into the back of a pickup truck, which then turns out to have first son Alfred and the bastard Nazi skeleton-child behind the wheel chuckling maliciously. They drive past Alfred's depraved sister, her dismembered torso singing effusively on the roadside and as the credits roll, a new image appears of a flaming Trabi.[42] While the film offers no obvious progressive message or clear political allegiances, it does point toward the ambiguity of postmodern theory—an ambiguity that is vulnerable to appropriation—, and exposes the difficulties of translating theory into progressive political practice.

Terror 2000: Intensivstation Deutschland (1992)

"If a Keystone Cops film were written by William S. Burroughs,
peopled with characters from George Grosz by way of Russ Meyer,
and directed in a style that suggests Jean-Luc Godard on speed,
you would have a movie with the style and mood of Terror 2000"
(Stephen Holden, New York Times *film review)*

Much in the same way that Nazi sexploitation films such as *Ilsa: She-Wolf of the SS* begin, formulaically, with referencing a "historical precedent" for the narrative that follows, *Terror 2000: Intensive Care Unit Germany* (1992) begins as a faux-documentary, framing the film as a "real-life event" by providing a voiceover that reports in monotone earnestness over an idyllic soundtrack and images of the town of Gladbeck: "The following film describes an authentic case from 1992."[43] Whereas Nazi sex-horror sets up plot as "real" ostensibly in order to partially justify the portrayal of brutal sex acts, the documentary style used in *Terror 2000* seems intended to de-legitimate its subject, which, broadly conceived, can be described as the discourse surrounding immigration in post-cold war Germany (including both multiculturalism and neo-Nazism). The plot revolves around the disappearance of a social worker, along with the Polish family he was escorting to an immigrant camp. The chaos of the immediate post-reunification period is related in the voiceover that continues:

> Germany has changed. The homes for asylum seekers are overflowing. The government is in retreat. The local police are on their own. A large part of the population is out of control and openly resisting. Only the experts are attempting to find a solution, but in vain up to this point. Ladies and gentlemen, dear little boys and girls, enjoy with us in the next few minutes a world full of love, fear, sex, and death. Enjoy with us the world in which we live. Have fun.[44]

While most of the voiceover is accompanied by a tour through the refugees' camp with various images of immigrants and their families, the word "death" is accompanied by a medium close-up of a black man looking directly into the camera, following which we hear the words "have fun," and we see the first image from the actual narrative: a group of men carousing around in a jeep, including a priest and a figure in a white, pointed hood (resembling the garb of the KKK). The plot develops from here in small segments that are subtitled and narrated in the manner of a TV crime drama. The first segment, entitled "Germany Out of Control" introduces us to the social worker Peter Fricke, who is in the process of warning a frightened family of Poles about the dire situation that awaits them in Germany: "[...] there's no social security, but anyway, it's not your problem, because ich bin Peter Fricke, euer Sozialarbeiter [...] and I bring you in an Asylantenheim mit Türken und Juden und Neger [sic]".[45] From the outset, the social worker is depicted as incompetent and naive: he can hardly speak German, he addresses the family in the informal *du* form, which effectively infantilizes them, and, as we learn later in this scene, he has an annoying penchant for singing old socialist hymns, accompanying himself poorly on guitar, while clinging to antiquated ideals of tolerance and bemoaning the decline of social welfare.[46] At this point in the narrative, the men from the jeep appear, shooting Fricke along with several of the Poles, and they rape the young girl. The next segment ("The Inspector Is Coming") fast-forwards a few days and introduces us to the private detective Peter Körn (played by Peter Kern) and his assistant Margret (played by Margit Carstensen), who have been sent to the provincial town of Rassau to investigate Fricke's and the Poles' disappearance.[47] We discover in short time that the authorities, represented by Körn, Margret, and

the occasional appearance of the local police, turn out to be as violent and perverse as the thugs. Following a disturbance at a town event, Körn tracks the men
from the jeep—who turn out to have a shared history with Körn that goes back
to "Gladbeck"—and violently assaults them.[48] As he explains to Margret later, it
has become necessary even for those charged with enforcing the law to use violence: "The German courts don't work any longer—Germany must get tougher
again!"[49] As the violence escalates—from a Nazi rally and the arrival of Michael
Kuehnen (a leading figure in Germany's neo-Nazi scene, played here to the
campiest extreme by Schlingensief himself) to the discovery of the Poles' dismembered bodies by a "miracle healer" and the outbreak of riots in the refugee
camp—it becomes increasingly difficult to differentiate authorities, government
officials, and "regular" Germans from Nazis, terrorists, and gangsters. When the
prime minister arrives in town to attend the funeral of the Polish family, which
is presided over by the homicidal priest who killed Fricke, it becomes clear that
Körn and Margret will not get any help from the government in pursuing the
gang of murderous Nazis. The priest delivers the "eulogy" and explains that the
Poles really only had themselves to blame: "They sought harbor, where there is
no harbor! Germany is not America! We are not an immigration country!"[50]
Instead of reacting with outrage or some measure of emotion, the minister simply adds in nonchalant monotone, "This is not Germany. This is a black spot. It
must be removed," whereupon he tosses a wreath onto the grave "as a warning"
against future attacks.[51]

     The plot makes countless allusions that merit further exploration (and a
more detailed analysis than I have space to provide here). To point up just a few
of these, it bears noting that Schlingensief is playing with several different political discourses throughout the film. As becomes apparent with phrases such as
"Germany must get tougher again!" and "Germany is not an immigration country!", the main object of critique (and butt of Schlingensief's progressivist joke)
is the post-reunification turn back toward conservative policies aimed at curbing
immigration and tightening social welfare. With the increased presence of foreign workers—particularly from the Eastern Block—in Germany, as well as
workers from the former East moving westward, unemployment rose sharply
after the fall of the Wall, prompting renewed ethnic violence. In this context, it
is also important to note the phonological (not to mention political and social)
similarity between the fictional town of Rassau and the actual German town of
Rostock, the mention of which calls to mind for many Germans the wave of
right-wing violence against foreigners that hit this and other cities including
Hoyerswerda, Moelln, and Solingen in the first years following reunification.
The Rostock suburb of Lichtenhagen became famous in August 1992 for the
largest anti-foreigner pogrom since WWII. Denunciations of these attacks, however, were (and are) often themselves denounced by the right as "left-wing
enlightenment" or misplaced indignation. In this sense, the negative comparison
to America ("They sought harbor where there is no harbor") is offered as both
an apology as well as an excuse, part and parcel for right-wing and right-of-
center discourses on multiculturalism and the post-'90s Germany that attempts

to gloss over ethnic violence by situating Germany as a "victim" of invading multitudes bent on sucking on the marrow of the German welfare system. The "black spot" ["schwarzer Fleck"] of ethnic violence, to which the priest makes reference, is also discursively loaded. This is the phrase typically used in reference to the Holocaust and, in general, to Germany's "dark past." Though he insists on its removal, as if it were a laundry stain that could be easily erased, the priest fails to recognize the structural and systemic underpinnings that support the "black spot," which one could read as the blind spot of democracy.

Liberal Democracy and Its Discontents

Splatter, for Schlingensief, is a medium for exposing the "dark side" of liberal democracy, the undercurrent of violence that precedes and in fact legitimates it. While liberalism and liberal democracy, as traditionally conceived, are founded on the elimination of violence, on the guarantee of "life" and the security of the individual above all else, Schlingensief's splatter aesthetic lampoons the politics of life and exposes the heart of liberal democracy as a precarious see-saw teetering between violence and hypocrisy. Underpinning liberal democracy is its public sphere, represented in *Terror 2000* by the throngs of reporters that flock to each catastrophe and encapsulate the complexities of xenophobic violence into sound bites prepared to assuage the anxiety of its viewing audience. Schlingensief's main target, then, is not right-wing radicalism, terrorism, or racism, but rather, liberal democracy itself. By situating his methodology outside the scope of liberalism's prescribed avenues of critique (especially outside the realm of high art), Schlingensief steps outside the circular argumentation of self-righteous indignation that plagues liberalist debates founded on reason and tolerance, debates which, at the turn of the twenty-first century, continue to falter in the face of right-wing attacks on the life, liberty, and happiness that democracy struggles to uphold.

Notes

1. "Gerade die Geschmacklosigkeit erscheint in diesem Zusammenhang als einzig mögliche Antwort auf Deutschland." Michael Althen, *Süddeutsche Zeitung*, November 3, 1992, p. 13. All translations, unless otherwise noted, are my own.

2. "Tötet Helmut Kohl!" was Schlingensief's resounding cry at the 1997 Documenta X in Kassel. See Roland Koberg, "Freiheit für Christoph," *Berlin Online: Berliner Zeitung Archiv: Feuilleton*, p.33, November 1, 1997. Accessed on September 21, 2005. www.berlinonline.de/berlinerzeitung/archiv/.bin/dump.fcgi/1997/0901/feuilleton/0052/index.html. Also available as "Mein Filz, mein Fett, mein Hase—48 Stunden überleben für

Deutschland" at *Schlingensief: Arbeiten: Aktionen: mein Filz, mein Fett, mein Hase (1997).* September 21, 2005. www.schlingensief.com/projekt.php?id=t011.

3. "Ausländer raus! Bitte liebt Österreich." See Schlingensief's website regarding this and other "actions": *Schlingensief: Arbeiten: Aktion.* May 24, 2005. www.schlingensief.com/aktion.php. See also Stefan Keim, "Theater als Teufelsaustreibung [Theater as Exorcism]," *Frankfurter Rundschau,* July 2, 2002. Also available at *Aktion18: Pressespiegel.* May 24, 2005. www.aktion18.de/presse.htm.

4. See "Hamlet," *Schlingensief: Arbeiten: Theaterinszenierungen: Hamlet.* September 26, 2005. www.schlingensief.com/projekt.php?id=t034.

5. A subgroup of film, media, and culture studies scholars is working with the notions of trash cinema and trash aesthetics. For the most part, they also agree to the extent that they locate trash *not* as a feature of postwar society, late capitalism, or postmodernism, but rather, they insist that trash has always been a part of film production. The division between "high" and "low" culture is, according to scholars of trash, an arbitrary one and, moreover, one that needs to be interrogated and differentiated from postmodern notions of, for example, parody, which relies on a certain elite, often socio-economically conditioned, enculturation in order for the "jokes" to be recognized. These scholars include Ian Conrich, Joan Hawkins, Kevin Heffernan, Ernst Mathijs, Tamao Nakahara, Eric Schaefer, Steven Jay Schneider, Jeff Sconce, Linda Williams, and others. In the context of German cinema, scholars such as Linnie Blake, Randall Halle, Steffen Hantke, and Patricia MacCormack are also interrogating the high/low divide within horror and Euro-trash film specifically.

6. "Die Würde des Menschen ist unantastbar" is the first article of Germany's *Grundgesetz,* or Basic Law, equivalent to its constitution. It came into effect in 1949 with the postwar establishment of the state of West Germany and, after reunification, continued in force for all Germany.

7. Steffen Hantke, "Horror Film and the Historical Uncanny: The New Germany in Stefan Ruzowitsky's *Anatomie,*" *College Literature* 31.2 (2004). 121.

8. Schlingensief's term is "Selbstprovokation." For background on the development of this philosophy, see the documentation in, for example, Matthias Lilienthal and Claus Philipp, eds., *Schlingensiefs Ausländer Raus* (Frankfurt/M.: Suhrkamp, 2000).

9. For excellent investigations into the specifically political valences of horror, see Peter Biskind, "Pods, Blobs, and Ideology in American Films of the Fifties," *Seeing Is Believing: How Hollywood Taught Us to Stop Worrying and Love the Fifties* (NY: Random House, 1983) and Joan Hawkins, *Cutting Edge: Art-Horror and the Horrific Avant-Garde* (Minneapolis and London: University of Minnesota Press, 2000). Also, on the double-codedness of parody, see Linda Hutcheon, *The Politics of Postmodernism* (New York and London: Routledge, 1989).

10. John McCarty, *Splatter Movies: Breaking the Last Taboo of the Screen* (St. Martin's Press, 1984). See also Judith Halberstam's chapter "Bodies That Splatter" from her book *Skinflicks: Gothic Horror and the Technology of Monsters* (Durham, N.C.: Duke UP, 1995).

11. Höltgen's term is "Ästhetik der Distanzverlust." See Works Cited.

12. With "distanciation," I am referencing Brecht's *Verfremdung.* While "alienation" is often used for *Verfremdung,* I agree with Fredric Jameson that this translation tends to invite confusion, based on the common usage of alienation for Marx's *Entfremdung.* Jameson, following on Shklovsky, uses the term "estrangement," which gets closer to the spatial metaphor I am invoking here. See Fredric Jameson, *Brecht and Method* (London and New York: Verso, 1998). On the various translations and uses of both *Verfremdung*

and *Entfremdung* across political, theatrical, and sociological terrains, see Ernst Bloch's "Entfremdung, Verfremdung: Alienation, Estrangement," in Erika Munk, ed., *Brecht* (Toronto: Bantam Books, 1972).

13. "vom innen aus" (*Terror 2000*, DVD). As Dietrich Kuhlbrodt notes with reference to *100 Jahre Adolf Hitler*, there is a distinct expressionist undertone in Schlingensief's work. In *Terror 2000*, this expressionist vibe works through the character of the detective-turned-Nazi-madman, who is reminiscent of Robert Wiene's schizophrenic doctor Caligari. In *Terror 2000*, every sector of society is corrupt: not only the neo-Nazi scene, but also the justice system and the social welfare system are contaminated by an almost atavistic violence. In this sense, Schlingensief's meta-cinematic discourse follows a post-Kracauer path: from Caligari to Hitler to Everyman.

14. For readers unfamiliar with this term, it is important to note the play on *Vergangenheitsbewältigung*, a term used frequently in discussions of the Holocaust and the legacy of the Third Reich to refer to the process of "coming to terms with the past." "Gegenwartsbewältigung" means "coming to terms with the present" and is a common variation of the former term, used mostly in the post-reunification context.

15. "Filme[...] in denen Hitler, Vergewaltiger und Amokläufer orgiastischen Unfug anstell[en]" (anon., "Schlingensief: Ein Portrait," *Schlingensief: Schlingensief*, September 21, 2005. www.schlingensief.com/schlingensief.php.

16. Schlingensief is frequently referenced—in venues ranging from his own website to film and theater reviews—as the "enfant terrible des deutschen Kinos." This is a title previously reserved for Rainer Werner Fassbinder.

17. On the subject of "Unification Horror," see Randall Halle's illuminating essay in the volume *Light Motives*.

18. "Schlingensiefs filmische Methoden kennzeichnen seine ästhetische Nachbarschaft zu Fassbinder: Die Neigung, die Bearbeitung eines Stoffs auf einen Einfall oder einen aktuellen Anlass zurückzuführen, Anarchie und Unbedenklichkeit im Umgang mit den Formen der szenischen Darstellung, die Spontaneität des Spielens als minderwertiges Nachstellen von Alltagsrealität und auch ein leichtfertiger, verstörender Hang zur Aggressivität. Der Imitation und der Irritation fallen Schlüsselbedeutungen zu. Es geht um den kürzesten Weg zur Dokumentation eines einmaligen, unwiederholbaren Ereignisses, das somit theatrale Züge trägt. Seine Filme sind persönliche Äußerungen, nicht nur über die Zeit, in der sie spielen, sondern ganz besonders auch über die Zeit ihrer Entstehung" (anon., "Schlingensiefs Filme," *Schlingensief: Arbeiten: Film*, December 1, 2004. www.schlingensief.com/film.php.

19. Fassbinder's German Trilogy consists of *Die Ehe der Maria Braun* (The Marriage of Maria Braun, 1979), *Lola* (1981) and *Die Sehnsucht der Veronika Voss* (Veronika Voss, 1982). On the use of individual bodies as "metaphors for the national body at large," see Caryl Flinn, *The New German Cinema: Music, History, and the Matter of Style* (Berkeley: University of California Press, 2003).

20. The inability to "get over" the past is a tragic flaw of postwar German identity explored most famously by Alexander and Margarete Mitscherlich in their book *Die Unfähigkeit zu trauern. Grundlagen kollektiven Verhaltens* (Munich: Piper, 1967), translated as *The Inability to Mourn: Principles of Collective Behavior* (New York: Grove Press, 1975). It is also interesting to note that, in the German, "getting over" is etymologically related to the words for violence (*Gewalt*) and rape (*Vergewaltigung*). That is, one could argue that the kind of approach to memory and recovery suggested by the term *Vergangenheitsbewältigung* is one that is bound up with (patriarchal) discourses of force and coercion (also lingering in phrases such as "mastering" or "surmounting" the past).

21. Hawkins traces European horror film's fascination with Nazism in the sixties and seventies to Georges Franju's art-horror film *Les Yeus Sans Visage* (*Eyes Without a Face*, a.k.a. *The Horror Chamber of Dr. Faustus*, 1959), which relates the story of a surgeon who murders young girls in order to steal their faces and graft them onto his daughter's, whose visage was mutilated in a car accident for which he feels responsible. As Hawkins writes, the film combines "traditional Sadeian motifs with what might be called the horror of postwar anatomical economy—(too few faces to go around)" (87).

22. The familiar phrase was "Papas Kino ist tot [Dad's cinema is dead]."

23. For most paracinephiles, as Hawkins calls fans of trash and sex-horror, eroticized violence in European horror calls to mind, before all others, Spanish filmmaker Jésus (Jess) Franco. Most fans and critics credit Franco with revolutionizing European horror, beginning with his *Gritos en la noche* (*The Awful Doctor Orlof*, 1962), which Hawkins notes is Franco's "first feature-length horror film" and "first reworking of Franju's *Les Yeux sans Visage* [1959]." The explicit eroticization of violence found in this film is, as Hawkins notes, typical for Franco's brand of sex-horror: "The implied connections between sex and death, blood and semen, cruelty and sexuality, that haunt all horror are laid bare in Franco's work" (97). As Tohill and Tombs note, "Before *Orlof*, horror films had opted for the poetic approach, playing down the sexual element, only hinting at the dark recesses of the human psyche. With *Orlof*, sex sizzled into the foreground, changing the face of Euro horror for the next twenty years" (77). Schlingensief's work can be situated as descendant from this line of explicitly sexual horror.

24. "Waren bis in die 50iger und 60iger Jahren noch Sexualität der Zensur Anlaß, so wandelte sich das Bild mit dem Aufkommen der 'neuen' Horrormovies. Die neue Qualität der Darstellung von Gewalt und Sexualität verursachte eine Sittendiskussion und höchst kontroverse Meinungen des Betrachters. 1973 wird in Deutschland der 'Gummi-Paragraf' § 131 Abs. 3 StGB verabschiedet, und ein neues Zensurinstrument wurde geschaffen. Gewaltdarstellungen (Gewaltverherrlichung) und auch das Sympathisieren mit eben dieser ist ab jetzt kriminalisiert. Als einziges Land der Welt schafft Deutschland einen Regulativ[,] der effektiv und gezielt eingesetzt werden kann (Seim/Spiegel 1995). Etliche Filme wurden auf Grund der harten strafrechtlichen Gangart auf den Index gesetzt oder sogar verboten. Von Seiten des Jugendschutzes wurden Schlagwörter wie 'Jugend desorientierend', 'verrohend', 'sittengefährdend,' oder 'Gewalt verherrlichend' zu Schlagwörtern, und eine regelrechte 'Gewalt-Paranoia' machte sich mit der in der Presse aufgebauschten Video-Welle in den 80iger Jahren breit" (Weinrich, n.p.).

25. Regulars in Schlingensief's films include actors such as Margit Carstensen, Udo Kier, Volker Spengler, Peter Körn, and Alfred Edel—these and others appearing in his work are faces familiar from New German Cinema, especially from Fassbinder films, and avant-garde cinema of the 1960s and onward.

26. "Ein Medium darf nicht in die Liste aufgenommen werden 1. allein wegen seines politischen, sozialen, religiösen oder weltanschaulichen Inhalts, 2. wenn es der Kunst oder der Wissenschaft, der Forschung oder der Lehre dient, 3. wenn es im öffentlichen Interesse liegt, es sei denn, dass die Art der Darstellung zu beanstanden ist." *Jugendschutzgesetz*, Abschnitt 4, §18, Absatz 3. For an overview of the history of the *Bundesprüfstelle*, see *Wikipedia: Bundesprüfstelle für Jugendgefährdende Medien.* (September 22, 2005) at: de.wikipedia.org/wiki/Bundespr%C3%Bcfstelle_f%C3%BCr_ jugendgef%C3%A4hrdende_Medien. The current law went into effect in April 2003 following a Columbine-esque incident in Erfurt, replacing the *Gesetz über die Verbreitung jugendgefährdender Schriften* from 1954. The first item to be placed on the original Index was a Tarzan comic. More recently indexed, well-known films include *The Texas*

Chainsaw Massacre (available only in edited form) and *The Texas Chainsaw Massacre 2* (banned throughout Germany since 1990). Within the past year, online reproductions of the Index are no longer available on the internet (for fear that the list itself is an "advertisement" for youth-endangering films).

27. "[...]die Bilder der Welt zu verbessern, um die Welt zu verbessern" (Kuhlbrodt, n.p.).

28. "Das Monstrum will Grossmacht sein."

29. "100 JAHRE ADOLF HITLER korrespondiert mit einem aktuellen Bedürfnis, Hitler nicht mehr als Phänomen des Bösen zu behandeln (wie war es doch bequem, den Führer zeitlich und örtlich auszugrenzen, um dann selbstzufrieden zu erklären, dass man damit nichts zu habe). Heute gilt vielmehr: 'Hitler bin ich' (André Glucksman). Sich selbst (und uns) Mut machend, überwindet Schlingensief vorsätzlich Berührungsängste, so eklig das auch ist und so viel Abweichung heute auch darin gesehen wird, und beschwört das Nicht-Geheure. Indem er Mythen des Stummfilms aktiviert, bindet er die alte Expressivität, die er—wie Werner Schroeter—freigesetzt hatte, an die Generation der Väter, Großväter und Vorderen. Und damit ist er einzigartig im deutschen Film" (Kuhlbrodt, n.p.).

30. "Das war damals für Thomas Mitscherlich beim Hitler-Film natürlich ein unglaublicher Faux-Pas, ich hab' gesagt, ich glaub', ich wär exzellenter Aufseher in einem Konzentrationslager geworden," from Christoph Schlingensief and Anonymous, interview, *100 Jahre Adolf Hitler: Die Letzte Stunde im Führerbunker,* dir. Christoph Schlingensief, 1988/89, DVD, 451 Filmgalerie, 2004.

31. "Da war er irgendwie 'Ja, was soll denn das jetzt heißen?' aber nein, ich sag' mal, [...] ich hab' diese Angst in mir, ich hab wahrscheinlich solche Moleküle, vielleicht war da irgendwann—ich bin über einige Ecken mit Goebbels verwandt, meine Großmutter ist eine geborene Goebbels, das ist die Kusine der Kusine gewesen oder so was, vielleicht gibt's da Moleküle in mir, [...] hoffentlich kommen die nicht zur Wirkung, also muss ich's doch vorher schon abnutzen, bevor es nachher vielleicht sich selber so aufbläht, und sagt, 'da ist es jetzt, da bin ich wiedergekommen" oder so [...]' (Schlingensief, interview excerpted from *100 Jahre Adolf Hitler,* DVD).

32. For a good overview of the *Historikerstreit*, see Rudolf Augstein et al., eds., *Historikerstreit: Die Dokumentation der Kontroverse um die Einzigartigkeit der nationalsozialistischen Judenvernichtung* (Munich/Zurich: Piper, 1987) and also the special issue on the *Historikerstreit*: *New German Critique* 44 (Spring/Summer 1988).

33. *Historikerstreit,* p.32, quoted in *Wikipedia: Historikerstreit.* September 25, 2005. de.wikipedia.org/wiki/Historikerstreit.

34. "[D]as ist ja auch das Problem vom ganzen Neo-Nazis Szene und von den ganzen Dingen, es wird nicht abgenutzt, den Hitler hat man leider seit '45 nicht abgenutzt, man hat ihn nicht zum Gebrauch hingeworfen, halt gesagt, lässt die Scheiße oder so, nutzt es ab, nutzt es, und dann wird's sich zerschleudern und zerfleddern und keiner wird mehr Interesse haben, diese kaputte Jacke anzuziehen. Das passiert nicht, weil natürlich immer diese Hochadelskultur einsetzt und sagt, 'Nein, um Gottes willen, Käseglocke drüber, Tempelanlage bauen, Wahnsinn, Vorsicht, Achtung, kein falsches Wort jetzt' und so weiter, und auch da hat Deutschland immer versucht, Punkte mitzumachen, indem es sagt, 'Ja, wir wissen worum es geht. Jetzt haben wir gerade Probleme, weil wir nicht mehr wissen, was sollen wir denn mit Israel anfangen.'" (Schlingensief, ibid).

35. "Alptraum-Inszenierung der Vereinigung," description by Inga Meißner, "Das Deutsche Kettensägenmassaker," *Das Deutsche Filminstitut: Sozialgeschichte des*

bundesrepublikanischen Films: Die Neunziger Jahre (2002), accessed on June 1, 2005.
www.deutsches-filminstitut.de/sozialgeschichte/dt103.htm.

36. Usually abbreviated hereafter as *GCM*.

37. "Es geschah am 3. Oktober."

38. "Seit Öffnung der Grenzen am 9. November 1989 haben Hunderttausende von
DDR Bürger ihre alte Heimat verlassen. Viele von ihnen leben heute unerkannt unter uns.
Vier Prozent kamen niemals an."

39. Variations and elements of the slasher can be found in movies such as Tobe
Hooper's *The Texas Chainsaw Massacre*, 1974; John Carpenter's *Halloween*, 1978; Sean
S. Cunningham's *Friday the 13th*, 1980; Wes Craven's *A Nightmare on Elm Street*, 1984;
Jim Gillespie's *I Know What You Did Last Summer*, 1997; and in parodic form, in so-
called "neo-slasher" films like Wes Craven's *Scream*, 1996 or Keenan Ivory Wayans'
Scary Movie, also known as *Scream If You Know What I Did Last Halloween*, 2000. See
also Vera Dika's seminal essay on the topic of stalker films, which are closely related to
the slasher, if perhaps not as extreme in their depictions of bodily violence. Stalkers and
slashers are characterized primarily by elements such as a "masculine controlling vision"
(the point of view of the killer, who remains predominantly off-screen and is represented
through the camera's eye), a "two-part temporal structure" that introduces the killer's
motivation (usually psychosexual in nature, originating in a childhood "primal scene"),
victims who are sexually active and attractive, and a heroine who triumphs over the killer
by taking up the active role, often by means of a phallic instrument such as a knife or
stake. Vera Dika, "The Stalker Film 1978-1981," in Gregory A. Waller, ed., *American
Horrors: Essays on the Modern American Horror Film* (University of Illinois Press,
1988) 86–101. On the figure of the serial killer and the move toward graphic, violent
spectacle in slasher films, focusing especially on *Henry: Portrait of a Serial Killer*, see
Cynthia Freeland, "The Slasher's Blood Lust," in *Dark Thoughts: Philosophic Reflections on Cinematic Horror*, eds. Steven Jay Schneider and Daniel Shaw (Lanham, MD
and Oxford: The Scarecrow Press, 2003) 198–211.

40. "Du bist jetzt im Westen, Klara!"

41. In terms of intertextuality, *The German Chainsaw Massacre* has an obvious ante-
cedent in Hooper's classic, but it also quotes films such as Hitchcock's *Psycho* and Romero's *Night of the Living Dead*. While it is typical of more recent horror film to use
postmodern elements such as citation or self-referentiality, it is usually done for comic
effect, whereas Schlingensief uses it in a critical way, and while his use of postmodernism may also produce some comic effect, it is a decidedly "blacker" humor. As Steven
Jay Schneider notes, satire and intertextuality are both characteristic of the "postmodern
treatment of horror generally, whereby audience overfamiliarity with character types and
narrative conventions is offset (in theory, if not always in practice) by the knowing laugh-
ter generated from self-referential dialogue and plot devices" (189). Yet, where the films
Schneider is talking about (mostly the "neo-slashers" such as *Scream* and *Scary Movie*)
are intended to poke fun, Schlingensief's use of intertextuality, while it may also aim to
entertain, makes use of texts gleaned from "high" and "low" culture in order to interro-
gate the categories of taste constructed through practices of cultural and socio-economic
exclusion.

42. The Trabbi (short for Trabant) is a make of automobile that is iconic for East
Germany.

43. "Der nun folgende Film schildert einen authentischen Fall aus dem Jahr 1992."

44. "Deutschland hat sich verändert. Die Asylantenheime sind überfüllt. Die
Regierung befindet sich auf dem Rückzug. Die Polizei vorort ist allein gelassen. Ein

grosser Teil der Bevölkerung ist ausser Kontrolle geraten und leistet offen Widerstand. Nur die Fachexperten bemühen sich um Klärung der Lage doch bisher vergeblich. Meine Damen und Herren, liebe Jungen und Mädchen, geniessen Sie mit uns in den nächsten Minuten eine Welt voller Liebe, Angst, Sex und Tod. Geniessen Sie mit uns die Welt, in der wir leben. Gute Unterhaltung" (voiceover, *Terror 2000*, VHS).

45. "[...] because I am Peter Fricke, your social worker, and I bring you to an asylum with Turks, Jews, and Negroes" (the translation is not provided in-line here in order to maintain the ridiculous-sounding nature of the German-English mix from the original).

46. This undoubtedly calls to mind Germany's most prominent political singer-songwriter Wolf Biermann, expatriated from East Germany in 1976.

47. See Liane von Billerbeck, "'Ich war Teil der Meute': Zehn Jahre nach dem Pogrom von Lichtenhagen: Täter, die zu Märtyrern gemacht werden, eine Mordanklage und ein ungewisses Urteil ['I was part of the mob': Ten years after the pogrom of Lichtenhagen: Perpetrators made into martyrs, a murder accusation, and an uncertain judgment]," *Die Zeit: Politik: Justiz* 25/2002.   September   21,   2005. www.zeit.de/archiv/2002/25/200225_lichtenhagen.xml.

48. "Gladbeck" references the actual hostage crisis originating in Gladbeck, Germany, during which Dieter Degowski and his accomplice Hans-Jürgen Rösner took captive over 29 hostages, fatally shooting two, including a woman named Silke B., and led the police on an international chase that was followed closely (and sensationally) by both radio and television media. The sensationalism that accompanied the crisis led to many public debates about the representation of violence in the media, among other things.

49. "Deutsche Justiz funktioniert nicht mehr—Deutschland muss wieder härter werden!"

50. "Sie suchten Hafen, wo kein Hafen ist. Deutschland ist nicht Amerika! Wir sind kein Einwanderungsland!"

51. "Das ist nicht Deutschland. Das ist ein schwarzer Fleck. Es muss weg."

Works Cited

Clover, Carol. *Men, Women and Chainsaws: Gender in the Modern Horror Film*. Princeton: Princeton University Press, 1992.

Creed, Barbara. *The Monstrous-Feminine: Film, Feminism, Psychoanalysis*. London: Routledge, 1993.

Das Deutsche Kettensägenmassaker [The German Chainsaw Massacre]. Dir. Christoph Schlingensief. Perfs. Karina Fallenstein, Susanne Bredehöft, Artur Albrecht, Volker Spengler, Alfred Edel, Brigitte Kausch, Dietrich Kuhlbrodt, Reinald Schnell, Udo Kier, Irm Hermann, Eva Maria Kurz, Ingrid Raguschke, Mike Wiedemann. Videocassette. Filmgalerie 451, 1990.

Flinn, Caryl. *The New German Cinema: Music, History, and the Matter of Style*. Berkeley: University of California Press, 2003.

Halle, Randall. "Unification Horror: Queer Desire and Uncanny Visions." *Light Motives: German Popular Film in Perspective*. Eds. Randall Halle and Margaret McCarthy. Detroit: Wayne State University Press, 2003. 281–304.

Hantke, Steffen. "Horror Film and the Historical Uncanny: The New Germany in Stefan Ruzowitsky's *Anatomie*." *College Literature* 31.2 (2004): 117–42.

Freeland, Cynthia A. "The Slasher's Blood Lust." in Schneider and Shaw, 198–211.

Halberstam, "Bodies That Splatter." *Skinflick: Gothic Horror and the Technology of Monsters.* Durham, N.C.: Duke University Press, 1995.

Hawkins, Joan. *Cutting Edge: Art-Horror and the Horrific Avant-Garde.* Minneapolis and London: University of Minnesota Press, 2000.

Holden Stephen. "Absurdist Spoof of Nazism." *The New York Times,* November 18, 1994, C20.

Höltgen, Stefan. "Distanzverlust als Motiv des modernen Horrorfilms [Loss of Distance as Motif in the Modern Horror Film]." *Splatting Image* 54 (2003) n.p.

100 Jahre Adolf Hitler: Die Letzte Stunde im Führerbunker [100 Years of Adolf Hitler: The Last Hour in the Führer's Bunker]. Dir. Christoph Schlingensief. Perfs. Udo Kier, Margit Carstensen, Alfred Edel, Brigitte Kausch, Dietrich Kuhlbrodt, Volker Spengler. DVD. Filmgalerie 451, 1989.

Jameson, Fredric. *Postmodernism, or, the Cultural Logic of Late Capitalism.* Durham: Duke University Press, 1991.

Kern, Louis. "American 'Grand Guignol': Splatterpunk Gore, Sadean Morality, and Socially Redemptive Violence." *Journal of American Culture* 19.2 (1996) 47–59.

Kuhlbrodt, Dietrich. "Portrait: Christoph Schlingensief." *Filmzentrale: Gesammelte Filmkritiken,* March 28, 2005. www.filmzentrale.com/rezis/schlingen siefdk.htm. [Article first appeared in epd film, 1989]

McCarty, John. *Splatter Movies: Breaking the Last Taboo of the Screen.* New York: St. Martin's Press, 1984.

Niesel, Jeffrey. "The Horror of Everyday Life: Taxidermy, Aesthetics, and Consumption in Horror Films." *Journal of Criminal Justice and Popular Culture* 2.4 (1994) 61–98.

Rectanus, Mark W. "Populism, Performance, and Postmodern Aesthetics: Christoph Schlingensief's Politics of Social Intervention." *Gegenwartsliteratur* 3 (2004) 225–249.

Schneider, Steven Jay. "Murder as Art / The Art of Murder: Aestheticizing Violence in Modern Cinematic Horror." in Schneider and Shaw, 174–97.

Schneider, Steven Jay and Daniel Shaw, eds. *Dark Thoughts: Philosophic Reflections on Cinematic Horror.* Lanham, MD and Oxford: The Scarecrow Press, 2003.

Sconce, Jeffrey. "Trashing the Academy: Taste, Excess, and an Emerging Politics of Cinematic Style." *Screen* 36.4 (1995) 371–93.

Terror 2000. Dir. Christoph Schlingensief. Perfs. Margit Carstensen, Peter Kern, Susanne Bredehöft, Alfred Edel, Udo Kier, Artur Albrecht, Kalle Mews, Brigitte Kausch, Dietrich Kuhlbrodt. Videocassette. Filmgalerie 451, 1992.

Tohill, Cathal, and Pete Tombs. *Immoral Tales: European Sex and Horror Movies 1956–1984.* New York: St. Martin's Press, 1995.

van der Horst, Jörg. "Schlingensief United." *Schlingensief: Arbeiten* (2002). May 25, 2005. www.schlingensief.com/arbeiten.php.

Weinrich, C. "Zensur und Verbot im Genrefilm. Die große Schnittparade des Horror- [sic] und Splatterfilms [Censorship and Banning in the Genre-Film. The Great Cut-Parade of Horror and Splatter Film]." September 21, 2005. www.censuri ana.de/texte/genrefilm/genre.htm.

Buttgereit's Poetics: *Schramm* as Cinema of Poetry

Mikel J. Koven

How does one theorize the work of extreme German filmmaker Jörg Buttgereit? His films, while highly controversial for their themes of necrophilia, murder and pornography, are likely to disappoint fans of extreme horror movies, as they are filmed with an aesthetic sensibility more akin with experimental and low-budget art-cinema than exploitation.[1] And yet, Buttgereit's cinema is often too rough, raw and graphic for modernist bourgeois art-cinema goers; his films do not reflect the kinds of intellectual rigor, meaning-making, or thematic exploration one would expect from art-cinema. Being "neither fish nor fowl" makes Buttgereit's work difficult in the extreme to theorize or make sense of. At least, it is difficult to make sense of it beyond its creator's sobriquet of pretentious shock-master with delusions of profundity—which may be equally appropriate. But before damning Buttgereit outright, viewers might want to think of his cinema within the framework of Pier Paolo Pasolini's theory of "the cinema of poetry," which the author/filmmaker proposed in 1965. It may just be that through this lens of "cinema of poetry" Buttgereit's films can be appreciated. To get to this point, I will first summarize Pasolini's definition of "poetical cinema" and then apply it to Buttgereit's 1993 film *Schramm*.

Telling the story of the final days of serial killer Lothar Schramm (Florian Koerner von Gustorf), and of his friendship with his prostitute neighbor Marianne (Monika M), *Schramm* progresses in a highly nonlinear way. The film opens with Schramm literally whitewashing his blood-splattered apartment after murdering what we eventually discover to be two Christians who have knocked on the wrong door in their evangelical mission. Schramm falls from his ladder, cracking his skull open on the floor. As he lies there, alone and bleeding to death, his red blood mixing with the spilled white paint, he reflects back on his life as killer and his friendship with Marianne. On one level, *Schramm* is a highly conventional horror film, but the *narration* of the film—how we are presented with this information, rather than how we reconstruct it in our minds—is completely within the conscious and subconscious awareness of Schramm himself as he lies dying, and underlines the highly subjective nature of Buttgereit's cinema in general.[2] This is a story we can never fully "trust" because we are never outside of Schramm's own mind.

The Cinema of Poetry

During a round-table discussion at the 1965 Pesaro Film Festival, Pier Paolo Pasolini, along with Christian Metz, Umberto Eco, and G. D. Volpe, began formulating what is commonly referred to as the discourse of film semiology (Greene 92). However, Pasolini's presentation, titled "Il cinema di poesia" ("The Cinema of Poetry"), liberally peppered as it was with generalized and simplistic slogans about the nature of cinema and reality, was heavily criticized as naive in its approach to film semiotics. Even today, Pasolini's essay is still largely dismissed due to what is seen as flaws within his perception and representation of cinematic sign-systems. Scholars such as Teresa de Lauretis and Gilles Deleuze have, respectively, tried to return to the central components of Pasolini's thesis, but still "poetic cinema" as discourse remains marginalized within Film Studies.[3] This paper, in part, attempts to redress this omission, though space, or inclination, prevents me from engaging too much with Pasolini's thoughts on film semiology. Although escaping entirely from those debates is impossible, as they are directly entangled with his thoughts on "the cinema of poetry," my focus will be more on what potentially makes cinema "poetic" rather than on the semiotics of cinema.

To begin with, Pasolini conceives of "the cinema of poetry" as being dream-like, that is, anti-rational, anti-narrational, and, therefore, anti-prosaic. He noted that the world *as conceived* is made up of image-signs (im-signs), but that the order and meaning given to these im-signs is linguistic (Pasolini 544). *Pre*-linguistic meaning transcends ideology, and thus becomes much more impressionistic and irrational (Pasolini 545). As Pasolini himself notes, "the word (linguistic sign) used by the writer is rich with a whole cultural, popular and grammatical history, whereas the filmmaker who is using an im-sign has just isolated it, at that very moment, from the mute chaos of things—by referring to the hypothetical dictionary of a community which communicates by means of images" (Pasolini 546). Cinema, therefore, in its most linguistically basic form, is a combination of these im-signs;

> Cinema, or the language of im-signs [...] is at the same time extremely subjective and extremely objective (an objectivity which, ultimately, is an insurmountable vocation of naturalism). These two essential aspects are closely bound together, to the point of being inseparable, even for the needs of analysis. The literary function also is double by nature: but its two faces are discernible: there is a "language of poetry" and a "language of prose" so differentiated that they are diachronical and have two divergent histories. (Pasolini 548)

Pasolini's grand project was to try to move cinema away from the rational and narratological world of the prose text towards a more "oniric nature of dreams ... of unconscious memory" (Pasolini 549). And to do this, the film poet needed to move away from an ideologically defined sense of "naturalism" towards an increasingly subjective cinema.

It is this combination of im-signs and language that was—and in many respects still is—heavily contested in 1965. Critics, like Antonio Costa, saw little value of studying Pasolini's theoretical writings as they "are of little or no use for the development of a scientific semiology of the cinema, nor for film theory and/or film criticism" (qtd. in de Lauretis, 159). But, as de Lauretis notes, neither was Pasolini himself interested in a *scientific* study of film semiology, thereby rendering Costa's criticism largely moot; nor was there much value in exploring Pasolini's insights into "the relation of cinema to reality and to what he called human action" (de Lauretis 159).

Pasolini proposed this combination of reality and human action with the cinema through a cinematic equivalent of "free indirect subjective" discourse within the film. While naturalism and realism are conveyed through the standard (and for Pasolini, prosaic) filmic system of continuity, such representations can be considered similar to omniscient narration within written prose. But when moving towards a cinema of poetry, Pasolini equated the subjective shot (the shot-reverse-shot, or an eye-line match) with the cinematic equivalent of direct discourse within literature (Pasolini 550). For Pasolini, true cinema of poetry would be that cinema which abandons altogether the distinction between character and camera or other cinematic apparatus; a cinema which, for him, only exists theoretically. As he noted, "I do not believe any film exists which is an entire 'free indirect subjective,' in which the entire story is told through the character, and in an absolute interiorization of the system of allusions belonging to the author" (Pasolini 551). One example Pasolini cites as coming close to a true cinema of poetry is Michelangelo Antonioni's *Il Deserto Rosso* (*The Red Desert*, 1964), on which he comments:

> The "cinema of poetry" [...] characteristically produces films of a double nature. The film which one sees and receives normally is a "free indirect subjective" which is sometimes irregular and approximate—in short, very free. This comes from the fact that the author uses the "dominant state of mind in the film," which is that of a sick character, to make a continual *mimesis* of it, which allows him a great stylistic liberty, unusual and provocative. Behind such a film unwinds the other film—the one the author would have made even without the pretext of *visual mimesis* with the protagonist; a totally and freely expressive, even expressionistic, film. (Pasolini 555; emphasis in original)

For Naomi Greene, Pasolini's "free indirect subjectivity" was his search for a cinematic equivalent of the literary "free indirect discourse" which "denotes the technique whereby an author conveys a character's thoughts or speech without either the quotation marks that accompany direct discourse or the 'he/she said' of indirect discourse" (113). For Deleuze, as Greene argues, the idea of "free indirect subjectivity" needed to be re-examined: "Deleuze now suggests that free indirect subjectivity refers to a kind of mimesis between a character's subjective vision and the camera, which sees both the character and his vision in a transformed manner" (Greene 117).

But how does "free indirect subjectivity" manifest itself on the screen? In both Pasolini's theoretical construct and his own filmmaking, one needs to recognize a contrast between cinemas of poetry with cinemas of prose: to wit, Hollywood's continuity system. If the objective of Hollywood continuity filmmaking was never to let the camera's presence be felt, then the cinema of poetry must demand the opposite (Pasolini 556). Pasolini does note that those moments of poetry within classical Hollywood cinema were often due to poetry as linguistic *technique*, and not a specific poetic cinematic *language*. For "the cinema of poetry" properly, Pasolini argued for a rupture in the continuity system of filmmaking.

> Thus one feels the camera, and for good reason. The alternation of different lenses, a 25 or a 300 on the same face, the abuse of the zoom with its long focuses which stick to things and dilate them like quick-rising loaves, the continual counterpoints fallaciously left to chance, the kicks in the lens, the trembling of the hand-held camera, the exasperated tracking-shots, the breaking of continuity for expressive reasons, the irritating linkages, the shots that remain interminably on the same image, this whole technical code was born almost of an intolerance of the rules, of the need of unusual and provocative liberty, a diversely authentic and pleasant taste for anarchy, but it immediately became a law, a prosodic and linguistic heritage which concerns all the cinemas in the world at the same time. (Pasolini 556–7)

The excesses of style and drawing attention to the film's formal construction create cinema's "double nature," as Pasolini refers to it above. When our attention is focused not on the narrative but on the formal construction of the image, we are invited to contemplate the materiality of that image, only partially with regards to its mimesis. "Since this 'other' film is created totally through formal means, its true protagonist—and, by extension, the true protagonist of the cinema of poetry—is style itself understood, essentially, as a stylistic liberty that calls attention to itself by breaking the rules" (Greene 120).

So, for Pasolini, when stylistic liberties rupture the narrative prose and we are asked instead to contemplate the formal means of the image's construction, and when that rupture derives from a character's subjectivity thereby fusing the character's subjectivity with mechanical reproduction of the camera itself, we are invited, if not *required*, to question the very poetics which are presented to us. At this point, Greene turns into a detractor of Pasolini's detractors, who in accusing the writer of naivety, reveal merely their own (Greene 108). Greene cites Deleuze's observation that what Pasolini was wrestling with was the establishment of "the ontological ground for cinema" (Greene 108). For de Lauretis, Pasolini

> is concerned with film as expression, with the practice of cinema as the occasion of a direct encounter with reality, not merely personal and yet subjective; he is not specifically taking on, as [his critics were], cinema as institution, as a social technology which produces or reproduces meanings, values and images *for* the spectators. [...] [For Pasolini] cinema, like poetry, is *trans*linguistic: it exceeds the moment of the inscription, the technical apparatus, to become 'a dynamics of feelings, affects, passions, ideas' in the moment of reception. (de Lauretis 164; emphasis in original)

What Pasolini was offering was a means of, in de Lauretis's words, "reclaim[ing] iconicity ... not so much *from* the domain of the natural or *from* an immediacy of referential reality, but *for* the ideological" (emphasis in original). De Lauretis's example is Pasolini's own film *Salo* (1975), wherein the atrocities depicted on-screen are so dispassionate and extreme, "one simply *can not* see: one must decide, choose, will oneself to see it, to look at it, to listen to it, to stay in one's chair, not to get up and leave" (emphasis in original). Choosing to watch and subjecting oneself to someone else's images—whether to *Salo*, for de Lauretis, or to *Schramm*—becomes both ideological and ontological; a distanced engagement with the social act of watching a film and the questions such an act raises about *our pleasure.*

Schramm as Cinema of Poetry

One wonders what Pasolini would have made of a film like *Schramm*. For, like the Antonioni film Pasolini praised as poetry, Buttgereit presents us with a film that is almost exclusively "free indirect subjective"; a film which takes place almost entirely within the (untrustworthy) mind of its protagonist. The extended use of "free indirect subjective" disrupts the generic familiarity one may experience watching a serial killer horror movie, where one would normally expect a more linear and "objective" representation of the horror. Buttgereit's films tend towards highly neurotic characters as protagonists, a feature Pasolini himself identified as representative of the director's own "obsessive vision" and as one of the central hallmarks of "the cinema of poetry" (Greene 118). Greene herself notes: "Free indirect subjectivity ... implies a degree of mimesis between the author's vision and that of the neurotic protagonists—and an 'abnormal' stylistic liberty; this liberty, in turn, betrays an obsessive relationship with reality even as it breaks with the conventions of film syntax" (120). Through a close textual analysis of certain key sequences in *Schramm*—to date,

Buttgereit's most recent film—Buttgereit's cinema in general, and *Schramm* in particular, I would like to argue that we are dealing with examples of Pasolini's "cinema of poetry."[4]

The film's opening sequences underline the narrative conceit: the credits on a black background are intercut with highly distorted images of Schramm's naked chest and blurry footage of legs running in a city marathon. After the credits we are presented with perhaps the only non-subjective image in the film (and even this may be part of Schramm's fantasy)—a newspaper with a photograph of Schramm and a headline reading "the lonesome death of the lipstick killer" ("Einsamer Tod des Lippenstift-mörders"). We are then presented with a series of abstractly constructed images of Schramm lying dead, naked except for a pair of boxer shorts, in a pool of white paint. Again, intercut within these images is footage of the city marathon. The camera spins closer to Schramm and the soundtrack features impatient knocks on the door. We see, filmed in reverse action, Schramm's artificial leg, which appears bloody and righting itself from the ground. We see a quick montage, accompanying the impatient knocking on the apartment door: Schramm answering the door, first, for two Christians on a mission, then for Marianne, Schramm's neighbor, a prostitute, who briefly talks about her latest trick. The impatient knocking on the soundtrack continues, however. Finally, we are fully sutured into the filmic world as Schramm answers the door and invites the Christians in once again, only to murder them moments after serving them drinks. But as naturalistic as this murder sequence apparently is, the screams of both victims and Schramm himself are heavily distorted and filmed in slow motion.

The world of *Schramm*, as poetical cinema, from the very first frame on, is oneiric. We are denied any context as to what the images we see and the sounds we hear are attached to within a concrete and realist narrative cinema (for that would be "prosaic cinema"). Even the newspaper we are presented with, which should be keying us towards seeing the film as a stereotypical serial killer narrative, becomes dreamlike since we are not given any context beyond Schramm's subjective as to whether or not the newspaper is real. As Schramm lies dying, alone, suffering an "Einsamer Tod," as the newspaper pointed out, we are presented with too many questions for a cinema of prose. Sounds are distorted throughout this sequence, including a replay of the dialogue between Schramm and the two Christians, which, the second time around, is heavily distorted and overdubbed with images of the two people naked and dead, posed in various positions while photographs, presumably by Schramm himself, are being taken.

After these two murders (and we are only led to assume this chronology), Schramm paints his entire apartment white to cover up the blood-splattered walls in a textbook example of the relationship between language and im-sign. Schramm is literally covering up his crimes, whitewashing them, as home movie footage of Schramm's childhood (we are again to assume) is intercut. Buttgereit presents us with a series of image-signs, which have larger linguistic connotations (in English: "whitewashing"), while in a purely denotative sense, we see him attempt to cover up the evidence of his crimes (both in English and in German: to paint over, "übertünchen"). But the home movies intercut within this sequence also echo a larger sense of the past—not just in the immediate past (the murder of the Christians) but also Schramm's own past. If we are to believe Linnie Blake, Buttgereit's obsession with "the past," which occurs in a variety of manifestations across his *oeuvre*, echoes his own feelings of national identity within a post-Nazi Germany. "Buttgereit's films dwell on the existential isolation of the desiring German subject and the libidinally ambiguous re-animation of the deeply repressed historical past" (Blake 192). In *Schramm*, this murderer is happily whitewashing over the evidence of his crimes, which reinforces the political echoes of this image. But complicating this even further, particularly at the ideological level of a cinema of poetry, is that the home movie footage used in this sequence, according to the director in the audio commentary on the DVD, was found footage. That is, these images are of other people's memories, not belonging to Schramm or any of the actors or crew working on the film, but random memories of someone else entirely. The pastoral image of children playing on a beach, of an almost bucolic idyll of childhood lost, is juxtaposed against Schramm painting over the blood splatters on his wall. This melancholic referral to the past, and *anybody's past*, is clearly gone, and replaced by a murderous present.

True cinema of poetry, however, turns the techniques of prosaic realism back on themselves. Schramm's loneliness and alienation from other people comes across via his eavesdropping through the ventilation shaft on Marianne having sex with one of her clients in her own apartment. Schramm becomes so aroused by this sound, which dominates the soundtrack, that he reveals a cheap sex-toy he keeps in his bed: a rubber torso of a woman, just breasts and a vagina. We first see, from an overhead shot, Schramm fondling something under the covers of his bed. The camera does not cut away, but Schramm gets out of his bed and walks off camera. He returns to pull back the sheet revealing the sex-toy and then disappears from the shot again. He returns, naked and begins to fondle the breasts of the torso, before moving into position to "mount" it. The only camera movement in this shot is a track backwards away from Schramm as he begins to have sex with the toy. The only cut we get is to an even more explicit shot, as the camera picks up on Schramm in a medium side view where we see him fully inserted into the rubber vagina. As we hear on the soundtrack Marianne's client's climax, Schramm changes position slightly to co-ordinate his climax with the client's (this is an assumption since the event and the action do coincide). The camera pans and tracks backwards almost discretely away from Schramm and his toy, out of his bedroom and into the bathroom, finally focusing on the bathtub itself. Schramm's climax is added to the soundtrack. But rather than an act of cinematic discretion, this camera movement sets up the second part of this single shot, wherein we witness Schramm bringing the sex-toy to the tub to rinse out his semen.

These two shots are exactly two minutes in length total; the first shot is 45, the second shot 75 seconds long. Here, attention is drawn to the filmic construction, not through heavy montage, as during the film's opening sequence, but by its *refusal* to edit, to cut away. We are confronted with what is normally a private activity, masturbation with a rubber sex-toy, but are shown this with almost documentary realism. By not editing the sequence, at least into shorter individual shots, Buttgereit draws attention to the mechanisms of construction and the pleasure of watching onscreen sexual activity, even if masturbatory. But Buttgereit takes this even further in the second of these two shots, by panning and tracking in what we assume at first to be a moment of uncharacteristic discretion. Instead the shot reveals its utter banality as Schramm must now clean up his own semen out of his toy. Again, like the images of the murderer painting over his crimes, Schramm must literally clean up after his own desire. Sex and gore, the staples of exploitation cinema, are here revealed to be not only messy, but events after which someone has to clean up, too.[5]

In both the cases so far discussed, the cinematic techniques of montage and realism/*mise-en-scène* are heightened to draw attention to themselves and the poetical echoes they may incur. But the horror or gore set-piece during which the special effect or prosthetic body part is introduced, can be equally poetic— particularly when dealing with horror cinema, even low-budget, or even exploitation cinema with delusions of grandeur (like Buttgereit's films). Again, due to the oneiric structure of the film, it is difficult to ascertain how certain scenes fit into the chronology of the film's story. Hence one must look at how these sequences fit within the context of their surrounding scenes. For example, Schramm drives Marianne to a wealthy client's party and she instructs him to wait for her while she does her job. She pokes her head out of the party at one moment, revealing that she is wearing a Hitler Youth costume. We then cut away to Schramm visiting the dentist. While the editing of the dentist sequence is handled in a fairly straightforward manner, maintaining stylistic and chronological continuity, the dentist is shot from Schramm's perspective in the chair, with the dental light dominating the left side of the frame and the dentist's face beside it dominating the right side of the frame. As the dentist painfully extracts one of Schramm's teeth, the scene is intercut with reaction shots of Schramm. Once the tooth is removed, the shot holds steady, following the editing pattern we saw above with the rubber torso. The dentist has seen something else that "looks quite bad" and picks up another pair of tongs to try and remove it. But unlike the dental pliers that came towards the camera at the bottom of the frame in the earlier shot, these tongs now move directly towards the center of the camera lens. The insert shot, although of Schramm again, is from a different angle, and the tongs are used to pry open his eyelids, causing his eyeball to pop forward. The dentist returns, but this time with a scalpel and proceeds to cut out Schramm's eyeball. Once the eyeball has been fully removed and grasped with forceps, what should be a return to the same shot of the dentist is still the same visual composition, except that now Marianne, dressed as the dentist, has taken the dentist's place. She holds up the eyeball and looks at it fascinated. The following shot returns us to the car, as Marianne returns after her job. The sequence is thus revealed to be yet another fantasy.

This fantasy, however, is not actually Schramm's but Buttgereit's himself:

> To me this was the most direct commentary by Jörg himself on how he feels about his movies, because the whole eye thing [in *Schramm*], the dentist taking out an eye after he has taken out a tooth, was a dream he had. He wanted to incorporate it and I thought we should. In my opinion, the taking out of the eye, like the loss of teeth in dreams, is closely connected psychologically with castration, and this whole fear of castration is running strongly in the movie. I found it a nice in-joke that it was really Jörg's dream. The taking out of the eye to me is a heightening that at the same time, is a punishment for having looked. He is imagining that his gaze has a kind of life of its own, for which he is punished. (Franz Rodenkirchen in Perks, 213)

This biographical interpretation notwithstanding, the removal of Schramm's eye is fully in keeping with the other castration images which permeate the film. Throughout the film, Schramm fantasizes about his own leg being lost, removed or otherwise incapacitated. His running in the marathon stands as an im-sign of virility, strength and power. It is this imagined artificial leg which causes him to lose balance on the ladder and the fall to his death. Perhaps Schramm's imagined injuries are a stand-in for Buttgereit's own fears about his virility and masculinity. But then, with the pop-sociology and psychology about serial killers and their sexual virility issues being so commonplace, reading the film as autobiographical, even by the film's producer and co-screenwriter, is perhaps a bit naïve or disingenuous.

However, a reading more appropriate to the "cinema of poetry" offers itself elsewhere in the film. In perhaps the most extreme moment of the film, Schramm nails his own foreskin to a chair. We first of all see him carefully choose a color of lipstick (he rejects one before making his decision) from a drawer in which he keeps mementos from his kills. Again, this is all assumption, since we are never allowed any information external to Schramm's own subjective. Intercut is Schramm presumably fantasizing about a previous murder during which he fondled the corpse. Schramm takes his penis, pulls at his foreskin, and marks it with the lipstick. He picks up a small finishing nail, lines it up with the lipstick mark, and begins to hammer the nail into his foreskin. Again, intercut with these images are scenes of his fondling the corpse of a previous victim. Mercifully, the extras provided on this DVD edition of *Schramm* confirm that for the actual nailing shots a prosthetic penis was used, but up until that shot, it is the actor's own penis. Buttgereit's commentary on this sequence is thematically useful here; he notes that Schramm is trying "to close his dick so he can't do any more harm" and that he is "closing the danger down."

The position of this sequence within the overall film complicates matters further. The eye-removal sequence occurs between those sequences of Marianne on the job while she is dressed in a Hitler Youth costume for the titillation of her wealthy clients. However, with all these sequences conveyed through free indirect subjectivity, if Schramm is trying to "close down the danger" of his murderous objectification of women, the fantasy in the dentist's office is about his own refusal to look, or refusal of *the desire* to look, at Marianne on the job. Furthermore, Marianne's costume, combined with Schramm's eye-removal fantasy, further implies a refusal to look towards the past. Within Schramm's subjectivity, he would rather have his own eye removed than confront the *historical* truth. This interpretation is verified by Linnie Blake, who notes "at the heart of Buttgereit's *oeuvre*, it seems, is an awareness of the politically problematic dimensions of visual pleasure, the uses to which that pleasure has been placed in the past and the linkage of that past to the present" (198). But here in *Schramm*, that pleasure is punished; first by the removal of Schramm's eye, punishing both Schramm and the spectator for watching (or at least *desiring* to look) and finally the ultimate punishment of male genital mutilation.

Conclusions

Shock-cinema, to which, for all its artistic pretensions, *Schramm* like the rest of Buttgereit's films ultimately belongs, is predicated upon transgressive images of sex and violence. *Schramm* is structured around these four shocking set-pieces—the violence of the murder of the two Christian missionaries, Schramm having sex with the sex-toy (and perhaps, more significantly, rinsing out the toy after he has ejaculated into it), the removal of Schramm's eyeball in the dentist's office, and finally Schramm nailing his own penis to a chair. In between these sequences, the mundane and almost prosaic story is almost never removed from Schramm's own subjective narrative position, calling into question any external verification of the events depicted in the film.

Clearly, the film's subjective position within the psychotic mind of Lothar Schramm makes *Schramm* a good candidate for a cinema of poetry; its stylistic fusion of a character's subjectivity with the mechanical documentation of cinema itself point to that conclusion. But the set-pieces themselves structure the cinematic poem, keying the spectator to interpret this free indirect subjective with particular intensity. Blake notes that this "makes Buttgereit a highly self-referential director, one who consistently references, and re-configures, the cinematic medium in his work" (200).[6] Within these set-pieces we are continually distracted by their material construction—through montage, continuous shots, and prosthetic special effect "appliances" (the penis, the eyeball). Endowed with self-referentiality, the set-pieces, on the one hand, take "as their premise the horrors of a past prematurely buried." On the other hand, they "work to expose the complicity of the film medium in acts of ideological manipulation of the subject, and, in turn, point to the ways in which that medium can bring about a re-sensitisation to the horrors of the past" (Blake 202), in particular of German filmmakers refusing to look to their own past (the removal of Schramm's eye), preventing their doing any more harm (the nailing down of Schramm's penis) or whitewashing over the past crimes. For scholars such as Blake, these images directly echo Germany's National Socialist past. Or, taking the route of de Lauretis and Deleuze, we can argue that in *Schramm*, as cinema of poetry, Buttgereit challenges the very ontology of cinema itself, challenging individual spectators to question their own pleasures in watching Schramm/*Schramm*, and thereby questioning the very pleasures of cinema.

My own position lies somewhere in between: while *Schramm* may offer up interpretations like Linnie Blake's, I can equally recognize the more general ontological issues pointed out by de Lauretis or Deleuze. "Shock" cinema, of which *Schramm* and Buttgereit's other films clearly are examples, shocks us for a reason. We may deconstruct these shocking sequences and images for their technical composition or their use of special prosthetic effects, but we do this specifically because the film's verisimilitude has been ruptured. These shocking sequences call attention to themselves through a kind of Brechtian *Verfremdungseffekt*, by which we are jolted out of our cinematic complacency to think not only about the "how" of such a sequence, but, more importantly, about the "why." More than just interesting because of their shock value, these sequences—not only in Buttgereit's films but in any shocking sequence in a film—demand from us that we think about the very ontology of cinema and our pleasures in exposing ourselves to such images. In *Schramm*, Buttgereit dares his audience to watch—watch the private interaction between a man and his rubber sex toy, watch a killer kill—but then also punishes that pleasure through images of eye-removal and penile mutilation. Pasolini's "Cinema of Poetry" allows us to see these ruptures in a film's verisimilitude as ontological acts.

Such ruptures must be inherently political too; after all, both Brecht and Pasolini were nothing if not political theorists. The kind of reading to which Linnie Blake subjects Buttgereit's films, and those Buttgereit himself performs on his films in commentaries and interviews, open up these films to historical and political interpretations, particularly in regard to contemporary German culture and its relationship to the crimes of the Nazi past. But we do not need to go so far in our analysis to see how a "Cinema of Poetry," even in horror cinema, can be political: in violating the verisimilitude of bourgeois realist cinema through shocking set-pieces, films like *Schramm* challenge the taste culture of high modernist art (particularly in cinema). As I noted from the outset, Buttgereit's films are too "artsy" to appeal to shock-horror fans, and too shocking to appeal to bourgeois modernist high-art cinemagoers. Buttgereit's "cinematic poetics" shock the complacency of the bourgeois film audience, challenging their definitions of representation.

Pasolini's forty-year-old essay "Il cinema di poesia" throws new light on the analysis of exploitation cinema, allowing us to view "corpse-fucking-art," as

Buttgereit himself characterizes his own work, as poetical cinema (Kerekes 40). But, as anyone who has read the doggerel written on the inside of any public toilet or greeting card can attest, just because something is identified as poetry, is no guarantee that it is of *quality*. *Schramm* may be poetic, but it is not very good poetry.

Notes

The author would like to thank Kelly Jones, whose valuable comments helped to fashion a better essay.

1. One comment on the Internet Movie Database page for *Schramm* reflects this dissatisfaction with blending an art-house sensibility with extreme splatter in terms of fan disappointment. "Some ... reviews have compared this to *Henry: Portrait of a Serial Killer* [(1986, John McNaughton)] but I think that they should all get their heads examined because this one doesn't even come close. It's too arty and boring for that ..." (comment by Macabro357. IMDb. www.imdb.com/title/tt0108053/usercomments). Accessed on July 27, 2005).

2. Terms and usage derive from Bordwell and Thompson, 69–72.

3. This may be due, at least in part, to academic film studies moving away from semiotics in the 1970s.

4. Since *Schramm*, Buttgereit appears only to have directed a single episode of the German-Canadian science fiction series *Lexx* (syndicated, 1997–2002); episode 2.09 "791."

5. Perks notes a similar theme running through all of Buttgereit's films. "There is no back story, as if the characters have no history, and often little dialogue, no explanation for why these characters do the things they do. Disturbing images simply have to be dealt with: thus, dead bodies are sought, washed and prepared" (Perks 210–11).

6. Linda Ruth Williams, writing in *Sight and Sound* in 1994, discusses how the extreme *mise-en-scène* of Dario Argento's horror films are a self-conscious awareness of the medium's artifice in a way that is equally appropriate to my discussion of *Schramm*. Her interpretation of Argento's use of violence to eyeballs reframes it as a self-reflexive "punishment" of the audience for looking.

Works Cited

Blake, Linnie. "Jörg Buttgereit's *Nekromantiks*: Things to Do in Germany with the Dead." *Alternative Europe: Eurotrash and Exploitation Cinema Since 1945.* Eds. Ernest Mathijs and Xavier Mendik. London: Wallflower Press, 2004. 191–202.

Bordwell, David and Kristin Thompson. *Film Art: An Introduction.* Seventh edition. London: McGraw-Hill, 2004.

de Lauretis, Teresa. "Re-Reading Pasolini's Essays on Cinema." *Italian Quarterly* 82.3 (1080): 159–66.

Greene, Naomi. *Pier Paolo Pasolini: Cinema as Heresy.* Princeton, NJ: Princeton University Press, 1990.

Kerekes, David. *Sex Murder Art: The films of Jörg Buttgereit.* Manchester: Critical Vision, 1998.

Pasolini, Pier Paolo. "The Cinema of Poetry." Trans. Marianne de Vettimo and Jacques Bontemps. *Movies and Methods Vol. 1.* Ed. Bill Nichols. Berkeley: University of California Press, 1976. 542–58.

Perks, Marcelle. "A Very German Post-Mortem: Jörg Buttgereit and Co-Writer/Assistant Director Franz Rodenkirchen Speak." *Alternative Europe: Eurotrash and Exploitation Cinema Since 1945.* Eds. Ernest Mathijs and Xavier Mendik. London: Wallflower Press, 2004. 203–15.

Williams, Linda Ruth. "An Eye for an Eye." *Science Fiction/Horror: A Sight and Sound Reader.* Ed. Kim Newman. London: BFI, 2002. 13–17.

Necrosexuality, Perversion, and *Jouissance*: The Experimental Desires of Jörg Buttgereit's *NekRomantik* Films

Patricia MacCormack

The grave's a fine and private place,
But none, I think, do there embrace.
Andrew Marvell, "To His Coy Mistress"

In spite of being rarely recognized as a subgenre of horror cinema, necrophilia films have a varied genealogy. One of the earliest examples of necrophilia in film was Germanic. Fritz Lang's *Metropolis* (1927) shows the automaton Maria (Brigitte Helm) as the fetishized lover devoid of volition. While not technically dead, Maria is Galatea to Rotwang's (Rudolf Klein-Rogge) Pygmalion, a relatively immobile but nonetheless compelling object of desire. The camera closes in on Maria deliriously while she is static, and it is before her "life" that she becomes a cinematic icon. In the 1960s and 1970s modern horror revisits the necrophile in the Roger Corman cycle of Poe adaptations, particularly in *The Fall of the House of Usher* (1960), *Tales of Terror* (1962), *The Premature Burial* (1963) and *The Tomb of Ligeia* (1965). These lyrical hymns to lost love developed a cadaverial viscerality primarily in Italy. The suggested necrophilia in Riccardo Freda's *The Terrible Secret of Dr. Hichcock* (1962) and Mario Bava's *Lisa and the Devil* (1973) was transformed into exercises in baroque gore in Antonio Margheriti's *Flesh for Frankenstein* (1973) and Aristede Massacesi's *Beyond the Darkness* (1979). With the exception of *Dr. Hichcock*, the story of a surgeon intent on recreating his dead wife through the murder of his new wife, these films lack the hierarchical power dialectic one would expect from these films, whereby placing themselves in positions of power and dominance, the living fetishize the dead.[1] One could argue that *Lisa, Beyond,* and *Flesh* are about fascinated and delirious desire rather than any form of aggressive control that may be involved in owning and manipulating a corpse for one's own pleasure. The corpse is simultaneously an object of desire as well as a facilitator of onanistic pleasure, problematizing positions of object, subject, memory and fantasy. In 1985, *Lucker the Necrophagous* (1986) returned the corpse to the status of a symbol, representing the quickening of violent and aggressive desire at the expense of the object. Lucker is a killer whose drive to destroy women is the reason for and means to fetishizing the corpse. This can also be seen in the recent *The Necro Files* and *The Necro Files 2* (Matte Jaissle, 1997 and 2003) and *I'll Bury You Tomorrow* (Alan Rowe Kelly, 2002). While never addressed as entries in an independent horror genre, many horror films about necrophilia have offered examples of the immobilized body as variously symbol of perverse desire, control, love, experimentation with the flesh, nostalgia and loss. Clearly, while these films all share a focus on the dead body, they do not share the same definitions of perversion, desire, power or intent.

German director Jörg Buttgereit's *NekRomantik* (1987), *Der Todesking* (1989) and *NekRomantik 2* (1991) introduced specific gender paradigms into necrophilia, ordinarily presumed a male form of sexuality. While *Todesking* is more a cinematic contemplation of death, the *NekRomantik* films present complex and intriguing examples of a variety of forms of necrophilia. All three of Buttgereit's death films share a sense of domestic banality and emphasize practicalities of death and necrophilia, such as preservation, decomposition, and abject fluid by-products. This ordinariness, juxtaposed with such an extreme form of sexuality, creates a unique representation of necrophilia and death, or, more particularly, of the residual matter of the dead, "who" are as enigmatic as they are repellent. Buttgereit's films have been maligned as offensive. They remain banned in many countries, including Finland, Norway, Singapore, Australia, and the United Kingdom.[2] There is still a sense that even in "serious" studies of horror films Buttgereit's necrophilia films are examples of the lowest form of horror as art and even pseudo-porn.[3] Analyzing these films seems to come with the need for vindication of film choice and also a theoretical contextualization which neutralizes the sensationalistic elements of the film as social phenomena, extricated from the purely conceptual aspect of their content. While the point of this essay is to analyze the films in relation to their philosophical paradigms, I feel it necessary to mention the state of these films as social pariahs in reference to issues of censorship, licit and illicit pleasure, and most importantly, the fact that the concept of necrophilia is one which is intensely repudiated, repressed or met with outrage. One could argue that extreme reactions occur because these films are particularly visceral, though, as I will argue below, no more aggressive or violent than relatively banal horror or action films. The films show in detail what is only suggested in other films. Ironically the banality and practicality of the messy business of necrophilia, distanced from the hermeneutic fetishized body seen in a variety of representations from the cinematic to the artistic, is precisely what offends many people. The desensationalized aspects of the film seem to elicit sensational responses. These films evoke a primal "yuk" factor which is subsumed and neutralized by a sense of moral outrage, or a dismissal of the films as childish. Perhaps Buttgereit's "childish" films tap into a childish plateau of disgust which escapes signification? This essay, however, is not about the psychoanalytic relationship, cathartic or antagonistic, between the viewer's sense of decency and the images, and so while mentioning these issues seems salient here, the essay analyzes Buttgereit's films purely through a variety of philosophical issues to do with abjection, corporeality, perversion and feminism.

Perhaps the sensationalist aspect of Buttgereit's films can contextualize their place in German cinema. Another film which emerged in 1987 was *Violent Shit* (Andreas Schnaas), the story of a butcher who escapes from an asylum and kills people violently and gruesomely, with an added scatological element thrown in. And really that is all that happens. Both films were victim either to the censor's scissors or banned outright and so both became part of a certain mythos of extremity that was as much to do with their procurement as their content. Before the World Wide Web, sourcing banned titles was not easy, and the look of fifth- and sixth-generation copies added to their perceived seediness. This association with the act of discovery and procurement connects *Violent Shit* and *NekRomantik*. Both include violence, both are low-budget and both are viscerally explicit. I would argue that *Violent Shit* sets out to be so, emphasized in the title, while *NekRomantik*'s title already suggests a strange juxtaposition of two seemingly irreconcilable terms. The main commonality is the extremity of gore in both films. In terms of narrative, *Violent Shit* shares more with the stalk-and-slash films of a similar era from America, the prime difference being the level of gore associated with the murders, and the budget. The zenith of the British "video nasty" phenomenon occurred in the late 1980s. The majority of films banned were European. The status of *NekRomantik* and *Violent Shit* represented a perceived malaise in "European" cinema which did not conform to the more "civilized" hygienic representations of violence in films from English speaking countries. The distance between the U.S. and U.K., and "Europe," was both geographical and moral. In regard to textual context, Linnie Blake has suggested that the *NekRomantik* films belong more to the German literary tradition of Faust and Goethe than the video nasty canon. Blake places the films at the end of the evolution of New German Cinema, which deals primarily with issues of memory and forgetting, burial (metaphoric and actual) and trauma.

> Like Syberberg before him, Buttgereit is a director who engages creatively with that strand of Romantic irrationalism that has lain at the heart of German culture since long before the nation's first unification in the 1870s— an irrationalism that once manifested itself in Goethe's rendering of the Faust legend, Hoffman's tales of the *Unheimlich* in prose and, much later, in the horror tales of Weimar cinema. Existing somewhere between the nightmare world of the ghost train, the crazy logic of dreams and the representational strategies of avant-garde or experimental cinema, Buttgereit's films joyfully participate in this irrationality—especially through the frequent inclusion of lengthy or repeated sequences of highly perplexing viscerality. (Blake, 2003)

With one exception, even the images selected for Blake's article are "arty"-looking—black and white, nuanced and somewhat lyrical. What Blake's article shows, and what my essay will attempt to continue, is the place of Buttgereit's films as part of larger cinematic and philosophical paradigms which are ablated when the sensationalism of the images is privileged over their ideological or theoretical context.

Concerning the Corpse

Discourse on necrophilia varies between epistemes. Psychiatry describes necrophilia as aggressive pathology, psychoanalysis as an externalized hatred of self. Both systems of knowledge share an overvaluation of reified subjectivity which is invested as a microcosmic version of the macrocosm of society. Sick individuals virally threaten to infect the arbitrary cultural definitions of normality, threatening as much because they fail at self-regulation as they do obedience to an enforced regulation of behavior. Pathological individuals pose a threat to definitions of normality because they do not internalize concepts of normalization. This means they refuse social concepts of normality, and thus the self as valuable only within strict definitions of what makes subjectivity valuable. Put simply, not *wanting* to fit in is as threatening as not fitting in. About the scientific pathologization of aberrations, Michael Foucault claims:

> This was in fact a science made up of evasions since, given its inability or refusal to speak of sex itself, it concerned itself primarily with aberrations, perversions, exceptional oddities, pathological abatements and morbid aggravations. It was by the same token a science subordinated in the main to the imperatives of morality whose divisions it reiterated under the guise of the medical norm...strange pleasures, it warned, would eventually result in nothing short of death; that of the individual, generations, the species itself. (53–54)

This system of normality defined not positively but only in relation to aberrations reflects the way in which subjects are interpellated by their deviation from the base level of subjectivity as white, male, able-bodied and so on, or, conversely, as woman, black, gay, diffabled, old, young, deviate. Necrophilia seems particularly resonant in this case as the value of subjectivity is repudiated for the object of desire. The corpse makes demarcations of object and subject ambiguous. But in spite of being devoid of will and capacity to act, the corpse is also overvalued by the necrophile, taken as sacred. In spite of being in control of the sexual paradigm, the necrophiliac subject tends to disappear when the corpse is overvalued. The corpse in necrophilia (rather than in necro-fetishism where it functions as object of conceptualization, admiration or contemplation) does not function purely to affirm the subject positioned in opposition to it. It does not represent the affirmation of the self as not-corpse. The corpse is situated through connectivity rather than alterity.

The majority of films and art dealing with "necrophilia"—or more frequently with the fetishization of the purity of the body as perfected in death—concern the female body. Buttgereit's films are rare because they focus on male corpses, used both heterosexually by women and homo- and bisexually by men. "To represent over her dead body," writes Elisabeth Bronfen, "signals that the represented feminine body also stands in for concepts other than death, femininity and body—most notably the masculine artist and the community of survivors" (xi).

Desire for the dead is repudiation of the very systems of which Foucault speaks, resulting in the conceptual death of the subject who materializes via traditional structures and values in society based on opposition, function and corporeal signification. This will become a key aspect of my analysis of the female necrophilia seen in *NekRomantik 2* as a potentially phylic form of sexuality entirely independent of the bisexual necrophilia of *NekRomantik*. But it is difficult, if not redundant, to attempt to decide whether the necrophile values death of these systems themselves, or desires upon a paradigm independent of that which it refuses. The question is whether it is death that is desired, or something entirely unique found in the dead? Foucault, however, would ask not what the necrophiliac desires, but what drives the compulsion to ask. After all, this is not a form of pleasure which is inherently violent or challenging to the rights of another living entity. Technically, from a Kantian perspective it is at worst a transgression of another's property, and therefore is not even relevant within a discussion of ethics. But the medical compulsion to analyze necrophilia is an example of Foucault's claim that science continues rather than breaks with morality. The pathologization of desire for the corpse masquerades as respect for the dead subject, assuming—though not explicitly confessing to—the belief that the subject within the body will live beyond its death in some form of afterlife. The pathologization of necrophilia then is a Christian rather than a logical clinical one. In psychoanalysis, necrophilia is an issue of mental health. To "save" the patient from this tendency is to both save his "self" and save him from himself. Freud's patient Schreber is exemplary. Schreber's belief that he, his parents, and his love objects had become corpses is the most famous incarnation of the relationship between the inability to demarcate the living from the dead as a symptom of psychosis.

Concurrent with this attitude toward the corpse is another inherent ambiguity, which is the urgent need to get rid of the corpse as filth. Everyday filth, such as excrement, blood and saliva, must be extruded from the subject to reiterate the borders of self as separate to the dirt it produces. When a subject becomes filth by shifting from person to corpse the contradiction of it being beloved friend and horrific object is irresolvable but nonetheless real. If filth threatens to make us materially dirty, sticky or messy, the corpse is the ideological filth that sticks to the very idea of self. Foucault's emphasis on generational and social continuity is an example of the death of self repudiated through thinking in broad social terms instead of individual deaths. Social norms, the family name, and traditions help us believe that man does not die. It shocks us to face the fact that, while traditions "live" on, we will inevitably not be part of that living. Burying the corpse allows the subject to transform from matter to memory. Necrophilia reminds us we are only matter. Religious faith both ritualizes the ridding of the corpse from the world, and claims that the corpse has nothing to do with subjectivity once the soul has fled. This belief, however, in no way prevents deep shock and outrage at the corpse being used after death.

Capitalism continues these traditions. The corpse has expended its use as subject and should be thrown away. Extending this analysis from film to other German corpse-art forms, Professor Gunther von Hagens, pathologist and artist, has recently caused outrage by using donated corpses to create art.[4] Von Hagens' baroque sculptured configurations of bodies, organs, and flesh may be considered strange, morbid, or shocking. But essentially the simple fact of the corpse being on display is the root of the outrage. Recently Von Hagens performed a public autopsy on Britain's Channel 4 and presented a four-part program entitled *Anatomy for Beginners*. The faces of the corpses were concealed in plaster to protect their "identity," a decision which really protects both relatives and the public from being exposed to the face, which is the primary site of recognition of "personhood." Von Hagens' subjectivity has been transformed from everyday pathologist, with its associations both of power and will indivisible from institutional interests, to one whose morbid interest in corpses is dubious, purely because it is creative and public. The scientist who deals daily with the corpse conceals his work when he conceals the corpse's identity, a fact that resonates with Foucault's point that the scientist analyzes the aberrant but is himself never analyzed.

Von Hagens' work shares with cinema the notion of spectacle. The spectacle of the corpse makes matter of the empty signifier "corpse." Witnessing the corpse re-anchors the subject as dead matter. Kristeva states: "If dung signifies the other side of the border, the place where I am not and which permits me to be, the corpse, the most sickening of waste, is a border which has encroached upon everything ... No, as in true theatre, without makeup or masks, refuse and the corpse *show me* what I permanently thrust aside in order to live" (3, original emphasis). We can neither separate our proper borders from those of the corpse as we can with personal filth, nor separate the filth of the corpse—the corpse not as filthy but as filth—from the subject it once was. The corpse does not represent or signify death, it is subjectivity as pure matter.

> Dirt then is never a unique, isolated event. Where there is dirt, there is a system. Dirt is the by-product of a systematic ordering and classification of matter, in so far as ordering involves rejecting inappropriate elements. This idea of dirt takes us straight into the field of symbolism and promises a link up with more obviously symbolic systems of purity. (Douglas 35)

The corpse cannot be considered a by-product because it cannot be extricated from the identity or subject it once was. To reject a corpse is to reject a loved one, to ritualize the rejection through the funeral allows the necessary contradiction of rejection, remembrance, and respect resolution. Concealing the corpse allows us to signify it as soul and hermetic body, not rotting flesh. Seeing the corpse, in all its sticky filthiness, makes us bear witness to subject become cadaver, as Kristeva states, without the masks of signification. It cannot be symbolized. To classify it as filth again classifies a loved one as both rejected and impure. The cleaned-up, white-frocked, best-suited, preserved, and embalmed cadaver suspends the classificatory boundary between purity and dirt for as long as the deceased is publicly visible.

Sexual practice, while historically contingent in its aspects and values, has also been subsumed as part of a rigid system of classification. Sex, whatever its incarnation, has been ritualized as one of the three most important life phase rituals, all deeply associated with the flesh and with the disgusting by-products it produces. Birth and death are occurrences usually concealed from public view. Marriage, in Christianity at least, vindicates sex, by limiting its availability to the marriage partner and focusing on reproduction over pleasure. Sex with the corpse allows it to transform from coffin/pure to decomposing/impure, refusing the suspended symbolism the funeral affords, simultaneous with expressing a form of sexuality become filthy. Necrophilia both de-ritualizes and de-symbolizes the already tentative grip classification has on the messy business of vital, irrefutable, and inescapable incarnations of the body, or subject as only body. Thus the subject who marries the risks of sex, including all its fluids, sounds and smells, with the corpse, both intensifies sexual activity as including desire (for the love object) and disgust (in fluids, flesh and vulnerability) with the respect and disgust found in facing the corpse.

Von Hagens' spectacles mingled with sexual desire can be seen in earlier Germanic art, such as N. M. Deutsch's 1517 painting "Death embraces the Maiden." Here death's "embrace" is also without pretty signification. Death, who, one could argue, is not gendered as it is skeletal and thus without flesh, "embraces" the maiden without pretty signifiers of love. It is interesting that the body is non-gendered and the necrophile is female. More frequently we see the female corpse fetishized by the male. Death pushes its hand between the maiden's legs, and her hand assists quite adamantly. Like death, sex is abstracted through signification, aberrations are emphasized to detract from the already rather aberrant nature of this brutally corporeal act. Sexual ecstasy—what Bataille calls "ex stasis" which he defines as out of body and out of self—and the corpse show self outside of flesh but nothing more than flesh. In its focus on flesh and the anxieties the flesh produces, sexual pleasure challenges stable subjectivity by emphasizing matter and abjection—body fluids, smells, vulnerability and loss of control. Can we say sexual pleasure evokes abjection even before it is placed in proximity to the obvious abjection of necrophilia?

NekRomantik

Jörg Buttgereit's *NekRomantik* (1987) and *NekRomantik 2* (1991) offer two very different examples of necrophilia. *NekRomantik* tells the story of a couple, Rob (Daktari Lorenz) and Betty (Beatrice M) as they explore their necrophilic drives with third-party corpses—necrophilia *a trois*, if you like. Their house is decorated with images of fashion models metonymically juxtaposed with pictures of serial killers. This suggests that their desires see beauty as inextricable from destructive impulses. Their necrophilia, however, is complex. Rob procures corpses for himself and Betty through his job in a clean-up crew for accidental deaths. His inner drives are associated with aggression and frustration. He kills Betty's cat in a rage and then bathes in its entrails. He also kills a prostitute, both out of anger that, while being alive, she cannot excite him, and to create the corpse he desires.

The couple's house is adorned with jars of human organs in formaldehyde. This is the first signifier that the pleasure these two achieve from corpses is not altogether contingent on mimicry of banal sexual acts with a perverse object choice. Rather perversion constitutes a form of pleasure which celebrates the body as dis- or re-organized, a body beyond traditional organization. This is what Gilles Deleuze and Félix Guattari would call a body-without-organs, not a body devoid of organs but of its traditional organization and the signification of each part. For examples, genitals are the organs which contextualize the body as belonging to one or another gender, skin writes race on the body, internal organs have both physiological and symbolic meaning (e.g. the heart pumping blood and representing love). During the sex between Betty, Rob and the corpse, Rob sucks ecstatically on the cadaver's eyeball. The organs in the house are objects of desire unto themselves; they do not need signification within the context of a body or subject. Even though he is "with" a male corpse, it would be reductive to claim this act was one of homosexuality. The eyeball as sexual object is neither gendered, nor is its sexual function pre-signified. How do we signify the eyeball as a sexual object? If we are compelled to do so are we back in the world of fetishism? The de- and re-organization of the significations of the body and its libidinal parts both challenges gender and the desirability of some parts at the expense of others. Sexuality is not organized around genitals, nor sex around the appropriate use of appropriate parts. All that matters is the matter of the corpse.

The most interesting moment of necrophilia occurs at the film's end, with Rob killing himself. Lying on the bed with an enormous erection, he plunges a knife into his abdomen. The jet of semen spouting from his erection becomes red as he shudders in both orgasm and death throes. His death elucidates discrepancies between the body's inside and outside, the object of desire as both living (just barely) and dead (almost), self and other, subject and object, *petite* and actual *mort*. The oppositions are neither removed nor exchanged. Rob's death involutes rather than polarizes binary terms, proposing desire within not beyond a frontier—masturbation, necrophilia, murder, suicide, pain, pleasure (but not masochism, not pain for, or at the expense of, pleasure), sexual ecstasy and death. The abject serves as a

> frontier, a repulsive gift that the Other, having become *alter ego*, drops so that the "I" does not disappear in it but finds, in that sublime alienation, a forfeited existence. Hence a *jouissance* in which the subject is swallowed up but in which the Other, in return, keeps the subject from foundering by making it repugnant. One thus understands why so many victims of the abject are its fascinated ones—if not its submissive and willing ones. (Kristeva 9)

Rob gives himself as a gift to what Bataille calls sexual plethora, that is to say, proliferation through alterity within the self. Sacrifice—of the prostitute, of the cat—is a means to an end dependent on the relation of will by one power against and through the destruction of another. The other must become object in order to be sacrificed. The gift takes the self as sacrifice, as other. Unlike a sacrifice, a gift is not an end but an object whose function is to instigate infinite pleasure rather than finite appeasement. Rob and Betty's corpse threesome and Rob's final act refuse an aggressive power diagesis because they reorganize bodies, desire, and binary dialectics. "The seductive, the marvelous, the ravishing," states Bataille, "wins every time over the need to organize things to last, over the resolute intention to become more powerful" (236).

Ironically, Betty and Rob seek to make their corpses last in the most pragmatic way through attempts to preserve them against decompositions. Still, they renegotiate sexual paradigms, adamantly refusing the organizing significations of the body which maintain and make the persistent definitions of acceptable desire last. Consequently, they have forsaken the need to have power over their sexual drives through knowledge of these drives anchored in established and reified understanding of the lasting definitions of bodies, sex and desire. Death, however, does not truncate Rob's sexual life, as we shall see when he is excavated by Monika M in *NekRomantik 2*. While cognizant of the irreducible split within the self when positioned toward the abject, Kristeva's theory on abjection, as it relates to desire, maintains a notion that there must be an abject or abject-ed object (being or made abject) positioned against the self. Although challenged in Rob's death scene, Rob and Betty's sexuality is disorganized through opposition to the dead as much as through a perversion of desire. There is a resonance seen in Rob's violent outbreaks that the procurement of the corpse as abject object is always present alongside disorganized desire.

Because *NekRomantik* is primarily the story of a male necrophile (Betty is essentially a secondary character), and because *NekRomantik 2's* protagonist is female, I will now shift my discussion to the ways in which we can position desire as seen in each film as gendered. This is not a simple comparative study, however, since each protagonist shares many features with the other. Gender confusion of object and act as they relate to sexuality is a frequent feature of sexual perversion. As binaries such as desire/disgust, alive/dead and object/abject are challenged in the films, so too is the clear demarcation of male and female desire. However, I will tactically suggest here that Rob's aggressive drive to find his abject object elucidates a masculine desire for an owned object in opposition to a subject. It is when he takes himself as object that the film's representation of desire is most engaging. While emphatically deconstructing traditional sexual paradigms, the resonance of an (abject) object in relation to a male subject is sufficient in *NekRomantik* to offer residue of a sexual dialectic. In *NekRomantik 2* a different (dis)organization of desire is shown —one of *jouissance*. In the following section I will explore *NekRomantik's* sequel and the desires of Monika (Monika M) as a particularly feminine example of necrophilia.

NekRomantik 2: Perversion as *Jouissance*

Abject desire, including the act of rendering something abject, relies on the notion that in order to fall away from clean, proper and hermetically sealed identity, one must already have this identity established and socially acknowledged. Before one is placed in a sexual dialectic in opposition to an object, one's subjectivity must be stabilized and reified in order to be recognized. Many feminists have pointed out that within patriarchal society, which defines gender through the identification or absence of the phallus and what it represents, the female is defined not by difference but lack. Similarly an established discourse on feminine sexuality is seen as annexed to its conformance with or failure to resonate with male sexuality rather than as an independent form of desire. Feminine desire is not in opposition to male sexuality. It is indefinable. Thus in their failure to be properly demarcated and defined, both female subjectivity and female identity are always and already vaguely abject and perverse. Oppositional dialectic desire is the exertion of power from subject toward object—*puissance* (properly speaking, force as "affective" rather than power as "oppressive"). Feminine desire is *jouissance*. "This is a signifier characterized by being the only signifier which cannot signify anything but which merely constitutes the status of the woman as being at all," writes Lacan, "There is a *jouissance* of the body which is, if the expression be allowed, *beyond the phallus*" (145). The subject is neither stable nor overvalued and thus a breakdown or reorganization of the sexual dialectic cannot threaten it.

NekRomantik 2 opens with Monika digging up Rob's corpse. She takes him home, has sex with him, sits on the couch with him, takes snapshots of herself with him, and watches television with him. Their relationship is as much domestic as sexual. She later meets Mark (Mark Reeder), with whom she shares her affection but not her secret. The film ends with her decapitating Mark during sex. She replaces Rob's decomposing body with Mark's fresher one and replaces Mark's head with Rob's. *NekRomantik 2* affirms and challenges feminine sexuality beyond the phallus. Monika seems interested in the phallus, which she keeps in the fridge, but even more so in the head of Rob's corpse. When she kills Mark she is happy to retain his penis but it is the head she wants to exchange.

In a weird conundrum, the identity of the corpse as "Rob"—inherently both an object devoid of identity and endowed with the resonance of an identity Monika actually never knew—is what Monika seeks to retain. While Rob shows an enjoyment of the death of things, Monika prefers things which are already dead—post-mortem objects, so to speak. Most often clinical studies of necrophiles, from Krafft-Ebbing to modern studies of necrophilia, have focused on male necrophiles and the relationship between violence and sex with the dead. Lorna Campbell states:

> Although Eros and Thanatos are indeed different psychic drives, the combining intensities of the life and death instincts can freely mutate through the process of de-sexualisation and re-sexualisation of libidinal energy...It is at this point, the vanishing point of disavowal, that the crucial production and reproduction of energy takes place. The moment of de-sexualisation projects libidinal energy forward to a new dimension of reality...the new horizon has been opened and the repetitive process of the transference of libidinal energy can proceed, causing not only liberation and *jouissance* but also failure. (101)

Monika's murder of Mark comes as rather a surprise. Indeed Mark points out, "she bewilders me ... she's really nice but I think she is somehow perverse." And the fact is, she *is* really nice, far nicer than Rob. Her pleasure is perverse, bewildering, but seemingly incommensurably "nice." Similarly Monika's interest in the penis of her lover may suggest that her pleasure is not beyond phallic sexuality. Nonetheless she is having sex with a corpse. The ability to answer the question "why does she desire the corpse?" reflects the persistent question asked by psychoanalysis: "what does woman want?" This question leads to the question "how is woman defined beyond castration/lack?" Kristeva points out that "the advent of one's own identity demands a law that mutilates [unbound desire], whereas *jouissance* demands an abjection from which identity becomes absent" (54). If woman is yet to have discursive "identity," then her close proximity to both *jouissance* and abjection is established. Castrated, woman is discursively (and literally) mutilated, as is her phallic desire. Taken not as failure but excess, *jouissance* cannot recognize the acceptable from the pathological—all desire and "identity" are already a mutilation of the normal.

The film does not attempt rudimentary vindications of Monika's desires. They are unapologetic and lack the pop psychological genesis of Rob's childhood trauma of seeing a beloved pet rabbit killed by his father, thus associating love with loss. Rob's murder of Betty's cat is mimetic catharsis; however, it associates perversion with the aggression clinical psychologists often see as concurrent. Animals, rather unethically, figure frequently in films which seek to show "authentic" suffering, violence and gore, and indeed Monika watches the autopsy of a seal with her friends for pleasure, but she does not watch the animal's death.[5] She hangs Mark upside down, like a gutted deer. Douglas emphasizes the loathing the animal evokes in its proximity to humans who urgently need to see themselves as superior and evolved. "Primitive" tribes make symbols of the animals they fear while anthropomorphizing their valuable attributes. Christianity classifies animals in order to control them, defining ambiguities between these classifications as filth. This is most evident in the Book of Leviticus and the classification of food it proposes. As an aside, the primary use of animals is as cadavers, to eat, another deeply ritualized act. Like Leviticus' taxonomy of the edible and the forbidden, Levi Strauss's *The Raw and the Cooked* draws up primary classifications between man and animal, primitive and civilized. Cooking as a ritual transforms the animal's corpse into "meat" to signify it as food rather than dead sentient being. Perhaps one could see the funeral and the grave as 'cooking' the corpse in order to civilize and symbolize its threat. "On the one hand there is bloodless flesh (destined for man) and on the other, blood (destined for God)" (Kristeva 96). Bleeding animals drains their existence as sentient beings equivalent to man, and transforms them into flesh. Here sex enters back into the food, waste, death equation. "But blood, as a vital element, also refers to women, fertility and the assurance of fecundation. It thus becomes a fascinating semantic crossroads, the propitious place for abjection where *death* and *femininity, murder* and *procreation, cessation of life* and *vitality* all come together" (Kristeva 96).

Embalmed corpses are not particularly "bloody"; however, another form (or properly, aspect) of sexuality and in particular the excesses of flesh in sex is menstruation. Like necrophilia, the visibility of menstrual blood in film is seen as either fetishistic or aberrant. While excrement is defined as unclean, the classification of blood is ambiguous. The life-blood of man, like the blood of Christ, is a ritualized, symbolically charged sacred fluid, but the blood of a menstruating female defiles (Leviticus' advice for compulsory rituals for societies to deal with women menstruating border on the hilarious). The blood of the hymen is key in the most rigid of marriage rituals. Taking Kristeva's comment further, while menstruation may signify fertility, it also explicitly signifies a failure to conceive, suggesting female sexuality for its own sake (i.e. not for procreation).

Monika's necrophilia is not simply pleasure for its own sake but *without* the possibility of conception. Vampiric seductions seem to evoke an air of romanticism, blood being the symbol of desire, pleasure and also the prevention of blood loss allowing the female victim to be saved and the traditional male to be redeemed (even though female victims of vampires are rarely unwilling). There is no redemption possible in Monika's world. How can a woman be "saved" from the corpse she herself has selected for her pleasure? How can we construe her as a "victim" of her own perverse desires, as we can construe the female victim of the vampire? Ironically, while vampire films deal with the loss of blood, the image of the red trail on the white neck is a salient symbol almost equivalent to the moment of ejaculation in pornography. It is visible proof of the sexual narrative's completion. Where does the necrophilic act begin and end? If it ends with Monika's orgasm, the female orgasm, as Linda Williams points out, it does not come with visible proof equivalent to male ejaculation. In capitalist terms, there is no visible proof or pay-off for the spectator watching female orgasm. In female necrophilia, woman cannot be used in the narrative as objects exchanged between the male protagonists—from father to suitor—or even, in the case of the lesbian vampire film, the villain and the hero. Finally the necrophilic woman is unable to conceive. The corpse is a useful *concept* (not object) for the memory of a person, particularly in a funeral rite. The flesh as an object is used as a text to be read in forensic pathology. The pathologist is constructed as devoid of drive, even epistemological desire. The scientist is objective, thus rendered invisible. The scientist is not a subject who desires the corpse as an object. Those who are situated as desiring-subject with corpse-object shift the purity of the dead body, as scientifically or mnemonically useful, to desecrated by a dangerous libidinal energy, which in many films, is precluded through violence in order to procure the body. However, Monika's murder of Mark is purely functional, *not* a natural progression of her unnatural drives. She seeks to procure certain objects for the already dead body with which she is in love; she does not kill to create that body. Monika's pleasure does not stem from the violent power of making subject into corpse but from submitting to her desire for the already abject corpse.

Eating and cadavers are not joined only through anthropological studies of food. The zombie film resonates entirely around the reanimated corpse (another ambiguous aberration—a living-dead) which eats its victims. Vampires, also living-dead creatures, confuse sexuality and food. Monika stores Rob's penis in the fridge, for preservation as we store food. Interestingly, the least visceral and most noble part of the sex act, the kiss, is what makes Monika vomit. She leans down in a moment of tenderness during intercourse with Rob to kiss him, and the sticky corpse resin, which she cannot help but accidentally ingest, makes her ill. Again Buttgereit's fascinating focus on the technicalities and banalities of necrophilia means that sex is acceptable and pleasurable but a kiss will make one sick, emphasizing that the signification and value of sexual acts has as much to do with practicalities as with their nobility. Necrophilic kissing in this scene is judged as more disgusting than intercourse—both an ironic and poignant concept. Resisting a simple Freudian oral compulsion analysis, my point is simply to draw connections between rituals concerning animals, food, and the historical associations between rituals, sex, femininity, gender, animals, food and death.

Woman has often been associated with the animal, whether in her animal sexual appetites or her position in natural taxonomy between man and animal.[6] Creatures that are half-man and half-animal, particularly those with animal heads rather than bodies—the werewolf, the vampire—are aberrant. The monstrous Minotaur was the result of an aberrant sexual union between Pasiphae and a bull. However, in spite of this brief discussion, I think abjection associated with animals is most pertinent when resonating with the unbound and unclassifiable aspects of female desire which deviate from or exist upon independent trajectories to phallic sexuality. Thus the value of the animal and the value of the woman, while not symbolized nor quantified identically, place both in the risk category that makes classifications of purity and danger ambiguous. Neither entirely fulfills the requirements of human subjectivity. Both are notionally less-than-human, seen as a direct threat to, and yet to receive ethical recognition equal to, the huMan. *NekRomantik 2* is an interesting example of a non-masculine heroine represented as expressing desire that is independent from masculine paradigms of both ritual and value. I would argue Buttgereit's heroine is volitional without being masculine, abject without being (persistently) violent. She kills for pragmatic purposes, not for pleasure. The strength of her character lies in its ambiguities. She explores rather than affirms or exemplifies fluid sexuality. She is perverse only against the traditional classifications of "normal" sexuality, gender placement and subject valuation. But to what extent is this simply a continuation of female desire as already defined as perverse? What is she if we take her desires beyond being defined purely through isomorphic comparisons to the normal sexual subject with its appropriate object choice?

Monika's is a kind of pleasure that is not necessarily enjoyable. The first time we see her having sex with Rob's corpse she leans in to lick him and rushes to the toilet to vomit. The viscous matter covering Rob's body, yet another signifier of a lack of boundaries, is the fluid, sticky, sexual and sour, that blurs rather than separates the two. Corpse treacle, if you will: "Treacle is neither liquid nor solid; it could be said to give an ambiguous sense-impression. We can say that treacle is anomalous in the classification of liquid and solid, being in neither one nor the other set" (Douglas 37). Odd as corpse treacle sounds, viscous matter is a frequent feature of *NekRomantik 2*. Replacing the phallic knives of *NekRomantik*, we see images of slugs and snails, which are potentially clitoral symbols. Their slimy efflux is neither dissimilar to corpse treacle, nor to female sexual fluid.[7] As stated above, female blood is not present in sex films which do not specifically fetishize it, and the not-quite-visible female sexual fluids similarly "fail" to offer the more clearly signified fluid of semen.

Fluid itself is a risky concept. *Jouissance* is a fluid form of sexuality, involving fluid identities and fluid values invested in acts and pleasures. Where identity is about demarcation, fluidity, more than impinging on it, resists the paradigm of clear identity altogether. Rob's fountain of sperm does not produce an abject fluid. "Excrement and its equivalents (decay, infection, disease, corpse) stand for the danger to identity ... neither tears nor sperm, for example, although they belong to the borders of the body, have any polluting value" (Kristeva 71). Sperm comes *out*, corpse treacle neither begins nor ends. It sticks to the subject and is not easily ejected. Corpse treacle and other viscous fluids are the borderland between bodies. Corpse treacle connects Monika with Rob. Like the definition of her *jouissance* corpse treacle is ambiguous, anomalous, undefined, but not any *thing* in itself. It is not fetishized. Monika washes her hands, and she keeps Rob's penis in the fridge so it will not turn into a rotted mess. Hers is not a sexuality which indulges in disgust. Like her sexual and domestic relationship with Rob, Monika's pleasures are at once repulsive and pleasurable, pragmatic rather than deliberately transgressive.

Buttgereit's films occupy a problematic subgenre of horror. Necrophilia remains an issue which cinema tentatively walks around or suggests in abstract ways. Those films that deal with it are often written off immediately, and unfairly, as trash. The viscerality of Buttgereit's films intensifies their potential to offend while ironically making them far more realistic and everyday than many cinematic representations of sexual acts in general. While I am not trying to laud Buttgereit's necrophilia films as particularly radical or revolutionary, each does deal with unique representations of gender and of entirely different versions of necrophilia, troubling the ease with which we can espouse rudimentary judgments of the characters as perverse. Their very potential to offend transfers their function from the desire to shock to their ability to emphasize the essentially arbitrary systems of classification, taxonomy and value which society maintains in order to maintain subjectivity itself, and particular forms of subjectivity defined through their gender, desires and adherence to rituals. Sadly, Buttgereit's follow-up to *NekRomantik 2, Schramm,* made in 1993, presented viewers with a relatively traditional, repugnant, and generally uninteresting and socially misfit masculinist murderer. The seminal nature of the *NekRomantik* films are part of a group of European horror films of the 1980s and 1990s which presented alternatives to the horror cinema in America that had become somewhat sanitized through the clean blade of the slasher film's knife. The frequently masculinized heroine is not present in Buttgereit's film. As texts themselves they are ambiguous, neither celebratory nor critical of the subject matter, but seem to seek to express ruptures and ambiguities of pleasure, power and perversion rather than a redeeming resolution of existing paradigms of traditional power. These elements rupture the spectator's own ambiguous but nonetheless fascinated relationship with the extreme images and desires, taking the films as our own abject objects of desire. "One thus understands," writes Kristeva, "why so many victims of the abject are its fascinated victims—if not its submissive and willing ones" (9).

Notes

1. *Lisa* and *Beyond the Darkness* are poignant stories of nostalgia and loss, in which the corpse stands as an attempt to resurrect desire which remains intact. In both, the corpse is preserved in terms of putrefaction, lacking the visceral and viscous physical breakdown of more obviously decomposed cadaver lovers. *Flesh for Frankenstein* is one of the most engaging hymns to necrophilia in modern cinema, where female desire is awakened when the body is signified differently by being corpse. The sexual act is transferred from genitals to entrails, reorganizing the body's traditional striation as well as rejecting the need for animation.

2. In Australia, according to the Internet movie database, *NekRomantik* is cut to a restricted certificate. *NekRomantik 2* is still banned, taking into account that technically films are not "banned" in Australia, but are refused rating. This rhetoric is used to suggest that nothing in Australia is outright illicit and thus people are still "free" to choose, but possession of refused films carries the threat of heavy fines and, in extreme circumstances, jail sentences. The first conference paper I ever presented as a young graduate student, in 1996, was a feminist analysis of *NekRomantik 2*, which included showing two minutes of footage. Even within its academic context, a complaint to the ABFLC resulted in threat of legal prosecution of my university, and to a loss of my bursary and potentially my candidature status. While I refused to make a formal apology, I remained both funded and a student. However, this led to research and publication in the field of censorship and I dropped any research to do with the film until this essay!

3. Even though there is sex and nudity it is no more explicit than many traditional films which deal with sex. Porn is clearly used as a derogatory generic term in these instances.

4. The notion of willing the body after death is another, no less interesting and ambiguous argument which I do not have room to discuss here. For more information, see Brown and Cowan.

5. Many video nasties include actual animal killing, particularly mondo films and the Indio films of Italy.

6. Both Aristotle and Kant place woman between man and beasts.

7. This kind of sticky, unclassifiable substance is seen in another German film about female sexuality, Andrzej Zulawski's *Possession* (1981), where Anna's (Isabelle Adjani) refusal to align her desire with phallocentric sexuality leads to her breeding, from a lump of slime she has produced, a tentacled animal-vegetable-insect creature which eventually becomes her full-fledged human lover.

Works Cited

Bataille, George. *Eroticism.* Trans. Mary Dalwood. London: Penguin, 2001.

Blake, Linnie. "Sex, Selfhood and the Corpse of the German Past." *Kinoeye* 3.6 (2003) www.kinoeye.org/03/06/blake06.php.

Bronfen, Elisabeth. *Over Her Dead Body.* Manchester: Manchester University Press, 1992.

Brown, Michael, *Nurses: The Human Touch.* New York: Ivy, 1992.

Campbell, Lorna. "Anteros and Intensity." Ed. Joan Broadhurst. *Deleuze and the Transcendental Unconscious.* Warwick: University of Warwick, 1992.

Cowan, Dale H. *Human Organ Transplantation: Societal, Medical-legal, Regulatory and Reimbursement Issues.* Michigan University Press: Ann Arbor, 1987.

Deleuze, Gilles, and Félix Guattari. *A Thousand Plateaus: Capitalism and Schizophrenia.* Trans. Brian Massumi. London: The Athlone Press, 1987.

Douglas, Mary. *Purity and Danger: An Analysis of Concepts of Pollution and Taboo.* London: Routledge and Keegan Paul, 1966.

Foucault, Michel. *The History of Sexuality Vol I.* Trans. Robert Hurley. London: Penguin, 1990.

Krafft-Ebing, Richard von. *Psychopathia Sexualis.* Trans. Domino Falls. London: Velvet, 1997.

Kristeva, Julia. *Powers of Horror: An Essay on Abjection.* Trans. Leon Roudiez. New York: Columbia University Press, 1982.

Lacan, Jaques. *Feminine Sexuality.* Trans. Jacqueline Rose, and Juliet Mitchell. London: Macmillan, 1982.

Lèvi-Strauss, Claude. *The Raw and the Cooked.* Trans. John and Doreen Weightman. London: Cape, 1970.

Williams, Linda. *Hard Core: Power, Pleasure and the Frenzy of the Visible.* Berkeley: University of California Press, 1989.

Part 5:

Interviews: Three German Horror Film Directors

Good News from the Underground: A Conversation with Jörg Buttgereit

Marcus Stiglegger

Filmmaker, film journalist, projectionist, DJ, director of radio plays: born and raised in Berlin, Jörg Buttgereit has made a name for himself as a likeable *enfant terrible* wearing all of these hats at one time or another. Regardless, however, of the critical accolades and awards that his short films and radio plays have garnered, one title will always remain synonymous with his name: *NekRomantik*. What started as a "buddy movie," inspired by a youthful desire to provoke and shock, has become the most publicly recognised and notorious "necrophiliac love story" of all times.[1] Nonetheless, it became an amazing success story on pirated videotapes and DVDs worldwide. However, none of this global success made its director a single cent. Buttgereit's later films *NekRomantik 2* and *Der Todesking*, a compilation film about suicide, made him more popular with international film critics. *NekRomantik 2* was instantly banned in Germany but was later officially recognized as a "work of art" by the German courts. The serial killer drama *Schramm*, Buttgereit's most recent film to date, was screened on a German cable channel, along with a long interview conducted by Alexander Kluge, the *maestro* of the New German Cinema of the 1960s and 1970s. Though recognized as an underground artist, Buttgereit works mainly in radio broadcasting these days, refining and completing his macabre *vision du monde*.

Jörg, did you have a happy childhood in Berlin?

The answer to this question is an unequivocal yes. (laughs)

In your award-winning short film Mein Papi (My Daddy)*, you document a few moments you shared with your father. What was your relationship toward each other?*

I think the film makes a clear case that my relationship toward my father—and that of all children to their parents—was never clear-cut but always ambivalent. The film was shot in 1981, was shown first at the Risiko, a club in Berlin, and became the favorite movie of the bartender at the club, Blixa Bargeld. But the film did not consist entirely of raw footage I had shot secretly of my father.

Since Super Eight is not really all that light-sensitive, I'd bought particularly fast stock, Kodak 160, and with that, I could secretly photograph my father at home without having to use extra lighting. This was sort of an act of revenge. I did get a kick out of seeing those drunk punk rockers and artists looking at images of my father and finding them amusing. But after my father had died . . . he had a "benign" cyst at the back of his brain, which was surgically removed. It made him lose his sense of balance, and it changed a few other things about him as well, like giving him a sudden appetite for sweets. After that, he could never walk unaided again; out in the street, he always had to use a wheelchair. This turned our relationship upside down because I became the one who had to take care of him. Which improved our relationship considerably. After his death, I realized that I couldn't really show the material anymore as it was; and so I re-edited it, added a few title cards and extra photos I had taken of him when I was still a kid. To give it a final boost, I'd had the whole thing blown up to 35 mm. After that, I was finished, though I didn't quite know what I'd wanted to accomplish with all this . . . During the first few showings, there were protests whenever I told people that my father had had no idea that these images of him even existed.

Even though we don't see you taking care of him in the film it does become quite clear that you two have a good relationship.

It must have been the Berlin film critic Annette Kilzer, who described the film in positive terms as "an experience of ambivalence." And if one person catches on, why not others as well? By the way, this was my last "home movie" if you will—after that, it was all over. (laughs)

How would you describe the subcultural climate of Berlin during the Eighties? You did experience it all quite consciously, didn't you?

The climate back then was such that anyone who could strap on a guitar used to think of himself as a musician. And since I was always convinced that I had no musical talent at all . . . This was the way Felsenheimer's punk band Soylent Green turned into Die Ärzte, and bartenders in weird latex pants started arthouse bands called Einstürzende Neubauten. This was the moment when I picked up a camera. A cinema movement was also in the works back then, it was just that most people were into documentary-style experimental films. Recently, I gave a lecture, together with the art historian Claus Löser, about the movement of experimental filmmakers back then. This was the first time I had a chance to watch some of the films again that had struck me as artsy crap back then. Suddenly, however, they all made sense to me. What I liked even back then was *Das Leben des Sid Vicious* (*The Life of Sid Vicious*) by Tödliche Doris.

Is this the one in which the kid in the swastika shirt is walking around Berlin?

That's the one. I liked it though I'd always wanted to stay away from the arthouse scene. This even includes Derek Jarman's *In the Shadow of the Sun*, with its industrial soundtrack by Throbbing Gristle, which was pretty exhausting. I was more into getting back to childhood experiences and shooting Godzilla movies with my friends.

Did the body art performances that you saw back then influence your own view of the body?

I saw all that stuff—SPK, for example, who, on stage, worked on bloody sheep's heads from the Turkish butcher store next door. I did take all that seriously back then, though it strikes me as somewhat banal today. But my image of the body had always been a little different since the time when I started, years earlier as a great fan of Bruce Lee, to practice martial arts. This is why I'd always been concerned not to "abuse" my body unnecessarily. That is to say, I've always been thinking about the vulnerability of the body, in my films as well, but back in those days of punk rock, I wouldn't even as much as touch a glass of beer. Later on, at the Risiko, I did on occasion have an OJ with champagne. But I would still say no to everything else that went into people's veins and up their noses. If you're supposed to show up for training the next day, you can't afford to indulge. I used to train with a bunch of Koreans back then.

You live in Schöneberg, Berlin's "Red Island," and have never moved away either. What is it that appeals to you about that place?

I never had a reason to leave. Schöneberg used to be a workers' district, and today, many artists have moved there as well. It was never as cool as Berlin Mitte is today, and never as decrepit as Kreuzberg. The SO 36 was in Kreuzberg, but the Risiko was right on the border between Kreuzberg and Schöneberg. I was always happy to come home to my apartment, where the Bruce Lee poster was on the wall right next to the TG poster.

How did your relationship to Bela B. Felsenheimer develop?

We attended a trade school together. We did a lot of things together, for example *Manne the Muwie* (*Manne the Muwie*), *Captain Berlin*, *Die schönsten Zerstörungen* (*The Most Beautiful Destructions*). That last one—it didn't get released. In it, we destroy objects of consumer society.

Which is typical of the Berlin performance art movement "Aktionismus"?

Exactly. The only thing that's well-known from it is *Der explodierende Turnschuh* (*The Exploding Sneaker*). In it, you see a no-brand sneaker explode in slow motion. By the way, it's even out of focus since we couldn't afford to do a reshoot. We only had that one sneaker. Inga Humpe from the band Ideal used to show the film on her program *Sieben Fragen an Punks und Polizisten* (*Seven Questions for Punks and Cops*).

You don't have any connections to the punk scene anymore?

I guess not. Recently, I was in Dresden for a screening of *Das Leben des Sid Vicious*, and I asked the art students in the audience whether it made sense to them. Back in the days, it used to be a provocation to most people. The students didn't even have anything to say, except for one who raised his hand and asked, "Who exactly is Sid Vicious?" (laughs). This made me wonder whether I was old, or whether punk is dead. I guess there's no more punk. Back then, it used to represent the mood of a new era. And the SO 36 was a kind of temple for it. It stood for the mixture of experimental art and punk, just how I tried to show it in my documentary *So war das SO 36* (*This Was the SO 36*)]. Back then, I used to work with Manfred Jelinski, who was to become my producer, and who never seemed to fit in with his long hippie hair.

This is where you two met?

Yes, I came to him as a a kid of supplicant, and together we shot the documentary about the SO 36.

Which turned out to be pretty rough . . .

You think so? I used to think the film was much too mainstream . . . we were only allowed to use German bands because they were the only ones for which we could secure the rights. If you watch the film today, it feels like a glimpse of another world.

Let's talk about your films. There are some recurring motifs that would qualify you as an auteur—like the classic monsters of film history, the complex interrelations of love, death, putrefaction, and wounds, and the hyperbolic and sexualized links to national socialism.

Really?

As in Blutige Exzesse im Führerbunker (Bloody Excesses in the Fuehrer's Bunker) *and* Der Todesking.

(laughs) *Blutige Exzesse im Führerbunker* premiered at the Risiko as well, but before that, I ended up in a police raid during which fliers for the film were discovered. I was let go, but during the premiere there were plainclothes cops everywhere—who happened to be extremely conspicuous because the rest of the audience consisted of emaciated junkies and avant-garde artists. And among those folks, those "Schimanskis" tried to blend in.[2] But they started leaving as soon as they realized that this was no neo-Nazi rally.

How do you account for your relationship to these topics? Isn't there another reference to German fascism in Todesking?

Yeah, from *Ilsa, She-Wolf of the SS*. I think of this as an act of liberation, an homage to all those things that were kept from us in Germany presumably for our own good. Once you discover that these things exist, you are equally horrified and intrigued. *Ilsa* was punk rock for me—same thing as Sid Vicious with his swastika shirt.

Did you ever think about making an entire film of this type, a kind of 'Sadiconazista'?

I wouldn't have minded, but it would have been impossible to finance. And Jelinski would have refused to take part. In *Der Todesking*, we made everything as authentic as we possibly could. Had we tried to take it even further, we would have probably ended up doing something similar to Monty Python.

Where did you get the period costumes?

They came from the uniform collection of Mark Reeder, the current owner of the MFS-Techno label. Today, he's a famous DJ. Back then he had a role as a Nazi in *Todesking* and later another role in *NekRomantik 2*. In the booklet to the *NekRomantik 2* DVD, a British scholar reads the film as a working through of "the German responsibility for National Socialism," which made sense to me and the writer. But we never actually thought of this ourselves.

Well, I guess the artist can return to the unconscious and doesn't necessarily have to be aware of his own motifs. Were you criticized or attacked for that?

No, never. My critics tended to get hung up on the representations of violence themselves, and thus never made it that far.

In Schramm *and the WDR radio play* Sexy Sushi, *an increasing number of sadomasochistic elements begin to surface. In your own opinion, what role does sadomasochism play in your work?*

I guess it's used rather playfully. I find the whole artificial situation that is created to celebrate the sexual act somewhat banal. I for one would prefer films that are more "hands on," like *Salo* (laughs). All this goes back to the evenings we'd get together around the VCR as teenagers. Whenever all levels of horror had been played out, we'd turn to other kinds of movies, like, for example, *Die Gummiklinik (The Rubber Clinic)*. The most convincing material of that type was this gay porn flick in which people used to stuff all kinds of things up their butts. This went so far as one guy inserting both arms, up to the elbow, and when he started getting his foot ready as well, we turned the thing off. And I thought to myself: alright then, this is true to itself, I can accept that. (laughs) S&M in magazines I find mostly playful and cute.

But nobody ever claimed that it was anything else. It's more about the public's idea than the thing itself.

Well, yes, but it would still bother me. Another one that was pretty cool was *Der Arschwühler* (*The Ass Digger*), a piece of American gay porn. In the closing scene, they call the fire department and then stick the phone up one guy's ass: "Hello, Fire Department!" (laughs) And then the guy would yell, in good "American" fashion, "You *Sau!*" This one did raise my personal bar in regard to S&M considerably. It's interesting that the people who make these kinds of films don't think of them as extreme at all. It's the same with my own work. I never thought any of it was really that bad.

After Schramm, *you were not able to make another feature-length film. How did that happen? And does this development bother you?*

Well, this was a self-imposed limitation. I told myself: I'm never going to shoot under such low-budget conditions again. And as long as I cannot do it at the level of a Cronenberg or Lynch, I'm just not going to make any more films at all. It's just no fun any more. The commercial work for *Lexx—The Dark Zone* and *Das Kondom des Grauens* (*Condom of Horror*) didn't do anything for me artistically. And so I started concentrating on dealing with my own past by way of my books. Only with the WDR radio plays, did I regain a full sense of artistic control. My monumental project *Body Play*, which is based on *Sexy Sushi*, isn't completely dead and buried, but I don't really think it's ever going to get made.

You did shoot a number of music videos for bands from the gothic scene (Die Krupps, Shock Therapy, Dance or Die) and usually you get an invitation to the Wave-Gotik-Treffen (Wave Gothic Meeting) in Leipzig. What is your attitude towards all that?

The bands come and ask me. Some of the musicians I even know from before. And I do think it's really cute when the little Goth girls are watching *NekRomantik*. Of course, I'm flattered. But in the films themselves, I tried to steer clear of the scene in order not to treat it as a fashion, a fad. But then Beatrice does look pretty Goth in the first part of the film, with her shades in the bathtub.

*You published a book about Godzilla films and another one about horror model kits (*Nightmares in Plastic*). What other projects do you have currently under development?*

Rumour has it that there will be something about "Treasures of the Low Budget Cinema in the 1970s in Germany" and a book about Cronenberg published by the Bertz-Verlag. But neither of those projects is a sure thing yet. There will be an English version of the Godzilla book published by David Kerekes in 2006.

Why are you still working as projectionist at the Berlin gay cinema Xenon? Out of nostalgia or out of necessity?

Back in the old days, it wasn't a gay cinema yet. I used to watch Godzilla movies there as a kid. Come to think of it, that used to be guys in rubber suits, too . . . Today, I can put down that job on my tax return so that I can move more freely.[3] The theatre is just around the corner from where I live and it's full of memories.

In recent years, you've been one of the few German film journalists who stood up for the French filmmaker Gaspar Noé and his film Irreversible. *Do you know each other personally?*

I met Noé in Helsinki a few years ago when he was a struggling novice director. A year and a half ago, he came to one of my DJ gigs in Berlin.

Which filmmakers do you appreciate right now?

That's difficult to say. I used to answer that question by mentioning Cronenberg and Lynch. Today, it's more difficult. I could mention Gaspar; given the uncompromising nature of his work, he is definitely far more interesting than many others who no longer have anything to worry about. Since *Irreversible* was such a failure in Germany, he'll probably remain as aggressive as before.[4] And that's a good thing.

Does it bother you that you are more famous and popular abroad than you are at home? In Germany, you're still stuck with that label of the "icon of splatter films."

Yes and no. The label doesn't really apply any longer since I've been active in very different fields. When it comes to my radio plays, I get to work with outstanding actors like Axel Milberg. It's more satisfying to work with such people on a radio play than to have to shoot a movie with amateurs. At the same time, my public image is helpful, too, because it draws attention to my new projects.

Jörg, best of luck with all those future projects.

Notes

1. This interview was conducted during the Exground Festival in Wiesbaden in the fall of 2003. It was translated by Steffen Hantke in consultation with Marcus Stiglegger. The original audio track of this interview can be heard on the German Code-0-DVD of *Hot Love—Jörg Buttgereits Super-8-Filme* (JB Films, 2005). It was first published in German in *:Ikonen:* 4 (Spring 2004), pp. 31–35.

2. The name of a popular character on the German crime show *Tatort*; the German equivalent of the action-oriented tough cop familiar from American film and television; see also the interview with Nico Hoffmann in this volume.

3. Buttgereit quit this job in 2005 due to insurance issues.

4. This remark is only true for the short life of *Irreversible* on the cinema circuit; the film later sold very well on German Code-2-DVD (Legend films/Universal, including extensive liner notes by Marcus Stiglegger).

Hunting the Innocents: A Conversation with Robert Sigl

Marcus Stiglegger

Fantasy has always been a rare commodity in contemporary German genre cinema—especially in the 1980s. At the same time Italian horror reached yet another peak with Dario Argento's *Opera* (1985), "easy comedy" ruled mainstream film production in Germany. And so it appeared as a kind of miracle when twenty-seven-year-old writer/director Robert Sigl was awarded the Bavarian Film Prize in 1988 for his debut feature, the gothic horror fairytale *Laurin*.[1]

Robert Sigl graduated from Munich film school after submitting a long analysis of Roman Polanski's *The Tenant* (1976) as his thesis. Immediately afterwards he managed to sell his script *Laurin* and raised the necessary money to shoot the film in Hollokö and Szentendre, Hungary, a part of Eastern Europe "where there are places where we didn't even have to change anything—it still looked like a hundred years ago," as he says. Though made on a shoestring budget, the film manages to evoke the brooding atmosphere of some of Werner Herzog's historical dramas, even replicating the magical realism of Herzog's *Nosferatu the Vampyre* (1979). Polanski, Herzog, Jacques Tourneur, Alfred Hitchcock, and Stanley Kubrick are clearly among Sigl's influences. There are also glimpses of Dario Argento's and Lucio Fulci's gothic horror films of the 1970s (e.g., *Inferno* [1980] and *The Beyond* [1981]) in *Laurin*. Sigl highlights the psycho-thriller structure by creating an almost surreal atmosphere, using colored lights to contrast the monochrome historical settings with more expressionist set-pieces. His fetishizing of certain details—a doll, a robe, a nail, a photo of a young girl's mother, etc.—is also reminiscent of the excessive close-up style of Argento. In *Laurin*, all of these elements seem to have a life of their own. Sigl's *vision du monde* is an animistic one indeed.

Viewers of Sigl's early short film *Der Weihnachtsbaum* (*The Christmas Tree*, 1983) will also notice another familiar element: a conflict between father and son, driven by a dark and destructive homosexual desire which creates a disturbing mood of latent violence and repression. The relationship between the father and son in *Laurin* is characterized in precisely that way. It is also important to note that the father in *Laurin* is a radical millenarian Catholic priest. "I hate the Christian church and especially the Pope," says Sigl, whose other projects so far—most of them unfilmed at this point—also include elements of gothic horror, occultism, heresy, and a perverse homoerotic undertone.

These elements also resurface in the "Giga Shadow" episode Sigl directed for the German-Canadian television series *Lexx: The Dark Zone* (1997). Occult elements are present even in the family fantasy-series *Stella Stellaris*, while gothic horror reappears in his German made-for-TV teen slasher movie, *Schrei denn ich werde dich töten! (School's Out*, 1999).[2] *Laurin*, meanwhile, has gained a growing number of fans since its release, fans who appreciate the idiosyncratic merging of influences, from Friedrich Wilhelm Murnau to E.T.A. Hoffmann, and who know that in years to come Robert Sigl is a German genre auteur to watch.[3]

Robert, would you talk about your time at the Film Academy in Munich?

In 1981, when I was nineteen, I was accepted at the film academy immediately after I graduated from high school. I shot two films there—the student film *The Cottage (Die Hütte)*, which has not been preserved, and *The Christmas Tree (Der Weihnachtsbaum)*. *The Cottage* deals with a black African girl who takes care of a crying baby, until we find out in the end that the baby is just a doll. Already you can see here anxieties revolving around pregnancy and abortion, anxieties surrounding the death of children. We were shooting in a wooden shed in the Botanical Gardens in Munich, which seemed to work very well. After that, I became interested in depth psychology and absurd theater, which resulted in the desire to shoot a more claustrophobic version of Polanski's *Cul-de-sac*. The twenty-minute film *The Christmas Tree* turned out to be a piece for two actors about a pathological father-son relationship. I played the young son, who returns from a long sea voyage to visit his father, to whom he is bound in a masochistic relationship. In retrospect, I would say the atmosphere is somewhat reminiscent of David Lynch's *Eraserhead*. For example, you can hear the late mother walk around the house, the sea roaring in the background.

So already at this point, you're working with disruptive elements and the theme of the overbearing father?

Yes, this is a theme I've been preoccupied with—the latent sexual violence emanating from the dominance of the father. The loss of a female role model within the family can exacerbate these tendencies. I'm extremely concerned about exactly that.

For personal reasons?

Yes, the female aspect of myself is something I wouldn't want to miss. I always want to give it as much play as possible. After all, the physical violence inherent in an exclusively male family context was what brought me to horror film, or rather to the psychological thriller, which works more with the psychological side of fear. The episode of *Alarm für Kobra 11* I am currently working on also deals with this motif—the father as a murderer of his child.[4]

It's also crucial to Laurin.

Exactly. However, I didn't make any more films at the Munich Film Academy after *The Christmas Tree* because the response was extremely negative.

Why was that?

I guess some people felt personally offended because of the psychosexual symbolism and theme. In *Laurin*, I packaged all this by phrasing it in the psychosexual terms of a fairy tale by the Brothers Grimm, which made it more palatable to a broader audience. This way, it's more subliminal. Because I do want to reach a lot of people, even entertain them. But that doesn't matter much in one's first efforts as a filmmaker; they're usually more about refining one's style anyway. As a matter of fact, an idiosyncratic style doesn't seem to be much in demand these days. Someone like Polanski, Lynch, or Cronenberg would have a hard time if they were starting out today.

Were Laurin *or* The Christmas Tree *intended as your "thesis" for graduating from film school?*

Ordinarily, everyone makes one film that is submitted as a graduating requirement. But not me, I had just turned twenty-three, and so I delved straight into the script for *Laurin*. Wolfgang Laengsfeld helped me get a scriptwriting grant from Niedersachsen, which is where I kept working on the project. At first, the film was supposed to take place on the North Sea coast, which, I hoped, would give it an atmosphere like that in Theodor Storm's *Schimmelreiter*.[5] Then the Südwestfunk, one of Germany's regional radio and TV channels, became interested in the project. In every case, I had to change the script a little. Looking back on it now, I would say the first draft of the script was perhaps the best. The final draft is much more invested in a poetic, almost lyric tone. These days I would call it a mixture of Black Romanticism and a fairy tale by Grimm or Andersen, something carrying a small but stark stain of blood.

You already mentioned directors who served as role models for you. Were there others as well?

Yes. When I was eleven, I saw the posters for *The Fearless Vampire Killers*, which was pure magic to me. I knew that this was exactly what I wanted to do myself. Early on, I went to watch movies that were intended for older audiences: *Rosemary's Baby*, Roeg's *Don't Look Now*, *The Elephant Man*, *Repulsion*, *The Tenant*, *Psycho*, *The Birds*, *Vertigo*, Clayton's *The Innocents*, and *Night of the Hunter*. *The Shining* was a little too sterile for my taste, even though it's a film that revolves around the family and its conflicts. I also found the scene in *Psycho* extremely impressive in which Vera Miles enters the bedroom of Bates's mother. I'm fascinated by the subtle psychological shocks in this scene. Psychology and black humor always have to be present in the dramatic presentation of shocking moments. After all, comedy and horror are only separated by a thin line.

Were you influenced by Werner Herzog at all? I was thinking of Nosferatu *or* Heart of Glass.

No. I am familiar with his imagery, but what I'm missing are real characters, their charisma, their wit, their vivacity. A languid desire for death should only arise out of the dramatic events themselves.

Other films I was reminded of while watching Laurin *were Jordan's* Company of Wolves, *Argento's* Phenomena, *and Fulci's* Don't Torture a Duckling.

The Company of Wolves was an important influence. I hadn't seen *Phenomena* back then, but there was a scene in *Inferno* that left a deep impression with me—the one in which Irene Miracle dives down into the basement room. It directly influenced the scene in which Laurin's mother plunges into the water. What I wanted was this effect of the warm glowing water . . . Unfortunately I've never seen a film by Fulci, though I know all of their titles.

Don't Torture a Duckling *also deals with a child murderer, though of course it's far more explicit in its imagery.* Laurin *is told from a child's point of view. Do you think this perspective is important for horror films?*

Not just for horror films, for all genres! Spielberg, for example, always tells his stories from a child's perspective, even in *Schindler's List*. I think our childhood fears are extremely important because they're always repressed when we become adults. Cinema allows us to relive these childhood fears, whenever we consider ourselves unobserved.

How important were literary influences?

As a child, I was very impressed with Bram Stoker's short stories. I almost like them better than a novel like *Dracula*. And that novel, in turn, is much darker than all of its cinematic adaptations. I would immediately agree to making a film based on *Dracula*, as dark as I see it. Then there were *Melmoth the Wanderer* by Charles Maturin, Mark Twain, Roald Dahl—whose adaptation by Roeg I also liked very much—and Henry James's "The Turn of the Screw." The adaptation by Clayton was a strong influence on *Laurin*. The one by Michael Winner (*The Nightcomers*) and the recent one with Patsy Kensit I didn't much care for.

The faded colors in Laurin *are reminiscent of Eastern European directors like Borowczyk or Zulawski. Is that a result of shooting the film in Hungary, or does it require a specific technique?*

It's a matter of the location and its unique light. Imagine shooting a horror film during a summer in Munich—the atmosphere . . . like Lego . . . That green! A green for the petit bourgeois! Awful! Right now, I've had an offer to work on an American script called *Capital Offender*—a serial killer story. And I'd love to do it in Berlin.

Bornedal did a good job preserving the atmosphere of Denmark when he re-made Nightwatch *in the U.S.*

Another great film! I hope that *Capital Offender* would turn out like this. There are so many good actors here; it's just they have only those bad scripts to work with!

In Laurin, *as well as in your miniseries* Stella Stellaris, *you are using elements of the occult. Is this something that is important to you?*

Well, the occult elements all come from the fairy tales that constitute the foundation of the stories. I always thought of the occult as a possibility, something to explore playfully, but I'm certainly not actively involved in anything esoteric. I find it's missing something sensual, something erotic. To me, it doesn't have a strong enough connection with real sexuality, with real life. However, I did have encounters with the supernatural; back in Hungary, I used to live in a haunted house. And while I take the occult seriously during the shoot, I would never go as far as Polanski, who called in a genuine Satanist, Anton LaVey, for the shooting of *Rosemary's Baby*. But then I'm superstitious.

You seem to prefer a relatively calm directorial style.

Yes, because this way it's easier to develop a more subtle psychological suspense.

How does that apply to your work in television, like on the show LEXX?

The people in charge keep telling me that everything's too slow. Surprisingly enough, you have much more creative freedom if you're working as a director for hire for U.S. television.

When the little boy Stefan is running through the woods in his sailor suit in Laurin, *I was reminded of Tadzio in* Death in Venice. *What role does homosexuality play in your work?*

How kind of you to mention the sailor suit! First let me say that I really don't care for Thomas Mann. So he didn't really matter that much. I never thought much of Visconti's film either. To me, the boy's outfit signifies the double father figure in the film—Laurin's father, who is a sailor, and VanRees, who comes from the sea. Homosexuality is more important on the psychological level. Originally, a sailor suit is supposed to underline the masculinity of the person who wears it. But when a child wears a sailor suit, it comes across as a travesty of masculinity. The girl Laurin, by the way, is far more masculine than the little boy.

Right . . . which is why there is a scene in which she plays a man and the little boy Stefan plays a woman.

I also just found out that there was a child murderer during the Third Reich who killed little boys in sailor suits—someone nicknamed "the Sandmann." I would love to make a film about that. But as far as the motive for murder is concerned, homosexuality doesn't really matter all that much. VanRees is definitely a homosexual, but he kills the boys because he wants to protect them from his father, at whose hands he himself had to suffer terribly. Clearly, he identifies with the victims.

In a style reminiscent of Argento, the film celebrates the gruesome death of the killer. But then the audience may not even want to see that, or wish that upon him.

This is exactly the reason why I don't want the audience to be satisfied by the death of the killer. The real evil is represented by his father, and his father survives.

Are you satisfied with the version of the film that is available on Redemption video—making the film known to a worldwide audience?

It's alright. It's converted to the wrong format, though—into a full-screen image. At least it's the English dubbed version. The two German-language versions sound incredibly mannered and theatrical, uneven somehow. I'm not happy with them at all. I discovered that about the video version at the exact same moment when I spotted it in a video store in Berlin. Which was a shock to begin with. The distributor had sold it without telling me. The problems had started as early as the theatrical release of the film. The first dubbing was so awful that it almost cost me the Bavarian Film Award. The Filmbewertungsstelle rejected even the second version.[6] Then Heinz Badewitz rejected the film for the Film Festival in Hof, telling me that I wouldn't be "doing myself a favor" if I released it as it was. At least I won the Bavarian Film Award, which helped me regain my composure somewhat. I also received a nomination from Saarbrücken, but then I didn't win the Bundesfilmpreis because, as they told me, the film had to be shot in Germany to be eligible for the award. Europolis took over the theatrical distribution of the film, which was postponed again and again, so that all advertising turned out to be a waste of money. The two broadcasts of the film on television, which helped to give its publicity some momentum, came later. In 1996, I wanted to look for a global distributor for the film and, for general release, create a director's cut, which was supposed to be seven minutes longer and feature new dubbing. But when I went back to Andreas Bareiss, the producer, he told me that he had had all negatives of the film destroyed. So all my plans failed in the most miserable way imaginable. But now the film has been released, and my lawyer has taken care of all unsolved legal problems.

What happened after Laurin?

While I was co-writing a new horror script with Leo Gough, entitled *The Spider*, I made ends meet by working as a dubbing director. I was rescued by an offer from producer Iris Kiefer, who also turned out to be one of the co-authors of the project *Stella Stellaris*. I ended up shooting this satirical family story in Poland, with a number of visual effects and rather nice settings. The technical challenge of this miniseries really did a lot for me, and the final product helped me secure a job with the Canadian-German television series *Lexx—The Dark Zone*. The Americans really appreciate technically competent work.

Is there going to be another collaboration with Malcolm McDowall?

He agreed to be in *The Spider*, if the film ever gets made. As a matter of fact, working on *Lexx* was a pleasure from beginning to end. I had an extreme degree of creative freedom, which extended to the sexual innuendo and anti-clerical references in the show. Suffice it to say that I have a problem with the arch-conservative representatives of organized religion and their partially inhumane opinions.

Notes

1. *Laurin* is available as a Director's Cut special edition DVD in Germany (e-m-s media), which also features the English dubbed version of the film.

2. This film is available on video and DVD in the U.S. (Mti Home Video).

3. The following conversation took place in Cologne, courtesy of Bernd Kiefer and his hospitality. Its first publication in German language was in *Splatting Image* 29, (March 1997), pp. 37–40. It was translated by Steffen Hantke, in consultation with Marcus Stiglegger.

4. A German TV series in the mid-nineties of action-oriented thrillers, produced by the private cable station RTL.

5. A classic German gothic novel from the 19th century drawing heavily upon the local color of Northern Germany.

6. A state-sponsored institution that assesses the artistic value of a film prior to its general distribution.

Loneliness, Passion, Melancholia:
A Conversation with Nico Hoffmann

Marcus Stiglegger

Nico Hoffmann was born in 1959 in Heidelberg, and trained as a director at the Academy for Film and Television in Munich. In 1988, he received an award for his debut feature film *Land der Väter, Land der Söhne* (*Country of the Fathers, Country of the Sons*). During the early 1990s, he left a lasting mark on the German thriller with his films *Der Sandmann* (*The Sandmann*), originally produced for German private television, and his primary work *Solo für Klarinette* (*Solo for Clarinet*), which caused a scandal at its release thanks to sensationalist coverage by German tabloids. A footnote to these films is the adaptation of Friedrich Dürrenmatt's novel *Das Versprechen* (*The Pledge*), written by Hoffmann and released as *Es geschah am hellichten Tag* (*It Happened in Broad Daylight*). He subsequently founded the production company TeamWorx, and has since worked exclusively as a producer. TeamWorx has established itself successfully in television, devoting itself primarily to high-end productions, such as the award-winning drama *Wolfsburg*. Hoffmann has no plans to return to the director's chair.[1]

Nico, how would you characterize the current situation of genre cinema in Germany?

It's extremely problematic. For years, television has waged a war of attrition against genre pictures on the screen. You can observe this trend as directors like Dominik Graf are abandoning feature films for television productions. These days, the most important developments in regard to the genre of the thriller are taking place in television, especially in long-running shows and miniseries. Some episodes of *Tatort* could be considered extensions of the genre.[2] At the same time, attempts in recent years to produce genre pictures for the screen have failed, for a number of reasons.

During the 1960s, German crime and horror pictures experienced the peak of their popularity, as, for instance, in the case of the countless Edgar Wallace adaptations. Did these films have any influence on you when you were younger?

No, these films had no direct influence on me. Of course, I watched and enjoyed them as a kid, but I didn't experience any pronounced affinity to the thriller genre back then.

How about the horror genre? Did you ever consider branching out into this direction?

I always used to shy away from the horror genre. Still, I'd make a clear-cut distinction between thrillers and horror films. In the thriller, the director is granted a surprising amount of psychological leeway. This struck me most of all when I shot the *Tatort* episode "Tod im Häcksler" ("Death in the Woodchipper"), which revolved around the figure of a serial killer. The thriller format offers you the opportunity, within the confines of the genre rules, to explore the abyss of the human soul. This psychological aspect is always first and foremost on my mind, which is why this context is so interesting.

Are there any directors of genre cinema who influenced you in your youth?

The first I'd have to mention would be Jean-Pierre Melville, who managed to create such an intense atmosphere of solitude and melancholia around the figure of the loner in his film *Le Samourai*. This film had an enormous influence on my own film *Solo für Klarinette*. The characters Melville has Delon play in his films are the best example. Then I've also been fascinated by Francis Ford Coppola's *The Godfather* because he manages to show the complexity of family psychology in the context of criminality. I've often analyzed this complex film, just for myself but also with my students. Finally I'd also like to mention Martin Scorsese's urban thrillers, which impressed me mostly because of the physical aspect of his actors' performance. It's important here to recognize the connection between aggression, group dynamics, and sexuality—all mechanisms that also function crucially in my own films.

What was it that made you want to become a filmmaker yourself, and later a producer?

I'll have to make a fine distinction here because I've only been a director for a period of about fifteen years. It all developed from my background in journalism: I was driven by a sense of extreme curiosity to explore different characters and their environments, and the moving image provided an enormous range of possibilities in this respect. Along the way, I went through a number of different phases: first, an autobiographical one, then one concentrating on *milieu*. In my current role as a producer, I do have more options, though, to branch out. Even now the production schedule of TeamWorx is largely focused upon crime and thriller formats.

How did you get involved in the intense collaboration with Götz George, the actor who became a German TV icon playing the Tatort *inspector Schimanski?*

I first met George in the context of comedy when we shot the TV production *Schulz & Schulz*. The producer Markus Trebitsch introduced us. George knew me because of my Bernhard Schlink adaptation *Der Tod kam als Freund* ("Death Came as a Friend") and wanted to work with me. At this point, we embarked upon a long and productive working relationship.

The thriller you ended up shooting together, Der Sandmann, *was a great success for all of its fifteen TV broadcasts so far. Do you think the audience has developed a certain appetite for German genre films? Or was the film perceived mostly as a kind of singular specimen of the television crime show that German audiences are already familiar with?*

When *Der Sandmann* was first broadcast in 1995, it represented the beginning of productions for television that had a kind of cinematic scope and quality. Since then, we've seen plenty of made-for-TV movies that all aspire to the style of feature films. But I guess our film was the first that accomplished a full realization of this concept. *Der Sandmann* was a success because it treated genre conventions affectionately, looked sleek and professional, and delivered a tight, dynamic narrative. The story about an alleged serial killer who is seeking the attention of the media manages to combine a critique of the media with the drama of a dangerous seduction. My favorite scene is the final showdown during a talk show, in which George lays bare his murderous soul, layer by layer, for the female journalist played by Barbara Rudnik. When the film premiered, it was seen primarily as a critique of contemporary mass media, but I guess today it functions mostly, and simply, as a suspenseful thriller.

Der Sandmann *offers its audience a number of important actors who have become icons of this period, most of all George and Barbara Rudnik. Do you think the choice of these iconic actors was important for the success of the film?*

Yes, extremely important. In the case of George, we were deliberately attempting to reverse the well-known television image he had acquired with the role of the tough cop Schimanski. After all, we were shooting exactly one week after Karmakar finished his film *Der Totmacher*, in which George plays the serial murderer Fritz Haarmann. This was to become a pivotal year in George's acting career; he received pretty much all the important awards an actor can get.

Der Sandmann *plays, with a sense of daring and great virtuosity, with the mechanisms of mystery and suspense. Had these aspects already been developed during the scripting stage of the project?*

We were working with an excellent script in which all of these mechanisms were already in place. As I was reading, I could already see the final construction and feel the film's rhythm. In the final instance, however, it all depends on the chemistry among the cast. With other actors and actresses, this could have very well turned out to be a failure.

How much personal input did George have within the larger context of the production?

First of all, George and I had already been cultivating a fairly intense collaboration. The final talk show scene, for example, was shot during a period of three days, during which there was always a sense of great fragility. George started out playing the scene very quietly, then started raising the level of intensity until it reached a kind of climax. This way, he managed to express his character's sexual greed and yet show his extreme capacity for self-control. This presupposes an enormous amount of trust between us. Immediately afterwards, we both fell ill, which might indicate how high the level of intensity had been.

A little later, you made Es geschah am hellichten Tag *(It Happened in Broad Daylight). Do you think of this film more as a remake of the classic German mystery thriller from the 1950s, or as an independent literary adaptation of Friedrich Dürrenmatt's* Das Versprechen *(The Pledge)?*

Both. I liked the book very much and knew it inside out. Of course, I'd seen the film as a kid, and it had left a strong impression on me. However, Bernd Eichinger's script stays very close to the original, and as a result, the film suffered. I was tempted to approach the film classically and conservatively as a director. But I just couldn't find a contemporary angle by which to gain access to the material.

How would you situate the film in comparison to the old German version and the American version with Jack Nicholson?

It falls somewhere in between those two versions. We didn't quite succeed in striking the right balance with the love story between Barbara Rudnik and Joachim Krol and the interior drama of the psychopathic murderer Axel Milberg. It strikes me as somewhat too demonstrative now to have shown him masturbating onto the photographs of his victims in order to show his sexual compulsions.

The atmosphere in your version is significantly lighter and more positive than in the other two films. Was this a deliberate artistic choice?

That happened during shooting and is of course the result of the material and the setting. Had we put the psychopathic murderer more at the center of events, the film would have ended up being more sinister. But the script concentrated on the love story. And the rural setting isn't exactly somber either. The end result was a kind of sinister *Heimatfilm*; this would be one way of looking at the movie.

Your most recent large-scale project as a director, Solo für Klarinette (Solo for Clarinet), *was based upon an American novel. What were the consequences of moving the location of the film from New York to Berlin?*

There were no really significant consequences, since New York and Berlin are in fact quite similar. Right now Berlin is undergoing changes just like New York did ten years ago. I've lived in both cities for some time. If we'd shot *Solo für Klarinette* in New York, I'm sure we'd have chosen not Manhattan but Brooklyn or Queens as a location. It was important to me to focus on the Melville influences. The protagonists are seekers, desperately searching for love. The city merely had to provide the right background for their personal drama.

Do you think of Solo für Klarinette *in the context of classic American film noir of the 1940s and '50s?*

Not so much; for me, though, the influence of Melville is crucial. However, my cinematographer, who happens to be ten years older than myself and has, therefore, had a different kind of education, did draw his inspiration mostly from film noir. And he was the one who left his mark on the shades of light and perspectives that now look like classic film noir. What I mostly cared about was to show two lonely people who are looking for love but cannot really face it. Loneliness, desire, and aggression all converge for these two main characters, one man and one woman, in one act of self-annihilation. For George, this brought about yet another refraction of the Schimanski character. We were telling primarily the story of a disturbed sexuality that requires an element of violence whenever it is directed at a woman. The key scene in this regard is the one in which the protagonist buys himself time with a prostitute and then increasingly loses all measure of self-control with her.

For long periods of time, Solo für Klarinette *seems to be interested only marginally in the search for the murderer. Instead, it functions mostly as a melancholic drama about loneliness and desire. In this regard, the film reminded me of Jane Campion's recent film* In the Cut.

Yes, that's right.

Do you think that the audience back then was confused by this shifting between melodrama, eroticism, and thriller?

No question about it. The audience wants clear-cut distinctions. The solving of the crime was of absolutely no importance to me whatsoever. I was far more interested in the different forms of sexuality on display in the film, the problematic balance between proximity and distance that we can see in the scene that features the sexual encounter between George and Corinna Harfouch, their inability to establish genuine contact. The leitmotif of the film is this constant shifting, the seeming incompatibility of tenderness and sex. On the very first day of shooting I scheduled the scene in which Corinna bites off Dietmar Mühe's penis. She wants some tenderness, he wants hard, anonymous sex. I also wanted to find out how far the actors were willing to go. Sometimes I wish we'd gone even further with these experiments . . .

From the discussion in recent years triggered by films like Intimacy, Romance, *or* Irreversible, *I had the impression that the audience isn't even all that interested in an intense confrontation with sexuality.*

Apparently, the audience doesn't want that anymore, at least not in any pure form. Presented in a mixed format, in the context of genre, it does go over much better.

After Solo für Klarinette, *you have not directed any further films. Do you think you'll return to the director's chair anytime soon?*

No, I don't think so. At the moment, I'm very happy being a producer. I can work on several projects simultaneously. Things seem to evolve for me in a rhythmic cycle of about ten years . . . *Solo für Klarinette* gave me a very satisfying sense of closure in regard to my intimate cooperation with Götz George and the realization of my melancholic urban vision in the tradition of Melville. But then one should never say "never" . . .

Notes

1. The interview was conducted during the summer of 2004; the original German version was published in 2004 in the German magazine *Ikonen*. The interview was translated by Steffen Hantke, in consultation with Marcus Stiglegger.

2. *Tatort* (*Scene of the Crime*) is the longest-running crime show on German TV, produced by the ARD in collaboration with a different regional broadcaster for each episode. Every region has established its own protagonist, some of whom have become popular icons of German television history (e.g. Götz George as Horst Schimanski, a macho inspector at work in the blue-collar town of Duisburg).

Index

About the Editor and Contributors

Linda Badley is professor of English at Middle Tennessee State University, where she teaches literature, gender and cultural studies, and film, and co-directs the film series for the biennial Women and Power Conference. She has written widely on literature, television, and film, especially on horror literature and cinema and their interconnections, and is the author of *Film, Horror, and the Body Fantastic* (Greenwood, 1995) and *Writing Horror and the Body: The Fiction of Stephen King, Clive Barker,* and *Anne Rice* (Greenwood, 1996). Her work in film studies is presently concerned with the theory and practice of auteurism and with contemporary international and American independent film. She is general editor (with R. Barton Palmer) of the Traditions in World Cinema series at Edinburgh University Press and co-edited the flagship volume (2005). Current projects include *American Commercial-Independent Cinema* (with R. Barton Palmer, Edinburgh) and *Lars von Trier* (Illinois).

Eugenie Brinkema is a Ph.D. student in modern culture and media at Brown University in Providence, Rhode Island. Her article "Pleasure in/and Perversity: *Plaisagir* in Liliana Cavani's *Il portiere di notte*" appeared in 2004 in *The Dalhousie Review,* and "Rape and the Rectum—Bersani, Deleuze, Noé" appeared in *Camera Obscura* in 2005. An abridged version of her senior thesis from Yale (B.A., 2002), entitled "The Lady Van(qu)ishes: Interiority, Abjection, and the Function of Rape in Horror Films," is forthcoming in the journal *Paradoxa,* as is an article on anamorphosis and courtly love in the films of Tod Browning for a new anthology on that auteur.

Blair Davis is a Ph.D. candidate in the Department of Communication Studies at McGill University in Montreal. He has been an instructor in film history and aesthetics with the School for the Contemporary Arts at Simon Fraser University since 2003. His essays are featured in *Horror Film: Creating and Marketing Fear* (University Press of Mississippi, 2004) and *Reel Food: Essays on Film and Food* (Routledge, 2004), and he is the co-editor of, and contributor to, a forthcoming book on director Akira Kurosawa entitled *Kurosawa, Rashomon and Their Legacies.*

Richard J. Hand is reader in theatre and media drama at the University of Glamorgan in Wales (UK). He is the co-author of *Grand-Guignol: The French Theatre of Horror* (2002) and the author of *Terror on the Air: Horror Radio in*

America, 1931-52 (2005) and numerous essays on horror in popular culture including theatre, film, comics, television and radio.

Steffen Hantke is associate professor at the English Department of Sogang University in Seoul. He serves as area chair for horror at the Southwest/Texas Popular Culture and American Culture Association and on the editorial board of *Paradoxa: Studies in World Literary Genres*. He is the author of *Paranoia and Conspiracy in Contemporary American Literature: The Works of Don DeLillo and Joseph McElroy* (Peter Lang, 1994). He is the editor of *Horror Film: Creating and Marketing Fear* (University Press of Mississippi, 2004) and of a special topics issue on horror of *Paradoxa* (2002). His reviews and articles on popular literature and film have appeared in *Paradoxa, Literature/Film Quarterly, Science Fiction Studies, Foundation, Kinoeye, The Rocky Mountain Review, Studies in the Novel, The Journal of Popular Culture, Post Script, College Literature, Film Criticism, Scope*, and in a number of anthologies, both in English and in German.

Mikel J. Koven is lecturer in film and television studies at the University of Wales, Aberystwyth. His main research areas involve the interrelationship between popular cinema and folklore, urban legends, contemporary American television and representations of the Holocaust. *Blaxploitation Films* (Pocket Essentials, 2001) was his first book, and he is currently finishing up his second, the first academic study in English on the Italian *giallo* film, *La Dolce Morta* (Scarecrow Press, 2006). He is also series editor of *Television and Genre*, with David Lavery (University of Wales Press) and will be editing one of the series' first volumes, *Horror TV*. With Sharon Sherman, he has just finished editing a special issue of *Western Folklore* on "Folklore and Film" and again with Sherman, co-edited a collection, *Filmic Folklore* (Utah State University Press, 2007). He is also editor of the forthcoming collection *Cool Jewz: Contemporary Jewish Identity in Popular Culture* (University of Wales Press, 2007). He has published in such journals as *Journal of American Folklore, Literature/Film Quarterly, Scope, Contemporary Legend* and *Culture & Tradition*.

Patricia MacCormack is senior lecturer in communication and film at Anglia Ruskin University, Cambridge. Her Ph.D. was awarded the Mollie Holman Doctorate Medal for Best Thesis. She has published on perversion, Continental philosophy, French feminism and Italian horror film. Her most recent work is on cinesexuality, masochism and becoming-monster in *Alternative Europe, Thirdspace, Theory Culture and Society, Body and Society*, and *Rhizomes*. She is currently writing on Blanchot, Bataille, and cinecstasy.

Ernest Mathijs is currently lecturing on film at the University of Wales, Aberystwyth. His research focuses on the reception of contemporary alternative cinema. He has published in *Screen, Social Semiotics, Cinema Journal, Litera-*

ture/Film Quarterly, Kinoeye, and *History of Political Economy.* He edited *The Cinema of the Low Countries, Alternative Europe,* and *Big Brother International.* He has just completed *The Cinema of David Cronenberg,* and three edited books on *The Lord of the Rings* (one with Murray Pomerance and one with Martin Barker). He is editor of the book series *Contemporary Cinema* (with Steven Schneider) with Rodopi Press, and of *Cultographies* (with Jamie Sexton and Xavier Mendik) with Wallflower Press.

Jay McRoy is associate professor of literature and film at the University of Wisconsin–Parkside. In addition to numerous contributions to books and film journals, he is the editor of *Japanese Horror Cinema* (Edinburgh University Press, 2006) and co-editor, with Richard Hand, of *Monstrous Adaptations: Generic and Thematic Mutations in Horror Film* (Manchester University Press, forthcoming 2007). His single-authored volume *Nightmare Japan: Contemporary Japanese Horror Cinema* will be published by Rodopi University Press in 2007.

Philip L. Simpson is professor of communications and humanities at the Palm Bay campus of Brevard Community College in Florida. He has served as department chair of communications and humanities, and is currently serving as Academic Dean of Behavioral/Social Sciences and Humanities at Brevard Community College. He also serves as Area Chair of Horror for the Popular Culture Association, and is book reviewer and elected Member-at-Large for the Association. He is a member of the editorial board for the *Journal of Popular Culture.* His book, *Psycho Paths: Tracking the Serial Killer Through Contemporary American Film and Fiction,* was published in 2000 by Southern Illinois University Press and is currently being revised and updated for a second edition. His essays of literary, cultural, and/or cinematic criticism have also been published in journals such as *Cineaction, Paradoxa, Clues,* and *Notes on Contemporary Literature;* encyclopedias such as *Encyclopedia of the Documentary Film* (2005), *Twenty-First Century British and Irish Novelists* (2003), *The Guide to United States Popular Culture* (2001), *War and American Popular Culture* (1999), and *The Encyclopedia of Novels into Film* (1998); and books such as *Horror Film: Creating and Marketing Film* (2004); *The Terministic Screen: Rhetorical Perspectives on Film* (2003); *Car Crash Culture* (2002); *Jack Nicholson: Movie Top Ten* (2000); and *Mythologies of Violence in Postmodern Media* (1999).

Marcus Stiglegger teaches film studies at the University of Mainz in Germany. His dissertation *Sadiconazista* (on sexuality and politics in film) is now published in a second edition. He is editor and author of several books on film history and film aesthetics (Abel Ferrara, Pop & Cinema, War Films, Western, mainstream-auteurs, Holocaust cinema, Nicolas Roeg). He has also directed short films (*Sister Mine...*) and video clips (*Sopor Aeternus: Like a Corpse Standing in Desperation*), and has written screenplays for German television

(*Der Fahnder*). He is the editor of the cultural magazine *Ikonen*. His new theoretical book *Ritual and Seduction,* on seductive strategies in cinema, is currently in preparation.

Kris Thomas-Vander Lugt is a doctoral candidate in Germanic studies at Indiana University in Bloomington, where she is completing her dissertation on representations of dead and undead bodies in German and Austrian literature, theatre, and visual culture after the 1960s. She has taught courses on international horror film and postwar German culture, and has written on topics ranging from the plastinated cadavers of anatomist Gunther von Hagens to depictions of the monstrous-feminine in recent fiction by young German female authors such as Thea Dorn and Tanja Dückers. In her research, she focuses on theories of identity as mapped on and through the body. Her current fascinations include the aesthetics of skin and the spaghetti westerns of Klaus Kinski.

Tony Williams is professor and area head of film studies at Southern Illinois University at Carbondale. He has recently authored *The Cinema of George Romero: Knight of the Living Dead* (2003) and *Body and Soul: The Cinematic Vision of Robert Aldrich* (2004), and has co-edited *Horror International* (2005) with Steven Jay Schneider. Two of his forthcoming articles on British and Hong Kong gangster films will be published in *The Gangster Films Reader*, edited by Alain Silver and James Ursini.